Running QuickBooks® 2008

Premier Editions

Kathy Ivens

CPA911 Publishing, LLC
Philadelphia PA

Running QuickBooks 2008 Premier Editions

ISBN Number 10-digit: 1-932925-03-1 13-digit: 978-1-932925-03-6

Published by CPA911 Publishing, LLC December 2007

A Note to the Reader

From the Publisher

The QuickBooks Premier editions have features not available in QuickBooks Pro. This book provides explanations and instructions for the features of interest to users of the Premier editions of QuickBooks 2008.

This book does not contain basic instructions for all the features in QuickBooks; instead, it's assumed that you have some knowledge of the software. Covering all the features of the Premier editions, as well as all the information on using QuickBooks basic features, would require a book of over 1200 pages; it just can't be done in one volume.

If you're just starting with QuickBooks, you can learn all the basics by reading *QuickBooks 2008: The Official Guide*, from McGraw-Hill Publishing. Throughout this book you'll find references to that book (e.g. "To learn how to set up printing, read QuickBooks 2008: The Official Guide").

The references to *QuickBooks 2008: The Official Guide* in this book are specific references to the edition that's sold in your favorite bookstores, written by Kathy Ivens. This is ***not*** the same book that Intuit makes available as a download file to users who purchase QuickBooks Premier editions (the download book is also named QuickBooks 2008: The Official Guide).

Acknowledgments

Cover Design: Matthew Ericson

Production: InfoDesign Services (www.infodesigning.com)

Indexing: After Words Editorial Services (www.aweditorial.com/)

The author owes a great debt of gratitude to the people at Intuit, Inc. for diligent attention to my questions, and unfailing generosity and expertise in providing explanations. In particular I want to thank George Jaquette, Victoria Dolginsky, Nicholas Tolstoshev, and Sharon Hallock for their timely and clear responses to my questions as I prepared this book.

Kathy Ivens

Table of Contents

Chapter 1

Getting Started

Updating existing company files

Creating a new company file

Configuring the QuickBooks window

Creating opening balances

QuickBooks Premier editions offer features not available in other versions of QuickBooks. If you previously worked with QuickBooks Pro, you'll find that your Premier edition of QuickBooks has all the features available in QuickBooks Pro, plus the advanced features built into the Premier editions.

Many of the advanced features are in both the generic Premier Edition and all the industry-specific Premier editions. However, each of the industry-specific Premier editions has additional features and tools that are helpful for running QuickBooks for that specific industry. If you have the Accountant Edition, you also have all the tools that are in the industry-specific editions. This makes it easier to support clients who install any of the QuickBooks Premier editions.

Company File Setup

You have several options available for setting up your company file in QuickBooks 2008 Premier.

- If you upgraded from an earlier version of QuickBooks (any edition), you must update your existing company file.
- If you're new to QuickBooks, you need to create a company file, either by going through the EasyStep Interview, or creating the file manually.

(In QuickBooks terminology, the word "version" means year, and the word "edition" means Pro or Premier.)

Opening an Existing Company File

If you installed QuickBooks 2008 Premier in the same folder that held your previous version of QuickBooks, the first time you launch QuickBooks the software opens the company file that was open when you last closed QuickBooks in the previous version. Then the system begins the process of updating the file to Premier 2008.

If you installed QuickBooks 2008 Premier in a new folder in order to preserve the previous version (a common scenario for accounting firms), no existing company file opens when you first launch QuickBooks Premier.

If you already have a previous version of QuickBooks, and you installed QuickBooks 2008 in a new folder, you can copy existing files to your QuickBooks 2008 data folder (the files you want to update to QuickBooks 2008). Then select File → Open or Restore Company. Follow the prompts in the wizard, locate the copy of the file, open it, and let QuickBooks begin updating it. This is a good way to install QuickBooks, because it lets you learn the new version without permanently updating your company file from the older version. If something goes wrong with QuickBooks 2008, you can continue to get your work done in the older version. When everything is working smoothly in QuickBooks 2008, you can uninstall the previous version and remove the old company file.

***NOTE**: You can open any file created in QuickBooks in any edition, as long as the file is moving within editions of the same version (year). That is, a file created or used in a Premier edition can be opened in any other Premier edition or in Pro Edition, and vice versa.*

Restoring a Backup File

If you have a backup of your company file and you want to restore it and update it to QuickBooks 2008, choose File → Open or Restore Company. Select the option Restore a Backup Copy and click Next. Follow the prompts to locate the file, restore it, and update it to QuickBooks 2008.

Creating a New Company File

If you're just starting with QuickBooks, you need to create a company file. Choose File → New Company and then select the EasyStep Interview (a wizard), or select Skip Interview to create your company file manually. I cover both methods in the following sections.

Using the EasyStep Interview

The EasyStep Interview is a wizard that walks you through all the processes involved in setting up your company data file.

***TIP**: Most of the tasks the wizard walks you through can be accomplished manually, using the QuickBooks menus, commands, and configuration dialogs. See the section "Manual Company Setup", later in this chapter.*

The first window welcomes you to the wizard. Click Start Interview to begin. (If you want to set up your company file manually, click Skip Interview, and read the section "Manual Company Setup".)

Company Information Section

In the first window, enter your company information. Notice that there are two fields for your company name:

- The Company Name field is for the company name you use for doing business (your d/b/a name), and that name (along with your address) is used on printed transaction forms, and the reports you generate in QuickBooks.
- The Legal Name field is used only if the legal name of your company differs from the company name you use for doing business. That name is used for government forms (if you do your own payroll, or you export your QuickBooks files to a tax preparation application).

For many companies, both entries are identical, and when you type the data in the Company Name field and press the Tab key, QuickBooks automatically duplicates it in the Legal Name field. Change it if necessary.

Enter your Tax Identification Number. This may be an EIN number, or your Social Security number, depending on the way you organized your business. When all the information is filled in, click Next.

Continue to click Next to move through the windows, entering the following information:

- Choose your industry from the list of industry types the wizard displays. If no listing exactly matches your business, select the industry that comes closest.
- Select the legal organization type for your business (e.g. sole proprietorship, partnership, corporation, etc.).
- Enter the first month of your fiscal year.

Creating an Administrator

In the next window, you can assume the role of administrator, just by virtue of the fact that you're the person setting up the company file, and the decision about the password is yours to make.

If you're ready to set up an administrator for this company, enter a password, and then retype it to confirm it. This doesn't have to be done during company setup, and many people wait until later to set up the administrator and additional users. Click Next to move on.

Saving the File

The next window is an announcement that you're about to save your information in a QuickBooks company file. Click Next again to get to the Filename For New Company dialog, in which you save the data file.

You don't have to accept the default location for the company file; in fact, I prefer to create a folder on the root of the hard drive (e.g. C:\QB2008Files), or in the My Documents folder (because in most businesses the My Documents folder is backed up regularly – or should be).

QuickBooks automatically uses the company name for the filename, but you can change the filename if you wish. It takes a few minutes to save the file, and then the wizard presents the next windows.

Choosing Features for Your Company File

The next section of the EasyStep Interview is designed to help you set up your company file to suit your business and accounting needs. Whatever data you enter in these windows can be changed at any time in the future. This interview is just a quick way of making sure you cover all the important topics before you start creating transactions in QuickBooks.

In the following windows, the wizard asks a series of questions about the way your business operates. You must indicate whether you sell products or services or both, whether you collect sales tax, create estimates for your customers, make cash sales, track accounts payable, and so on. Go through all the windows, indicating your answers and clicking Next.

Nothing you select is immutable; you can change any Yes to No (or the other way around) at any time in the future, using the Preferences dialog.

Setting Up the Chart of Accounts

After you complete all the questions about the types of transactions you'll use in QuickBooks, the wizard displays a page indicating it's time to establish the accounts you need.

Selecting the QuickBooks Start Date

When you click Next, the wizard wants to know your start date for using QuickBooks. This is your "go live" date, and it means that every financial transaction before that date is historical, and every financial transaction after that date must be created in QuickBooks. QuickBooks uses this date to manipulate some of the information in the following wizard windows.

You should select the option to start tracking your finances on the first day of the fiscal year, because that's the only way to get complete accurate reports about your business finances. You don't really have to enter every single transaction between the first day of the year and the day you're setting up the company file—see the section Creating Opening Balances later in this chapter to learn how to enter historic balances.

Creating a Bank Account

The next window asks if you want to set up a bank account. If you select No, you can add the bank account yourself when you set up your chart of accounts (covered in Chapter 2).

If you select Yes the wizard asks for the bank name (the name you want to use in the chart of accounts, such as Operating Account), and optionally, the account number. You're also asked to indicate whether you opened this bank account before your QuickBooks start date.

Don't Enter Opening Balances for Accounts

If you indicate that the bank account existed before your start date (a highly likely scenario), in the next window you're asked to enter the last statement date, and the reconciled bank balance as of that date. Do *not* enter any amount in the bank balance field, leave it as zero.

When you enter an opening balance for a bank account or any other type of account that has a field for the opening balance, QuickBooks automatically counterposts that amount to an account named Opening Bal Equity.

The Opening Bal Equity account is something QuickBooks invents to hold balancing postings for opening balances, and after you start using QuickBooks you or your accountant must clear that account. It's almost impossible to figure out which accounts should really have received those postings (most of the amounts really belong in revenue, liabilities, receivables, retained earnings for prior years, and so on). You can post the opening balances properly later, when you set up your Opening Trial Balance (covered later in this chapter).

Selecting Income and Expense Accounts

Next, QuickBooks displays the income and expense accounts that have been selected for your chart of accounts, based on the industry type you selected (see Figure 1-1).

This is not a complete chart of accounts, and you need to create additional accounts (covered in Chapter 2). Select and deselect accounts by toggling the check marks next to each account.

The EasyStep Interview ends in the next window; click Finish.

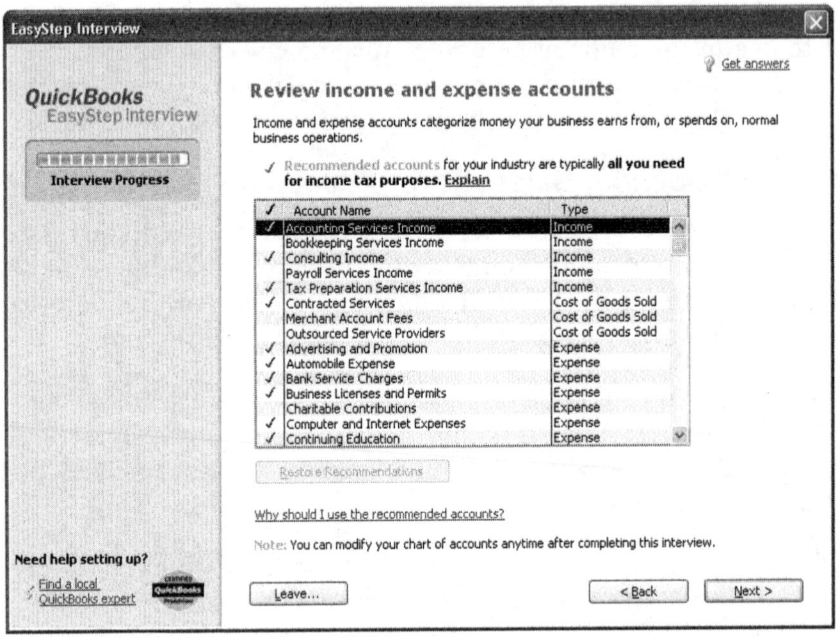

Figure 1-1: Select or deselect accounts you want to install to get a head start on creating your chart of accounts.

Manual Company Setup

If you click the Skip Interview button when the EasyStep Interview opens, QuickBooks displays a dialog in which you can enter basic information about your company (see Figure 1-2).

Enter the company name the way you want it to appear on the forms you create. If the company's legal name differs from the "Doing Business As" name, enter it in the Legal Name field.

In the following windows, select the legal organization type for your company (proprietorship, corporation, etc.), enter the first month of your fiscal year, and select a type of business so QuickBooks can install the appropriate chart of accounts. (You can also choose the option "No Type" to enter or import your own chart of accounts.) Finally, save the file.

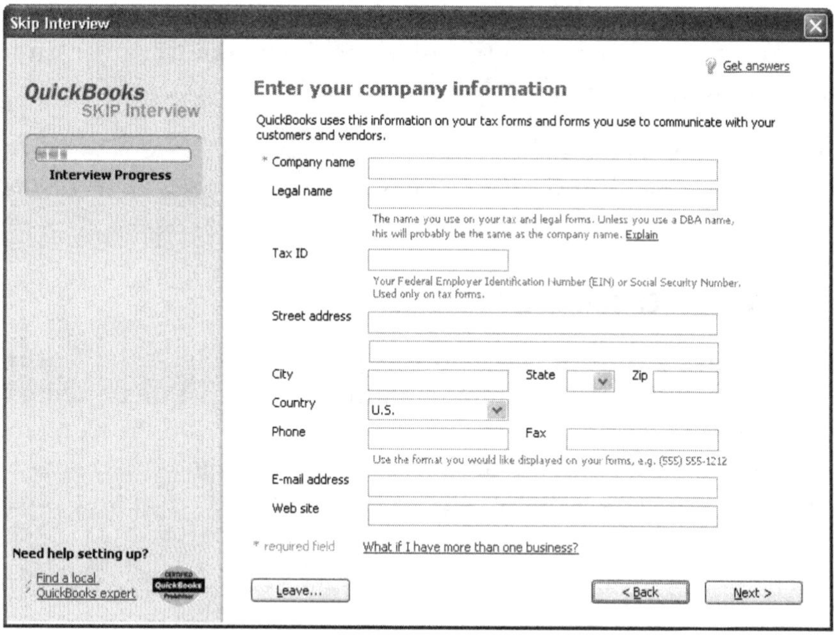

Figure 1-2: Enter basic information about your company.

Now you can set up a full chart of accounts, enable features, add entries to lists, and do all the other configuration tasks required to use QuickBooks efficiently.

Configuring the QuickBooks Window

By default, the QuickBooks software window contains a Menu Bar, an Icon Bar, and the Home page. If you upgraded from QuickBooks 2005 or earlier, or if you installed QuickBooks 2008 as a new installation and created a new company file, you also see the QuickBooks Coach on your Home page.

Home Page

The Home page is a central access point for commonly used QuickBooks functions. If the QuickBooks Coach resides on the Home page, you can use the Coach to view a tutorial (a video that explains the windows you use when you're working in QuickBooks), or to help you use the workflow icons on the Home page (hover your mouse pointer over an icon to see an explanation of the workflow).

You can stop loading the Home page, or customize it (including getting rid of the Coach) in the Desktop View section of the Preferences dialog.

Customizing the Icon Bar

The icons that appear on the Icon Bar may not include the features you use most frequently, so you should change the Icon Bar to make it more useful. You can also change the way the Icon Bar and its icons look. Choose View → Customize Icon Bar to open the Customize Icon Bar dialog, which displays a list of the icons currently occupying your Icon Bar.

Adding an Icon

You can add an icon to the Icon Bar from the Customize Icon Bar dialog, or by automatically adding an icon for the QuickBooks window you're currently using.

To add an icon from the Customize Icon Bar dialog, click Add to open the Add Icon Bar Item dialog seen in Figure 1-3.

Scroll through the list to select the task you want to add to the Icon Bar. Then choose a graphic to represent the new icon (QuickBooks selects a default graphic, which appears within a box). You can also change the name (the title that appears below the icon) or the description (the text that appears in the Tooltip when you hold your mouse pointer over the icon).

To position your new icon at a specific place within the existing row of icons (instead of at the right end of the Icon Bar), first select the existing icon that you want to sit to the left of your new icon and then click Add.

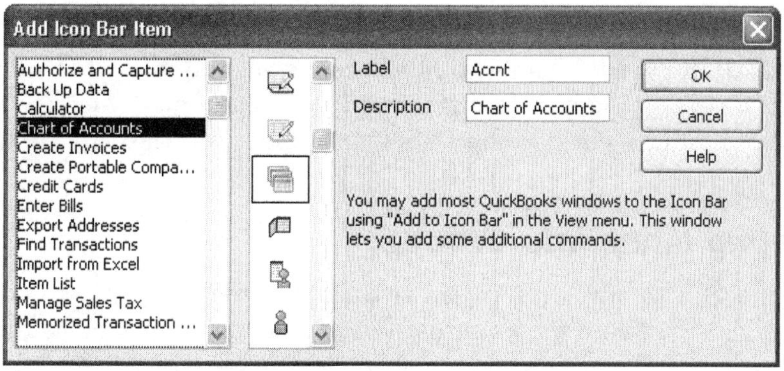

Figure 1-3: Design your own Icon Bar

Adding an Icon For an Open Window

If you're currently working in a QuickBooks window, and you think it would be handy to have an icon for fast access to that window, it's easy to add an icon to the Icon Bar.

While the window is open, choose View → Add <*Name of Window*> To Icon Bar. A dialog appears so you can choose a graphic, a title, and a description for the new icon.

Changing the Order of Icons

The list of icons in the Customize Icon Bar dialog reads top-to-bottom, representing the left-to-right display on the Icon bar. Moving an icon's listing up moves it to the left on the Icon Bar, and vice versa.

To move an icon, click the small diamond to the left of the icon's listing, hold down the left mouse button, and drag the listing to a new position.

Displaying Icons Without Title Text

By default, both icons and text display on the Icon Bar. You can select Show Icons Only to remove the title text under the icons. This makes the icons smaller, and you can fit more icons on the Icon Bar. Position your mouse pointer over a small icon to see a Tooltip that describes the icon's function.

Changing the Icon's Graphic, Text, or Description

To change an individual icon's appearance, select the icon's listing and click Edit. Then choose a different graphic (the currently selected graphic is enclosed in a box), change the Label, or change the Description (the Tooltip text).

Separating Icons into Groups

You can insert a separator between two icons, which is a way to create groups of icons. (Of course, you must first move icons into logical groups on the Icon Bar.) The separator is a gray vertical line.

To accomplish this, in the Customize Icon Bar dialog select the icon that should appear to the left of the separator bar and click Add Separator. QuickBooks inserts "(space)" to the listing to indicate the location of the separator.

Removing an Icon

If there are icons you never use, or use so infrequently that you'd rather replace them with more useful icons, you can remove them. Select the icon in the Customize Icon Bar dialog and click Delete. QuickBooks does not ask you to confirm the deletion; the icon just disappears from the Icon Bar.

Removing the Navigation Bar Icons

You cannot use the Customize Icon Bar dialog to remove the icons for Home page, Customer Center, Vendor Center, Employee Center, or Report Center. These icons, which are larger, are actually a discrete group called the Navigation Bar.

To remove the Navigation Bar from the Icon Bar, choose View → Navigation Bar. Selecting the Navigation Bar command toggles the check mark.

QuickBooks Centers

QuickBooks centers are windows that display data about specific areas of your company. You can see current data, analyze that data, and manipulate the way the data is presented. The following centers are available:

- Customer Center
- Vendor Center
- Employee Center
- Report Center

Open each center from its associated icon on the Navigation Bar (the left side of the Icon Bar). If you remove the Navigation Bar you can open all of the centers from their associated menus (e.g. Vendors → Vendor Center).

Creating Opening Balances

QuickBooks does not have a feature called the "Opening Balance," per se. However, every account register is sorted by date, so when you begin entering transactions in QuickBooks, you can follow these rules:

- Enter current transactions using dates on or after first day of your current fiscal year.
- Enter historic transactions using any date prior to the first day of your current fiscal year.

Understanding the Opening Trial Balance

The goal you seek when you enter historical transactions is to build an opening trial balance for the first day of your fiscal year. A trial balance is a list of all your accounts and their current balances.

However, the report called the *Opening Trial Balance* is a bit different from the trial balance reports you create normally. The opening trial balance is the balance of the accounts on the first day of the fiscal year (usually the same as the calendar year for small businesses).

On the first day of a fiscal year, you do not have any income or expenses. The previous year's income and expenses have been calculated as a net number by subtracting the total expenses from the total income. Let's hope the result is a positive number so you have a net profit (a negative number means a loss).

That net number is posted to an equity account (called Retained Earnings), and the income and expense accounts all show zero balances, waiting for your first sales and expense transactions of the year. Therefore, the opening trial balance only has balances for asset, liability, and equity accounts (generally referred to as *balance sheet accounts*).

To get to this point, you need to enter historical balances, and QuickBooks will automatically create the opening trial balance accurately for the first day of the current year.

***NOTE**: Before you start entering any transactions (historical or current), be sure your chart of accounts, items, vendors, and customers are in the company file. Instructions for performing these tasks are found throughout this book—check the Index or the Table of Contents to find the chapters you need.*

Entering Historic Transactions

To enter historic transactions, follow these guidelines:

- Enter open customer and vendor history using QuickBooks transactions windows.
- Use journal entries to record closed sales and expenses totals that contribute to last year's retained earnings figures.
- Use journal entries to record running balance sheet totals (assets, liabilities, and equity).

Confer with your accountant to check your work and develop your final opening balances, which often requires adjusting the equity accounts (which are affected by the historical transactions you enter) to match your final retained earnings as of last year.

In this section, I'm assuming the following:

- You're setting up your QuickBooks company file to track transactions from the first day of your fiscal year, even if you started using QuickBooks later in the year. This gives you all the information you need to create final reports on your business year, making it much easier to file your tax returns.

- You've entered your lists—customers, vendors, items, and chart of accounts.

Entering Current Transactions While Entering Historical Transactions

Because QuickBooks is date sensitive, you can begin using the software for current transactions before you've entered all your historical transactions. To make it easier for your accountant to validate the opening trial balance for your fiscal year, don't enter any current transactions that are dated the first day of the year.

Using a calendar year as an example (since most small businesses operate on a calendar year), that means that even if you had sales or wrote checks on January 1, 2008, enter those transactions with the date January 2, 2008. That leaves January 1, 2008 "pristine" and your opening trial balance on that date reflects only the totals of your historical transactions.

After you're sure your opening trial balance for January 1 is correct, you can edit the January 2 transactions that were really created on January 1 to correct the date (or you can leave the date as January 2).

Entering Open Customer Balances

You have to get all of your open customer balances as of the last day of the year into QuickBooks. If any of the invoices were paid this year (with any luck, all of them were paid, especially if you start using QuickBooks a couple of months into the current year), you enter those payments as current transactions. You also have to track any outstanding credits as of the end of last year.

Creating an Item for Historical Transactions

Since all sales transactions require you to use an item, one efficient way to do this is to create an item specifically for these historical open invoices. You can call the item Historical Sales or something similar and link it to an existing income account. Use a Service or Other Charge item type.

If you remitted sales tax for the last reporting period of last year with a check dated before the end of the year (which means you don't have to track sales tax for historical transactions), make the item nontaxable.

If you haven't yet paid sales taxes for the last reporting period of last year, create two items: HistoricalSalesTaxable and HistoricalSalesNonTaxable, and mark their tax status appropriately. See the next section "Tracking Historical Sales Tax" for more information on this topic.

For each customer, you can enter the open invoices in either of two ways:

- Enter each individual invoice, using the real date of that invoice. This works well for customers who send payments earmarked for a specific invoice and also permits you to generate an accurate A/R aging report.
- Enter one invoice representing the total outstanding balance, dating it December 31. This is less data entry but only works well if your customers send payments to be applied against a running open balance, and you don't track aging by due dates.

Tracking Historical Sales Tax

If you filed and paid all of your previous year sales taxes by the last day of last year, you don't have to worry about sales tax when you enter the historical transactions. However, if you hadn't yet remitted sales taxes for the last period of last year (either the last quarter or the last month, depending on the frequency of your tax reporting), you have to build the tax liability as you enter the transactions.

If you're using actual invoice dates as you enter historical transactions, do not use the taxable item in any transaction that falls in a period for which you already remitted your sale tax payment. For example, if you're a quarterly filer, make all transactions in the first three quarters nontaxable, and create taxable transactions for the last quarter. Then, in the current year, use the QuickBooks Sales Tax feature to generate the appropriate report for the quarter and remit the taxes.

If you prefer to enter summarized total transactions, you must create one summary nontaxable transaction for the periods covered by sales tax reports you remitted to the tax authorities last year (use the nontaxable item for those transactions) and another summary taxable transaction for the period yet to be reported (using the taxable item).

Creating Historical Invoices

Use the following guidelines to enter historical transactions that are still open:

- If you track individual invoices for customers (instead of using a balance forward system), use the original invoice date to make it easier to track aging.
- If you track individual invoices for customers (instead of using a balance forward system), use the original invoice number to make sure you and your customers can discuss open balances intelligently.
- In the Item column, select the historical transaction item you created.
- Move directly to the Amount column to enter the total for each invoice (skip the Qty and Description fields).
- Use the Memo field for any notes you think might be important if you have to discuss this invoice with your customer.
- Deselect any check marks in the To Be Printed or To Be E-mailed boxes at the bottom of the window.

***TIP**: I use the Intuit Service Invoice template for historical transactions because it has fewer fields and columns than other built-in templates.*

Figure 1-4 shows an invoice for a customer who pays against a running balance, so the invoice is a summary of open invoices through the third quarter and has no sales taxes that are still due (and the invoice is dated for the last day of the third quarter). A similar invoice is created for the last quarter, and that invoice has taxes applied, because the taxes hadn't been remitted as of the last day of the previous year.

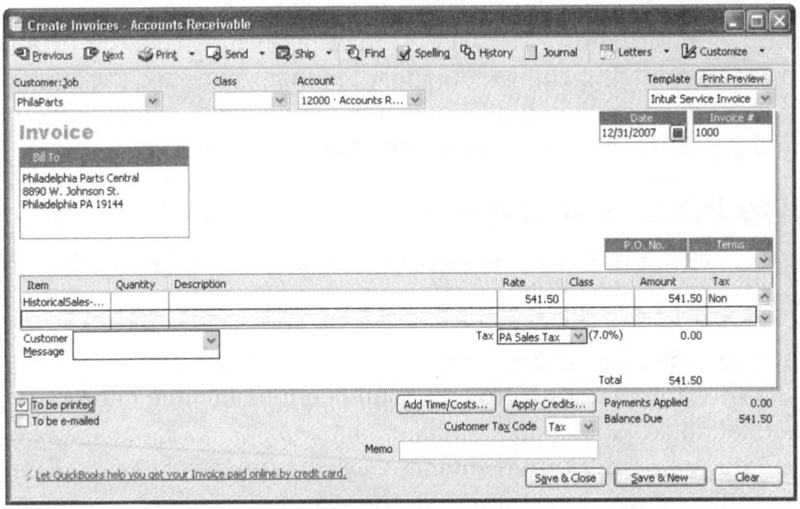

Figure 1-4: Enter historical customer balances by creating invoices.

***NOTE**: When you enter a transaction that is 90 days before the current date, or 30 days after the current date, QuickBooks issues a warning (which is a nifty idea because it avoids typos that can create some very strange financial reports). Click Yes to confirm that you want to use this date. If you're entering individual historical transactions and you don't want to click Yes after saving each transaction, you can turn off this function in the Accounting Preferences dialog, on the Company Preferences tab. Turn the warnings on again after you've completed your historical transactions.*

Creating Historical Credits

If any of your customers had outstanding credit balances at the end of the year, you must enter them. You can apply them against customer payments or invoices that are entered in the current year.

When you create the credit memo, use the real date from the previous year if you're tracking payments by invoices, or summarize multiple credit memos and use the last day of the year if you're using running balances.

Use the item you created for historical transactions. The same rules about sales tax apply as discussed in the previous section. When you save a credit memo, QuickBooks asks how to handle the transaction (see Figure 1-5). Since this is a prior year transaction that will be applied against a current year transaction, select the option Retain As An Available Credit.

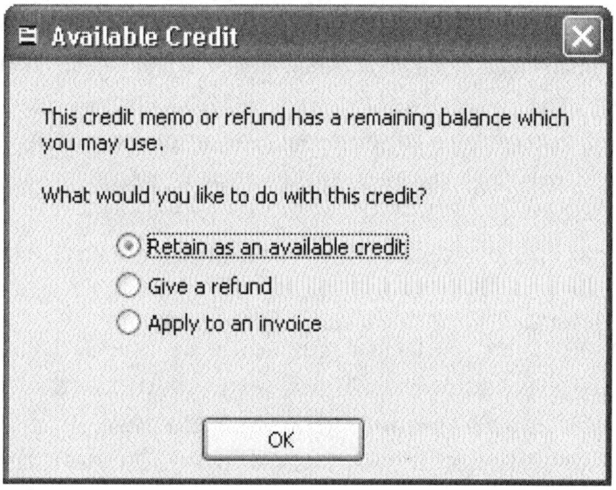

Figure 1-5: Create previously existing credits to apply to current year transactions.

Entering Open Payables

Enter all the vendor bills that were due as of the last day of the previous year (you record the payment as a current transaction). If multiple bills existed for any vendors, you can enter individual bills, or enter one bill to cover the entire amount.

If you normally pay your bills on a per-invoice basis it's best to enter each bill individually. This makes recording payments more straightforward and also makes it easier to have conversations with the vendor in the event of a dispute.

Entering Inventory

If you track inventory, enter the quantity and value of each inventory item as of the last day of the year. Choose Vendors → Inventory Activities → Adjust Quantity/Value On Hand. When the transaction window opens, click the Value Adjustment check box at the bottom of the window to add the Current Value and New Value columns to the window

For each inventory item, enter the appropriate numbers in the New Qty column and the appropriate costs in the New Value column. When you complete this task, you end up with the following:

- The total value of your inventory is posted (as a debit) to your inventory asset account as of the last day of the year.
- The cost per unit of your inventory items has been calculated by QuickBooks. This number is used to post amounts to cost of goods when you enter sales transactions in the current year.
- The inventory adjustment account has been credited with the offsetting total.

The inventory adjustment account requires some discussion with your accountant. If you're adding inventory as an adjustment instead of receiving goods via a purchase order and vendor bill (as is the case in this opening entry), the inventory adjustment account is credited. By default, QuickBooks creates the account as an expense type, but most accountants prefer a cost of goods account type (see the discussion on this issue in Chapter 2).

Creating the Trial Balance for Last Year

When your historical transactions are posted, you can begin to create a trial balance report as of the last day of the previous year.

Creating Reports on Historical Transactions

Start by viewing the current trial balance, which shows the totals posted for all the historical transactions you entered.

To generate the report, choose Reports → Accountant & Taxes → Trial Balance. When the report opens, set the date range to the previous fiscal year. You probably have balances for the following accounts (depending on the types of historical transactions you entered):

- Accounts Receivable
- Inventory
- Accounts Payable
- Sales Tax Payable
- Income (the account you linked to the item you created for entering historical invoices)
- Expenses (postings from the open vendor bills you entered)

Print this report; you need it as a reference when you create the journal entry to enter balances in all your accounts, because you don't want to enter these totals twice.

You also need to create a balance sheet report as of the end of the year, so you can see the effect of your entries on your balance sheet accounts, including equity accounts.

To generate the report, choose Reports → Company & Financial → Balance Sheet Standard. When the report window opens, select Last Fiscal Year as the date range.

Print the report, because you have to know what's already posted and calculated (net profit or loss in the equity account) when you enter the remaining account totals.

Entering the Remaining Account Totals

The totals for the remaining accounts can be entered as a journal entry dated the last day of the previous year. Remember not to use the accounts that received postings as a result of your transaction entries (with the exception of the sales tax liability account, which is discussed in the section "Entering Sales Tax Liabilities Balances").

The goal is to create an opening trial balance for the first day of the current year, which has only balance sheet accounts. The best way to get there is to create a journal entry as of the last day of the previous year that uses all your accounts (including income and expense accounts). Then let QuickBooks perform the calculations that turn the numbers into an opening trial balance on the first day of the current year.

Enter all the totals you calculate from your manual or spreadsheet-based former bookkeeping system. This puts all the income and expense totals into your QuickBooks company file, which makes it easier to create budgets for the current year and also lets you create reports comparing sales and expenses between the current year and last year.

Some of the entries in your journal entry are easy to figure out, but others require some thought. For example, the totals for accounts of the type Other Current Assets (excluding inventory) and Other Assets are usually easy to calculate. Most Current Liabilities and Long Term Liabilities totals are equally straightforward. However, the totals you enter for your bank accounts, fixed assets, and payroll liabilities merit special attention, explained in the following sections.

Entering Opening Bank Account Balances

To enter bank account balances, use the reconciled balance as of the last day of the last fiscal year in your journal entry (most banks generate statements as of the last day of each month for business accounts). Don't include any transactions that hadn't cleared as of the last day of the year.

After you save the journal entry, use individual transactions to enter the previous unreconciled transactions, which allows you to see those transactions when you reconcile the bank account in QuickBooks.

Enter each deposit total and check (and electronic transfers, if any exist), all of which should be dated earlier than the first day of the year. You can make the entries directly in the account register, which is faster than using transaction windows (Write Checks or Make Deposits).

Entering Fixed Asset Balances

You can enter your current balances for fixed assets in either of the following ways:

- Enter the net amount (the purchase amount less accumulated depreciation).

- Enter the original purchase amount and also enter the accumulated depreciation.

I prefer the latter, because I like my accounting system to provide as much information as possible.

Entering Payroll Liabilities Balances

If you ended the year with payroll liabilities still unpaid, enter them in the opening balance journal entry. They'll wash when you enter the transaction that paid them during the current year.

Entering Sales Tax Liabilities Balances

If you have taxable sales for the last reporting period, you have to enter the total sales tax liability for those transactions *not* included in the historical transactions you entered. Paid (not open as of the end of the year) transactions also contributed to your tax liability, and you have to add that total to the sales tax liability account in order to remit taxes accurately.

Entering Income and Expense Balances

If you're working with calculated totals from the previous year (that you calculated in your old bookkeeping system), you may have to "back out" the amounts you posted when you entered the open receivables and payables.

For example, if you know your calculated sales total from your old system includes the unpaid invoices you entered in QuickBooks, subtract the total of the entered transactions from your year-end total. Do the same for your expense balances.

Entering Equity Account Balances

When you enter equity account balances you have to build in the accumulated equity (retained earnings) for your business. The way you enter equity account balances depends on the way your business is organized. If your business is a proprietorship or partnership, and you track capital in and draws out, you need to enter those individual totals.

If your accountant has prepared an end-of-year trial balance, including final equity balances as of the last day of the year, you can use those figures as a starting point. However, you have to subtract the equity that resulted from the historical transactions you entered. Ask your accountant for help and advice on recalculating that equity.

Creating the Historical Journal Entry

To create the journal entry that populates the account balances as of the last day of the prior year, choose Company → Make General Journal Entries and enter the totals as seen in Figure 1-6

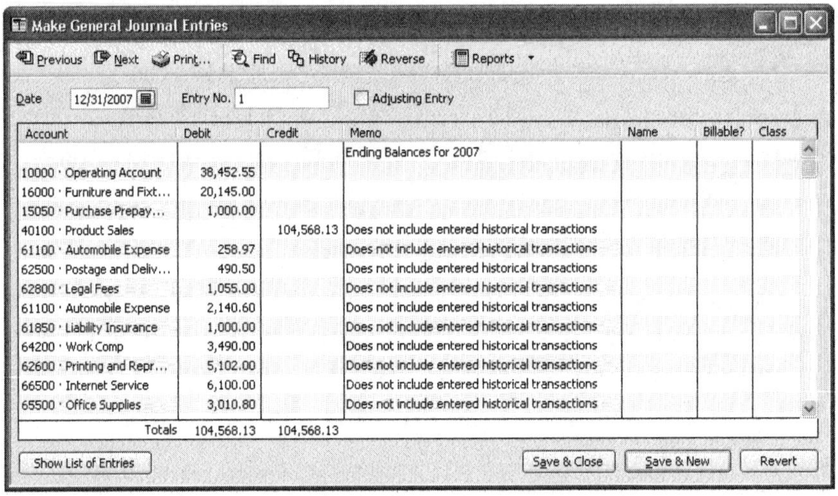

Figure 1-6: Enter the account balances for the previous year.

Remember to omit the balance sheet accounts you used when you entered your open transactions (except for sales tax liabilities as described earlier). For income and expense accounts, subtract the totals of the transactions you entered from the totals you have from your previous system (assuming those previous totals included open transactions).

Checking the Results

You need to check your work against two standards:

- The closing reports for the previous year, to make sure the numbers match your accountant's numbers, including the numbers used for your tax return.
- The opening trial balance for the current year, which should contain no accounts except balance sheet accounts, and the account balances should match your accountant's numbers.

Creating Reports on the Previous Year

To make sure your previous year numbers are correct (they're the basis of your tax return in addition to being the basis of your starting numbers for the current year), run the standard financial reports and set the date range for each report to the previous year.

- Profit & Loss Standard
- Balance Sheet Standard
- Trial Balance

Check the numbers against your accountant's figures. If they don't match, you can drill down through the reports to find the entries that are causing the problem.

Generating the Trial Balance for the Current Year

Run a trial balance report for the first day of the current year. Only the balance sheet accounts should display on the report; if you see any income or expense accounts drill down to the offending transaction (which has a date entered incorrectly). Congratulations, you're starting off in QuickBooks with accurate numbers!

Chapter 2

The Chart of Accounts

- Designing a chart of accounts
- Creating accounts
- Using subaccounts
- Manipulating accounts
- Importing a chart of accounts

The most important step in your company setup is the creation of your chart of accounts. QuickBooks may have created some accounts for you during the initial setup of your company file, but you'll need many additional accounts in order to keep books accurately. In this chapter, I'll discuss creating the chart of accounts, as well the various ways in which you can manipulate the accounts you've created.

It's easier to configure your company file if you create the chart of accounts before you create the other lists you need in QuickBooks. Some of the lists you work with require you to link the list elements you create to accounts. For example, service and product items are linked to income accounts.

Designing a Chart of Accounts

If you're designing your own chart of accounts, be sure to do so carefully, because you have to live with the results every time you use QuickBooks. Discuss the design with your accountant, who can help you devise a scheme that works for the types of transactions you have to enter, and the reports you need.

You have several decisions to make about the general format you'll use for your chart of accounts. You need to decide whether to use numbered accounts, and if so, how many digits to use for each account. You should also design a system for the use of subaccounts. Subaccounts make it possible to post transactions in a way that makes it easier to identify the specific categories you're tracking. In addition, you must create a protocol for account naming, and make sure everyone who works with the QuickBooks data files understands the protocol and applies it.

Using Account Numbers

By default, QuickBooks does not assign numbers to accounts, and you should switch your QuickBooks configuration options to correct that oversight. A chart of accounts with numbers is easier to design, and easier to work with. Numbered accounts also have account names, of course, but you can categorize accounts by number, which makes the chart of accounts easier to work with.

The advantage of using numbers is that you can arrange each section of the chart of accounts by category and subcategory, because within each type of account QuickBooks displays your chart of accounts in numerical order (without numbers, QuickBooks displays each section of your chart of accounts in alphabetical order).

For example, if accounts of the type Expense are arranged numerically instead of alphabetically, you can list related expense accounts contiguously. This means you can export reports to Excel and insert subtotals for related categories, which makes it easier to analyze where you're spending your money.

You can also use subaccounts in a numbered chart of accounts to provide subtotals for related expenses (or income) right on your QuickBooks reports, without the need to export the report to Excel in order to perform calculations.

Numbered accounts have proved to be useful in avoiding data entry errors when using a bank account. It's best if your main (most commonly used) bank account is at the top of the drop-down list. If your money market account is named for the bank (AlfaSavings), or even if you name the account Money Market, an alphabetic listing puts that account at the top of the bank account list when your operating account is named OperatingAccount, or it's named for the bank, which might be RiversideBank.

My experience with clients shows that this became extremely important when companies changed banks. Suppose the people who enter data in your company file have gotten used to selecting the second account on the list (because that's where your general operating account sits in alphabetic order), and your new account is now the third account on a drop-down list (or the first account, depending on the alphabetical sort and whether you made the old bank account inactive so it doesn't appear at all).

By the time everyone notices, figures out, and gets used to, the new bank list, you'll have a lot of research to do, followed by a lot of journal entries. You'll discover this when you try to reconcile your bank accounts. If you use numbered accounts, you can make sure the bank accounts always appear in the most convenient order. Even if your old bank was number 10000, and you want your new bank to use that number, it's a simple task to edit the original bank number to 14990 (moving it to the bottom of the list) and give the new bank the 10000 number to keep it at the top of the list.

Enabling Account Numbers

To switch to a number format for your accounts, you have to change the QuickBooks preferences as follows:

1. Choose Edit → Preferences from the menu bar to open the Preferences dialog.
2. Select the Accounting icon in the left pane.
3. Click the Company Preferences tab.
4. Select the Use Account Numbers check box.

All the accounts included in the chart of accounts you selected during company file setup are automatically switched to numbered accounts. These numbers are built in by QuickBooks and you can change them to match the order of accounts you prefer (see "Editing Accounts" later in this chapter).

When you select the option to use account numbers, the option Show Lowest Subaccount Only becomes accessible (it's grayed out if you haven't opted for account numbers). This option tells QuickBooks to display only the subaccount on transaction windows instead of both the parent account and the subaccount, making it easier to find the account you need in the narrow field of a drop-down list. (Subaccounts are discussed later in this chapter in the section "Using Subaccounts.")

QuickBooks does not automatically number accounts you added manually, so you must edit those accounts to add a number to each account record. If some accounts lack numbers, when you select Show Lowest Subaccount Only, QuickBooks displays an error message that you cannot enable this option until all your accounts have numbers assigned. After you've edited existing accounts that lack numbers, you can return to this preferences dialog and enable the option.

Designing the Number Scheme

After you've converted your chart of accounts to numbered accounts, you must use the numbers intelligently as you create or edit accounts. It's best to assign ranges of numbers to account types.

You should check with your accountant before finalizing the way you use the numbers, but the example I present here is a common approach. This scheme uses five-digit numbers, because that's the default in QuickBooks 2008, and the starting digit represents the beginning of a range:

> ***NOTE:*** *You can have as many as seven numbers (plus the account name) for each account.*

- 1xxxx Assets
- 2xxxx Liabilities
- 3xxxx Equity
- 4xxxx Income
- 5xxxx Expenses (of a specific type)
- 6xxxx Expenses (of a specific type)
- 7xxxx Expenses (of a specific type)
- 8xxxx Expenses (of a specific type)
- 9xxxx Other Income and Expenses

You can, if you wish, have a variety of expense types and reserve the starting number for specific types. Many companies, for example, use 5*xxxx* for sales expenses (they even separate the payroll postings between the sales people and the rest of the employees), then use 60000 through 79999 for general operating expenses, and 8*xxxx* for other specific expenses that should appear together in reports (such as taxes).

Some companies that track inventory use 5xxxx for Cost of Goods Sold and begin grouping expenses with 6xxxx. Other inventory-based companies start the Cost of Goods Sold accounts in the 45xxx range (since most companies don't have a large number of income accounts, the number range 40000 to 44999 is sufficient for income).

Some companies use one range of expense accounts, such as 70000 through 79999 for expenses that fall into the "overhead" category. This is useful if you want to track overhead expenses so you can apportion them to appropriate classes or jobs.

Also, think about the breakdown of assets. You might use 10000 through 10999 for cash accounts and 11000 through 11999 for receivables and other current assets, then use 12000 through 12999 for tracking fixed assets such as equipment, furniture, and so on.

Follow the same pattern for liabilities, starting with current liabilities and moving to long term. It's also a good idea to keep all the payroll withholding liabilities together.

Usually, as you create new accounts, you should increase the previous account number by 100, so that if your first bank account is 10000, the next bank account is 10100, and so on. These intervals give you room to create additional accounts that belong in the same general area of your chart of accounts.

Accounts Sort Order

You have to create a numbering scheme that conforms to the QuickBooks account types because QuickBooks sorts your chart of accounts by account type. If you have contiguous numbers that vary by account type, your reports won't be in the order you expect. QuickBooks uses the following sort order for the chart of accounts:

Assets:

Bank

- Accounts Receivable
- Other Current Asset
- Fixed Asset
- Other Asset

Liabilities

- Accounts Payable
- Credit Card
- Other Current Liability

- Long-Term Liability

Equity

Income

Cost Of Goods Sold

Expense

Other Income

Other Expense

Non-Posting Accounts

Non-posting accounts don't post financial amounts to the general ledger. They are created automatically by QuickBooks when you enable features that use those account types, such as Estimates, Purchase Orders, Sales Orders, etc. You can open the account register of non-posting accounts to see the transactions that fall into the appropriate account category, but you don't have to worry about any amounts impacting your financials.

Displaying Accounts Alphabetically in Reports

As convenient as it is for you (and your accountant) to have numbered accounts so you can track your finances by category and subcategory, suppose you have to submit financial reports to a bank because that's part of the requirements of your line of credit? Your bankers have certain financial categories they look at first, and it's easier for them if your accounts, especially your expenses, are in alphabetical order.

To produce reports without account numbers, putting each account type list back into alphabetical order, turn off the account number feature by deselecting the option in the Preferences dialog. Print the reports, and then turn the feature on again to restore the numbered order.

Account Naming Protocols

You need to devise protocols for naming accounts, whether you plan to use numbered accounts, or only use account names. When you're posting transactions to the general ledger, the only way to know which account should be used for posting is to have easy-to-understand account names.

Your protocol must be clear so that when everyone follows the rules, the account naming convention is consistent. This is important because without rules it's common to have multiple accounts for the same use. For example, I frequently find expense accounts named Telephone, Tele, and Tel in client systems, and all of those accounts have balances. Users "guess" at account names, and if they don't find the account the way they would have entered the name, they invent a new account (using a name that seems logical to them). Avoid all of those errors by establishing protocols about creating account names, and then make sure everyone searches the account list before applying a transaction.

Here are a few suggested protocols—you can amend them to fit your own situation, or invent different protocols that meet your comfort level. The important thing is to make sure you have absolute rules so you can achieve consistency.

- Avoid apostrophes
- Set the number of characters for abbreviations. For example, if you permit four characters, telephone is abbreviated "tele", a three-character rule produces "tel".
- Decide whether to use the ampersand (&) or a hyphen. For example, is it "Repairs & Maintenance" or "Repairs - Maintenance"? Do you want spaces before and after the ampersand or hyphen?

Creating Accounts

After you've done your homework, made your decisions, designed your protocols, and checked with your accountant, you're ready to create accounts. Start by opening the Chart of Accounts List by pressing Ctrl-A.

Press Ctrl-N to open the Choose Account Type dialog (see Figure 2-1), and select the type of account you want to create. The major (most used) account types are listed on the dialog. Accounts that are less frequently created by users are listed in the drop-down list you can open when you select Other Account Types.

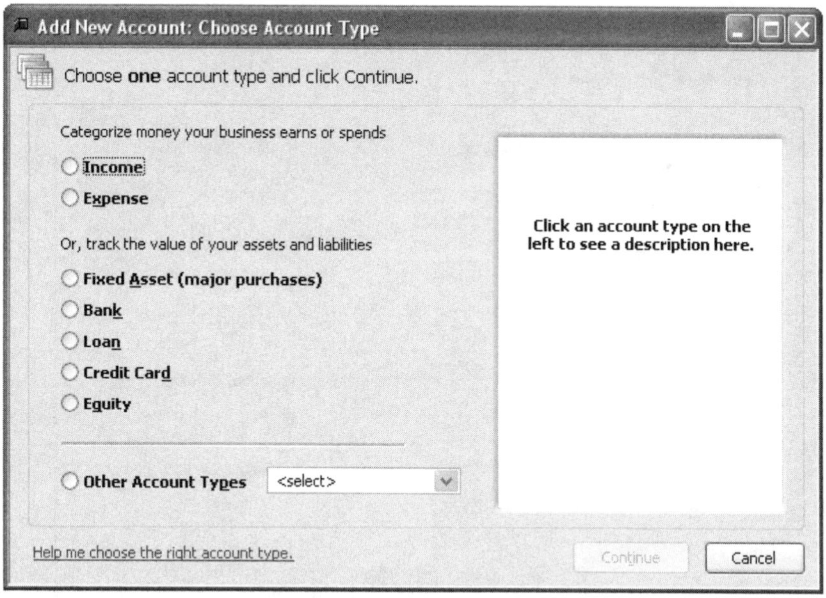

Figure 2-1: Creating an account starts by selecting the type of account.

After you select the account type, click Continue to open the Add New Account dialog. The dialog for creating a new account changes its appearance depending on the account type you select, because each account type contains particular fields to hold relevant information. Figure 2-2 shows the New Account dialog for an expense account.

The Tax Line field is only useful if you're planning to prepare your own business tax return using TurboTax®. If you didn't specify the type of tax return you use when you created your company, and you didn't add that information to the Company Information dialog later, the Tax Line field doesn't appear on the New Account dialog.

As you finish entering each account, click Save & New to move to another blank New Account dialog. By default, QuickBooks uses the same account type as the account you just created, but you can change the account type by selecting another type from the drop-down list at the top of the New Account dialog.

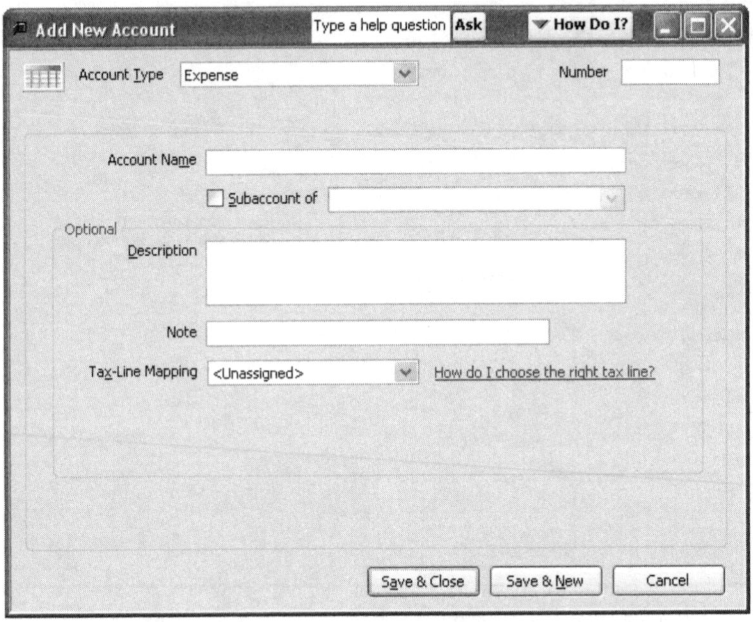

Figure 2-2: The only required entries for a new account are a number (if you're using numbers) and a name.

When you're finished entering accounts, click Save & Close, and then close the Chart of Accounts list.

Select From Examples

If you created your company file in QuickBooks 2008 (instead of updating the file from a previous version of QuickBooks), when you add a new account you may see a button labeled Select From Examples. Click the button to see a list of accounts that QuickBooks thinks you might want to consider adding to your chart of accounts.

If you used the EasyStep Interview to create your company file, you were able select accounts that were not already selected, or to deselect accounts that QuickBooks had selected. Accounts that remained unselected appear in the Select From Examples list.

If, during the EasyStep Interview, you selected an account for which QuickBooks suggests subaccounts (which did not appear in the account list during the interview), the account appears in the Select From Examples list, it's grayed out (because it was selected and does not need to be added to your chart of accounts). The suggested subaccounts are listed.

If you skipped the EasyStep Interview, QuickBooks installed the accounts that were preselected by default for the industry you chose during company file setup. Accounts that were not in the preselected list appear in the Select From Examples list.

If you did not select an Industry during company file setup (instead, you selected "None"), the Select From Examples button is grayed out and inaccessible.

NOTE: *If you add an account from the Select From Examples list, that account is removed from the list. If you delete the account from your chart of accounts, it is put back on the Select From Examples list.*

The following account types do *not* display the Select From Examples button:

- Bank
- Credit Card
- Equity
- Account Receivable
- Accounts Payable
- Long Term Liability

Automatically Created Accounts

QuickBooks has some "special" accounts that the software automatically creates. Some of these are added when you create a company file. Others are added when you enable a feature in one of the Preferences dialogs, or when you open a transaction window for a feature you've enabled in one of the preferences dialogs.

Most of these special accounts have a hidden marker that QuickBooks stores to indicate the fact that the account has a special use.

***TIP**: The hidden marker is visible when you export your chart of accounts to an .IIF file, and you can also create these special accounts, including the data for the hidden marker, when you prepare a chart of accounts in an .IIF file and then import the chart of accounts into a company file. See Appendix B for more information.*

In the following sections I'll explain these special accounts, and also offer solutions for the special accounts that might cause problems if you create similar accounts manually.

Special Accounts in All Company Files

The following special accounts are always automatically created when you create a company file.

- Opening Bal Equity
- Retained Earnings

Both of these accounts are equity account types, and aren't accounts you would normally create manually.

Feature-based Special Accounts

The following special accounts are added when you enable the attendant feature in the Preferences dialog:

- Estimates (a non-posting account) when you enable estimates in the Jobs & Estimates Preferences dialog.
- Sales Tax Payable (Other Current Liability account type) when you enable Sales Tax in the Sales Tax Preferences dialog.

***CAUTION**: Don't create a sales tax liability account when you're creating your chart of accounts, because you have no way to link that account to transactions. QuickBooks only uses its own sales tax account, which it creates when you enable the sales tax feature.*

The following accounts are added the first time you open a transaction window, after you enable the feature:

- Sales Orders (Non-Posting account type), which is added when you open the Create Sales Orders transaction window.
- Undeposited Funds (Other Current Asset account type), which is added when you open either the Receive Payments transaction window or the Enter Sales Receipts transaction window.
- Purchase Orders (Non-Posting account type), which is added when you open the Create Purchase Orders transaction window.

These are not accounts you'd normally create when you're creating your chart of accounts, so you don't have to worry about duplicates or conflicts with the accounts QuickBooks creates automatically.

The following accounts are added the first time you open a transaction window if you did not previously create the account:

- Accounts Receivable (Accounts Receivable account type), which is added when you open the Create Invoices transaction window, unless you created the account manually.
- Accounts Payable (Accounts Payable account type), which is added when you open the Enter Bills transaction window, unless you created the account manually.

When you open any of the transaction windows mentioned in this list, QuickBooks checks to see if the appropriate account exists in the chart of accounts. If so, QuickBooks does not add the account automatically.

Accounts Receivable and Accounts Payable do not have special hidden markers, because they're earmarked as unique accounts by their account type. Accounts Receivable is an account type Accounts Receivable in QuickBooks, even though it's technically a current asset in standard accounting terms. Accounts Payable is an account type Accounts Payable in QuickBooks, even though it's technically a current liability in standard accounting terms.

QuickBooks created these account types to make sure the software linked transactions properly. As long as you created these account types, no matter what account name you assigned the accounts, QuickBooks uses the accounts appropriately.

One advantage of this approach is the ability to have multiple A/R and A/P accounts. For example, some professional service businesses prefer to track retainer A/R separately from A/R for clients who are billed for hourly fees. Many nonprofit organizations have one A/R account for grants and another for individual pledges. Some companies like to separate A/P for inventory products separately from A/P for other expenses.

Using Multiple A/R and A/P Accounts

If you create multiple A/R or A/P accounts, you must be careful about posting transactions to the appropriate account. When you create invoices and enter bills, you must remember to select the appropriate A/R or A/P account from the drop-down list at the top of the transaction window.

Each A/R account has its own set of numbers. When you enter the first invoice number in a transaction linked to one A/R account, all invoices linked to that A/R account will use the next available number. For the second A/R account, start the invoice numbers with a totally different number scheme, so that customer and aging reports show the A/R links clearly. For instance, if you start numbering invoices for one A/R account at 101, start numbering invoices in the other A/R account at 2001.

When you receive payments from customers, you must remember to select the appropriate A/R account at the top of the Receive Payments window. The only invoices that appear when you select a customer are those linked to the selected A/R account.

Similarly, when you pay bills the A/P account selected at the top of the Pay Bills transaction window determines the bills that display.

Inventory Special Accounts

If you enable inventory and purchase orders in the Items & Inventory Preferences dialog, no accounts are added to your chart of accounts. Instead, QuickBooks waits until you create an inventory item to install inventory accounts.

As soon as you open a New Item dialog and select Inventory Part as the item type, QuickBooks automatically creates the following accounts:

- Inventory Asset (Other Current Asset account type)
- Cost of Goods Sold (Cost of Goods Sold account type)

The accounts are created before you fill in any data for the new inventory item, and are automatically entered as the default posting accounts. Figure 2-3 shows the way the New Item window looks when you select Inventory Part as the item type.

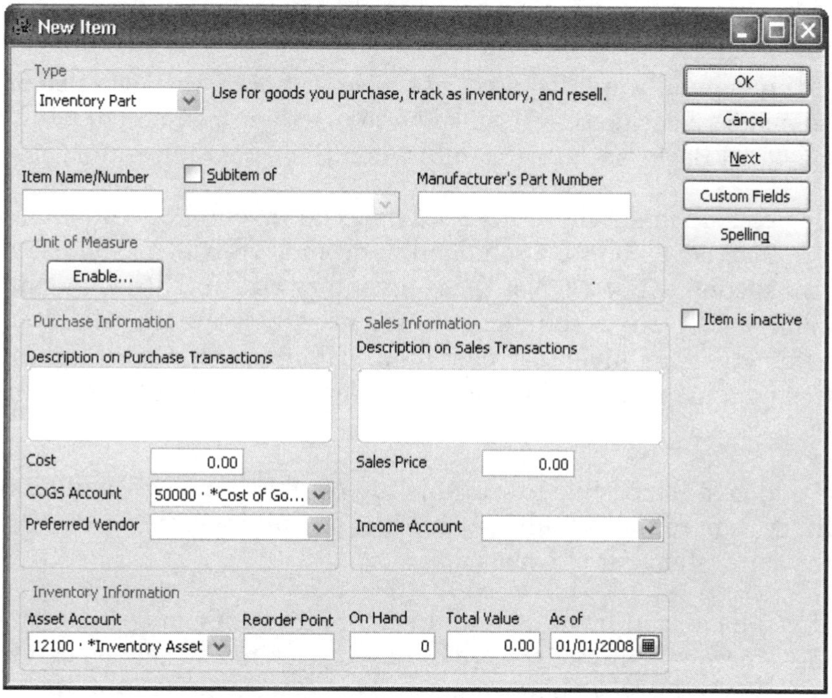

Figure 2-3: Before you enter any data for a new inventory part, QuickBooks has assigned some posting accounts.

Notice the account numbers in Figure 2-3 for the posting accounts for COGS Account and Asset Account; they provide clues for future problems. The asterisk in front of the account name means that these are duplicate accounts, because the user had already created accounts with these names.

This chart of accounts now has two accounts named Inventory Asset (both Other Current Asset types) and two Cost of Goods Sold accounts (both Cost of Goods Sold types).

However, every time you create an inventory part, QuickBooks automatically uses its own accounts as the default accounts for the Inventory Asset account and the COGS account.

If you haven't used the accounts you created yourself, delete them, and then edit the QuickBooks accounts to remove the asterisk from the name.

If the manually created accounts have balances, they can't be deleted, and some users decide they'll continue to use their own accounts by replacing the QuickBooks special accounts when they create inventory items.

Some users make the QuickBooks special inventory accounts inactive, because inactive accounts are hidden in drop-down lists as you use dialogs and transaction windows. Not these inventory accounts! Inactive, hidden, it doesn't matter; the accounts are automatically made the default accounts when you create an inventory part item. (Hiding accounts by making them inactive, and using hidden accounts, are topics discussed later in this chapter.)

It's almost impossible to win this tug-of-war; somebody will link an inventory item to the default QuickBooks special inventory accounts and throw your system out of whack.

If you have your own manual inventory accounts, and they contain postings, merge them into the QuickBooks accounts. Then you can remove the asterisk from the account name and change the account number of the QuickBooks accounts to match your own numbering system. Merging accounts is covered later in this chapter.

Don't Enter Opening Balances

Some account types have a field for an opening balance. Do *not* enter a balance while you're creating new accounts. The best way to put the account balances into the system is to enter historical transactions and historical totals via a journal entry (see Chapter 1 to learn how to enter your historical information and create opening balances).

The account types that offer an opening balance field (remember, this is the field to ignore and avoid) are the following:

- Asset accounts except Accounts Receivable
- Liability accounts except Accounts Payable
- Equity accounts

Creating Subaccounts

Subaccounts provide a way to post transactions more precisely, because you can pinpoint a subcategory. For example, if you create an expense account for insurance expenses, you may want to have subaccounts for vehicle insurance, liability insurance, equipment insurance, and so on.

Post transactions only to the subaccounts, never to the parent account. When you create reports, QuickBooks displays the individual totals for the subaccounts, along with the grand total for the parent account.

To create a subaccount, you must first create the parent account. If you're using numbered accounts, when you set up your main (parent) accounts, be sure to leave enough open numbers to be able to fit in all the subaccounts you'll need. If necessary, use more than five digits in your numbering scheme to make sure you have a logical hierarchy for your account structure.

When you view the chart of accounts, subaccounts appear under their parent accounts, and they're indented. When you view a subaccount in the drop-down list of the Account field in a transaction window, it appears with a colon between the parent account and the subaccount.

Because many of the fields in transaction windows are small, you may not be able to see the subaccount names without scrolling through the field. This can be annoying, and it's much easier to work if only the subaccount to which you post transactions is displayed.

That annoyance is cured by enabling the preference Show Lowest Subaccount Only, discussed earlier in this chapter. When you enable that option, you see only the last part of the subaccount in the transaction window, making it much easier to select the account you need.

QuickBooks offers two methods for making an account a subaccount: the New Account dialog, or dragging an account listing to an indented position.

Creating Subaccounts in the New Account Dialog

To use the New Account dialog for creating subaccounts, create the parent account, and then take the following steps:

1. Open the Chart of Accounts list.
2. Press Ctrl-N to create a new account.
3. Select the appropriate account type.
4. Enter an account number
5. Name the account
6. Click the Subaccount check box to place a check mark in it.
7. In the drop-down box next to the check box, select the parent account.
8. Click OK.

The new subaccount appears indented below its parent account in the Chart of Accounts window.

Creating Subaccounts by Dragging Account Listings

You can omit the extra steps of selecting the Subaccount check box and selecting the parent account. Create all the accounts you need, as if they were all parent accounts. However, be sure you assign account numbers with subaccounts in mind.

After you create all your accounts, open the Chart of Accounts window (if it isn't still open), and position your mouse pointer on the dia mond symbol to the left of the account you want to turn into a subaccount. Your pointer turns into a four-way arrow.

Drag the diamond symbol to the right to indent it. QuickBooks configures the account as a subaccount of the unindented listing immediately above this account. If you open the account's dialog, you'll see that the Subaccount Of option has a check mark, and the parent account referenced is the account name of the unindented listing above the subaccount. Repeat the action for the remaining listings under the parent account.

If the potential subaccount isn't currently listed directly below the account you want to use as a parent account, drag it up or down until it's positioned properly. Then drag the listing to the right to create a subaccount of the account directly above. This is only necessary if you don't use numbers, because if you designed your numbers properly, the accounts are in the right order for this step. (If you don't use numbers, the listings are alphabetical.)

Using Subaccounts for Easier Tax Preparation

One clever way to design your parent accounts and subaccounts is to design your chart of accounts around your tax return. This saves your accountant time, and that means you save money.

For example, the tax return you use may have a line into which you enter the total for office expenses. However, for the purpose of analyzing where you spend your money, you prefer to separate office expenses into multiple accounts, such as Computer Ribbons & Toner, Paper & Other Consumables, and so on. Office Supplies becomes the parent account, and any specific subcategories you care about become the subaccounts.

In fact, to save even more money on accounting services, arrange the order of your income and expense accounts and subaccounts in the order in which they appear on your tax return.

***NOTE**: CPA911 Publishing has created import files for the chart of accounts that are specifically designed for tax returns. Each chart of accounts is arranged in the order in which categories and totals are entered for the tax return in question. These files are included in the QuickBooks 2008 Accountant's Client Kit CD, which is available on our web site (www.cpa911publishing.com).*

Manipulating Accounts

You can edit, delete, hide, and merge accounts, and you'll probably perform some or all of these actions as you tweak your chart of accounts into a state of perfection. Tinkering with the chart of accounts is an ongoing process, because you'll find things you want to change as you use transaction windows and create reports.

Editing Accounts

If you need to make changes to an account, open the chart of accounts window, click the account's listing to select it, and press Ctrl-E. The Edit Account dialog appears, which looks very much like the account dialog you filled out when you created the account.

Adding and Changing Account Numbers

One of the most common reasons to edit an account is to add or change account numbers for existing accounts. After you enable the account number feature, QuickBooks automatically attaches numbers to any existing accounts that came from a predefined chart of accounts, but fails to attach numbers to any accounts you created manually. Therefore, you must add the missing numbers. In addition, if you don't like the numbering scheme that QuickBooks used, you can change the account numbers.

If you want to make wholesale changes in the numbering system QuickBooks used, it's easier to export the chart of accounts to Excel, make your changes with the help of the automated tools in Excel, and then import the changed chart of accounts into your company file. This works as long as you make no changes to anything except the account numbers, because QuickBooks will use the account name to accept the accounts properly (they won't appear to be duplicates).

Be sure to back up your company file before trying this, in case something goes awry. To learn how to export/import the chart of accounts, see Appendix A (importing Excel files) and Appendix B (importing IIF files).

Editing Optional Account Fields

You can edit any field in the account, including (with some exceptions) the account type. For example, you may want to add, remove, or change a description. For bank accounts, you might decide to put the bank account number in the dialog, or select the option to have QuickBooks to remind you to order checks when you've used a specific check number. If you want to change the account type, the following restrictions apply:

- You cannot change A/R or A/P accounts to other account types
- You cannot change other account types to be A/R or A/P accounts
- You cannot change the account type of accounts that QuickBooks creates automatically (such as Undeposited Funds).
- You cannot change the account type of an account that has subaccounts. You must make the subaccounts parent accounts (it's easiest to drag them to the left), change the account type of each account, and then create the subaccounts again (drag them to the right).

Deleting Accounts

To delete an account, select its listing in the Chart of Accounts window, and press Ctrl-D. QuickBooks displays a confirmation message, asking if you're sure you want to delete the account. Click OK to delete the account (or click Cancel if you've changed your mind).

Some accounts cannot be deleted, and after you click OK, QuickBooks displays an error message telling you why you cannot complete the action. Any of the following conditions prevent you from deleting an account:

- The account is linked to an item
- The account has been used in a transaction

- The account has subaccounts

If the problem is a link to an item, find the item that uses this account for posting transactions, and change the posting account. Check all items, because it may be that multiple items are linked to the account. (When you open the Items list, you can view the posting accounts in the Account column.)

If the problem is that the account has been used in a transaction, you won't be able to delete the account. QuickBooks means this literally, and the fact that the account has a zero balance doesn't make it eligible for deletion. I know users who have painstakingly created journal entries to move every transaction out of an account they want to delete, posting the amounts to other accounts. It doesn't work.

If the problem is subaccounts, you must first delete all the subaccounts. If any of the subaccounts fall into the restrictions list (usually they have transactions posted), you can make them parent accounts in order to delete the original parent account. (To turn a subaccount into a parent account, either drag its listing to the left in the Chart of Accounts window, or edit the account to remove the 'Subaccount Of' checkmark.)

An account that was created automatically by QuickBooks can be deleted (as long as it doesn't fall under the restrictions), but a warning message appears to tell you that if you perform actions in QuickBooks to warrant the use of the account, the system will automatically create the account again. For example, if QuickBooks created an account for Purchase Orders, you can delete it if you haven't yet created a Purchase Order. When you create your first Purchase Order, QuickBooks automatically recreates the account.

If you're trying to delete an account because you don't want anyone to post to it, but QuickBooks won't delete the account, you can hide the account by making it inactive. See the next section "Hiding Accounts".

If you're trying to delete an account because transactions were posted to it erroneously, you can merge the account with the account that should have received the postings. See the section "Merging Accounts".

Hiding Accounts

If you don't want anyone to post to an account but you don't want to delete the account (or QuickBooks won't let you delete the account), you can make the account inactive. In the Chart of Accounts window, right-click the account's listing and choose Make Inactive from the shortcut menu.

Inactive accounts don't appear in the account drop-down list when you're filling out a transaction window, and therefore can't be selected for posting. By default, they also don't appear in the Chart of Accounts window, which can be confusing. For example, you may have money market bank accounts that you don't want anyone to use during transaction postings. However, if you don't see the account in the Chart of Accounts List window, you won't know its current balance. In fact, you might forget it exists.

To view all your accounts in the Chart of Accounts window, including inactive accounts, select the option Include Inactive at the bottom of the window. A new column appears on the left side of the window with a column heading that's a large black X. Inactive accounts display a large black X in this column. To make an inactive account active, click the black X (it's a toggle).

***TIP:** If the Include Inactive option is grayed out, there are no inactive accounts.*

Using a Hidden Account in Transactions

Sometimes, in an office with multiple QuickBooks users, the bookkeeper or owner wants to prevent other users from posting transactions to a certain account. For example, it's not unusual for equity accounts (such as Draw) to be misused, and it's rather common to see inappropriate postings to Miscellaneous Expenses. It's better if only people with some expertise post transactions to these account types.

You can hide an account (make it inactive), and still use it. When you're entering data in a transaction window, don't use the drop-down list in the Account field (because of course, the account won't appear). Instead, enter the account name or number manually.

QuickBooks displays a message asking if you want to use the account just once, or reactivate the account. Click the option to use the account just once. (You can use the account "just once" as many times as you want to.)

Merging Accounts

Sometimes you have two accounts that should be one. For instance, you may be splitting postings inappropriately, and your accountant suggests that one account would be better. Perhaps there's no reason to post some revenue for consulting work to an account named Income-Consulting, and other revenue to an account named Income-Fees.

Often, you may find that accidentally, two accounts were created for the same category. As I discussed earlier in this chapter, I've been to client sites that had accounts named Telephone and Tele, with transactions posted to both accounts. Those accounts badly need merging. Accounts must meet the following criteria in order to merge them:

- The accounts must be of the same type
- The accounts must be at the same level (parent or subaccount of the same parent account)

If the accounts aren't at the same level, move one of the accounts to the same level as the other account. After you merge the accounts, you can move the surviving account to a different level.

Take the following steps to merge two accounts:

1. Open the Chart of Accounts window.
2. Select (highlight) the account that has the name you *do not* want to use anymore.
3. Press Ctrl-E to open the Edit Account dialog.
4. Change the account name and number to match the account you want to keep.
5. Click OK.

QuickBooks displays a message telling you that the account number/name you've entered already exists for another account, and asking if you want to merge the accounts. Click Yes to confirm that you want to merge the two accounts. All the transactions from both accounts are merged into the account you chose to keep.

If you're doing some serious housekeeping on your company file, and you find three (or perhaps more) accounts that should be merged into a single account, merge the first two, then merge the surviving account with the third account.

Importing the Chart of Accounts

Importing a chart of accounts is an efficient way to get exactly the chart of accounts you need without going through all the work of entering accounts one at a time. Of course, to import a chart of accounts, you have to have an import file. You can import data into QuickBooks from either of these source file types:

- An Excel worksheet with a file extension .xls or .csv.
- A tab-delimited text file, with a file extension .iif.

If you're an accountant, creating import files that you can take to clients provides a valuable service for your clients, and also makes your own work easier—the chart of accounts is configured properly for your tax, planning, and analysis services. Many accountants create import file templates to create a customized chart of accounts for each QuickBooks client.

The steps required to import an Excel file are in Appendix A, and the steps required to import an IIF file are in Appendix B. Because you can import a variety of QuickBooks lists, I thought it was more efficient to put the instructions for accomplishing the import in one place (the appendices), instead of repeating the rather lengthy steps in every chapter of this book that discusses imported files.

Chapter 3

Lists and Classes

Creating lists

Creating custom fields in lists

List limits

Creating classes

Lists are mini-files within your QuickBooks data file, and they contain the data you use when you create transactions. For example, the names of your customers and vendors are held in QuickBooks lists. (Database developers usually refer to these files-within-the-file as *tables*.)

Most of the fields in the QuickBooks transaction windows require you to make a selection from a drop-down list. If the selection you need isn't there, you can create it while you're creating the transaction (which is called *on the fly* data entry). However, that interrupts the process of creating a transaction, which makes you less productive. Take the time now to get this basic data into your system.

Creating your lists is one of those "which came first, the chicken or the egg" exercises. Some lists have fields for other list items, such as the Customer:Job list, where each dialog contains fields for data that's contained in auxiliary lists (Terms, Price Level, Type, and so on).

In this chapter, I present an overview of the lists, providing some of the things I've learned from clients about creating and using them in a useful way. The basic instructions for creating, editing, merging, and deleting list items are in *QuickBooks 2008: The Official Guide*.

I'll start with the auxiliary lists, which QuickBooks calls the Customer & Vendor Profile Lists. After you create items for these lists, you can choose data from a drop-down list when you're creating data for the larger lists.

Customer & Vendor Profile Lists

Some of the Customer & Vendor Profile lists let you filter, sort, and categorize information about your customers, jobs, and vendors. Other lists in this category are for maintaining information that makes it easier to manage transactions.

When you create customers and vendors, you can pre-assign the entries in some of these profile lists as default settings, and the data will appear in transaction windows involving those customers and vendors. The default settings you specify aren't etched in stone; you can change any field's data in any transaction window.

To access these lists choose Lists → Customer & Vendor Profile Lists, which displays a submenu containing the following lists (all of which are covered in this section):

- Sales Rep List
- Customer Type List
- Vendor Type List
- Job Type List
- Terms List
- Customer Message List
- Payment Method List
- Ship Via List
- Vehicle List

Sales Rep List

The Rep field on transaction windows is used to link a sales representative to a customer. You need this information if you pay commissions to sales reps, but even if you don't have a commission structure, it's often helpful to know who the primary contact is for a customer (usually referred to as a service rep instead of a sales rep).

When you create a sales rep, you enter the name and initials. The initials become the code for the sales rep, and those initials appear in the Rep field of sales transaction forms.

Creating this list is one of those "chicken or the egg" situations, because in order to add a sales rep, the name must already exist in the Employees, Vendors, or Other Names list.

If the sales rep's name is not already on one of those lists, you can create the entry in the Sales Rep list, and when you press Tab to move to the next field, QuickBooks displays a dialog that lets you add the new rep to your Employee, Vendor, or Other Names list.

TIP: *Paying commissions to sales reps can be complicated. To avoid making it more complicated than it needs to be, and to make sure you don't have errors in the setup and configuration of commissions, see the troubleshooting information on commissions in Appendix C.*

Customer Type

Use the Customer Type list to sort your customers by a type you deem important or convenient when you create reports. For example, you may decide to signify wholesale and retail customers by type.

Types don't work well unless they're similar in category. If you want to use types such as "retail" and "wholesale" to categorize customers, then you can't use "yellow pages" or "local newspaper ad" to track the source of referrals.

If you mix categories, you won't be able to sort or filter reports properly to gain useful information. If you really need more than one category of customer type, use custom fields for some of the categories (see "Creating Custom Fields", later in this chapter).

Vendor Type

Use this list to classify your vendors by type, so you can create reports sorted by the criteria you establish when you invent your vendor type entries. As with Customer Types, Vendor Types don't work if you mix categories.

Job Type

The entries you create for this list help you classify jobs (if you track jobs or projects) so you can create reports sorted by different types of jobs. For example, you may want to have job types to separate fixed fee jobs from time and material jobs. Or, you may want to classify jobs by those you do with in-house personnel and those that involve outside contractors.

Terms

Terms, of course, refers to payment terms. The terms you create are linked to both customers and vendors, and you may need additional terms to make sure you've covered all your customer and vendor terms. QuickBooks supports two types of terms:

- Standard terms, which have a due date following a certain amount of time after the invoice date.
- Date driven terms, which are due on a particular day of the month, regardless of the invoice date.

Create a name for the new terms, using a name that makes it easy to understand the terms when you see it on a drop-down list in a transaction window. For example, if you create standard terms of 30 days, name the entry 30Days. If you create date driven terms where the payment is due on the 15th of the month, name the entry 15thMonth.

Creating Standard Terms

Select Standard, and fill out the dialog to match the terms. Net Due is the number of days you allow for payment after the invoice date.

To give customers a discount for early payment, enter the discount percentage and the number of days after the invoice date that the discount is in effect. For example, if you allow 30 days for payment but want to encourage customers to pay early, enter a discount percentage that is in effect for 10 days after the invoice date.

Creating Date Driven Terms

Select Date Driven, and enter the day of the month the invoice payment is due. Then enter the number of days before the due date that invoices are considered to be payable on the following month (for example, it's not fair to insist that invoices be paid on the 10th of the month if you mail them to customers on the 8th of the month).

To give customers a discount for early payment, enter the discount percentage and the day of the month at which the discount period ends. For example, if the standard due date is the 15th of the month, you may want to extend a discount to any customer who pays by the 8th of the month.

> ***NOTE**: Terms that provide discounts for early payment are commonly used by manufacturers and distributors of products. It's not standard practice to provide discounts for early payment if you sell services. If you need an incentive for customers to pay their bills on time, use finance charges.*

Customer Message

This list holds the messages you can print at the bottom of customer transaction forms (invoices, sales receipts, estimates, etc.). The messages can contain up to 101 characters (including spaces and punctuation).

Payment Method

This list contains specifies the various types of payments you receive from customers. Tracking the payment method for customers helps you resolve disputes because you have a detailed report of every payment you receive.

In addition, specifying the payment method lets you group deposits by the appropriate categories when you use the Make Deposits window. Your bank statement probably displays separate entries for credit card receipts, electronic transfers, and cash and checks. Depositing funds by payment method makes it easier to reconcile the bank account.

Ship Via

Use this list to specify the way products are shipped when you sell products to customers. The list is prepopulated with the major carriers, as well as the US Postal Service. If you have your own trucks or cars, add self-delivery to your list.

Vehicle

A vehicle list in the Customer & Vendor Profile list group? Don't ask me, I can't figure it out either. Use this list for vehicles for which you want to track mileage.

Once you've entered a vehicle in the vehicle list, you can track mileage for that vehicle by choosing Company → Enter Vehicle Mileage. The dialog that appears is easy to fill out and can be extremely useful (see Figure 3-1).

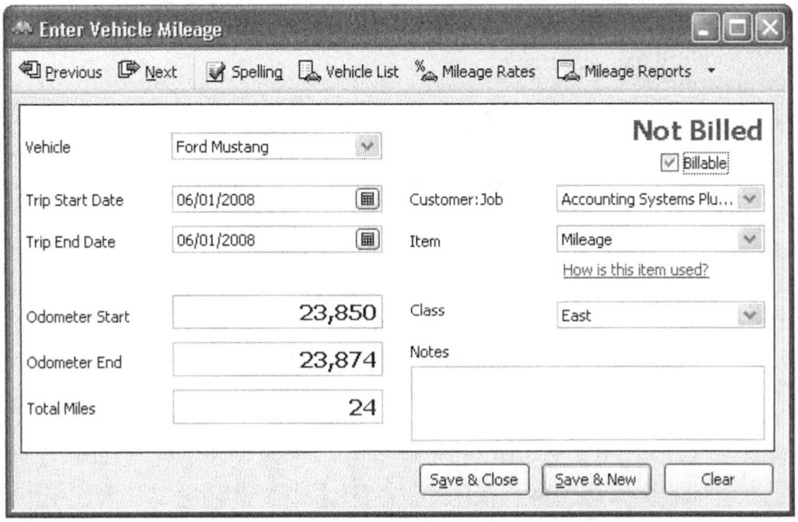

Figure 3-1: Track mileage for the vehicles in your Vehicle List.

Mileage data can be used for numerous purposes:

- Bill customers for mileage (reimbursement amounts for trips marked Billable are automatically available when you invoice the customer).
- Link trips to customers/jobs without billing the customers, in order to track job costs.
- Track mileage for tax deduction purposes.
- Track mileage for vehicle maintenance purposes.

Customers & Jobs List

In QuickBooks, customers and jobs are handled together, because jobs must be linked to customers. You can create a customer and consider anything and everything you invoice to that customer a single job, or you can have multiple jobs for the same customer. You can link as many jobs to a single customer as you need to.

***TIP**: If you are going to track jobs, it's more efficient to create all your customers first, and then create the jobs.*

Customer Name Protocols

You have to develop a set of rules, or protocols, for naming your customers. Some businesses use number codes, some use a combination of letters (using the first few letters of the customer name) and numbers, and some use the actual name. What's important is to have a consistent pattern for creating customer names; otherwise, you run the risk of entering the same customer multiple times. Imagine trying to track receivables under those circumstances!

When you create a customer in QuickBooks, the first field in the New Customer dialog is Customer Name. Don't take the name of that field literally; instead, think of the data you enter in that field as a code rather than a real name. This code is a reference that's linked to all the information you enter in the customer record (company name, primary contact name, address, and so on).

The code doesn't appear on printed transactions (such as invoices or sales receipts); the Customer:Job dialog has a field for the Company Name, and that's what appears on transactions, not the Customer Name. You must invent a protocol for the customer name (the code) so you enter every customer in the same manner.

Avoiding punctuation and spaces in codes is a good protocol for codes. This avoids the risk that you'll enter any customer more than once.

Consider the following customer codes I've found in client files (each of these represents a single customer entered multiple times):

- O'Neill and Oneill
- Sam's Pizza, Sams Pizza, and SamsPizza
- The Rib Pit, Rib Pit, and RibPit

Incidentally, the last listing in each entry of this list represents the best protocol. Customer names such as SamsPizza and RibPit have a capital letter in the middle of the name to make it easier to read the name. However, if you're typing the name in a list box (it's easier to select a name from a long drop-down list by typing than by scrolling), you don't have to capitalize any letters—data in drop-down lists is not case-sensitive.

If your business has most of its customers in the same industry, you may find that many customers have similar (or identical) names. I have a client who sells supplies to video rental stores, and at least seventy percent of the customer names start with the word "Video". A large number of those stores have identical names, such as Video Palace, Video Stop, Video Hut, and so on. In fact, some customers are individual stores that are owned by a chain; so all the names are identical (except for the store number). To make it possible for each customer in the system to have a unique customer name, we use telephone numbers (including the area code).

***NOTE**: You can use up to 41 characters in the Customer Name field.*

Importing the Customer List

If you've been keeping a customer list in another software application, you can avoid one-customer-at-a-time data entry by importing the list into QuickBooks. You have two methods at your disposal for importing the list:

- Import the list directly from an Excel file or a CSV file.
- Import the list from an IIF file.

If you've been using another accounting application, you must export the data from that application to create your import file. This is only possible if your current accounting application is capable of exporting data to one of the following formats:

- Excel file
- CSV (comma separated value) file
- Tab-delimited text file.

All three of these file types can be opened in Excel. If you use another spreadsheet application, you can use a CSV file or a tab-delimited text file (and some spreadsheet software is capable of loading Excel files and converting them to their own document type).

If you keep your customer list on paper, or in a software application that can't export to the required file type, you can enter the customer information in a spreadsheet and then import the data. It's much faster to work in the rows of a spreadsheet document than to move from field to field, one customer dialog at a time, in QuickBooks.

A QuickBooks customer import file can contain all the information you need to fill out all the fields in the customer dialog, such as customer type, sales tax status, and so on. It's unlikely you've kept records in a manner that matches these fields, but you can import whatever information you already have, and later enter additional information by editing the customer records.

Detailed instructions for creating and importing Excel/CSV files are in Appendix A, and detailed instructions for creating and importing IIF files are in Appendix B. These instructions include all the column headings and keywords for importing customers and jobs.

Vendor List

Your vendors have to be entered into your QuickBooks system, and it's easier to do it while you're setting up your company instead of during transaction entry.

Importing the Vendor List

If you've been tracking vendors in Excel, or even in Word, or in another software application, you can import the vendor list into QuickBooks, which saves all that one-customer-at-a-time data entry you'd have to perform in QuickBooks. You have two methods at your disposal for importing the list:

- Import the list directly from an Excel file or a CSV file.
- Import the list from an IIF file.

If you've been using another accounting application, you must export the data from that application to create your import file. This is only possible if your current accounting application is capable of exporting data to one of the following formats:

- Excel file
- CSV (comma separated value) file
- Tab-delimited text file.

All three of these file types can be opened in Excel. If you use another spreadsheet application, you can use a CSV file or a tab-delimited text file (and some spreadsheet software is capable of loading Excel files and converting them to their own document type).

If you keep your vendor list on paper, or in a software application that can't export to the required file type, you can enter the vendor information in a spreadsheet and then import the data. It's much faster to work in the rows of a spreadsheet document than to move from field to field, one customer dialog at a time, in QuickBooks.

A QuickBooks vendor import file can contain all the information you need to fill out all the fields in the vendor dialog. Detailed instructions for creating and importing Excel/CSV files are in Appendix A, and detailed instructions for creating and importing IIF files are in Appendix B. These instructions include all the column headings and keywords for importing vendors.

Fixed Asset Item List

Use the Fixed Asset Item List to track information about the assets you depreciate. As you can see in Figure 3-2, the dialog for a fixed asset includes fields that allow you to keep rather detailed information. The dialog also has fields to track the sale of a depreciated asset.

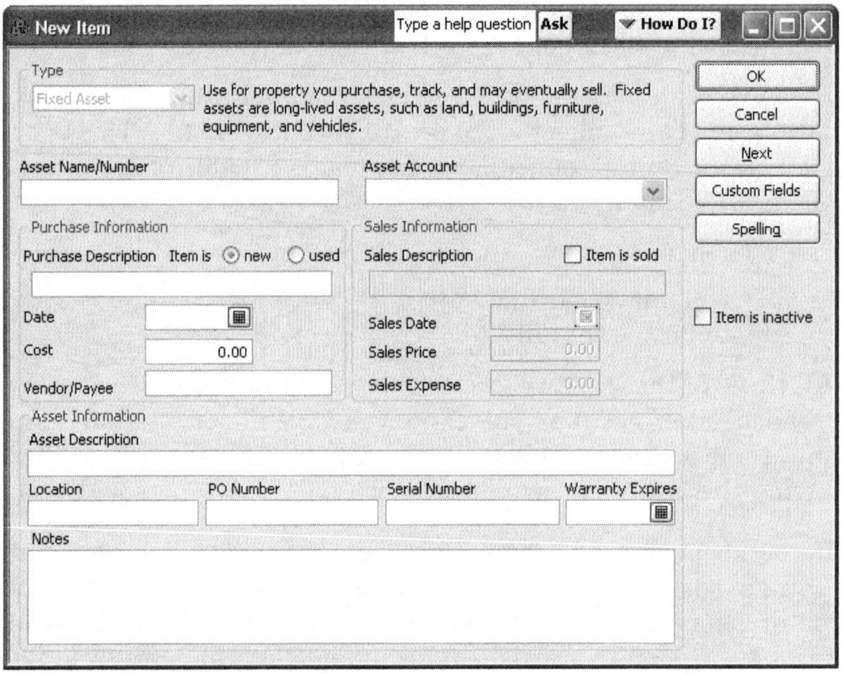

Figure 3-2: Track depreciable assets in the Fixed Asset Item List.

Should You use the Fixed Asset Item List?

The Fixed Asset Item List is inert. It doesn't do anything, and isn't used for any type of transaction in QuickBooks (except Premier Accounting Edition—see the next section, "When the Fixed Asset Item List is Useful").

When you enter a fixed asset in the Fixed Asset Item List, the financial information you enter isn't transferred to your Fixed Asset accounts, even though you must specify those accounts in the New Item dialog. You have to create separate transactions in your chart of accounts to enter that information into your fixed asset accounts. It doesn't work the other way around, either; the Fixed Asset Item List won't read the information from the fixed asset account you specify.

QuickBooks adds all the fixed assets you keep in this list to the Items list you see when you're creating a transaction. You have to scroll through all the fixed asset entries as well as your "regular" items to select an item for the transaction. If you have a lot of items and a lot of fixed assets, this is really a pain!

The Fixed Asset Item List is not any more useful than a list you could keep in Word or Excel. If you design a table in Word, with a column for each category you want to track, or you keep your fixed assets in Excel, you can sort the data to match whatever information you need to see. In fact, entering the data is much easier in Word or Excel, because you don't have to keep clicking OK to open a new blank dialog to enter each asset. Instead, you can just move down the columns and across the rows.

When the Fixed Asset Item List is Useful

QuickBooks Premier Accountant Edition includes Fixed Asset Manager (discussed in Chapter 10), a tool that *does* use the information in the Fixed Asset Item list to generate depreciation.

Fixed Asset Manager automatically performs depreciation transactions, applying depreciation amounts to the appropriate fixed asset accounts. If your accountant uses Fixed Asset Manager, you can send your company file or an Accountant's Copy file to automate the process of depreciating your assets. Since this may make your accountant's work easier and faster, it may reduce your bill for tax preparation. That trade-off may be worth the annoyances that come with the decision to use the Fixed Asset Item List.

Price Level List

The Price Level List is a nifty, easy way to fine-tune your pricing schemes. You can use price levels to make sure your customers are happy, and your bottom line is healthy.

***NOTE**: The Price Levels List only appears on the Lists menu if you enabled Price Levels in the Sales & Customers section of your Preferences dialog.*

QuickBooks Premier editions offer two types of price levels:

- Fixed percentage price levels
- Per item price levels (not available in QuickBooks Pro editions)

Fixed Percentage Price Levels

Fixed percentage price levels can be applied to a customer, a job, or an individual sales transaction. The price levels are applied against the standard price of items (as recorded in each item's record).

For example, you may want to create a price level that gives your favorite customers an excellent discount. Another common price reduction scheme is a discounted price level for all customers that are nonprofit organizations.

On the other hand, you may want to maintain your item prices for most customers, and increase them by a fixed percentage for certain customers. (You can also apply the price level to an individual sale, such as an estimate, invoice, or cash receipt.)

To create a percentage-based price level, open the Price Level List by choosing Lists → Price Level List from the QuickBooks menu bar. When the Price Level List window opens (see Figure 3-3), follow these steps:

1. Press Ctrl-N to open the New Price Level dialog.
2. Enter a name in the Price Level Name field. Use a name that reflects the algorithm you're using for this price level, such as 10Off (for a ten percent reduction).
3. In the Price Level Type field, select Fixed % from the drop-down list, if it's not already selected.
4. Specify whether the price level is a decrease or increase against an item price.
5. Enter the percentage of increase or decrease. (You don't have to enter the percent sign—QuickBooks will automatically add it.)

6. Click OK.

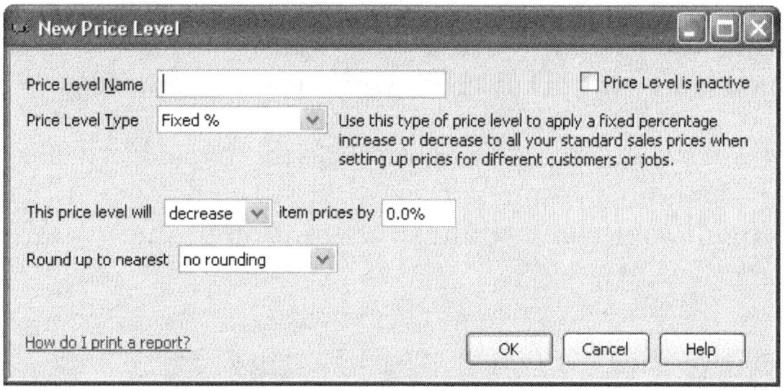

Figure 3-3: A fixed percentage price level is uncomplicated and easy to create.

Rounding Prices

When you use a percentage-based price level, the resulting price is usually not an even dollar amount. QuickBooks lets you set a rounding algorithm for your price levels.

To select a rounding algorithm, click the arrow to the right of the field labeled Round Up To Nearest, and select the rounding amount to apply to this price level from the drop-down list (see Figure 3-4).

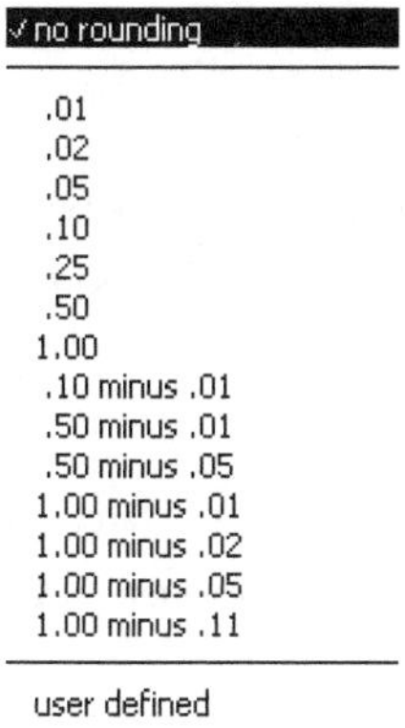

Figure 3-4: Tell QuickBooks how to round up the resulting price after this price level is applied.

Customizing the Rounding Algorithm

You can customize the rounding algorithm, which gives you more precision, and also gives you the ability to use standard, normal, rounding rules (which means you can round down when it's appropriate).

To create your own, customized, rounding scheme, select User Defined from the Rounding drop-down list (it's at the bottom of the list). The dialog adds fields to accommodate your creation of the custom rounding algorithm (see Figure 3-5).

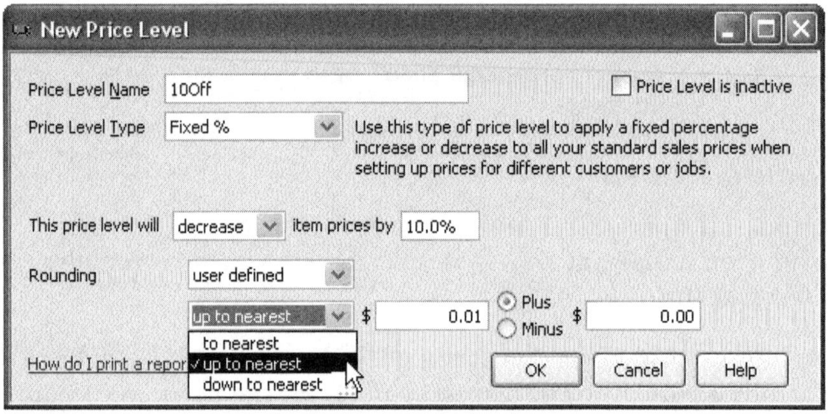

Figure 3-5: Create a rounding scheme that is precisely what you want.

Applying a Fixed Percentage Price Level

You can link price levels to customers and jobs, or apply price levels while you're creating sales forms (invoices, sales orders, sales receipts, and credit memos). The method you use produces different results, as follows:

- If you link a price level to customers or jobs, the price level is automatically applied to all items whenever you use that customer or job on a sales form.
- If you apply the price level while you're creating a sales form, the price level is applied against the standard price for the item. If the

item is already discounted because of a price level applied to the customer, that discounted price is ignored in favor of the price level you're applying to the sales form.

Linking a Fixed Percentage Price Level to a Customer or Job

To link a price level to a customer or a job, you need to edit the customer or job record to reflect the link. Open the Customers & Jobs list in the Customer Center and take the following actions:

1. Double-click the listing for the customer or job you want to link to a price level, to open the Edit Customer dialog.
2. Move to the Additional Info tab.
3. Click the arrow in the Price Level field to display a drop-down list of all the price levels you've created.
4. Select the appropriate price level.
5. Click OK.

Repeat this for all the customers and jobs you want to link to a price level. Be aware of the following "rules" governing the application of price levels to customers and jobs:

- If you link a price level to a customer, it does not apply to that customer's jobs. You will only see the price level applied if you create a sales form for the customer (which is hardly ever done when you're tracking jobs).
- If you link a price level to a job, only sales forms related to that specific job reflect the price level.

These rules make it possible to apply different price levels to each of a customer's jobs, if that's your plan. Unfortunately, that's hardly ever the plan (at least it's rare in the client sites I visit, and in the accountant seminars I give or attend).

QuickBooks didn't think to include a dialog that pops up when you apply a price level to a customer and asks if you want to apply that price level to all of the jobs for that customer.

It would be even nicer if such a dialog box included the selection "apply to future jobs for this customer".

It would be absolutely terrific if the dialog listed all the current jobs, so you could select those that should be configured for this price level, along with the "Apply this to future jobs" option.

Since none of these helpful tools are available, I created a workaround. See the section "Applying Price Levels to Customers and Jobs in Batches", later in this chapter.

Applying a Fixed Percentage Price Level in a Sales Form

You can change the price of an item on a sales form by applying a price level as you create the sales form. This gives you quite a bit of flexibility for passing along discounts (or price hikes) to any customer. Use the following steps to apply a price level to a sales form:

1. Fill out the sales form in the usual way.
2. Click the arrow in the Rate column to display your price levels (see Figure 3-6).
3. Select a price level to apply to the item.

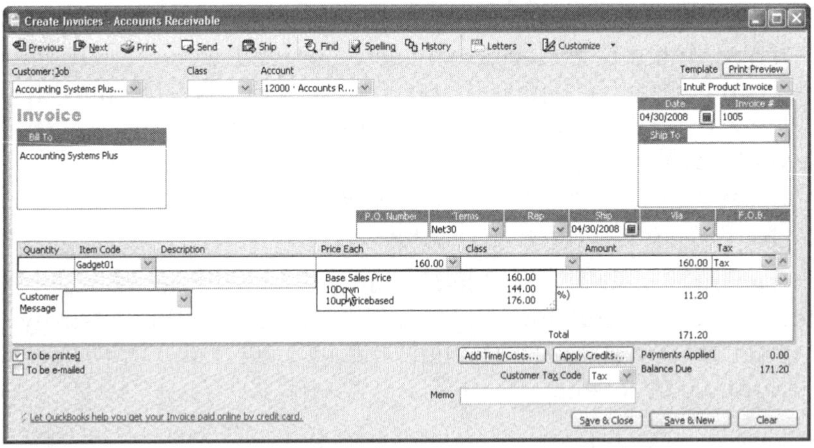

Figure 3-6: The drop-down list shows each price level, and its resulting price.

This can get complicated, because the price level you're selecting is applied to the recorded price of the item (the price you entered in the item's record when you created the item), which may not be the price displayed on the sales form, because *that* price may be linked to a price level you applied to this customer.

If you linked a price level to the customer, the price that appears on the sales form reflects the application of the price level. Applying another price level at this point may be butting into a rate that has already had a price level applied. The price level you select while you're working in the sales form wins—any amount calculated by a customer-linked price level is overwritten.

For example, the customer in the invoice seen in Figure 3-6 was linked to a price level that caused the item's price to be reduced automatically by 15%. If you select a 10% price level decrease from the drop-down list in the sales form, the customer pays more. While the ability to set a price level in a sales form gives you some flexibility in determining prices for a customer, you need to be careful about undoing a promised discount.

Applying Price Levels to Customers in Batches

If you already had a large number of customers and jobs in your system when you created percentage-based price levels, you have to open each customer record, and each job record, move to the Additional Info tab, and assign a price level by selecting one from the drop-down list in the Price Level field.

That's a lot of work, and besides, it's so boring! And, you have to do the same thing if you create new price levels that you want to assign to customers to replace existing price levels, or assign to customers for whom you hadn't previously assigned price levels. More time consuming, boring work!

There's an easier way. Export your customer list to an IIF file, and assign the price levels in Excel, which is a snap to do! Then import the new data into your QuickBooks customer records.

To export the file, take the following steps:

1. Choose File → Utilities → Export → Lists to IIF Files.

2. In the Export dialog select Customer List and click OK.
3. Select a location for the file and name it appropriately (e.g. CustList).

The following sections offer some tricks and tips to help you finish this task smoothly. But first, back up your company file before doing anything else. Whenever you're going to import data, you should have a current backup to restore in case something goes wrong.

Note the Names of the Price Levels

You must use the price level names that exist in your system in your import file, so you must make sure you have the names exactly right. Punctuation, spaces, etc. must be exactly the same as the price level names in your system. I have a foolproof system for this that you can use, too.

1. Open a word processing program (Word, WordPad, or Notepad).
2. In QuickBooks, double-click the first price level listing to open its record in edit mode. The price level name is highlighted.
3. Press Ctrl-C to put the highlighted text on the Windows clipboard.
4. Switch to the word processor and press Ctrl-V to paste the text.
5. Open each fixed percentage price level listing and repeat the process.

Save the document, and leave it open. It provides the text you'll paste into your worksheet when you create your import file.

***WARNING**: Remember that you can only assign Fixed Percentage price levels to customers, so don't use Per Item price levels for this task.*

Eliminate Unneeded Cells

It's easier to work in Excel if the columns and rows are straightforward and easy to locate. After you export the file and open Excel, select all the rows on top of the first row of *real* data. The first row of real data is the row that has !CUST in Column A.

To select the rows, click the row number header on the left edge of Row 1 and then hold the Shift Key and click the last row above the first row of real data. When all the rows are selected (see Figure 3-7), click Edit → Delete.

	A	B	C	D	E	F	G	H	I	J	K
1	IHDR	PROD	VER	REL	IIFVER	DATE	TIME	ACCNTNT	ACCNTNT	SPLITTIME	
2	HDR	QuickBook	Version 17	Release R		1	1/5/2007	1.16E+09	N	0	
3	ICUSTNAM	INDEX	LABEL	CUSTOME	VENDOR	EMPLOYEE					
4	IENDCUSTNAMEDICT										
5	CUSTNAM	0	ContractR	Y	Y	N					
6	CUSTNAM	1	RequiresD	N	Y	N					
7	CUSTNAM	2	Backorder	Y	N	N					
8	CUSTNAM	3		N	N	N					
9	CUSTNAM	4		N	N	N					
10	CUSTNAM	5		N	N	N					
11	CUSTNAM	6		N	N	N					
12	CUSTNAM	7		N	N	N					
13	CUSTNAM	8		N	N	N					
14	CUSTNAM	9		N	N	N					
15	CUSTNAM	10		N	N	N					
16	CUSTNAM	11		N	N	N					
17	CUSTNAM	12		N	N	N					
18	CUSTNAM	13		N	N	N					
19	CUSTNAM	14		N	N	N					
20	ENDCUSTNAMEDICT										
21	ICUST	NAME	REFNUM	TIMESTAN	BADDR1	BADDR2	BADDR3	BADDR4	BADDR5	SADDR1	SADDR2
22	CUST	InHouse	91	1.16E+09							
23	CUST	RetailCust	89	1.16E+09							
24	CUST	GrantJohn	88	1.17E+09	John Grant	John Grant	845 N. Wa	Philadelphia PA 19177			
25	CUST	House	80	1.14E+09	House						

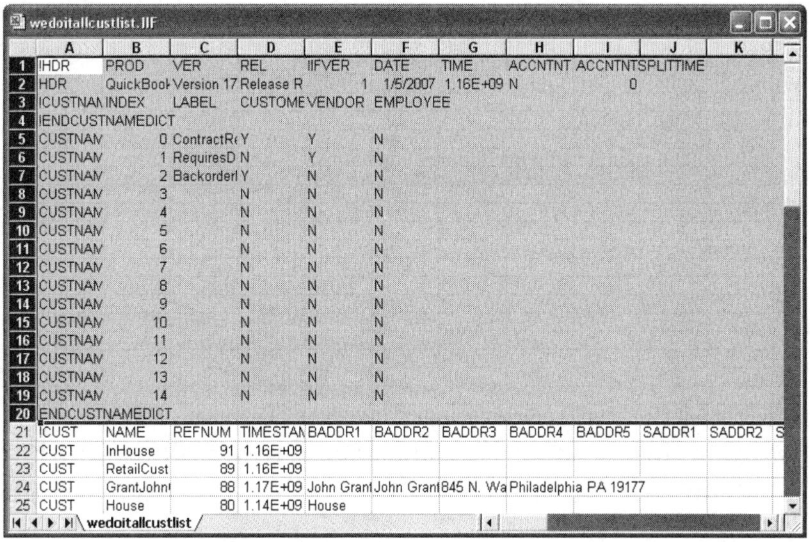

Figure 3-7: Eliminate unneeded data to make it easier to work in the spreadsheet.

Now your worksheet contains only the data about your customers, but some of the columns aren't needed, so let's get rid of them. The following two columns contain information you don't need when you import the file back into QuickBooks: REFNUM and TIMESTAMP.

However, you need a blank column near the NAME column, so you can enter the price level information (the PRICELEVEL column is way over to the right, and it's easier to move it next to the customer data so you can see your customers' names as you enter the price level data). Therefore, take the following steps:

1. Select one of the two unneeded columns (it doesn't matter which one) by clicking its column heading above Row 1.
2. Click Edit → Delete to remove the column.

3. Select the other column by clicking its column heading above Row 1.
4. Press the Del key to remove the data, but keep the column—you have a blank column.

Move the Price Level Column Next to the Name Column

It's easier to link price levels to customers when the data columns are next to each other. A QuickBooks import file doesn't have to be in any particular column order, so you can put the price level column next to the customer name column.

If you've already linked price levels to some customers, you don't want to lose that data, so use the following steps to move the data to a more convenient place in the worksheet:

1. Scroll all the way right to find the column named PRICELEVEL, and select the entire column by clicking its column heading, above Row 1.
2. Choose Edit → Cut
3. Move to the blank column you created (next to the NAME column), and click the cell in Row 1 to select it (don't select the column header, just click in the top cell).
4. Choose Edit → Paste.

Your existing price level data is in Column C, next to the NAME column. In Row 1 of the blank column, enter the text PRICELEVEL to create a column for receiving price level data.

Entering Price Level Data

When you're working in Excel, you can take advantage of the Windows clipboard and the Excel data entry tools to enter data.

1. In your word processor, select the first price level name you want to assign to customers. Press Ctrl-C to place the text in the Windows clipboard.
2. In the PRICELEVEL column, select the cell next to the first customer to whom you want to assign this price level
3. Press Ctrl-V to paste the price level name into the cell (or right-click in the cell and choose Paste).

4. Move to the cell next to the next customer you want to assign this price level to and press Ctrl-V to paste the text there. Continue to paste until you've pasted this price level for all the customers who should have it. (Once you have text in the Windows clipboard, you can continue to paste it endlessly, as long as you don't stop pasting to perform another task.)
5. Select the next price level from the word processor, press Ctrl-C to copy it to the clipboard, then return to the worksheet and paste the text in the PRICELEVEL column next to every customer who gets this price level.
6. Keep going until you've assigned all your price levels to all the customers who get price level assignments.

You've probably noticed that I said "customer" not "customer and job" when I discussed assigning price levels.

If you want all the jobs for a customer to have the same price level as you assigned to the customer, there's an easier way to accomplish that—you don't have to paste text one cell at a time.

1. Return to the first customer with a price level assignment, and select the cell that has the price level.
2. Position your mouse pointer in the lower right corner of the cell, until the pointer changes to vertical and horizontal intersecting lines.
3. Drag the right corner down the column, through all the job listings for this customer. Excel copies the text, and the same price level is now assigned to every job.
4. Repeat for every customer that has jobs.

If there are any jobs that have a different price level than that assigned to the customer, or any customer who has a job with a price level, but the customer doesn't have a price level assignment, you can enter that data manually.

Importing the Price Level Data

You can import the data back into your QuickBooks company file with an IIF file (see Appendix B).

***TIP**: You can do the same thing for any data you want to add to QuickBooks list records in one fell swoop instead of opening each record one at a time. For example, you may need to add or change Terms (for customers and vendors), Sales Tax Items, Types for customers and vendors, data for custom fields (for customers, vendors, and items), etc. etc.*

Per Item Price Levels

Available only in QuickBooks Premier editions, per item price levels let you set different prices for each item you sell, and then apply the appropriate price level when you're creating a sales form. This paradigm gives you a great deal of flexibility as you try to enhance your business by balancing individual customer activity and competitive prices.

A per item price level can be a fixed amount (an amount different from the standard price you entered when you created the item), or a percentage (higher or lower than the standard price).

To create an item price level, choose Lists → Price Level List to open the Price Level List window. Then, follow these steps:

1. Press Ctrl-N to open the New Price Level dialog.
2. Name the price level, using text that will remind you of the algorithm you're using for the price changes. If you're creating prices that have a fixed rate, use a name like 10$Off, if you're creating a percentage use 10%Off.
3. Select Per Item in the Price Level Type field. The dialog displays all the items in your Items list, as seen in Figure 3-8.

Now you can create a fixed price level, or a percentage-based price level, as described in the following sections.

***NOTE**: The Per Item Price Level dialog includes columns for the cost and the price of inventory items, so you can't inadvertently reduce a price to the point that you lose money. However, other item types (services, other charges, non-inventory items) have no costs associated with them. You must be aware of cost, including overhead, when you create reduced prices for these items.*

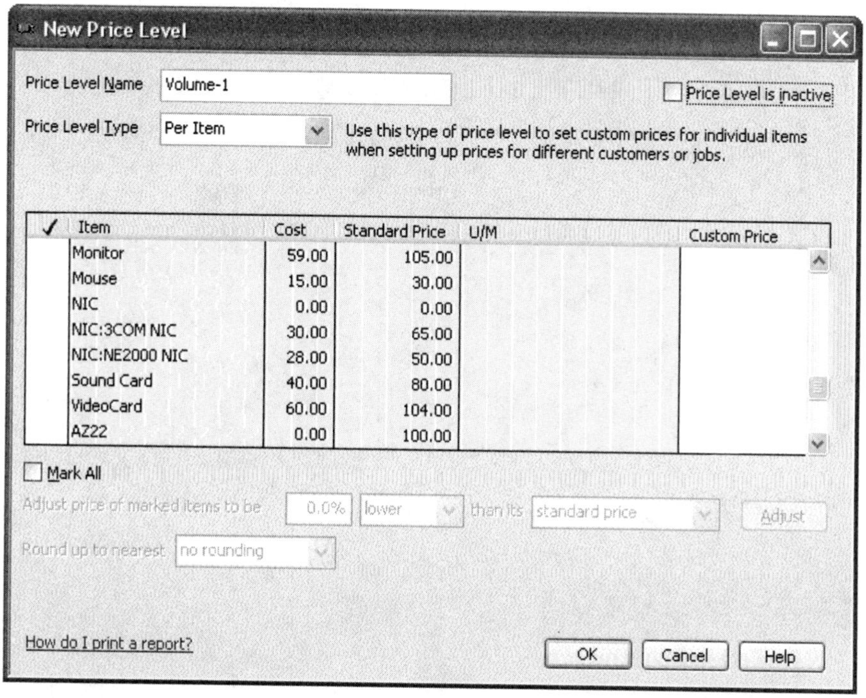

Figure 3-8: Create special price levels for specific goods and services.

Creating Fixed Rate Per item Price Levels

You can create a specific price as the new price level, and it can be higher or lower than the standard price (depending on the way in which you plan to use price levels).

To set a new price level for any item, click in the Custom Price column of the item's listing, and enter a new price (see Figure 3-9). You can perform this action on as many items as you wish. When you are finished entering the custom prices, click OK.

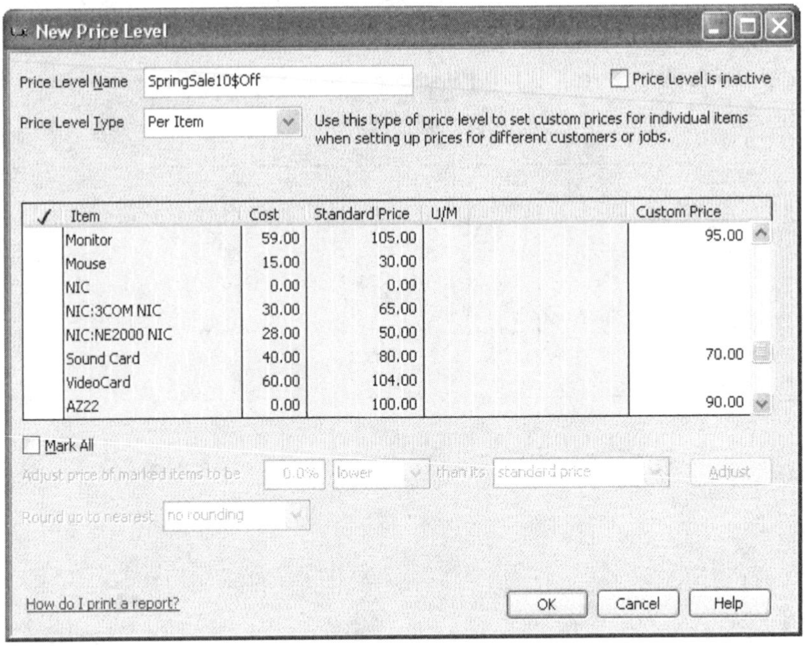

Figure 3-9: Prices for some items have been reduced for a special sale.

Creating Percentage-Based Per Item Price Levels

You can also create price levels for individual items that are based on a percentage of the item's standard price or cost.

Select an item, or multiple items, by clicking in the leftmost column to place a check mark in that column. You can choose the Select All option to select all the items, and if you want to exclude a few items, click the leftmost column to remove their check marks (the check mark is a toggle).

When all the items for this percentage-based price level are selected, fill in the fields at the bottom of the dialog (the section labeled Adjust Price Of Marked Items To Be).

Enter the percentage for this price level. You aren't restricted to whole numbers; you can enter 8.5 or 7.25 if you wish. You only have to enter the number—QuickBooks automatically adds the percent sign.

In the next field, select Lower or Higher from the drop-down list. Then select one of the following options from the drop-down list in the next field:

- Standard Price, which applies the percentage to the item's price as established in the item's record. Use this for a price level for which you selected Lower in the previous field.
- Cost, which applies the percentage to the item's cost as established in the item's record. Use this for a price level for which you selected Higher in the previous field.
- Custom Price, which applies the percentage to a custom price you created for the item (covered next).

Selecting a rounding algorithm, and then click the Adjust button to have QuickBooks calculate the prices (see Figure 3-10)

Creating Percentage Changes for Custom Prices

If you've created a Per Item price level that's a fixed amount (instead of a percentage change), you can apply a percentage-based price level against that custom price. This is useful for raising or lowering custom prices for a specific reason, commonly for a sale that lasts a specific amount of time.

To accomplish this, create a price level for Per Item fixed custom prices, changing the prices of selected items. Select the items that have custom prices that you want to include in this price level scheme. Then use the fields at the bottom of the dialog to enter a percentage amount, select Lower (unless you're raising prices, in which case select Higher), and in the last field choose Current Custom Price.

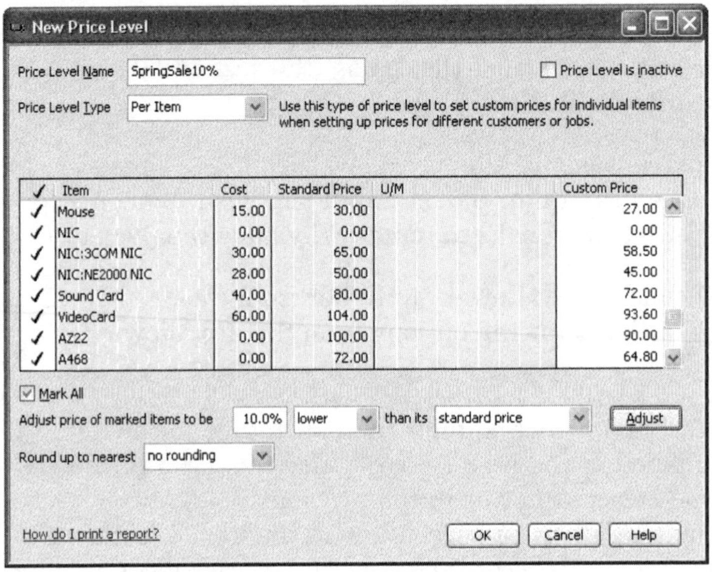

Figure 3-10: You can design a percentage-based price level based on the price or cost of selected items.

When you click Adjust, QuickBooks applies your percentage change against the custom price of the items you selected.

Printing Price Level Reports

QuickBooks provides printable reports on price levels, but they're not well thought out, and not well designed, so you have to modify the reports to make them useful. You can create and print a report on a specific price level, or on all the price levels in your system.

Printing a Specific Price Level Scheme

To create a report on a specific price level, right-click the price level's listing in the Price Level List window and choose Price Level Report from the shortcut menu.

The report that opens isn't suitable for printing and sending to customers, nor for your own use if you want to discuss special pricing with a customer. By default the report displays four columns: Item, Description, Preferred Vendor, and the prices for each item in this price level scheme.

You need to modify the report so it displays the standard price of each item, in addition to the price for this price level (so you can see the difference). Also, there's no need to include the preferred vendor. Follow these steps to modify the report:

1. Click Modify Report to open the Modify Report dialog with the Display tab in the foreground.
2. In the Columns list, deselect everything except Item, Description, and the Price Level Name.
3. In the Columns list, select Price.
4. Click OK.

If the report displays items that have no prices (the price is set at zero), use the Filters tab in the Modify Report dialog to remove them from the report. Select Price in the Filter list, and filter the criteria so only prices greater than .01 are displayed (see Figure 3-11).

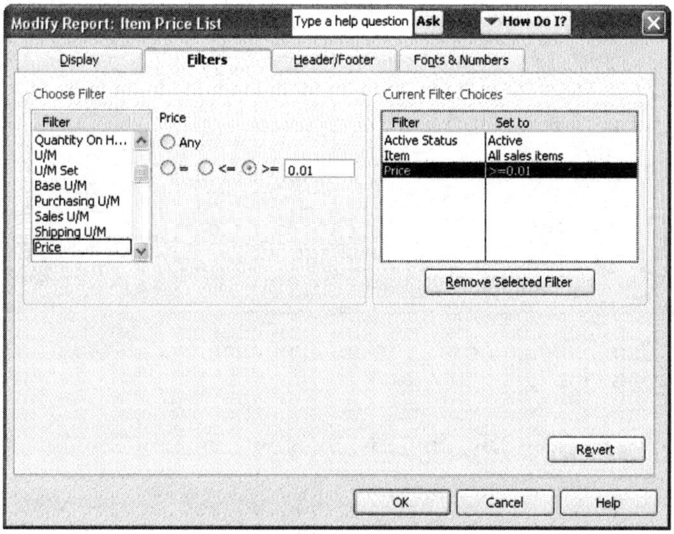

Figure 3-11: Remove items that lack prices.

If this price level scheme only applied price levels to one type of items (e.g., inventory items), you can remove the other item types from the report, which usually makes the report much shorter and easier to read.

To restrict the report to the single item type involved in this price level, go to the Filters tab and select Type in the Filter list. In the Type field, select the appropriate item type from the drop-down list.

Unfortunately, there's no way to have the report list only those items with prices that differ in this price level scheme, and eliminate the items that aren't affected.

If you want to send a printed copy of this report to customers, you can hope they'll notice which items are affected, or you can export the report to Excel, tweak it, and then print it from Excel.

To tweak the report in Excel, you can remove all the items that aren't affected by this price level, and enter formulas that show and "sell" the difference in price, as seen in Figure 3-12.

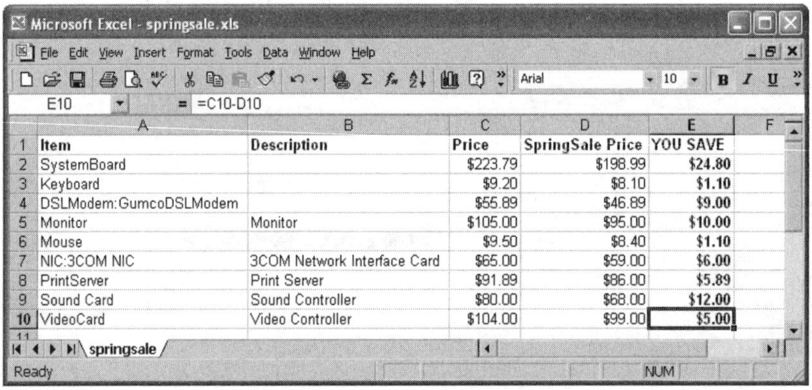

	A	B	C	D	E
1	Item	Description	Price	SpringSale Price	YOU SAVE
2	SystemBoard		$223.79	$198.99	$24.80
3	Keyboard		$9.20	$8.10	$1.10
4	DSLModem:GumcoDSLModem		$55.89	$46.89	$9.00
5	Monitor	Monitor	$105.00	$95.00	$10.00
6	Mouse		$9.50	$8.40	$1.10
7	NIC:3COM NIC	3COM Network Interface Card	$65.00	$59.00	$6.00
8	PrintServer	Print Server	$91.89	$86.00	$5.89
9	Sound Card	Sound Controller	$80.00	$68.00	$12.00
10	VideoCard	Video Controller	$104.00	$99.00	$5.00

Figure 3-12: Use the features in Excel to show customers how this price level saves them money.

Printing a Report on All Price Levels

It's a good idea to have a list of all price levels in the office, so your sales calls can quote accurate current prices. QuickBooks doesn't offer such a report, but it's rather easy to build one, using the following steps:

1. Choose Reports → List → Item Price List. All of your items appear, along with their recorded standard prices.
2. Click Modify Report.
3. In the Display tab Columns list, deselect the Preferred Vendor listing (I also remove the Description listing to make the report less crowded).
4. In the Display tab, scroll through the Columns list and select your price levels by name (the listings are at the bottom of the Columns list).
5. In the Filters tab, select price and then select Greater Than (>) .01.
6. Click OK to return to the report window, which now displays columns for each of your price levels.

***TIP**: Memorize this report so you don't have to go through all this customization again.*

Using Per Item Price Levels in Sales Forms

Because per item price levels can't be linked to customers, you can only apply the price level when you're creating a sales form. Enter the item in the sales transaction, click the arrow in the Rate column to display your price levels, and select the appropriate price level.

But wait! It's not as easy and straightforward as the previous paragraph implies. Assigning a Per Item price level is dandy if the price in the Rate column is the standard, recorded price that appears in the item's record. However, if the price displayed in the Rate column is the result of an assigned price level, be careful about assigning a Per Item price level that conflicts with customer expectations.

Billing Rate Level List

The Billing Rate Level list lets you assign a billing rate to a person performing a specific service (the *service provider*). This list is only available in the following Premier Editions:

- Accountant Edition

- Contractor Edition
- Professional Services Edition

After you create billing rate levels, and associate them with service providers, invoicing for services becomes automatic. Every time you create an invoice with billable time, QuickBooks automatically fills in the correct rate for the service, based on the person who performed the work.

To track services for each service provider and associated billing rate level, the service providers must use the QuickBooks Timesheet feature.

Creating a Billing Rate Level

To create a billing rate level, choose Lists → Billing Rate Level List. When the list window opens, press Ctrl-N to open the New Billing Rate Level dialog. You can choose either of the following types of billing rate levels:

- A Fixed Hourly Rate, which is a specific hourly rate assigned to certain service providers.
- Custom Hourly Rate per Service Item, which is a rate tied to a service, but it differs depending on the rate assigned to the service provider.

Creating a Fixed Hourly Billing Rate

To create a fixed billing rate that you can assign to a service provider, select Fixed Hourly Rate as the rate type. Then, enter a name for this billing rate level, and enter its hourly rate (see Figure 3-13).

After you link this billing rate to service providers, you can automatically invoice customers at this rate for any service performed by those people. Create all the fixed hourly rates you need.

Creating a Custom Hourly Billing Rate

To create a custom hourly rate, enter a name for the rate, and then select Custom Hourly Rate Per Service Item. The dialog changes to display all your service items (see Figure 3-14). Enter the hourly rate for each service that is performed by a person linked to this billing rate.

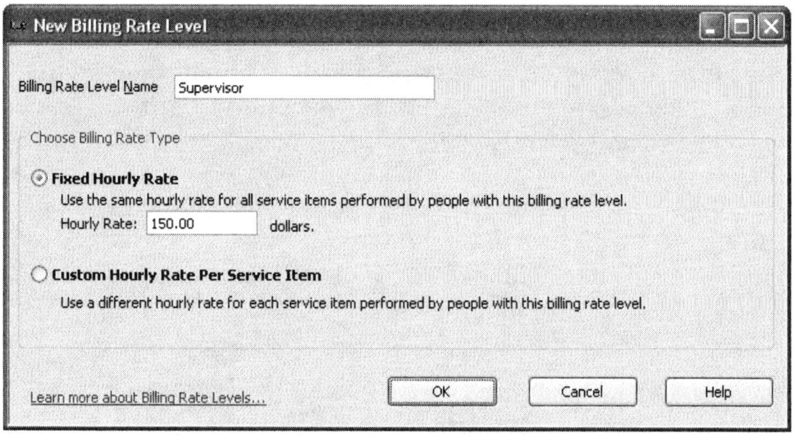

Figure 3-13: Establish an hourly billing rate you can link to specific service providers.

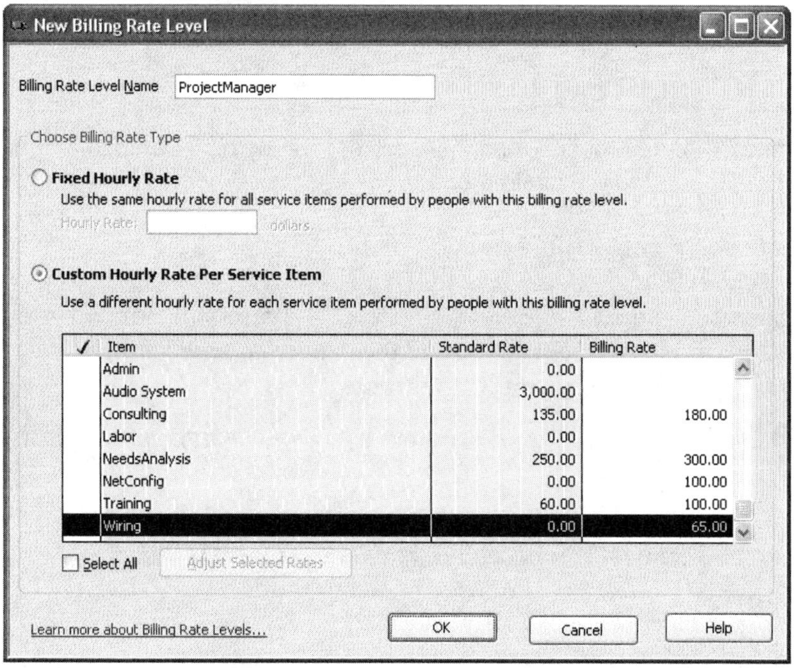

Figure 3-14: Select the services linked to this billing rate, and enter the hourly rates.

Creating a Percentage Based Custom Rate

You can also create a custom rate by applying a percentage against the standard rate for a service. For example, you might want to set a rate of 10% more than the standard rate for service providers linked to the rate.

To accomplish this, follow the instructions for creating a custom hourly billing rate in the previous paragraph. Select the services you want to include, and then click Adjust Selected Rates (see Figure 3-15). Configure the adjusted rate as follows:

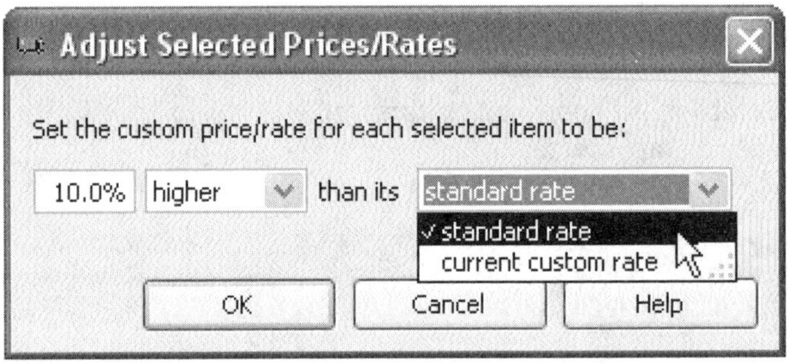

Figure 3-15: Automatically adjust a billing level by a percentage to create a custom rate.

- Indicate a percentage by which you want to raise or lower the rate based on the standard rate for the selected services.
- Indicate a percentage by which you want to raise or lower the rate based on the current billing rate level (one that you entered in the dialog before beginning the adjustment).

QuickBooks multiplies the amount by the percentage, and automatically fills in the rate.

Assigning Billing Rate Levels to Service Providers

After you've created billing rate levels, you must assign a level to each service provider. To do this, open the appropriate names list (Vendor, Employee, or Other Names) and select a service provider. Edit the record by selecting a rate from the Billing Rate Level drop-down list. (In the Vendor and Employee lists, you must go to the Additional Info tab to find the Billing Rate Level field.)

Invoicing with Billing Rate Levels

To prepare invoices that use billing rate levels, you must use the timesheets that each service provider hands in. When you invoice your customers, the appropriate billing rates are automatically added to the invoice from the Time and Costs dialog that's available on the Invoice window.

You can also apply any customer's percentage price level (usually a discount) to the billing rate invoice items.

Item List

Items are the things that appear on the sales forms you create, so your Items list contains all the goods and services you sell. However, there are other items you need to create because they, too, might appear on a sales form.

For example, sales tax is an item, as is shipping. Less obvious are some of the other items you need to add to sales forms as you sell your goods and services to customers, such as prepayments received, discounts applied, subtotals, and so on.

Understanding Item Types

Before you create the items you need to run your business, you should understand the item types that QuickBooks offers. Following are the names (and explanations) of the item types available when you create items:

Service

A service you sell to a customer. You can create services that are charged by the job or by the hour.

Inventory Part

A product you buy for reselling. This item type isn't available if you haven't enabled inventory tracking in the Purchases & Vendors category of the Preferences dialog.

Inventory Assembly

An item you build, usually from inventory parts. This item type is only available in QuickBooks Premier and Enterprise Editions. (See Chapter 7 to learn about using inventory assemblies.)

Non-Inventory Part

Use this item type for products that you don't track as inventory. This could be products you sell (without tracking inventory), or, if you do track inventory, the supplies you use for boxing and shipping inventory parts (e.g. tape, labels, and so on).

Other Charge

Use this item type for things like shipping charges, or other line items that appear on your invoices. In fact, some people create a separate Other Charge item for each method of shipping.

Subtotal

This item type adds up everything that comes before it on a sales form. You can use it to calculate a subtotal before you subtract any discounts or prepayments.

Group

You can use this item type to enter a group of items (all of which must already exist in your Item list) all at once. For example, if you frequently have a shipping charge and sales tax on the same invoice, you can create a group item that includes those two items.

Discount

Use this item type to give a customer a discount as a line item. When you enter an item of the Discount Type, you can indicate a percentage as the rate.

Payment

Use this item type to add a customer's prepayment to an invoice. QuickBooks automatically calculates the total appropriately

Sales Tax Item and Sales Tax Group

Use these item types to add sales tax to an invoice. Sales tax gets complicated in some states, and you have to be extremely careful about the way you set up sales tax items. Chapter 4 explains how to set up sales tax items and groups.

__TIP__: I've described all of the item types in terms of their use on your invoices, but some of them are used on purchase orders, too.

Creating Items

To create an item, open the Items List by choosing Lists → Item List from the menu bar. Then press Ctrl-N to open the New Item dialog.

Select the item type from the Type drop-down list. The item type you select determines the appearance of the New Item dialog, because different item types have different fields.

__NOTE__: For A to Z basic instructions about creating items, you can purchase a copy of QuickBooks 2008: The Official Guide from your favorite bookstore.

Creating Subitems

After you've created an item, you can create subitems. For example, for a particular product you can create subitems for different manufacturers. Or, you can create subitems for product sizes, types, colors, or other variations in the product. Not all item types support subitems—look for the Subitem Of field on the New Item dialog.

To create a subitem, use the same steps required to create an item, and then click the Subitem Of option, and select the appropriate parent item from the drop-down list.

Importing the Item List

If you've been keeping your list of items in another software application, or on paper, you can avoid one-item-at-a-time data entry by importing the list into QuickBooks. You have two methods at your disposal for importing the list:

- Import the list directly from an Excel file or a CSV file.
- Import the list from an IIF file.

If you've been using another application, you must export the data from that application to create your import file. This is only possible if your current application is capable of exporting data to one of the following formats:

- Excel file
- CSV (comma separated value) file
- Tab-delimited text file.

All three of these file types can be opened in Excel. If you use another spreadsheet application, you can use a CSV file or a tab-delimited text file (and some spreadsheet software is capable of loading Excel files and converting them to their own document type).

If you keep your item list on paper, or in a software application that can't export to the required file type, you can enter the information in a spreadsheet and then import the data into QuickBooks. It's usually faster to work in the rows of a spreadsheet document than to move from field to field, one item dialog at a time, in QuickBooks.

A QuickBooks item import file can contain all the information you need to fill out all the fields in the item dialog, but it's unlikely you've kept records in a manner that matches these fields. You can import whatever information you already have, and later enter additional information by editing the item records.

Detailed instructions for creating and importing Excel/CSV files are in Appendix A, and detailed instructions for creating and importing IIF files are in Appendix B. These instructions include all the column headings and keywords you need to import items into your QuickBooks company file.

Manipulating List Data

You can perform the following actions on the records in your lists:

- Edit the fields in the record (see the Note below for exceptions).
- Delete the record, providing no transactions are attached to the record.
- Hide the record by making it inactive.
- Merge two records to combine their histories.

***NOTE**: For an item record, you cannot edit the item's type unless the item is a Non-inventory Part or an Other Charge. All other item types are permanently assigned when you create the item.*

Using a Hidden Record in Transactions

Hiding a record means making it inactive, which you can do by right-clicking the listing and choosing Make Inactive. To see all the entries in a list, including inactive entries, take the following action:

- For the Customers & Jobs, Vendors, and Employees Lists, select All *<List Name>* from the drop-down list at the top of the tab.
- For all other lists, select the Include Inactive option at the bottom of the list window.

When you view all entries, the inactive entries have a large X in the leftmost column.

When a record is hidden, it doesn't appear in drop-down lists in transaction windows. Usually, you make a record inactive because you don't want anyone to use it, and you can't delete it (because it has been involved in transactions).

However, you may have other reasons to hide entries from users who create transactions, such as:

- A customer has a large overdue balance, and you don't want anyone to sell that customer more products or services.
- An item is seasonal, or will be out of stock for a long time (re-activate it when it can be sold again).
- Prevent purchasing goods from a vendor with whom you're having a dispute.

You can hide a record and still use it, which is a feature often used by business owners and bookkeepers who don't want other users to involve certain records in transactions (so don't tell other users about this feature).

When you're entering data in a transaction window, don't use the drop-down list in the appropriate field (e.g. Vendor) because of course, the record won't appear in the list. Instead, enter the record name manually.

QuickBooks displays a message asking if you want to use the account just once, or reactivate the account. Click the option to use the account just once. (You can use the account "just once" as many times as you want to.)

Creating Custom Fields In Lists

Custom fields are useful if there's information you want to track, but QuickBooks doesn't provide a field for it. You can add custom fields to the customer, vendor, employee, and item lists.

After you create a custom field, you must populate the field with data in each record that uses the custom field. In addition, you can add the custom field to transaction templates, so you can see the data you entered while you're creating a transaction.

***TIP**: You can customize most QuickBooks reports to include the data in custom fields.*

Custom Fields for Names Lists

You can add a custom field to the any names list except Other Names, which means you can add custom fields to the customer, vendor, and employee lists.

After you create a custom field, you can assign it to multiple names list. I had a client whose business participated in a softball league, and he added a custom field labeled Team Name to his employee, vendor, and customer lists (it was a league for businesses in his industry, and many employees of his local customers and vendors participated).

You can create up to fifteen custom fields, but you can only add seven fields to an individual list. A custom field that overlaps lists count as one field on each list. For example, if you add the same field to all three lists, you can still add six other fields to each list.

To add a custom field to your QuickBooks file that you can apply to a names list, open any employee, vendor, or customer record. It doesn't matter which list you use to create the custom field; after the new field exists you assign it to the names list (or multiple names lists) for which it's intended.

In the record you open, move to the Additional Info tab and click Define Fields. Enter names for the custom fields and select the list(s) to which you want to add this field (see Figure 3-16).

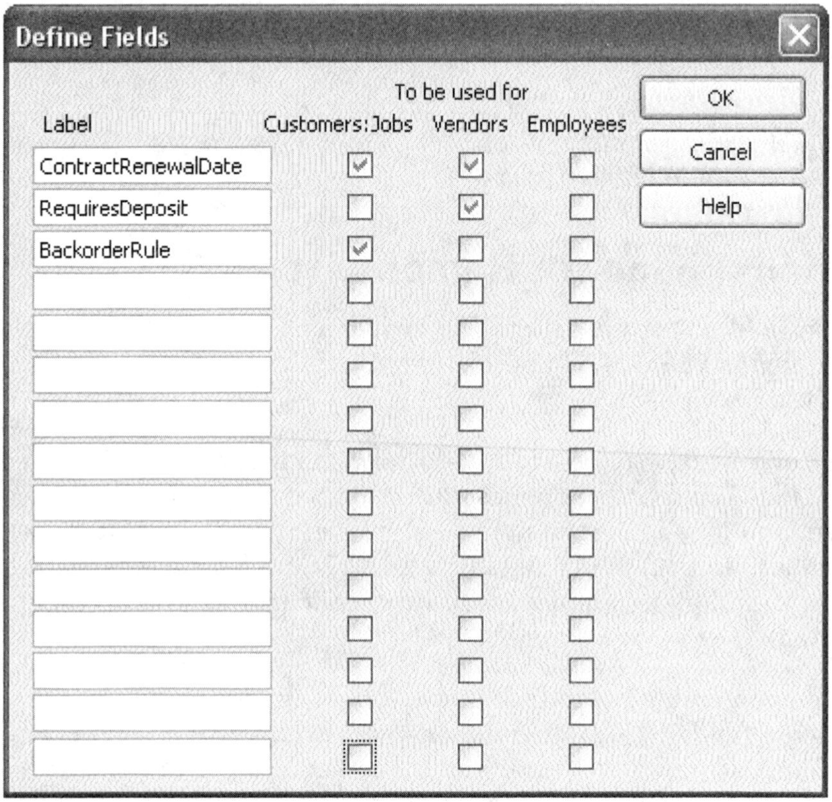

Figure 3-16: Create a custom field and assign it to as many names lists as necessary.

Custom Fields for Items

You can add up to five custom fields for items. However, your custom field won't be available for the following item types:

- Subtotals
- Sales tax items
- Sales tax groups

To create a custom field, open any item record, click Custom Fields, and then click Define fields. If this is the first custom field you're creat ing for items, QuickBooks displays a message saying that no custom fields currently exist, and telling you to click the Define Fields button to create a custom field.

In the Define Custom Fields for Items dialog, enter the custom field name, and select Use to place the field on item records (see Figure 3-17).

Figure 3-17: Add custom fields to items for information you need when you create reports or transactions.

After you've created your first custom field for items, when you click the Custom Fields button on an item record, the Custom Fields For Items dialog opens, displaying the existing custom fields. To create additional fields, click Define Fields.

Entering Data in Custom Fields

Custom fields aren't useful until you populate the fields with data in the names and/or item records.

To add data to a custom field in a Names list, open the appropriate record (e.g. a customer name) and move to the Additional Info tab. Enter data that's specific to this record, and continue to enter data in every record that requires information in the custom fields (see Figure 3-18).

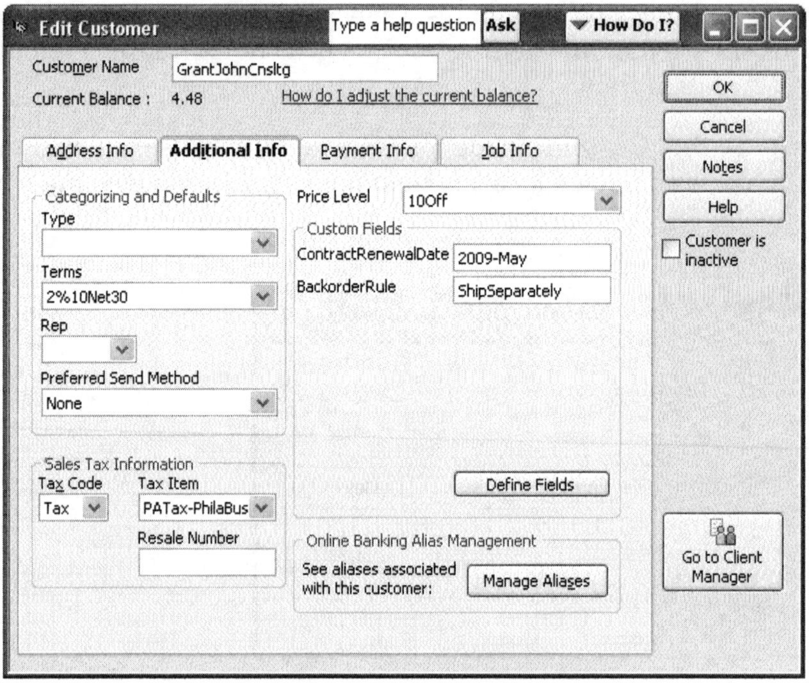

Figure 3-18: Each record in a names list requires its own specific data for a custom field.

To add data to a custom field in the Items list, open the appropriate item and click Custom Fields. Then add data for this item in the custom fields (see Figure 3-19).

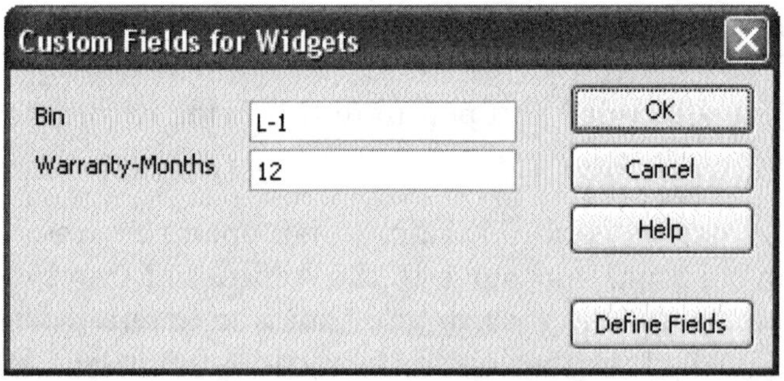

Figure 3-19: Track specific information about each item with the data you enter into custom fields.

The data you enter in custom fields should be consistent from record to record. For example, let's say you're tracking vendor information or item information in a custom field named Co-op Adv (to display the formula for co-op advertising revenue). If the formula is a certain percentage of co-op refunds for a minimum purchase, decide on the format of the text to use for every record. For example, you could enter 10%-20K if the co-op formula is 10% for a minimum purchase of $20,000.00. Don't enter the same type of data in different ways, such as:

- 10-20000
- 10%-20K
- 10-$20K

If your data is inconsistent, it's difficult (if not impossible) to produce reports that provide the information you need about the data in custom fields.

Adding Custom Field Data in Batches

If you have a lot of names or items for which you need to populate custom fields with data, you can export each list as an IIF file, add the data in an Excel worksheet, and then import the data back into QuickBooks.

You must import the data with an IIF file, because the Excel import feature in QuickBooks doesn't recognize custom fields. Appendix B has directions for working with IIF files, but here are some guidelines for adding custom field data:

- An IIF file in Excel is a single worksheet file. You cannot have multiple worksheets, so export, and work on, one list at a time.
- Custom field names are not exported; instead, data is held in columns with the keyword names CUSTFLD1, CUSTFLD2, and so on. Names list exported files contain 15 columns named CUSTFLD, the items list export file contains 5 columns named CUSTFLD.
- The CUSTFLD column numbers are linked to the order of the custom fields you created. Before you can enter data, view your

custom fields, and note the custom field names in top-to-bottom order. (You cannot change the column title to match the name; this is for your convenience when you enter data.

- Add custom field data to the first record in each list, to have sample data in the export file.
- In Excel, remove unneeded rows at the top of the file to make it easier to work. The first required row contains the list keyword preceded by an exclamation point in the first column, such as !INVITEM, !CUST, and so on. (IIF file keywords are in Appendix B.)

Adding Custom Fields to Transaction Forms

Some custom fields should appear in transaction templates, because the data in the field helps you create the transaction more efficiently.

For example, QuickBooks doesn't provide a field in customer records to indicate how the customer wants you to deal with backorders. There's no point in tracking backorders for a customer who indicates they want you to ship what's available and forget the rest of the order, or for a customer who wants you to hold shipment until backordered items are available.

Create a custom field named Backorders, and enter data for each customer to indicate how backorders should be handled. Then, customize sales transaction templates to include the customer's backorder data on the screen when you're creating the transaction.

You should be aware of the "rules" that govern the way custom fields are added to transaction windows. (According to the e-mail queries I receive, this rule isn't well known.):

- Custom fields in the Names lists are added to the transaction template as fields in the heading section.
- Custom fields in the Items list are added to the transaction template as columns in the line item section.

Customizing a template is a two-step process: First, duplicate the built-in template you want to use as the basis of the new template and give it a new name, and second, customize the new template.

Duplicating a Template

Use the following steps to duplicate a built-in template:

1. Choose Lists → Templates to open the Templates List window.
2. Right-click the listing for the template you want to customize and select Duplicate.
3. In the Select Template Type dialog, select the type of template and click OK.
4. The Templates List window displays a listing named Copy Of: <Template>,
5. Double-click that listing to open the Basic Customization dialog.
6. Click Manage Templates and in the right pane of the Manage Templates dialog, change the name of the template. Use a name that describes your customization—for example Invoice-BackorderInfo.
7. Click OK to return to the Basic Customization dialog.

In this dialog you can make minor changes to the template, such as changing fonts, colors, the company information that prints on the transaction document, and so on.

However, in this case you want to make major changes to the template, to add fields or columns to the document. The following section, Customizing the Template, covers those tasks.

Customizing the Template

With your new template displayed in the Basic Customization dialog, click the Additional Customization button at the bottom of the dialog. This action opens the Additional Customization dialog seen in Figure 3-20.

On the Header tab you can include or exclude fields for the on-screen version, the printed version, or both. For example, if you've created custom fields, the data in those custom fields might be needed only on the screen as you prepare the PO, and not on the printed document you send.

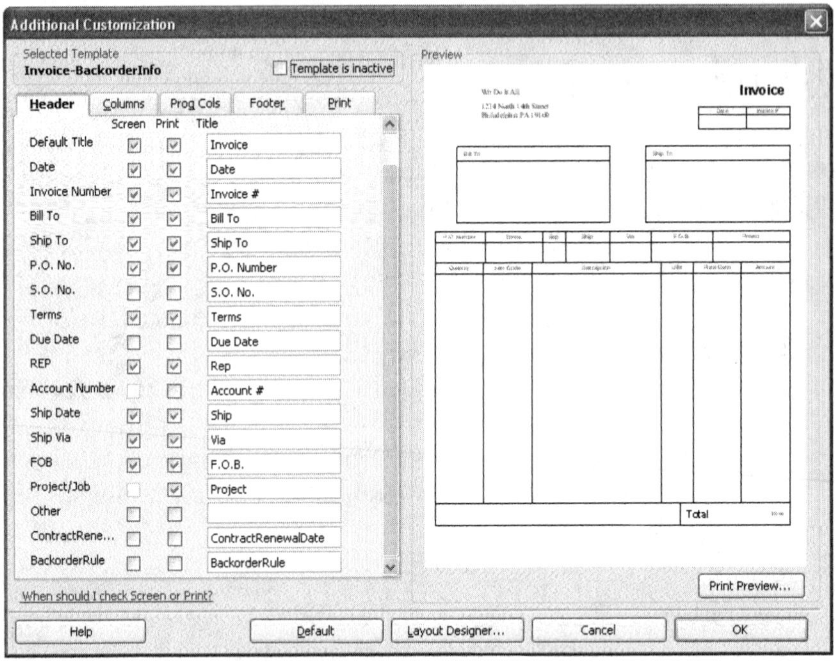

Figure 3-20: Customize the template to make sure all the information you require is included.

***NOTE**: As soon as you begin making changes QuickBooks displays a message about using the Layout Designer to make sure all the elements you're changing fit properly in the template. The message reappears every time you select a check box or change text. Most of the changes you make don't require a complete overhaul of the layout, so you can select the option to stop displaying the message. Keep an eye on the preview panel in the right pane, or click Print Preview to see if changes you're making cause fields or columns to overlap. If so, you can use the Layout Designer to move fields and columns. The Layout Designer is not difficult to use, but if you want assistance, it's discussed in detail in QuickBooks 2008: The Official Guide.*

Move to the Columns tab (see Figure 3-21) to see if there are any columns you want to select or deselect. The custom fields you created for items are included in the list. You can also change the order in which columns appear by changing the number in the Order list.

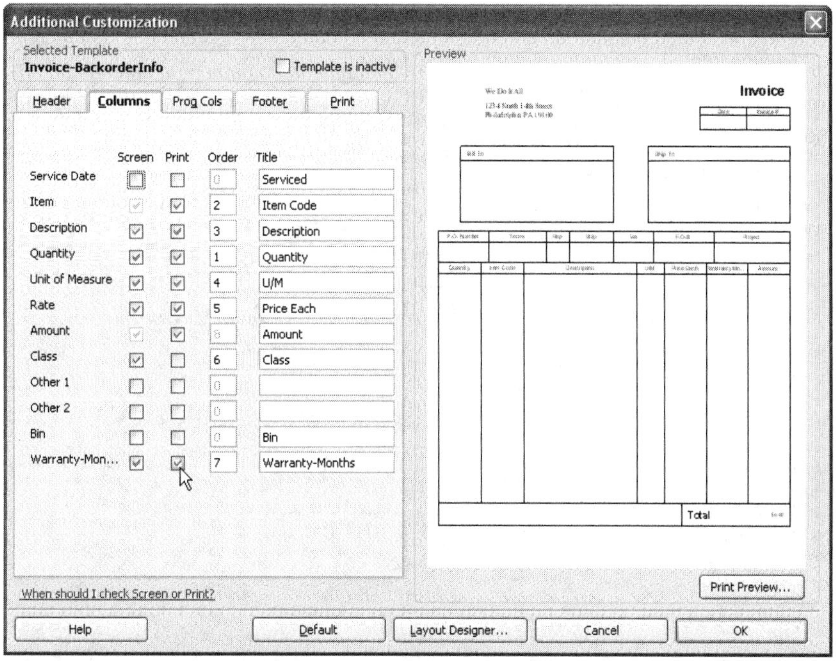

Figure 3-21: Customize columns for your new template.

Click OK when you finish customizing fields and columns, and then click OK in the Basic Customization dialog to save the new template. Now you can select it from the Template field when you create transactions.

List Limits

QuickBooks limits the number of entries you can have in a list (except for the Enterprise Editions). Table 3-1 specifies the number of entries for each list. The entry labeled Names includes the following lists:

- Customers & Jobs
- Vendors
- Other Names
- Employees

List	Maximum
Names (each list)	10000
Chart of accounts	10000
Items (excluding payroll items)	14500
Job types	10000
Vendor types	10000
Customer types	10000
Purchase orders	10000
Payroll items	10000
Price Levels	100
Classes	10000
Terms (combined A/R and A/P)	10000
Payment methods	10000
Shipping methods	10000
Customer messages	10000
Memorized reports	14500
Memorized transactions	14500
To Do notes	10000

Table 3-1: Maximum number of entries in lists.

However, the limits are a bit more complicated, and more stringent, than the table indicates. It's important to realize the following:

- The combined total of names for all the names lists cannot exceed 14,500.
- Once you have reached 10,000 names in a single name list, you cannot create any new objects for that list.
- Once you have reached 14,500 names in your combined name lists, you can no longer create any new names in any names list.

When you reach a list maximum, QuickBooks locks the list(s), and when a list is locked, that's a permanent decision. Deleting objects doesn't free up space for new entries. It's too late.

***TIP**: To view your current numbers press F2 to open the QuickBooks Product Information Window. The List Information box displays the list totals.*

QuickBooks also imposes a maximum on the number of transactions in a file, but since that number is 2,000,000,000 (yes, two billion), it's unlikely that a small business would exceed that number.

Every individual action you perform is a transaction. Filling out a transaction window is an obvious transaction, but when you edit, delete, or void a transaction, that counts as a transaction. If you reach the maximum number of transactions, your company file is locked and you can't work in that file. You can condense and archive older transactions to make your company file smaller and more efficient.

Classes

Classes let you group transactions to match the way you want to track and report your business activities. In effect, you can use classes to "classify" your business by some pattern, such as divisions, branches, or type of activity.

The ability to classify your business means you can produce P & L reports by class, so you can see how each department, division, or location is doing.

To use classes, you must enable the feature, which is listed in the Accounting category of the Preferences dialog. Once classes are enabled, QuickBooks adds a Class field to your transaction windows. For each transaction, you can assign one of the classes you create.

Classes only work well if you use them consistently, but it's common for users to skip the Class field in transactions. QuickBooks offers a feature to help everyone remember to assign a class to a transaction. You can enable that feature by selecting the option Prompt To Assign Classes, which is available in the same Preferences dialog you use to enable classes (the Company Preferences tab of the Accounting category).

When you enable this feature, any time a user tries to save or close a transaction without assigning classes, QuickBooks displays a reminder message about assigning a class. However, the message is merely a reminder, and QuickBooks will let the user continue to save the transaction without class assignments. You must train users about the importance of assigning classes, or you won't get the reports you want.

When you create your classes, include the following two classes in addition to the classes you create for departments, division, locations, etc.:

- Other, which users can select if they're not sure which class a transaction belongs to. Later, you can create a report on transactions linked to the Other class, and drill down through each transaction to apply the appropriate class.
- Administration (or Overhead), which you can use for posting expenses that aren't specifically applicable to a "regular" class. You can use the totals in this class to allocate that overhead to class expenses (via a journal entry).

Creating a Class

To create a class choose Lists → Classes to open the Class List. Press Ctrl-N to open a New Class dialog (see Figure 3-22), and enter the name of the class in the Name field.

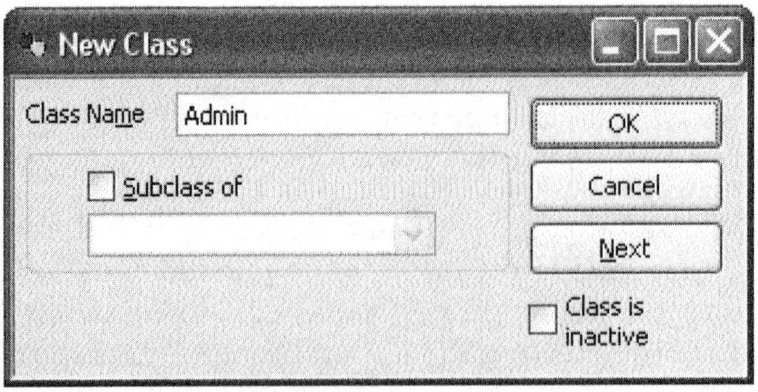

Figure 3-22: Creating a class is one of the easiest tasks in QuickBooks.

Using Subclasses

Classes work best for a single purpose, such as separating your business into locations or by type of business (wholesale and retail). If you need further classifications, you can use subclasses.

Create the broad classes you need, and then create subclasses for those classes that need additional classification. For example, if you create classes for locations, you might want to separate the classification of transactions between wholesale and retail for each location, or between sales and service for each location.

Class Reports

To generate a report on the Profit & Loss for each class, choose Reports → Company & Financial → Profit & Loss By Class. The report displays columns for each class, as well as a column titled Unclassified.

The Unclassified column contains all the totals for transactions in which the user failed to enter a class. You can drill down through those transactions to add the appropriate class.

QuickBooks does not offer a report on a class-by-class basis for balance sheet accounts (Assets, Liabilities, and Equity). However, I receive a lot of requests from readers who want to know how to do this, and I use a slightly kludgy trick to create a report that displays totals by class.

You can only generate a report for a single class when you're reporting on balance sheet accounts, so you have to generate multiple reports to include all your classes. However, you can export each report to the same Excel workbook (each class gets its own worksheet).

To create a balance sheet report for a class, use the following steps:

1. Choose Reports → Company & Financial → Balance Sheet Standard.
2. Click the Modify Report button at the top of the report window.
3. Move to the Filters tab and select Class in the Filter list, and then select the class you want to report on.

4. Move to the Header/Footer tab and change the text in the Report Title field to add the name of the class to the title (so you're not confused about which report you're viewing).
5. Click OK to display the report, which now reflects data that has been filtered by class.

It's important to remember that the postings to many balance sheet accounts don't involve transactions that have a Class column, so this report isn't a valid balance sheet; it's just a vehicle for tracking activities on a class basis for balance sheet accounts.

Chapter 4

Sales Tax

Configuring sales tax

Sales tax codes

Sales tax items

Sales tax groups

Remitting sales tax

Sales tax complications and workarounds

If you collect and remit sales tax, you need to configure the sales tax features in QuickBooks. Sales tax is becoming a complicated issue and has created an enormous administrative burden for small businesses.

In recent years, many states have created multiple sales tax authorities within the state (by county, city, town, or even a group of zip codes), and each location has its own tax rate.

Businesses in some of those states must remit the sales tax they collect to both the state and the local sales tax authority (or to multiple local sales tax authorities). In some states, businesses remit all the sales tax to the state, but must report taxable/nontaxable sales on a location-by-location basis.

As a result, tracking sales tax properly (which means in a manner that makes it possible to fill out all the forms for all the authorities) has become a very complicated process.

Because of the complications, and because of the importance of accurate reporting of sales tax (to avoid audits, fines, and annoying communications from a variety of tax authorities), you need to pay careful attention to the way you set up, configure, collect, and track, sales tax.

If your state hasn't instituted new, complicated, sales tax structures, you can skip some of the following discussion. But don't relax—your time is certainly coming soon.

Enabling the Sales Tax Feature

You enable sales tax by choosing Edit → Preferences and selecting the Sales Tax icon in the left pane of the Preferences dialog. Move to the Company Preferences tab to see the dialog shown in Figure 4-1.

Enable the sales tax feature by selecting the Yes option next to the label Do You Charge Sales Tax?

The sections of the dialog labeled Set Up Sales Tax Item and Assign Sales Tax Codes, each of which have several fields, are discussed in the sections "Sales Tax Codes" and "Sales Tax Items", later in this chapter.

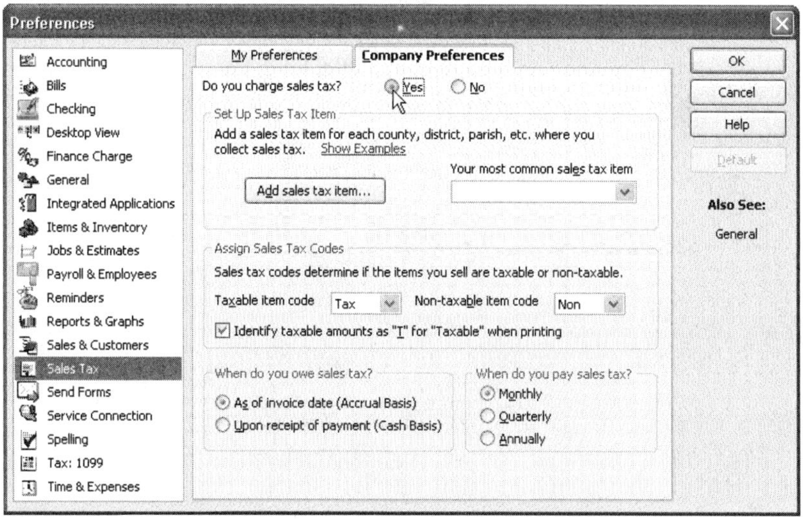

Figure 4-1: Start by enabling and configuring sales tax.

The bottom sections of the dialog ask whether you remit sales taxes when you invoice your customers (accrual basis), or when you receive payments from your customers (cash basis). The information that arrived with your sales tax license should clearly state these terms.

You also must select your payment interval. You don't get to choose—the notice that arrived with your sales tax license and reporting forms indicates the schedule you must use. Many states base the frequency on the amount of tax you collect, usually looking at your returns for a specific period—perhaps one specific quarter (the period they examine is usually referred to as the *lookback* period).

If your sales tax liability changes dramatically during the lookback period, you may receive a notice from the state that your remittance interval has changed. If that occurs, don't forget to return to the Preferences window to change the interval.

If you remit sales tax semi-annually, you have to force feed the system to accommodate your reports and payments, because QuickBooks doesn't support that interval. Select Quarterly and then, at the end of June, change the date range for reports.

***TIP**: The Sales Tax dialog has an option, which is selected by default, to print "T" next to the price of each line in a sales transaction that has a taxable item. Deselect it—it makes a very unattractive document, and your customers probably won't understand what it means.*

Understanding Tax Codes and Tax Items

QuickBooks has two discrete entities for configuring sales tax: Sales Tax Codes and Sales Tax Items. Many QuickBooks users get them confused, so I'll attempt to clarify everything, and I'll start by defining each entity:

- A sales tax **code** indicates tax liability, which means the entity to which it's linked (a customer or an item) is deemed taxable or nontaxable, depending on the code. Tax codes contain no information about the tax rate or the taxing authority; they just offer a Yes or No answer to the question "taxable?"
- A sales tax **item** contains information about the tax rate and the taxing authority to which you remit taxes and reports. Like all items, the sales tax item appears on sales forms. The amount of tax due is calculated when you add the sales tax item to the taxable line items (products and services configured as "taxable") on an invoice or sales receipt for a customer configured as "taxable".

Sales Tax Codes

Linking a sales tax code to customers and items lets you (and QuickBooks) know whether sales tax should be calculated for that item for this customer. A customer's sales tax liability is like a light switch; it's either on or off.

However, if a customer is liable for sales tax, it doesn't mean that every item you sell the customer is taxable, because some items aren't taxable—like customers, items have a tax liability switch that operates as an on/off switch.

For sales tax to kick in, both the item and the customer must have their tax liability status set to "taxable".

I can't give you a list of taxable/nontaxable categories, because each state sets its own rules. For example, in Pennsylvania, food and some other necessities of life aren't taxable, but some types of consulting services are. Other states don't tax services at all, reserving the sales tax for products. Some states seem to tax everything—California comes to mind.

QuickBooks prepopulates the Sales Tax Preferences dialog with the following two sales tax codes:

- Tax, which means liable for sales tax
- Non, which means not liable for sales tax

For many of us, that's enough; we don't need any additional tax codes for customers or for items. We can move on to creating sales tax items so tax rates can be calculated on sales forms.

However, for some companies, those two tax codes aren't enough. Some taxing authorities care about the "why"—most often they want to know why a customer *isn't* liable for sales tax.

If your state sales tax report form wants to know why a customer is taxable, it's probably asking about the tax rate for that customer. Many states are setting up multiple sales tax rates, basing the rate on location (county, city, town, or zip code). Identifying a customer as "taxable because he's in the Flummox County of our state" means the tax charged on sales to that customer are the tax rates assigned to Flummox County. (Tax rates are configured in sales tax items, not sales tax codes. See the section "Sales Tax Items".)

Most taxing authorities are only interested in the "why not" question. Is a customer nontaxable because it's out of state and the rules say you don't have to collect taxes for out-of-state sales? Is the customer nontaxable because it's a nonprofit organization, or a government agency? Is the customer nontaxable because it's a wholesale business and collects sales tax from its own customers? If your state requires this information, you must create tax codes to match the reporting needs required by your state.

Creating Sales Tax Codes

If you want to create codes to track customer sales tax status in a manner more detailed than "taxable" and "nontaxable," you can click the arrow to the right of either the Taxable Item Code or Non-taxable Item Code field in the Sales Tax Preferences dialog and select <Add New>. Or, you can choose Lists → Sales Tax Code List and press Ctrl-N. Either action opens the New Sales Tax Code dialog seen in Figure 4-2.

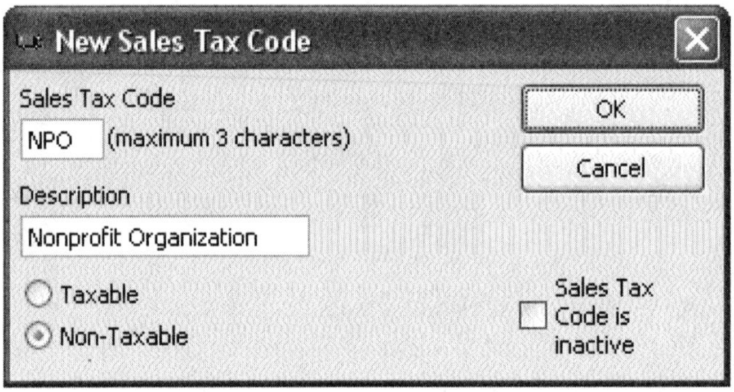

Figure 4-2: Create the tax codes your state requires.

1. Enter the name of the new code, using up to three characters.
2. Enter a description to make it easier to interpret the code.
3. Select Taxable if you're entering a code to track a specific reason for tax liability.
4. Select Non-taxable if you're entering a code to track a specific reason for a nontaxable status.
5. Click Next to set up another tax code.
6. Click OK when you've finished adding tax codes.

This procedure works nicely for specifying different types of nontaxable customers. For example, you could create tax codes similar to the following for nontaxable categories:

- NPO for nonprofit organizations
- GOV for government agencies
- WSL for wholesale businesses

- OOS for out-of-state customers (if you aren't required to collect taxes from out-of-state customers)

For nontaxable customers who are resellers, don't forget to record the tax exemption number (QuickBooks provides a field named Resale Number for this information on the Additional Info tab of the customer record.)

***WARNING**: In some states, tax-exempt reseller certificates that make a customer nontaxable are only for the state tax; some local tax authorities do not recognize reseller tax exceptions.*

For taxable customers, the permutations and combinations are much broader, of course. If you're required to collect and remit sales tax for some additional states, just create codes for customers in those states, using the postal abbreviations for each state.

Some states have specific codes for the state/local combo sales taxes, and you must include those codes in your reports. For example, Kansas has codes that specify each combo of state/local sales tax rates.

This would be a great use of the QuickBooks sales tax code, but alas, QuickBooks permits three characters only in the tax code field and most of the state jurisdictional codes have five or more characters.

The workaround for this is to use those codes as the name of the sales tax item and assign that item to the appropriate customer.

Sales Tax Items

A sales tax item is a collection of data about a sales tax, specifically the rate and the agency to which the sales tax is remitted. The agency has to be set up as a vendor.

Sales tax is an item because, like your service and product items, it's used on sales transaction forms. QuickBooks uses sales tax items to calculate the amount in the Tax field at the bottom of sales forms, and to prepare reports for tax authorities.

However, there are circumstances in which the sales tax rules under which you operate are so complicated that you must create sales tax items that are used in the line item section of the sales form, and in that case you must prevent QuickBooks from calculating a sales tax amount. You accomplish this by creating a "fake" sales tax that has a zero rate. Those circumstances are discussed later in this chapter.

Creating Sales Tax Items

When you enable sales tax in the Preferences dialog, you must specify the most common sales tax, which means you must create a sales tax item. Click the button labeled Add Sales Tax Item to open the New Item window with Sales Tax preselected in the Item Type drop-down list. Press Tab to display the New Item window seen in Figure 4-3:

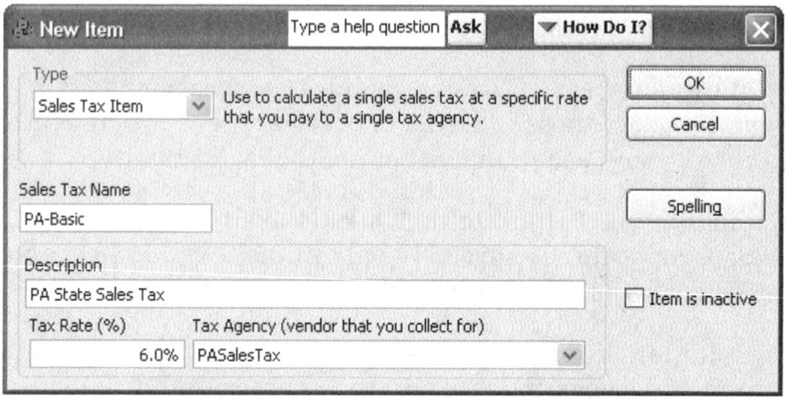

Figure 4-3: A sales tax item must have a name, a rate, and a tax agency.

It's entirely possible that your most common sales tax item is not an individual tax; instead it may be a sales tax group (two sales tax items, one for the state and one for the county or city). However, you can't create a sales tax group until you've created the sales tax items that make up the group (see "Sales Tax Groups", later in this section).

For now, let's assume you only have to worry about a single state tax, and finish configuring the sales tax dialog, using the following steps:

1. Enter a name for the sales tax, and make it descriptive. For instance, use your state abbreviation if your state has a single sales tax structure, or you do business in one of the state's counties or cities that isn't required to collect local taxes along with the state tax.
2. Optionally enter a description of this sales tax.
3. Enter the sales tax rate (QuickBooks automatically adds the % sign).
4. Select the Tax Agency from the drop-down list if you've already created a vendor record for the tax agency. If the vendor doesn't exist, select <Add New> and add the tax agency to your vendor list.

Notice that Figure 4-3 displayed an agency name that's a vendor code, not the real name of the sales tax authority. If you remit sales tax to your state's Department of Revenue, it's highly likely you remit other payments to the same department. Using vendor names that are codes ensures that the right vendor gets the right check for the right type of payment. Because QuickBooks has a field for the Payee in the vendor record, the checks are made out to the right payee. For example, I have the following vendors in my system, all of which have the Payee "PA Department of Revenue".

- PA501 (the vendor for remitting employee withholding for state income tax—501 is the form number).
- PACorp (the vendor for paying state corporate taxes).
- PACorpEst (the vendor for remitting estimated corporate taxes).
- PASalesTax (the vendor for remitting sales tax).
- PAUC (the vendor for remitting unemployment tax).

This paradigm makes it easy to create checks and track history.

If your state has a multi-tax structure, and you report the taxes individually, the name should indicate that this tax is part of a multi-tax unit by using text such as PA-Basic (for Pennsylvania basic state tax, which is part of a multi-tax structure for some cities in the state). Later, when you create the local tax, you can create a sales tax group made up of the two taxes, and use the sales tax group on sales forms (see "Sales Tax Groups" later in this section).

Some states have a complicated multi-tax structure and have invented tax codes where each code is already a group (a combination of the state tax and the local tax for the specific code), you can create a single sales tax item for each code, using the code as the sales tax item name.

When you finish configuring this sales tax item, click OK to return to the Sales Tax Preferences dialog. QuickBooks inserts this tax as the most common sales tax item. If this is the most common sales tax item (or the only sales tax item you need), you're finished.

When you click OK, QuickBooks displays the dialog seen in Figure 4-4, asking whether it should configure all your existing customers, non-inventory, and inventory items as Taxable.

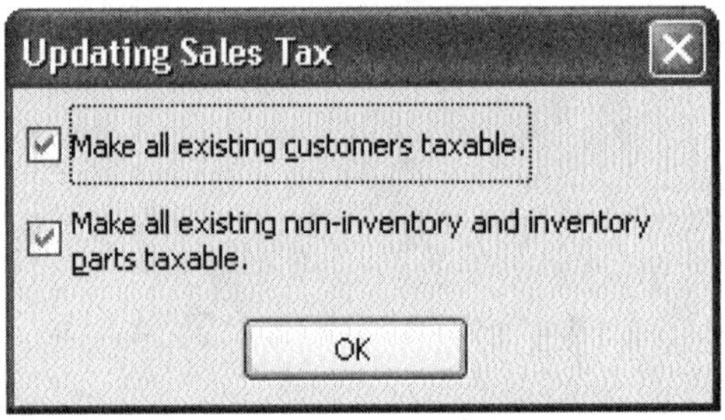

Figure 4-4: If most of your customers and items are taxable, let QuickBooks configure them automatically.

QuickBooks does not insert the most common sales tax you configured into the records of existing customers; however, as you create new customers the most common sales tax is automatically linked to the customer.

You can change any customer's tax code and tax item, either manually or in a batch import (those topics are covered later in this chapter).

Sales Tax Groups

In some states, the tax imposed is really two taxes, and the taxing authority collects a single check from you but insists on a breakdown in the reports you send. For example, in Pennsylvania, the state sales tax is 6%, but businesses in Philadelphia and Pittsburgh must charge an extra 1%, making the total tax to the customer 7%.

One check is remitted to the state's revenue department, but the report that accompanies the check must break down the remittance into the individual taxes—the total of the 6% tax, and the total of the 1% tax.

In other states, the basic state sales tax is remitted to the state, and the locally added sales tax is remitted to the local taxing authority.

The challenge is to display and calculate a single sales tax for the customer and report multiple taxes to one or more taxing authorities. Tax groups meet this challenge.

A sales tax group is a single entity that appears on a sales transaction, but it is really multiple entities that have been totaled. QuickBooks inserts the sales tax amount in the sales transaction window by calculating taxable sales at the "combo" rate—the total of the two rates in the group.

To create a sales tax group, you must first create the individual sales tax items, which you can do by clicking the Add Sales Tax Item button in the Preferences dialog, or (if you're performing this task after you've saved the preferences, by choosing Lists → Item List.

Create a sales tax item for each sales tax you need to add to a group. If you're liable for sales tax collection for five counties in your state, you'll need five groups. Each group contains the state's basic sales tax as well as one of the county sales taxes.

When you create the additional sales tax items you need, be sure to name them appropriately so you have an easy time creating your group. The county sales tax seen in Figure 4-5 is an example.

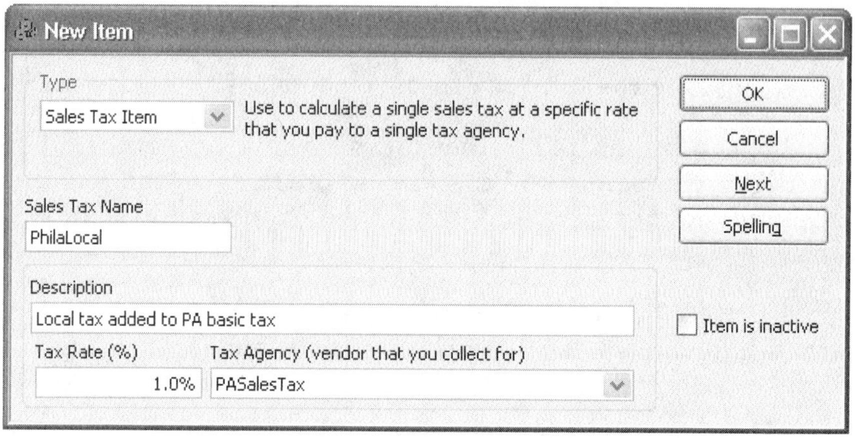

Figure 4-5: This is clearly a local tax that is always linked to a state tax.

Creating Sales Tax Groups

After all your individual sales tax items are in the system use the following steps to create a sales tax group item.

1. Open the Item List by choosing Lists → Item List.
2. Press CTRL-N to open the New Item dialog.
3. Select Sales Tax Group as the type.
4. Enter a name for the group.
3. Optionally enter a description.
5. In the Tax Item column, choose the individual sales tax items you need to create this group. As you move to the next item, QuickBooks fills in the rate, tax agency, and description (if one exists) of each sales tax item you select. The calculated total (the group rate) appears at the bottom of the dialog (see Figure 4-6).
6. Click OK.

Select this item for the appropriate customers when you're creating sales transactions.

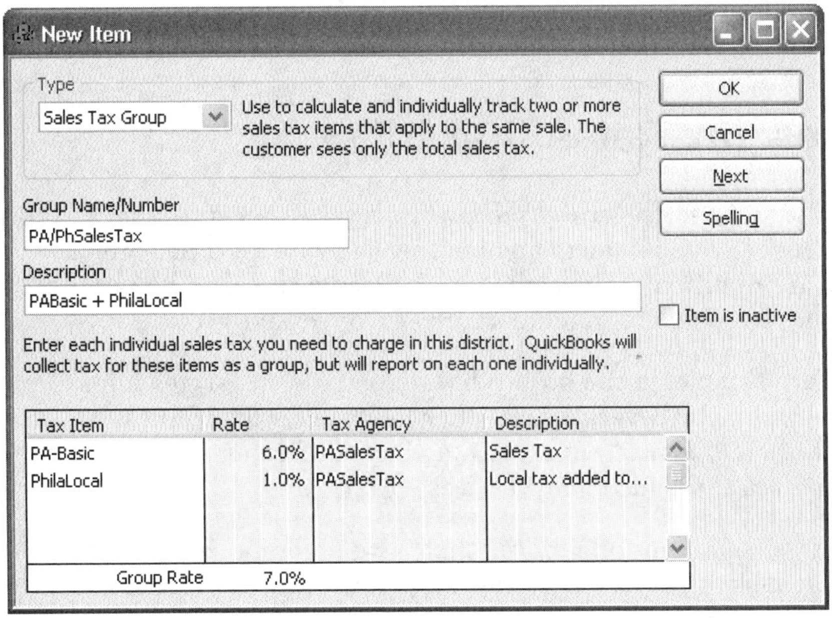

Figure 4-6: Create a Sales Tax Group to apply two taxes at once.

Assigning Tax Items to Customers

Each customer's taxable status (the sales tax *code*) and linked sales tax item are on the Additional Info tab of the customer's record, and you can edit each customer's record to make changes to either field.

Adding the sales tax item to every customer record can be a pain. If you already created a great many customers, opening each record to make changes is onerous, and there are two ways to remedy this:

- Wait until you use each customer in a sales transaction. Then, in the transaction window, change the customer's tax item. When you save the transaction, QuickBooks cooperates with this approach by asking you if you want to change the customer's tax information permanently. Click Yes.

- Export your customer list to an IIF file, change or create the tax code and tax item for each customer, and then import the file back into QuickBooks.

Sales Tax Rates that Differ by Item

Suppose you offer several products or services in a state that imposes one tax rate for some products and another tax rate for other products? The taxes are remitted to the same tax authority; this isn't a matter of "one rate for residents of X and another rate for residents of Y".

For example, in the hospitality industry, some states impose one tax rate for alcoholic beverages, another tax rate for food, and yet another tax rate for hotel rooms. Your state may have different rate structures for another set of products and services.

If you sell items or services that have different sales tax rates, it's not an easy task to prepare a single sales transaction for a customer who is purchasing items that have differing tax rates.

For tax rates based on an item, creating a Tax Group doesn't work, because a Tax Group represents the total of differing rates, and that's not what's needed in this case. The workaround for this complicated situation has two parts:

- Creating the items you need.
- Learning how to enter those items on a sales transaction.

Creating Items for Item-Based Tax Rates

You have to create multiple items to be able to apply different tax rates in the same sales transaction. Obviously, you have to create an item for each tax rate, but you also have to create two other items:

- A subtotal item (which you may already have) that enables you to create a subtotal for all items that bear the same tax rate.
- A fake tax item to satisfy the QuickBooks need for a tax rate for the entire invoice (the field that appears at the bottom of the invoice).

Creating the Tax Items

You need to create a tax item for each tax rate. Open the Item List by choosing Lists → Item List, and press Ctrl-N to create a new item using the following guidelines:

- The Item Type is Sales Tax Item
- The Tax Name is the specific tax, e.g. Food Tax. The Description should be specific, such as Food Tax. Don't leave the Description field blank, because you want the customer to see what the line item tax is (remember, there won't be a single item named "Tax").
- In the Tax Rate field, enter the appropriate rate (QuickBooks adds the % character automatically).
- In the Tax Agency field, enter the name of the tax authority (a vendor) to which you remit this tax.

Creating a Placeholder Tax Item

When you want to enter taxes as line items, QuickBooks throws up two impediments:

- It continues to tax the total taxable sale at the rate of the default tax item, which is displayed at the bottom of the transaction form.
- It won't let you enter a line item tax if that tax is already assigned to the customer or item, and is automatically listed at the bottom of the sales transaction (e.g. Food Tax).

The solution is to have a tax item that has a zero percent rate, and has a description that the customer will understand. Here are some guidelines for creating this item:

- The Item Type is Sales Tax
- The Item Name is Placeholder
- The Tax Rate is zero percent
- The Description is "Other Sales Tax"
- The Tax Agency is a vendor you must create named "No Tax", and the vendor has no address or other information, just the name.

TIP: *The vendor named No Tax will appear on all sales tax reports, but since no money is involved, it won't affect your numbers, nor will a check print when you remit your sales tax.*

Creating a Subtotal Item

In order to apply taxes as line items properly, you need a subtotal for each set of taxable line items. You have two ways to do this:

- You can create one item of the type Subtotal, named Subtotal (which may already exist in your Item List). Then, when you prepare a sales transaction, you can type in the description, such as "Total Taxable Food" before applying the applicable tax (in this case, the food tax).
- You can create one item for each subtotal you need, such as Subtotal-Food, and enter an appropriate description, such as "Total Taxable Food", which saves you the effort of entering the description when you prepare the sales transaction.

The second choice works best, because it's always more efficient to do a little extra setup work once to save the efforts needed on a daily basis.

Creating a Multi-rate Sales Transaction

In the Invoice or Sales Receipt transaction window, enter the Customer Name, and change the Tax field at the bottom of the line item section to the Placeholder tax item you created. Then, take the following steps:

1. Enter all the line items that are subject to one of the taxes.
2. Enter the subtotal item for these item types, which creates a total of the previous items. You must enter a subtotal item even if you only had one item in this group.
3. Enter the appropriate sales tax item. QuickBooks will calculate the tax based on the amount of the subtotal (which is why you must enter a subtotal even if you only had one item).
4. Enter the line items that are subject to the next tax.
5. Enter the subtotal item for these items.
6. Enter the appropriate tax item for this subtotal.
7. Continue to enter items, subtotals, and tax items.

You can make the printed version easier to read by inserting blank lines after each tax line (to separate the sections). To insert a blank line, place your cursor on the line below the place where you want the blank line, and press Ctrl-Ins (or Ctrl-Insert, depending on your keyboard's text).

Figure 4-7 shows an invoice that is prepared properly (although you can't see all the items because there's no way to let you scroll down in a printed figure). Notice that the taxes are applied properly, and the standard Tax field at the bottom of the invoice form has a zero amount.

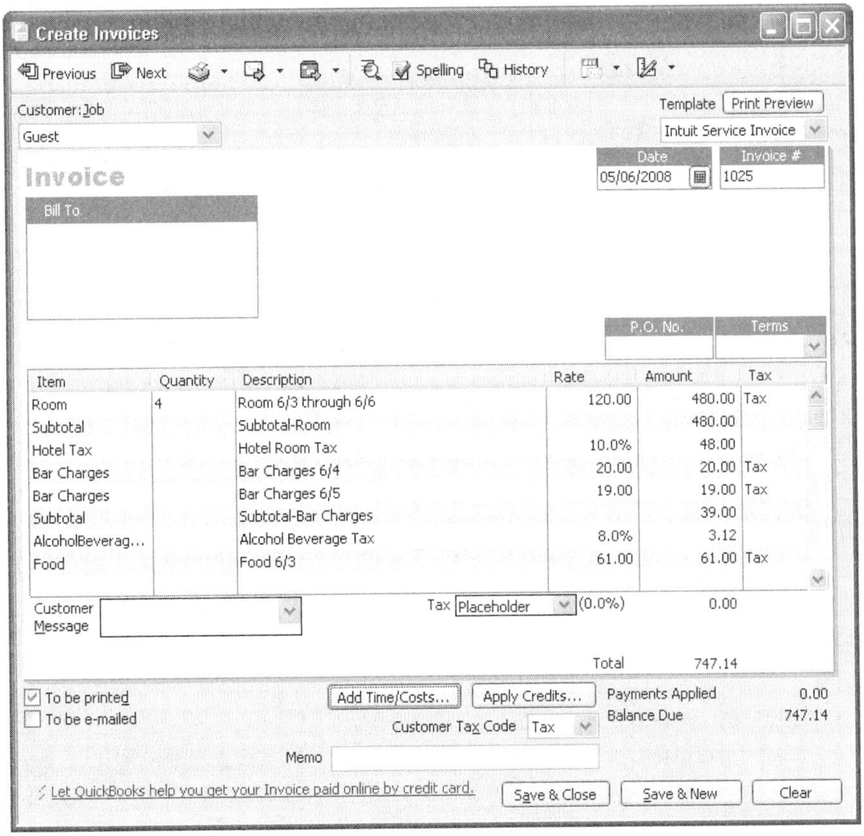

Figure 4-7: This invoice tracks all taxes properly, making it easy for the customer to understand the tax structure.

On Premises Vs. Off Premises Tax Rates

Some states or local tax authorities differentiate between goods that are used/consumed on your premises and goods that are purchased for use/consumption at home. The most common example (and perhaps the only example) is food. Sales tax on food works as follows in many states (usually, states that don't tax grocery items):

- You must apply tax to the diner's bill for food that is consumed on the premises.
- Take-out customers don't pay tax.

The solution for this is to create separate items, such as Food (taxable) and TakeOut (not taxable). QuickBooks calculates the total of the taxable item at the bottom of the sales form.

Incremental Sales Tax

In some states, the state sales tax is accompanied by local sales taxes, but to calm any public outcry about the additional local taxes, many local authorities devised incremental sales taxes.

An incremental local tax has a per-item limit for applying the tax. If the item limit is $5000.00, the local tax is only applied to that amount, and then it disappears. For example, if the local tax is 2%, then a $6000.00 item carries a tax burden of $100.00 (2% of the first $5000.00).

Remember this is per-item, so if a customer purchases two items at $5000.00 each, the tax is imposed on the entire $10,000.00; purchasing one item for $4000.00 and multiple other items that total $2000.00 has the same effect—the local tax is applied to the entire invoice/sales receipt.

Other states have devised incremental sales taxes that kick in with the opposite formula—tax exemptions at the beginning and tax applications at a particular point (essentially, a tax exemption with a maximum). For example, a state may say that the first $100.00 of a particular item type (e.g. clothing) is tax free (per item) and then the sales tax kicks in. For other item types no such scalable tax rate applies.

To make it worse, in some states (e.g. New York), the exemption to a certain amount for certain types of items is ignored by the local sales tax.

QuickBooks cannot manage incremental taxes, because, unlike most of its competition, it does not have a tax table that lets you create tax items with formulas (the way payroll items are configured). Hopefully this will change in the future.

I've looked at some QuickBooks users' workarounds for this, but none of them work properly. For instance, users have entered an item for the first $5000.00 (or other threshhold), applied the combo tax as a line item, and then entered the same item with the balance of the real price, selecting Non as the tax code for that item.

If the item is an inventory item, you've removed two pieces of inventory in QuickBooks (and one item from the physical inventory) and registered some really strange price structures and COGs calculations. In addition, the customers don't understand the printed sales receipt, and trying to explain it to each customer as a line of waiting customers grows impatient, is not good business.

You can build a set of formulas in Excel, calculate the taxes in Excel, and then enter the tax amount manually, but that's a lot of work and wastes a lot of time. Instead, think about using an external sales tax calculator.

Some states have online calculators (e.g. Kansas and Iowa, and perhaps others). You fill out the form (including the purchaser's address or local tax code), and the calculator provides the sales tax amount(s). Use a line item to apply the sales tax to the sales transaction form, and select a tax rate of zero to avoid additional tax being imposed automatically by QuickBooks (see the discussion on the zero-percent Placeholder tax, earlier in this chapter).

The Streamlined Sales Tax Project (http://www.streamlined-salestax.org/), the national organization that's working to streamline sales taxes, has certified two tax calculator solutions: Avalara (www.avalara.com) and Taxware (www.taxware.com). Avalara has a specific product for QuickBooks, and Taxware services small businesses using one of Avalara's products (AvaTax).

Remitting Sales Tax

This discussion assumes you've created the sales tax items you need, and each item is linked to the right vendor (tax authority).

Manage Sales Tax Feature

QuickBooks provides a feature called Manage Sales Tax (see Figure 4-8) that acts as a "home page" for information and help, and contains links to the reports and payment forms covered in this section. You can open the Manage Sales Tax window by choosing Vendors → Sales Tax → Manage Sales Tax.

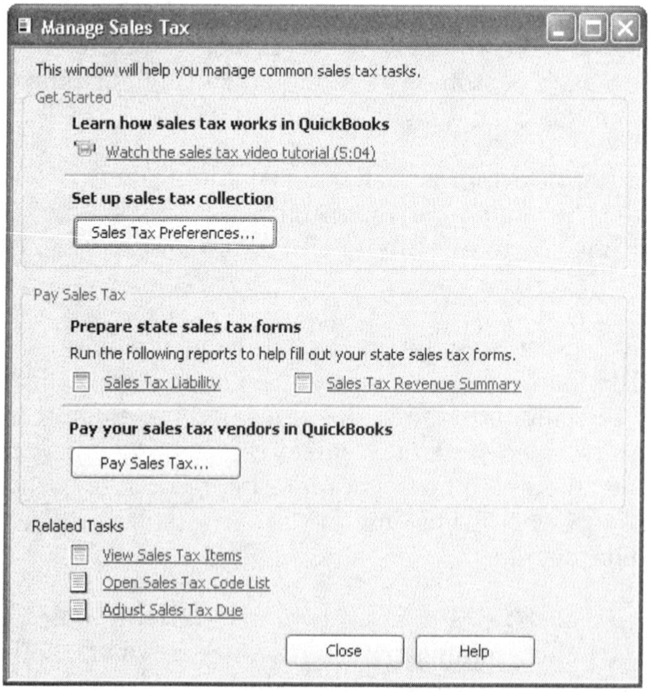

Figure 4-8: The Manage Sales Tax window has links to sales tax functions.

In the following discussions I'll provide the menu commands to access features and functions, but you can also use the links on the Manage Sales Tax window for some of these chores.

Sales Tax Reports

At some interval determined by your taxing authority (or multiple authorities), you need to report your total sales, your nontaxable sales, and your taxable sales, along with any other required breakdowns. And, of course, you have to send money.

Sales Tax Liability Report

The sales tax liability report helps you fill out your sales tax forms, and check your totals. To open this report choose Reports → Vendors & Payables → Sales Tax Liability.

Use the Dates drop-down list to select an interval that matches the way you report to the taxing authorities. By default, QuickBooks chooses the interval you configured in the Preferences dialog, but that interval may only apply to your primary sales tax. If you collect multiple taxes, due at different intervals, you must create a separate report with the appropriate interval to display those figures.

Tax Code Reports

If you have to report specific types of taxable or nontaxable sales, you can obtain that information by creating a report on the tax code you created to track that information.

Choose Lists → Sales Tax Code List and select (highlight) the tax code for which you need a report. Press Ctrl-Q to see a QuickReport on the sales activity with this tax code. Change the date range to match your reporting interval with the sales tax authority (this isn't a sales tax item report, so QuickBooks doesn't automatically match the settings in the Sales Tax Preferences dialog).

If you have multiple tax codes to track, you don't have to create these reports one code at a time; you can modify the report so it reports all of your tax codes, or just those you need for a specific tax authority's report.

In fact, you can modify the report so it reports totals instead of every sales transaction.

Click the Modify Report button on the report window. In the Display tab, use the Columns list to deselect any items you don't require for the report (for example, the Type, Date, and Number of an invoice/sales receipt, and the contents of the Memo field).

In the Filters tab, choose Sales Tax Code from the filter list. Click the arrow to the right of the Sales Tax Code field and select the appropriate option from the drop-down list, choosing one of the following options:

- All Sales Tax Codes, which displays total activity for the period for every code
- Multiple Sales Tax Codes, which opens the Select Sales Tax Code window, listing all codes, so you can select the specific codes you want to report on
- All Taxable Codes, which displays total activity for the period for each taxable code
- All Nontaxable Codes, which displays total activity for the period for each nontaxable code

Click OK to return to the report window, where your selections are reflected. Unless you want to take all these steps again when you need this report, click the Memorize button to memorize the report, and name it so it's easy to figure out what the contents are.

Remitting the Sales Tax

After you check the figures (or calculate them, if you have multiple reports with different standards of calculation), it's time to pay the tax, using the following steps:

1. Choose Vendors → Sales Tax → Pay Sales Tax, to open the Pay Sales Tax dialog (see Figure 4-9).
2. Select the bank account to use.
3. Check the date that's displayed in the field named Show Sales Tax Due Through. It must match the end date of your current reporting period (for instance, monthly or quarterly).

4. Click in the Pay column to insert a check mark next to those you're paying now. If you're lucky enough to have the same reporting interval for all taxing authorities just click the Pay All Tax button (the name of which then changes to Clear Selections).
5. If you're going to print the check, be sure to select the To Be Printed check box at the bottom of the dialog. If you write the check manually, or if you remit sales tax online using an electronic transfer from your bank, deselect the To Be Printed check box. (For electronic payment, open the bank account register and change the check number QuickBooks inserted automatically to ACH or another code indicating an electronic transfer.)
6. Click OK.

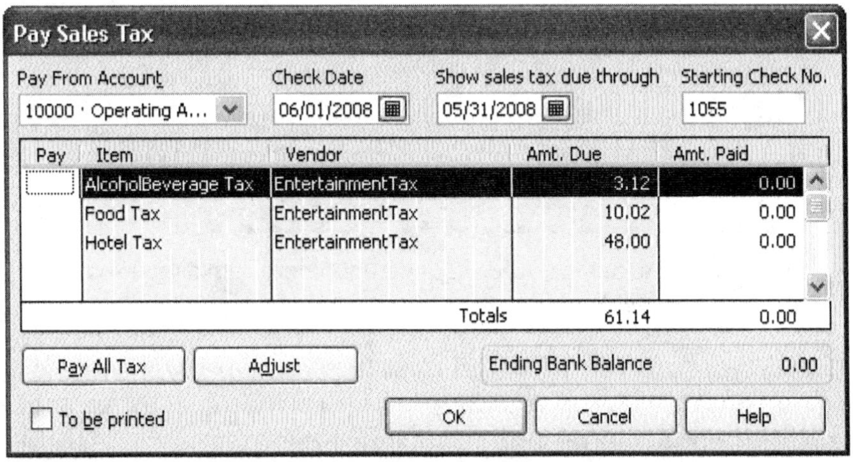

Figure 4-9: Remit your sales tax to the tax authorities.

***NOTE**: QuickBooks doesn't ask for a start date because it uses the period duration defined in your Sales Tax Preferences.*

Adjusting Sales Tax Amounts

If you need to adjust the amount of sales tax due (most states offer a discount for timely payment), select the appropriate sales tax item in the

Pay Sales Tax window and click the Adjust button to open the Sales Tax Adjustment dialog seen in Figure 4-10.

Figure 4-10: Adjust the sales tax amount before remitting the payment.

Specify the amount by which to reduce (or increase, if you're late and paying a penalty) the tax amount. Specify an Adjustment Account (you can create a specific account for this adjustment), and click OK to return to the Pay Sales Tax window, where the amount has been changed to reflect your adjustment.

Chapter 5

Payroll

Payroll tips

Garnishments

Managing outsourced payroll

Payroll causes more angst, confusion, and panic calls to accountants than any other element involved in running a business. Whether a business does payroll in-house, or has a payroll service, questions and problems abound.

In this chapter I'll pass along some explanations and tips for tracking payroll (either in-house or outsourced) I've learned from clients, or worked out in response to client problems with payroll.

Keeping Payroll Information Secure

The way QuickBooks Pro/Premier editions set up user permissions makes it very difficult for business owners to prevent users from viewing payroll information for employees, bosses, owners, etc.

The permissions you must give your Accounts Payable person mean that he can view net payroll checks. The permissions you must give a user who needs to transfer funds, create journal entries, or perform online banking chores also let her open the Employee Center (where everything you'd want to know about employees is available). Lots of other permissions needed to let users do their jobs provide access to employee payroll information.

The only way to keep payroll information secure is to create a separate company for payroll. Perform all payroll tasks from this company, and then use journal entries to move totals into the accounts in your real company. (The same way you use journal entries to transfer totals if you outsource your payroll, covered later in this chapter.)

Configuring Vendors For Payroll Liabilities

Businesses that remit their own payroll liabilities often have to go through some difficult maneuvers to create the liability checks properly. In many businesses the 941 and 940 liabilities are paid to the bank or to the IRS (for electronic payments), and the state payroll taxes, UC and SDI payments are all paid to the same state agency (e.g. Department of Revenue or Department of Labor & Industry).

The business owner or bookkeeper (or even the accountant) sets up the bank or the IRS as a vendor, and sets up the appropriate state department as a vendor. When it's time to remit liabilities, all the liabilities are selected, and QuickBooks creates one check for each vendor.

This doesn't work, because there are always forms to fill out, or coupons to attach to each individual liability payment, and the vendor won't accept one large check for multiple types of liability payments.

What's the solution? There are two solutions; one is a pain, the other is easy. At CPA911, we presented this topic as a newsletter puzzle (our newsletter readers can vie for prizes by answering our puzzles), and only a couple of respondents presented the easy solution, everyone else was using the "painful" solution.

The painful solution is to select each liability, one at a time, in the Pay Liabilities window. Create the check, print the check, attach the appropriate paperwork, and return to the Pay Liabilities window to process the next check for the same vendor. (For e-payments, substitute "record the check and fill out the appropriate form online".)

That's real work, and I'm far too lazy to do that. Besides, I'd probably lose track and cut the same check twice.

The easy solution is to take advantage of the fact that QuickBooks presents a "Print On Check As" field in each vendor record, so you can have separate vendors with the same payee name.

For the federal deposits, create one vendor named 940 and another vendor named 941. Both vendors have the same name in the Print On Check As field (either the bank or the IRS). For the state, create separate vendors for each separate liability (payroll taxes, UC, SDI, etc.). Enter the appropriate payee name in the Print On Check As field (possibly the same text for all vendors).

***TIP**: I name all my payroll liability vendors with the form name: 940, 941, PA501 (the form number for remitting payroll taxes in Pennsylvania), SUTA (for state UC), and so on.*

Edit your payroll items list to reflect the vendor names (not the payee text). After you've completed this one-time-only setup chore, paying liabilities is a snap. Select all the liabilities that are due and click Create. QuickBooks creates separate checks for each liability payment.

This system works well for garnishments, too. If you have employees with garnishments for child support, tax liens, etc. and the money is all sent to the same government agency, you can't send one check for all garnishments. (See the Section "Garnishments" later in this chapter.)

Social Security Numbers on Pay Stubs

I've had a great deal of e-mail from readers who use direct deposit and print pay stubs that are mailed to employees. The employees have asked that the social security number be omitted from the pay stubs, because they fear identity theft.

That's a valid fear, because by default the direct deposit pay stub prints not only the social security number, but also the bank account number—the kind of information someone bent on stealing identities revels in.

You can change the data that prints on pay stubs. Choose Edit → Preferences and select the Payroll & Employees category in the left pane. In the My Company tab, click the button labeled Printing Preferences.

The dialog that appears offers options for all the types of information that you can print, or not print (see Figure 5-1). You can disable the printing of the SSN altogether by deselecting it. You can also enable the option to print only the last four digits of the SSN and the bank account.

Some states require employers to print the SSN on direct deposit pay stubs, and if you live in one of those states, check to see whether the last four digits will suffice. If your state doesn't require this information, disable the printing of the SSN altogether.

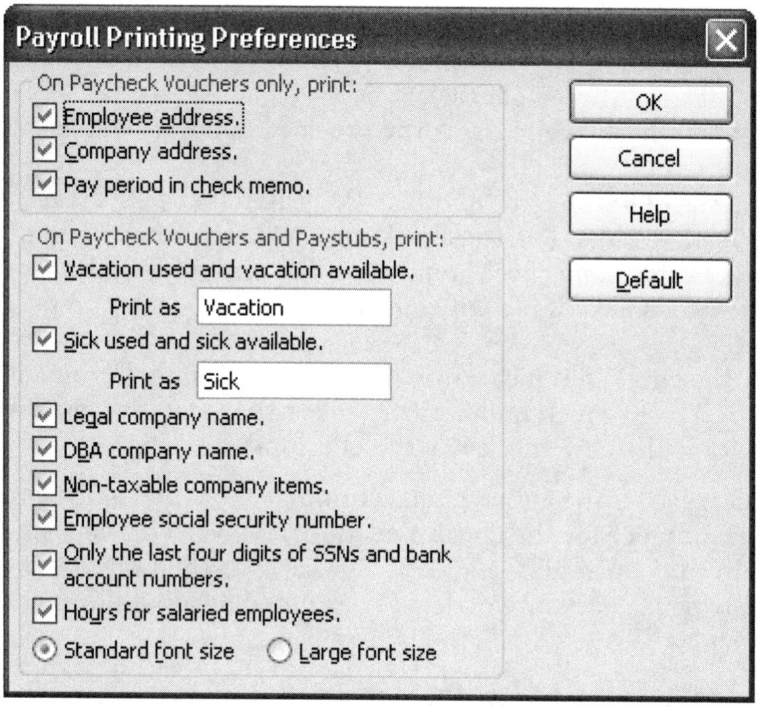

Figure 5-1: For safety and security, change the data that prints on pay stubs.

Re-issuing a Lost Paycheck

You can't manage the replacement of paychecks the same way you manage the replacement of lost or destroyed vendor checks. Payroll checks and their attendant postings are more complicated than ordinary vendor checks, but if you follow these step-by-step instructions, it's easy to accomplish this task.

1. Do NOT void the original paycheck.
2. Create the employee as an Other Name. You have to use a variation of the name in the Name field, because you can't have duplicate names in your company file.

3. Use the Write Checks function to write a check for the NET amount to the Other Name entry. Post the check to any expense account (e.g. Misc expenses).
4. Print the check, write down the check number, and give it to the employee.
5. Open the bank register and find the original check (the one that was lost). Write down the check number. Edit that original check so it has the same check number as the one you just issued. When QuickBooks asks if it's OK to have duplicate check numbers, say Yes.
6. Edit the check you just wrote to the Other Name. Change its number to the old check number (the check that was lost or destroyed).
7. Now that the new check has the old number, void it.

Your records show the correct check number for the voided check, the correct check number for the check that the employee will deposit, your liabilities haven't changed, the W-2 will be correct, the Other Name listing and the expense account you used does not show a balance for this transaction.

Payroll Deductions for Employee Purchases

If you do your own payroll, and you permit employees to purchase goods, and then pay for those goods with a payroll deduction, here's how to set up and use that function.

You can use the same paradigm presented here to track and repay employee loans and payroll advances.

Setting Up Employee Purchase Elements

Before you can create transactions for employee purchases, you have to set up the list components you'll need, which are the following:

- A customer record for the employee. You cannot duplicate the name you use in the employee record. Use a nickname, or use the format "employee name-cust", such as SmithJ-Cust.

- An account to track employee purchases. The account is of the type Other Current Asset. Name the account Employee Purchases (or something similar).
- An Item of the type Discount, which you can name Employee Purchase. The item is non-taxable, has a default amount of $0.00, and is linked to the Other Current Asset account named Employee Purchases.
- A Payroll Item that is a Payroll Deduction, named Employee Purchases. Link the payroll liability account for this item to the Other Current Asset account named Employee Purchases. Apply the item to Net pay (not Gross).

Creating an Employee Purchase Transaction

Here's how to create an invoice that will be paid from the employee's paycheck:

1. Create an invoice for the customer/employee.
2. Enter the services or items purchased by the employee/customer on the invoice, using the pricing structure for employees (which may or may not be the same as for other customers).
3. In the next item line, enter the discount item you created for employee purchases, and enter an amount equal to the total of the employee's purchases.

The balance of the invoice is now $0.00. However, the Employee Purchases Other Current Asset account has been increased by the amount for the discount item.

Deducting Payment from the Paycheck

When you create a paycheck for the employee, add the Employee Purchases payroll deduction item in the Other Payroll Items area of the Preview Paycheck window. You can either enter the full amount owed, or a partial amount (and deduct the rest from subsequent paychecks).

If the full amount is deducted, the Employee Purchases Other Current Asset account has no balance. If a partial payment is deducted, the remaining balance equals the balance in that account.

Tracking Multiple Employee Purchase Accounts

If multiple employees make purchases that are deducted from paychecks, you don't have to set up a separate asset account for each employee. Instead, you can track each employee's current balance by creating and memorizing a report, as follows:

1. Choose Reports, Custom Transaction Detail Report.
2. In the Date Range field, select All
3. Click Modify Report.
4. In the Display tab, select Sort by Customer.
5. In the Filters tab, select the Employee Purchases account.
6. Memorize the report (the name Employee Purchases seems appropriate).

The report provides a breakdown of employee indebtedness on an employee-by-employee basis. Run this report on payday so you know how much should be deducted from each paycheck.

Job Costing and Class Tracking in Payroll

Many businesses want to link payroll expenses to classes, customers, and jobs. Even if they don't bill customers for payroll expenses, the links are set up as an effective method of job costing.

NOTE*: Many nonprofit organizations have funding contracts that enable reimbursement for payroll expenses, either by a percentage or for a particular job title. To learn how to do this, read Running QuickBooks in Nonprofits from CPA911 Publishing. The book is available at your favorite bookseller.*

You can link your payroll expenses to classes and job costing through allocation journal entries (discussed in Chapter 6), or by setting up your QuickBooks payroll system to perform the allocations automatically when you issue paychecks. To accomplish this in the most effective way, you need to take advantage of two QuickBooks features:

- Configure your company file to track job costing and class tracking for paycheck expenses.
- Use timesheets to track employee time by job and class.

Configure Payroll for Class Tracking and Job Costing

To establish class tracking and job costing for paycheck expenses, first make sure you've enabled class tracking, and then set up class tracking and job costing for payroll.

Enable Class Tracking

To turn on class tracking, choose Edit → Preferences and select the Accounting icon in the left pane of the Preferences dialog. In the Company Preferences tab, select the option labeled Use Class Tracking.

You should also select the option Prompt To Assign Classes. The prompt (a message) appears whenever a user fills out a transaction window and fails to enter a class in the Class Column.

The prompt is just that; a prompt, a reminder—you cannot set up QuickBooks to force a user to enter class information in transactions. You have to make sure your users understand the importance of class tracking for developing accurate P & L reports by class.

TIP: *Class tracking doesn't work well unless you create a generic class for transactions that don't fit neatly into a "real" class. This is your "overhead" class, which you should name Admin or Overhead. You can use a journal entry to move portions of the totals from the generic class to a real class.*

Enable Payroll Class Tracking and Job Costing

To apply class tracking and job costing to payroll, in the Preferences dialog select the Payroll & Employees icon in the left pane. Move to the Company Preferences tab and select the option labeled Job Costing and Class Tracking for Paycheck Expenses.

You can opt to apply classes and jobs to an entire paycheck, or to each earnings item within a paycheck.

If you're tracking classes and not job-costing, and each employee is working exclusively for a specific class, the option to assign a class to a paycheck is sufficient. Otherwise, select the option to track classes and jobs to the payroll items that make up paychecks.

Using Timesheets to Track Employee Activity

You can use timesheets to track employee time in a way that lets you link the time they spend on service activities (service items in your Item List) to classes and jobs. You can use the information you gain from the timesheets to report on service activities by class, and link customers and jobs to service activities. You can bill customers for the activities, or merely maintain the information for job costing purposes.

To fill out timesheets choose Employees → Enter Time → Use Weekly Timesheet. The Weekly Timesheet provides a way to enter all the information you need to track the services employees perform by customer and class.

As you can see in Figure 5-2, you can decide on a job-by-job and service-by-service entry whether to bill the customer or merely track the information for job costing purposes.

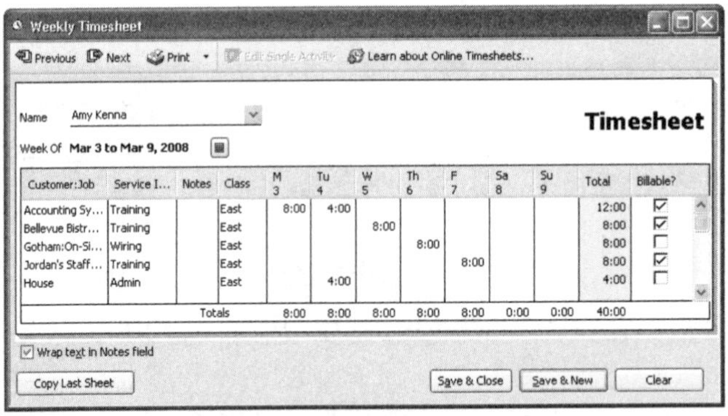

Figure 5-2: Timesheets provide a way to link jobs and classes to the work employees perform.

Notice the existence of a customer named House and a service item named Admin, to cover administrative work for the company that isn't connected to a customer for job costing or reimbursement.

Garnishments

I receive many requests for help from small businesses who have been on the receiving end of a garnishment order. Garnishments are extremely complicated, almost impossible to automate, and can't be avoided. If a garnishment order is delivered, employers are required to collect the garnished amount and remit it to the appropriate agency.

I've never found a simple way to deal with payroll garnishments, and as a result of experimentation and troubleshooting client protocols, I've come up with some rules. My rules were established for employers who have multiple garnishment orders to deal with, but the practices established with these rules work for companies that are managing only a single garnishment order.

- You need a separate payroll liability account for garnishments.
- You need a discrete payroll item for every garnishment order, even if the agency and/or employee are the same.
- Every garnishment payroll item has to have its own agency (vendor), even if the vendor is the same for multiple garnishments. The vendor code (Name) must vary, although the payee and mailing address is the same.
- You must preview payroll checks for every employee with a garnishment deduction in order to view or change the garnishment deduction. (Some deductions vary depending on the amount of the net check, and other deductions are eliminated if the net check isn't a certain minimum amount.)

Without following these rules you won't be able to track, report on, and remit garnished wages with any level of confidence. Remember, the onus is on you—you're under orders and are obligated to do this properly. After all, in most cases, if the employee could be relied upon to make these payments there wouldn't be a garnishment order.

Liability Account for Garnishments

You have to create a specific payroll liability account for garnishments. Actually, it's best to have separate payroll liability accounts for every type of payroll liability instead of posting everything to a single account named Payroll Liabilities.

Separate payroll liability accounts make it easier to track, and create reports about, what's due and what's paid on a tax-by-tax basis. In fact the best way to set up payroll liability accounts is as a series of subaccounts under the payroll liabilities parent account. As you can see in Figure 5-3, subaccounts provide individual balance totals, and a grand total for the parent account, when you view the chart of accounts list.

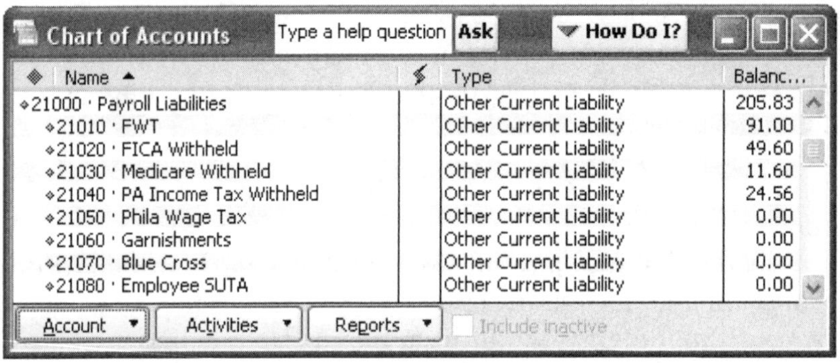

Figure 5-3: Subaccounts provide individual totals as well as a grand total for payroll liability balances.

Garnishment Vendors

Each garnishment needs to have its own vendor, and the way you create the vendor is directly connected to its garnishment order. The reason for individual, separate, vendors is to create individual, separate, checks for each garnishment remittance.

If you send one check covering multiple garnishments to the same agency, I can almost guarantee that the check won't be processed properly, no matter how detailed a report you attach to the check (besides, you don't want to go to the trouble of creating such a report every payday). In fact, many agencies insist on separate checks for each employee's garnishment order, and won't accept one check for multiple garnishment remittances.

Vendor Type for Garnishment Agencies

It's a good idea to set up a vendor type for garnishments; in fact, creating vendor subtypes for each type of garnishment is a better idea. Taking this step makes it easier to generate reports about garnishments—filtering a report on vendor type means you display only the specific information you need.

Garnishment Vendor Configuration

Setting up vendors properly takes a bit of time, but it's a one-time task, and that's certainly easier than going through multiple steps every payday to make sure each garnishment agency receives its remittance. Following are some guidelines for creating garnishment vendors.

In the Vendor Name field, create a code that identifies this vendor and the garnishment to which it's attached—include a reference to the employee in the code.

For example, if the employee Robert B. Whatsizname has a garnishment order for child support, and the agency is the Philadelphia County Division of Family Services, name the vendor PhilaFamServ-RBW. If the garnishment is for an unpaid student loan, and the agency is the Pennsylvania Higher Education Agency, name the vendor PHEA-RBW.

In the Company Name field, enter the name of the payee for the remittance check. QuickBooks automatically copies that name to the field labeled Print On Check As. No matter how many garnishments you have for child support from a single county agency, each check is processed individually, and each payment is posted against the individual deduction liability.

Move to the Additional Info tab and enter the garnishment reference in the Account No. field. Usually this is a case number, such as S112255. The data you enter here prints on the Memo Line of the check (if you print checks), or has to be entered manually if you don't print checks (this is yet another reason to print checks in QuickBooks; manual checks are a lot of work and prone to omissions or errors).

Payroll Item for a Garnishment

You must create a payroll item for each individual garnishment order, using the following steps (this is a wizard, so click Next to move through the wizard windows):

1. Choose Employees → Manage Payroll Items → New Payroll Item to open the Add New Payroll Item Wizard.
2. In the first wizard window, select Custom Setup.
3. In the next wizard window, select Deduction.
4. In the next wizard window, name the deduction, using text specific to the garnishment and the employee.
   For instance, for a child support order for employee R.B. Whatsizname, use ChildSupp-RBW.
5. In the next wizard window, enter the vendor specific to this garnishment, the account number that identifies this garnishment, and the liability account you created to track garnishments.
6. In the next wizard window, which asks about Tax Tracking, select None.
7. In the next wizard window, which establishes taxes that are deducted before this payroll item is deducted, click Default to select all the appropriate taxes.
8. In the next wizard window, which specifies the way the deduction is calculated, select Neither (meaning neither by quantity nor hours).
9. In the next wizard window, select Net Pay.
   If the garnishment is a percentage, it's always based on net pay; if the garnishment is a flat amount no calculation occurs when you apply it to the paycheck.
10. In the next wizard window, enter the rate for this deduction.
    If the garnishment is an amount, enter it, if it's a percentage remember to use the percent symbol (%). If there's a limit (which usually exists only for loan or other fixed-figure garnishments, not for child support) enter it. The window also has a check mark to

indicate an annual limit, but it's unusual for a garnishment to establish annual limits.

11. Click Finish to save the payroll item.

Now that the payroll item exists, you can apply it to the appropriate employee.

Assigning a Garnishment Deduction to an Employee

To link the garnishment item to the employee, open the employee record in the Employee Center. In the Change Tabs field at the top of the record, select Payroll And Compensation Info to display the Payroll Info tab seen in Figure 5-4.

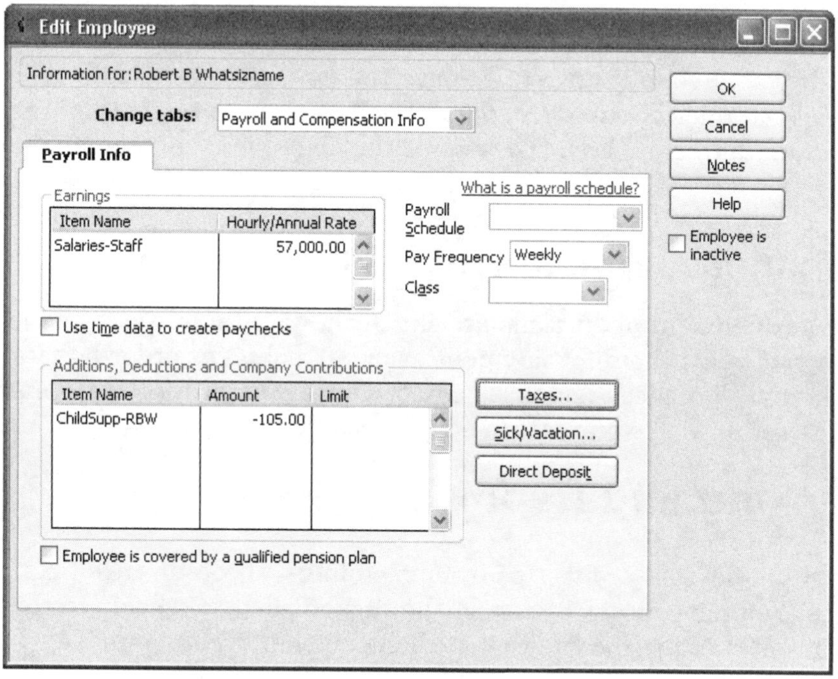

Figure 5-4: Enter the deduction for the garnishment in the employee's record.

You need to repeat all of these actions for every garnishment order you receive (with the exception of creating the liability account—you don't need a separate liability account for each garnishment order).

Viewing and Editing Garnishment Paycheck Deductions

You should always preview paychecks for employees who have garnishments, because you may have to adjust, or even remove, the deduction. Many garnishment orders include specifications about the net paycheck amount and its affect on the garnishment.

Some specifications limit the amount of the deduction depending on the amount of the employee's net pay. Other specifications remove the deduction entirely if the net pay amount is below a minimum figure.

The deduction can be edited in the Review Or Change Paycheck window. If you have to change or remove the deduction, you need to calculate the correct amount outside of QuickBooks—there is no method I know of to automate this process. (To remove the deduction, change its amount to 0.00.)

Remitting Garnishment Deductions

Your garnishment deductions appear in the Pay Liabilities window, and when you select them for payment each garnishment order has its own check, and that check is appropriately annotated with the case number. All the setup work you performed ensures this.

Tracking and Reporting Tips

If your employees receive tips from customers, those tips are taxable wages. You have to pay or report the tips on each paycheck, so that the tips are part of the income reported on the employee's W-2.

- You have to give the employees the tips if you collected the tips.
- You have to report the tips if the employee collected the tips.

In many businesses, you have to do both; that is, you have to add the employee tips you kept to the employee's paycheck, and you have to report the tips the employee kept. Usually the tips you have to provide in the paycheck are tips added to credit card charges that you didn't turn over at the time you processed the credit card. The tips that need to be reported, but not paid, on the paycheck are the cash tips the employee collected and kept at the time of customer payment.

In addition to these simple paradigms, there lots of possible combinations and permutations in the way tips are handled. Tips may be collected in a central place (a big jar) and split evenly, or split unevenly to account for job titles (servers get a larger percentage than the employees who bus the tables; colorists and stylists get a larger percentage than people who shampoo; etc. etc.

You must have a way to track tips, because if you don't the IRS will do it for you. Employees must report their tips, you must track the tips you kept and added to a paycheck, and you must track the tip jar's contents and the way those contents are distributed.

Creating an Account for Tracking Tips

You have to track the in-and-out of tip dollars, and the easiest way to do that is to create a single account for all tip activity. Commonly, the account is of the type Other Current Asset, and is named Employee Tips.

Everything you do regarding employee tips passes through that account. Tips are not a payroll liability, nor are they a payroll expense. They fall outside the payroll accounts you use to track payroll liabilities and expenses. The only connection tips have to payroll is the fact that they must be reported to the IRS, and the way to do that is to track them within paychecks (but not as liabilities or expenses).

Adding Tips to Sales Transactions

The way you manage sales transactions depends on the way your employees receive their tips:

If your employees collect their tips in cash, the tips don't affect the sales transactions. The employees must track these tips and give you the total before payday.

If you collect the tips and add them to the employees' paychecks (usually because the customer added the tip to a credit card transaction), you must post the tips to the Employee Tips account, not to the income count you use for the rest of the transaction. To do that, you need an item (a sales item, not a payroll item), and that's covered in the next section.

If you collect the tips and give the money to the employees from the cash register or petty cash, you must post the transaction to the Employee Tips account. The employees must track these tips as if they were directly received from the customer, and the amount must be included in the total they provide you before payday.

Creating a Sales Item for Tips

If you collect the tips, the sales transaction that includes the tips must account for those tips separately from the posting to income for the sale. That means you must have an item to use in the sales transaction. Create an item named Tips Held, using the following guidelines.

- The item type should be either an Other Charge or Service.
- The item is not taxable.
- The amount is zero (and is filled in when you create a transaction).
- The Account is the Employee Tips account you create as described earlier in this section.

Creating Payroll Items for Tips

You need to create payroll items to remit and report tips. An easy way to understand what these payroll items do is to think of them as Tips In and Tips Out.

- Tips In is an additional compensation payroll item you use to add tips to a paycheck.

- Tips Out is a deduction payroll item you use to remove the tips the employee already collected. It is a deduction from Net, not Gross.

Once both items are available for paychecks, any combination of held/collected tips can appear on a paycheck.

For example, let's say an employee received $200.00 in tips, and $100.00 of that amount was in cash and kept by the employee. The other $100.00 was added to credit card charges and you did not turn it over in cash; instead, you added it to the employee's paycheck.

- Tips In is $200.00. That's the taxable amount, and is used when creating W-2s.
- Tips Out is $100.00. That's the amount you're reducing from the Tips In total because you don't include that amount in the paycheck (the employee already has the money).

If the employee kept all $200.00 in cash at the time the customers left the tip, or if you turned over the cash after you processed the credit card transaction, then Tips In and Tips Out are both $200.00.

If you keep all the tips and remit them in paychecks, then Tips In is the amount of money you're giving the employee in the paycheck, and Tips Out is zero (and the Tips Out payroll item is omitted from the paycheck).

QuickBooks provides payroll items that work for tips, which makes configuring all of this easy. To create your tips payroll items, choose Employees → Manage Payroll Items → New Payroll Item.

In the Add New Payroll Item Wizard, choose Custom Setup, and then proceed as explained in the following sections.

Creating a Payroll Item for Tips In

For the compensation item (Tips In), use the following guidelines as you step through the wizard windows:

- The payroll item type is Addition.
- The payroll item name is Tips In.

- The expense account is the Other Current Asset account you created as described earlier in this section.
- The tax tracking type is Reported Tips.
- The taxes are the default taxes (all federal, state, and local taxes).
- The calculation basis selection is Neither (because it's not compensation based on quantity or hours).
- There is no default rate nor is there a limit.

Creating a Payroll Item for Tips Out

For the deduction that covers the tips employees already received, use the following guidelines to move through the wizard:

- The payroll item type is Deduction.
- The payroll item name is Tips Out.
- There is no agency (and therefore, no identification number with an agency).
- The liability account is the Other Current Asset account you created as described earlier in this section.
- The tax tracking type is None.
- No taxes are applied (all the taxes should be deselected in the wizard window).
- The calculation basis selection is Neither (because it's not a deduction based on quantity or hours).
- The item is calculated on net pay.
- There is no default rate nor is there a limit.

Adding Tips to Paychecks

Add the tips to employee paychecks in the Preview Paycheck window in the Other Payroll Items section (see Figure 5-5). When you enter the Tips In item, the totals in the Employee Summary section change (higher gross and higher taxes). When you enter the Tips Out item, the amounts are adjusted.

Tips and IRA Plans

If you provide a simple IRA that involves contributions from both the employer and employee, the order in which you add the payroll items to checks is important. Tips are compensation, and the amount entered for Tips In affects the IRA contribution calculation.

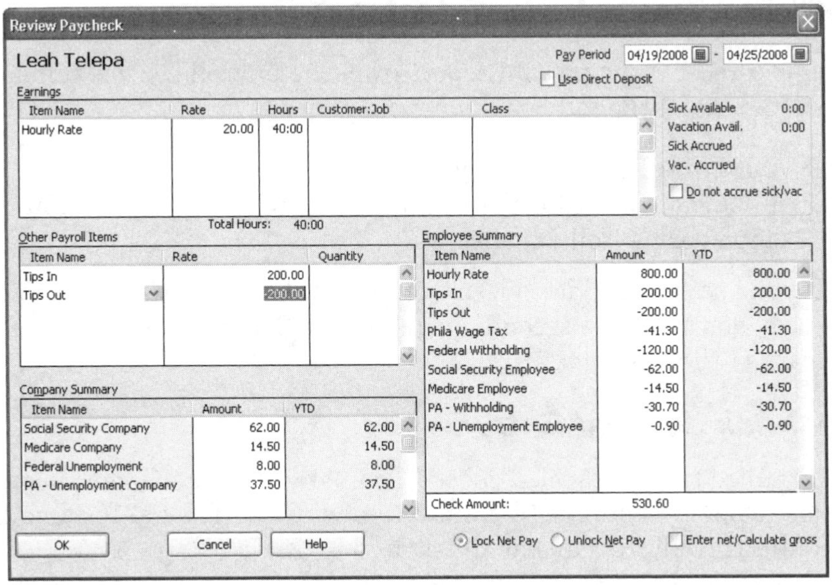

Figure 5-5: QuickBooks automatically adjusts the paycheck figures to manage tips.

QuickBooks calculates the totals "in order", which means you must enter the tips and the IRA payroll items in the following order:

- Tips In
- Tips Out
- IRA employee deduction
- IRA company contribution

If your IRA items are listed before the Tips In items the IRA calculations don't use the amount for tips.

Tracking Outsourced Payroll

If you don't do your payroll in-house, you have to track your payroll amounts using journal entries. If you maintain a separate bank account for payroll (recommended if you outsource payroll) you have to set up special tasks to reconcile the account. I cover both issues in this section.

Entering Payroll as a Journal Entry

When you receive the payroll report from the payroll service company, you should make the following journal entries:

- A Journal Entry for the payroll
- A Journal Entry for the remittance of withholding amounts and employer payroll expenses.

If your payroll service doesn't remit withholding and pay employer expenses, don't use the second journal entry. The checks you write will take care of the postings.

Paycheck Journal Entry

To journalize the paychecks, choose Company → Make General Journal Entries to open a blank GJE transaction window. Then enter amounts in the columns (Debit/Credit) as illustrated in Table 5-1.

Account	Debit	Credit
Salaries & Wages	Total Gross Payroll	
FWT		Total Federal Withheld
FICA		Total FICA Withheld
Medicare		Total Medicare Withheld
State Income Tax		Total State Tax Withheld
Local Income Tax		Total Local Tax Withheld
State SDI		Total State SDI Withheld
State SUI		Total State SUI Withheld
Benefits Contrib		Total Benefits Contributions Withheld
401(k) Contrib		Total 401(k) Withheld
Other Deductions		Total Other Ded Withheld
Payroll Bank Account		Total Of Net Payroll

Table 5-1: Sample journal entry for outsourced payroll.

Payroll Liability Payments Journal Entry

If you remit your own payments, the liability payments are posted automatically when you create those transactions (washing the liabilities you entered in the JE).

If your payroll service remits your payments, enter the payments in a separate JE as illustrated in Table 5-2.

Account	Debit	Credit
FWT	Total Federal W/H Remitted	
FICA	Total FICA Remitted	
Medicare	Total Medicare Remitted	
State Income Tax	Total State Tax Remitted	
Local Income Tax	Total Local Tax Remitted	
State SDI	Total State SDI Remitted	
State SUI	Total State SUI Remitted	
Benefits Contrib	Total Benefits Contributions Remitted	
401(k) Contrib	Total 401(k) Remitted	
Federal Unemployment (FUTA)	Total FUTA Remitted	
Other Payments	Total Other Deductions/Payments Remitted	
Payroll Account		Total Payments Made

Table 5-2: Sample journal entry for payroll liability payments.

Reconciling the Payroll Account When You Use a Payroll Service

The best way to track payroll when you use a payroll service is with a journal entry. However, the problem with journal entries for payroll is that when the bank statement comes for the payroll account, reconciling it is a bit difficult. When you open the payroll account in the Reconcile window you see the journal entry totals instead of the individual checks.

Most people find that the payroll checks are cashed quickly and clear rapidly, which always makes reconciliation easier. Payments to government agencies may not clear quite as fast.

Reconciling the Payroll Account Outside of QuickBooks

The report from the payroll service lists each check number and Payee, so you can set up a system to reconcile the account in a spreadsheet or a table in a word processing program.

Technically, you only need two columns: Check Number and Cleared. However, some users prefer to duplicate a real reconciliation window by adding columns for Date, Check Number, Payee, Amount, and Cleared.

Reconciling in QuickBooks with Fake Checks

You can't enter the paychecks in the normal fashion in your payroll account, because the JE you created already posted the amounts to that account. To create transactions that you can use when the statement arrives, you must enter the checks so they "wash", which means you post them back to the payroll account. This requires some setup, but after that one-time task you can enter each paycheck every payday.

It's easier to do this without tracking the individual payee names; instead, track the check numbers and amounts, because the statement only references that data. If a check doesn't clear, use the report from the payroll service to track the payee name against the check number. However, if you wish, you can enter the paychecks with both the check number and payee name in addition to the amount.

Create a generic employee in the Other Name list, naming it Payroll or Employee. If you want to track payee names, you have to create each employee as an Other Name list entry, using a slightly different version of the real employee name (because you can't have duplicate names in your company file). For example, you can insert a fake middle initial, such as X, in each name to create the listing in the Other Name List.

Enter the paychecks by opening the account register for the payroll account, and taking the following actions:

1. On the next available transaction line, enter the payroll check date.
2. Tab to the Number field and enter the first check number on the payroll service report.
3. Enter the generic payee you created (unless you've entered all your employee names as Other Name types, in which case enter the appropriate name).
4. Enter the amount of the net paycheck.
5. In the Account field, choose the Payroll account. QuickBooks displays a message warning you that you're posting the payment to

the source account. Click OK. (In fact, click the check box that tells QuickBooks to omit this warning in the future.)

6. Click the Record button to save this check, and then enter the next check.
7. Continue the process until all the checks are entered.

You can also enter the checks the payroll service wrote to transmit your withholdings and employer payments. As long as the postings were entered into the journal entry you can post everything back to the payroll account. You're "washing" every transaction, not changing the balance of the account. Then, when you want to reconcile the payroll account, the individual checks are there. The fact is, this procedure is quite easy and fast and you only have to do it on payday (or once a month if you want to wait until the bank statement arrives).

Net To Gross Paycheck Calculation

Available only in the QuickBooks Enhanced Payroll services, the net to gross feature is handy for special paychecks in which you want to make sure the employee receives a certain amount in the net check.

This scenario occurs when you want to give an employee taxable pay above and beyond the regular salary or wages—the most common reason is a bonus check. If you're tracking bonuses, be sure to create a payroll item for bonuses. You can also give a bonus amount as part of a Salary payroll item.

TIP: *If you don't subscribe to one of the QuickBooks Enhanced Payroll Service offerings, you can find net-to-gross calculators on the Internet. Enter the words **net to gross payroll** in your favorite search engine.*

Use the following steps to create a net to gross paycheck:

1. In the Enter Payroll Information window, make sure there's a check mark next to the employee's name, and then click the name to open the Review or Change Paycheck window.

2. In the Earnings section of the window, select a Bonus or Salary payroll item from the drop-down list in the Item Name column. Don't enter anything in the Rate column.
3. Click the option labeled Enter net/Calculate gross at the bottom of the window.
4. The Check Amount field displays the current amount of the net check (which is either 0.00, or a negative figure if the employee has an automatic deduction).
5. Replace the current amount of the check with the net amount you want this employee to receive.
6. Press the Tab key to automatically calculate the gross amount, the taxes, and any automatic deductions that result in the net amount you specified.
7. Click OK and then continue to follow the procedures for creating paychecks.

Chapter 6

Premier-Only Accounting Functions

Advanced functions for journal entries

Additional bank reconciliation features

The QuickBooks Premier editions include features that add efficiency, power, and added value to your accounting tasks. These features, which are unique to the Premier editions, are the subject of this chapter.

Some of the Premier accounting tools are only available in certain Premier editions, and I'll note those restrictions when I discuss those features.

Journal Entries

Journal entries provide a quick and efficient way to create transactions directly into the general ledger (such as depreciation entries), and to fine tune existing account balances (for job costing, class assignments, or allocation across classes). The Premier editions offer some nifty features that add convenience and power when you're creating journal entries.

If you're tracking classes, you can use a journal entry to post existing transactions to a class. All you have to do is journalize the original transaction (in and out of the original accounts), and add the class information. This is a great way to allocate overhead expenses to the divisions, departments, or programs (in nonprofit organizations) for which you established classes.

Similarly, journal entries provide a way to add job costs to existing account totals; merely create a GJE that applies customers or jobs against existing postings.

Entering a single JE transaction to include class or job information to multiple previous postings is faster than editing each original transaction to add the class or job.

However, I frequently hear from business owners and accountants about JEs created for job costing that don't seem to work. The job costing reports don't reflect the information that was entered in the JE.

Fine-tuning your account balances with JEs can be a trip down a rabbit hole if you don't understand the way QuickBooks stores information contained in JEs (see the section " JE Source and Target: Solving the Mystery ").

***NOTE**: I use the term journal entry, and abbreviate it JE, out of habit. QuickBooks call this transaction type a General Journal Entry, and uses the abbreviation GJE.*

Adding a JE Icon to the Toolbar

If you use journal entries frequently, add an icon to the toolbar, using the following steps:

1. Choose Company → Make General Journal Entries to open a blank GJE window.
2. On the QuickBooks menu bar choose View → Add "Make General Journal Entries" to the toolbar.
3. In the Add Window To Icon Bar dialog (see Figure 6-1), you can change the default Label or Description text, and also change the default graphic for the icon.
4. Click OK to place the icon on your toolbar.

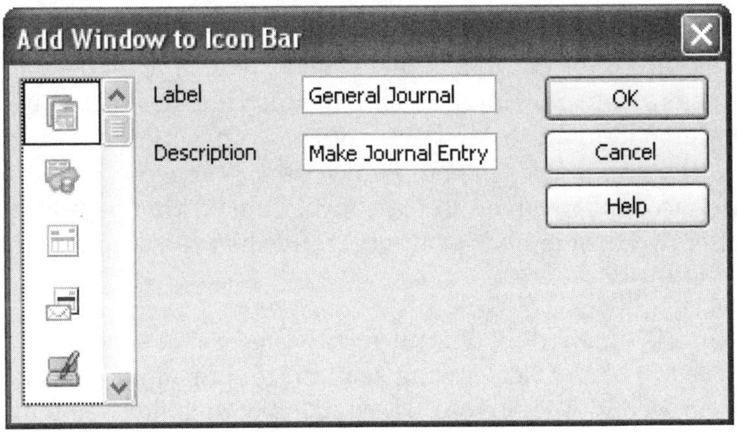

Figure 6-1: Create a toolbar icon for journal entries.

The text in the Label field represents the text that displays under the icon on the toolbar. The text in the Description field is the text you see when you hover your mouse over the icon (also called a *tooltip*).

AutoFill Memos in Journal Entries

In QuickBooks Pro, the text you enter in the memo field of any line in a journal entry stays with that entry line. This means you see your comments when you open the register for the account that entry line posted to.

For example, if you are entering a journal entry for a correction your accountant told you to make, you could enter the comment "Bob's Memo-9/4/07" (assuming your accountant's name is Bob).

Most people enter memo text only in the first line of the journal entry. Later, if they view the register of the account (or multiple accounts) to which the ensuing line(s) of the JE posted, there's no text in the memo field. You don't see any explanation for the transaction unless you open the original transaction. To avoid that problem, some users enter (or copy and paste) the text in the memo field manually, on each line of the General Journal Entry. That's extra work!

QuickBooks Premier editions offer a clever feature called AutoFill Memos in Journal Entries. This means that the text you enter in the Memo field on the first line of the transaction is automatically entered on all lines of the transaction. When you view the register of any account involved in the journal entry, the memo text is available to help you remember or understand the reason for the transaction.

This feature is enabled by default in the Preferences dialog, in the My Preferences tab of the Accounting section. If your memo text isn't repeated on the second line of your JE, somebody disabled the feature. Choose Edit → Preferences, select the Accounting section of the Preferences dialog, and enable it.

***TIP FOR ACCOUNTANTS**: For your clients who aren't using one of the QuickBooks Premier Editions, you might want to pass along the suggestion to Copy and Paste memo text to every line of a JE. This means you'll know the reason for the JE when you see it in an account register. Without the memo, you have to open the original transaction to see the memo that appeared only on the first line.*

Auto Reversing Journal Entries

Automatic reversing journal entries are only available in the QuickBooks Premier Accountant Edition. To create an auto reversing journal entry, open the Make General Journal Entries window by choosing Company → Make General Journal Entries.

The Help files in QuickBooks Premier Editions tell you to create a journal entry, save it, then redisplay it and click the Reverse icon on the GJE window. (To redisplay an entry, open the GJE window if it isn't already open, and click Previous to locate the entry you want to auto-reverse).

However, I'm pathologically lazy, and I find it's much quicker and easier to do everything at once, which is accomplished using the following steps:

1. Enter the data for the journal entry.
2. Click the Reverse icon (instead of clicking Save & Close, or Save & New).
3. QuickBooks displays the Recording Transaction dialog to tell you that you haven't recorded your entry, and offers to save it. Click Yes to record the entry.
4. The GJE window displays the reversing entry (don't worry, the original entry was saved, click Previous to see it if you don't believe me).
5. Click Save & Close if you're finished with the GJE window; click Save & New to enter another journal entry.

The Reversing Entry is automatically dated the first day of the following month, but you can change the date. If you're using automatic numbering for GJE transactions, the reversing entry number has the format *xxx*R, where *xxx* is the number of the original journal entry.

Adjusting Journal Entries

This feature, available only in QuickBooks Premier Accountant Edition, lets you specify a journal entry as "adjusting". The GJE window includes a check box labeled Adjusting Entry, which is enabled by default.

The way QuickBooks reports on adjusting entries, compared to journal entries that aren't designated "adjusting", is inconsistent. After you create an adjusting entry, when you view the registers of the affected accounts, the transaction type is GENJRNL. That's the same transaction type that QuickBooks records for a journal entry that's not configured as an adjusting entry.

However, you can view a report of adjusting entries by choosing Reports → Accountant & Taxes → Adjusting Journal Entries. This report, like the feature, is only available in Premier Accountant Edition.

If you upgraded to QuickBooks Premier Accountant Edition from a previous version of QuickBooks or from any edition of QuickBooks Pro, all the existing journal entries in your company file are marked as adjusting entries. In addition, if you perform a file cleanup (File → Utilities → Clean Up Company Data) QuickBooks condenses closed transactions by creating JEs, and marks all of those JEs as adjusting entries.

Discussing adjusting entries always makes me want to ask, "What's the difference between an adjusting entry and any other type of journal entry; aren't all JEs adjustments?" So, I literally asked the question of my own accounting firm, and the answer I received indicates that the difference is subtle, but apparently understood by all accountants. One of the accountants replied, "It's really a distinction without a difference; an adjusting journal entry is posted to correct or update an account in the general ledger." Another accountant told me, "Often when referring to an adjusting entry, the term is used in the sense of preparing a financial statement and not as a permanent entry". (Thanks, Craig and Steve.)

History and Reports in the JGE Window

In the Premier Accountant edition, the Make General Journal Entries transaction window displays existing (prior) JE transactions. Each time you open the GJE window, you can quickly check the existing journal entries. This means you won't re-enter a journal entry you already made, which is an occasional problem during end-of-period activities.

By default, the list includes all the journal entries created in the last month, but you can change the time period. Click the arrow to the right of the List Of Selected General Journal Entries text box to select a different time interval for displaying journal entries (see Figure 6-2). All journal entries that match the date range are displayed.

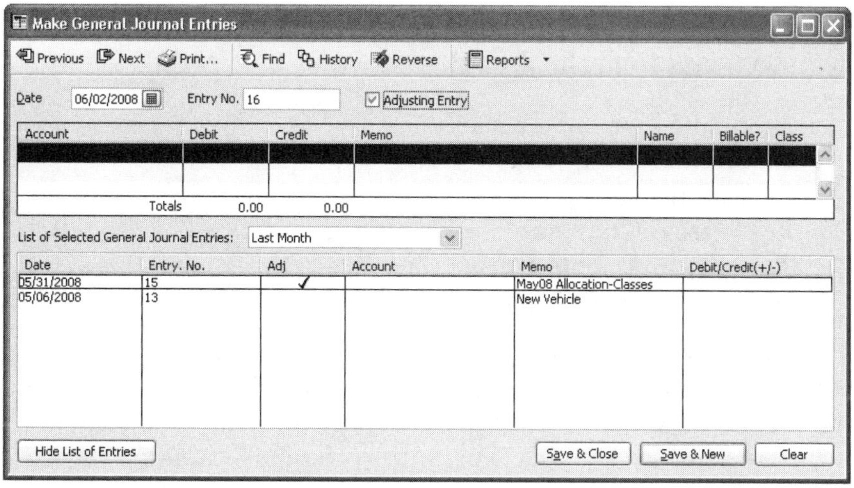

Figure 6-2: Previous JEs appear in the JE window in the Premier Accountant Edition.

When the previous entries are displayed, the number of lines that appear in the GJE transaction window is reduced. If you have a long journal entry to record, click the Hide List Of Entries button to reveal a full GJE transaction window. The button label changes to Show List Of Entries, so you can bring back the list with a click of the mouse.

When you close the GJE window, QuickBooks remembers its state (whether the list of previous journal entries is displayed, and if so, which time interval is selected), and the next time you open the window you see that same state.

Viewing and Editing Existing Journal Entries

The journal entries in the history list display the first line of the JE. To see the contents, click the appropriate item in the history list. The contents of that JE are loaded into the GJE transaction window, and the transaction becomes the current transaction. You can edit the JE, making changes to any part of the transaction, and selecting/deselecting the Adjusting Entry designation.

Quick Reports from the GJE Window

The GJE window also has a Reports button at the top of the transaction window. Click the arrow to the right of the button and select one of the following reports from the drop-down menu:

- Adjusting Journal Entries
- Entries Entered Today
- Last Month
- Last Fiscal Quarter
- This Fiscal Year to Date
- All Entries

When you open one of these reports, the report is collapsed, which means a total is displayed for each account used in each JE. Click the button labeled Expand to display each posting to any account that has multiple postings in the JE. (The button changes its name to Collapse).

JE Source and Target: Solving the Mystery

One common use of a JE is to allocate an expense across jobs to track job costs. It's easy, you debit the same expense account multiple times in order to select a customer or job for each applicable portion of the expense, and credit the original expense total so the general ledger totals aren't changed. You can do the same type of JE to allocate costs (usually overhead) across classes. Table 6-1 is a representation of a JE designed to track job costs.

Account	Debit	Credit	Memo	Name
Shipping	100.00		Jan 2 2008	Cust:Job #1
Shipping	50.00		Jan 9 2008	Cust:Job #2
Shipping	50.00		Jan 12 2008	Cust:Job #3
Shipping		200.00		

Table 6-1: Allocate expenses to track the cost of jobs.

After performing this task, it's a common complaint that the job costing reports don't show the expenses that were allocated in the journal entry. If you run an Unbilled Costs By Job report, some or all of the data in your JEs doesn't appear. If you marked the amount as billable in the JE, the billable costs show up when you invoice the customer, they just don't show up in reports.

Often, when you create a JE that moves expenses from one customer to another, the wrong customer receives the cost posting.

What's going on? The answer is that all transactions in QuickBooks have a source and a target, and if you don't get them right, you end up with unexpected results.

The source is the account where the transaction originates, and the target is the account where it is completed. When you write a check to a vendor, the bank account is the source (it's where the money starts) and the expense account is the target (it's where the money ends up).

If you attach additional information to the check, it travels with its source or target counterpart. For example, assigning a customer to the line that contains an expense account (for job costing) links the customer information and the amount to the target (because a line item, in which this data exists, is part of the target).

For JEs that perform job costing allocations there are two important facts to remember:

- QuickBooks assigns job costing or other information when it's part of the target, and ignores it when it is part of the source.
- The first line of a JE is the source and all other lines are targets.

This means that if you're moving job costing information from one customer to another or from one job to another for the same customer, you will almost certainly end up with one or more incorrect postings.

Creating JEs With No Source Accounts

I've learned that to play it safe, the best way to create a JE is to make every line in the transaction part of the target. Remembering that only the first line is the source, the solution is to avoid using the first line for anything "real".

In the first line of a JE, enter only a memo. Starting with the second line, enter real information. Because everything is a target, everything posts appropriately, and you can create reports that show your activities.

After I learned to do this, I never had a problem with job costing reports. In fact, I've used this method successfully to make adjustments to Form 1099 totals, which is not an easy task without this trick.

***NOTE**: Appendix C has troubleshooting tips for Form 1099 as well as workarounds for other source/target problems, including ways to customize reports to solve those problems*

If you've already encountered the source/target problem, you don't have to void and re-enter all the journal entries that had a source/target mix up. Just edit the journal entry to change the source line, as follows:

1. Open the JE transaction and click anywhere in the first line to select that line.
2. Press Ctrl-Ins (or Ctrl-Insert, depending on the label your keyboard uses) to insert a blank line above the current first line.
3. Enter text in the Memo field to create a source line.
4. Close the Make General Journal Entries transaction window.
5. QuickBooks displays a message that you've changed the transaction and asks if you want to save it.

6. Click Yes.

Everything posts correctly.... but you may have another problem. When you insert a line in a previous JE, QuickBooks loses track of the automatic numbering feature for JEs. In fact, the JE number may disappear from the JE window. Before you close the window, re-enter the JE number to kick-start automatic numbering again.

Allocating Overhead Expenses to Jobs

Real job costing includes the allocation of overhead and other expenses not specifically incurred for a job. These allocations are made in addition to the job costing entries you make during transaction data entry (when you enter an expense and then charge all or part of it to a job).

When you charge expenses to a job, if you select the option to bill the customer/job, the expense is available when you invoice the customer/job. If you deselect the option to bill for reimbursement, the amount you linked to the customer/job is saved and you can create reports that display your costs for each customer/job.

If you use timesheets to track employee and subcontractor time, you can either invoice customers for that time, or merely link that expense to jobs for the purpose of job costing. If you track mileage, you can accomplish the same thing for the cost of travel.

However, it's often the case that additional expenses contribute to the cost of a job, and you can use JEs to allocate those expenses to jobs. This is the only way to see the real cost of a job, and that information makes it easier to bid properly on future jobs. Some of the overhead expenses commonly used in job cost allocation include:

- Staff payroll, including employer tax and benefit expenses.
- Office supplies, including consumables such as paper, printer cartridges and toner.
- Telephone bills. (Long distance charges should be specifically applied to the job when you pay the telephone bill.)
- Vehicle expenses, if you're not using the QuickBooks mileage tracking feature.

You need to spend some time thinking about the staff, consumables, and other expenses that were connected to a particular job in order to come up with a figure. For short-term jobs, most businesses allocate overhead after the job is complete. For long-term jobs, you can allocate monthly to keep an eye on the totals. A job allocation JE is quite simple:

- Credit the original expense for the amount you're allocating to a job (or multiple jobs).
- Debit the original expense for the same amount, and select the appropriate job(s), deselecting the option to bill the customer.

Allocating Overhead Expenses to Classes

If you're already tracking divisions or departments of your business with classes, you can post overhead expenses to classes with a journal entry.

This works best if you create a generic class for overhead, or general expenses, and then move expense totals out of that class into your departmental classes. Common names for the generic class include Other, Administration, General and other generic terms that represent general office expenses.

During transaction data entry (entering bills or writing checks) always post expenses to a class, either the class specifically tied to the expense, or your generic glass. Then you can journalize the appropriate portions of overhead and general expenses. To do so:

- Credit the original expense for the amount you're allocating to classes, and link that line in the JE to the generic class.
- Debit the same expense the appropriate amount for each class, linking each line in the JE to the appropriate class.

Auto-calculating by Percentage

QuickBooks has a nifty function you can use to automate some allocations that would require the use of a calculator. For example, if you're splitting an expense unevenly—perhaps 55% to one class and 45% to another class, you can do the math right in the JE, as follows:

1. Enter the Memo text in the first line.

2. Enter the credit to the expense you're allocating (the next line automatically displays an equal amount in the Debit column).
3. Tab to the Debit column in the next row and enter an asterisk (*) to open the QuickBooks calculator.
4. Enter the percentage in decimal form, as seen in Figure 6-3.
5. Press Tab to have QuickBooks perform the calculation against the number that was originally in the column. The new amount appears in the Debit column.
6. The next line contains the correct amount for the debit to the next row.

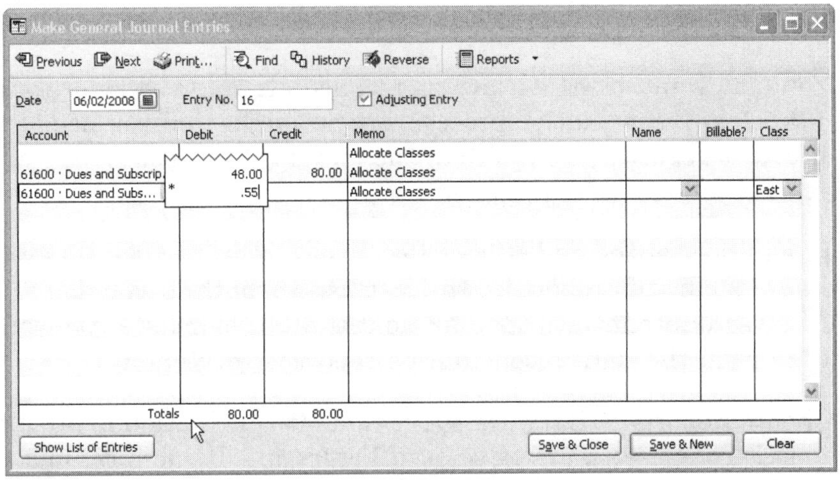

Figure 6-3: Let QuickBooks do the math.

You can also use this function to split an allocation evenly across three classes:

1. In the Debit column of the JE line for the first class, enter *.33.
2. In the Debit column of the next JE row, enter *.50 (half of the amount that appeared after you calculated the previous row).
3. The last JE row is automatically calculated correctly.

For more than three classes, this gets a bit complicated, and you'll probably need a calculator to figure out the formula.

Previous Bank Reconciliation Reports

The Premier editions automatically save bank reconciliation reports, even if you don't print or display the reports when you finish reconciling your bank account.

Without this feature, the only way to see previous bank reconciliation reports is to remember to print a report every time you reconcile a bank account. When you need a previous report, go to your filing cabinet. That's what users of QuickBooks Pro have to do, because they only have access to the last reconciliation report. Luckily for you, QuickBooks Premier editions store multiple reconciliation reports.

You may want to see a previous reconciliation report before you begin the next reconciliation process, or you might find you need to look at a previous report when you're in the middle of reconciling the current month, and you run into a problem.

In addition, at the end of your fiscal year, most accountants want to see the reconciliation report for the last fiscal month. If you don't meet with your accountant until several months after your fiscal year end, the ability to print the right reconciliation report is very handy.

Choose Reports → Banking → Previous Reconciliation to open the Previous Reconciliation dialog seen in Figure 6-4. If you have more than one bank account, select the appropriate account from the drop-down list in the Account field. Then select the report you want to see by choosing its statement ending date.

Choosing the Type of Reconciliation Report

You have a variety of choices for the type and format of the reconciliation report for the statement period you select. The Type Of Report section at the top of the dialog has three options: Summary, Detail, and Both.

- Select Summary to see the totals for transactions that were cleared and not cleared at the time of the reconciliation. The report also lists the totals for new transactions (transactions entered after the reconciliation). Totals are by type, so there is one total for inflow (deposits), and another total for outflow (payments).

- Select Detail to see each transaction that was cleared or not cleared in a previous reconciliation, and also see each new transaction since that reconciliation.
- Select Both to open both reports (not one report with both sets of listings).

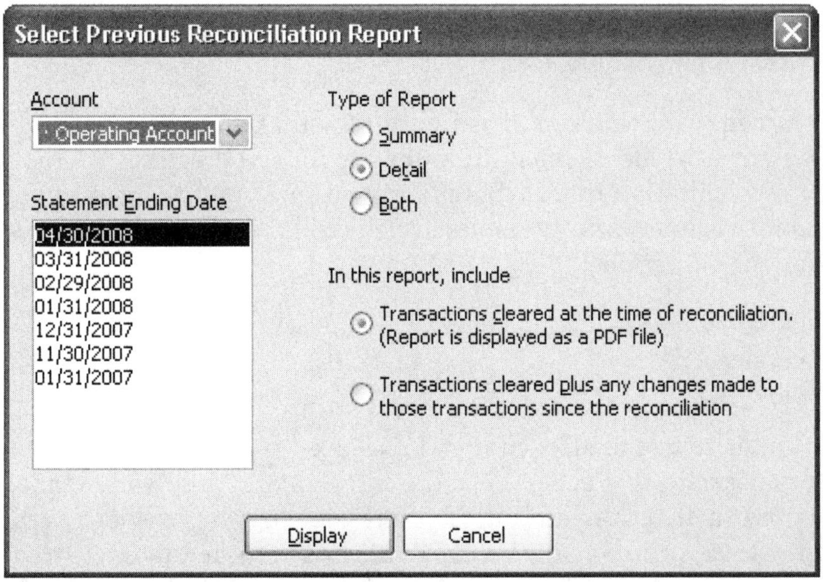

Figure 6-4: Previous reconciliation reports are available in Premier editions.

After you select the type of report, select the type of content you want in the report.

Selecting the option Transactions Cleared At The Time Of Reconciliation (Report Is Displayed As A PDF File), results in a Portable Document Format (PDF) file.

To view a PDF file, you must have Adobe Acrobat Reader installed on your computer. If you don't, when you select this report QuickBooks opens a dialog with a link to the Adobe website, where you can download Acrobat Reader (it's free).

PDF files are graphical and let you view and print information. You cannot drill down to see details, because this report is not directly linked to your QuickBooks data. However, the report gives you an accurate report of the last reconciliation. (If you printed a reconciliation report the last time you reconciled the account, the PDF file matches your printout.)

Selecting the option Transactions Cleared Plus Any Changes Made To Those Transactions Since The Reconciliation opens a standard QuickBooks report window.

Unfortunately, this report is neither useful nor accurate if you need to see a report on the reconciliation for the date you selected. This is not really a reconciliation report. It's merely a report on the current state of the account register, and it displays the account's transactions sorted by the following categories:

- Cleared
- Uncleared
- New

If you, or someone else, changed a cleared transaction, the new information appears in this report, not the information that was extant at the time you reconciled the account. If you're viewing the previous reconciliation to try to determine whether any changes were made to cleared transactions, this report fools you—it's dangerous to rely on its contents.

If you need to see an accurate, trustworthy, previous reconciliation report in order to track down discrepancies, either use the PDF file or make sure you print and file a detailed reconciliation report every month when you reconcile your bank account.

Resolving Reconciliation Problems

Often, the reason you open a previous reconciliation report is to investigate problems in the current reconciliation. Usually, this means the Begin Reconciliation dialog displays a beginning balance that differs from the opening balance shown on your bank statement.

Click the Locate Discrepancies button on the Begin Reconciliation dialog to open the Locate Discrepancies dialog (see Figure 6-5). You have access to your previous reconciliation reports in this dialog, as well as a discrepancy report that may help you locate the reason for the difference between the beginning balances.

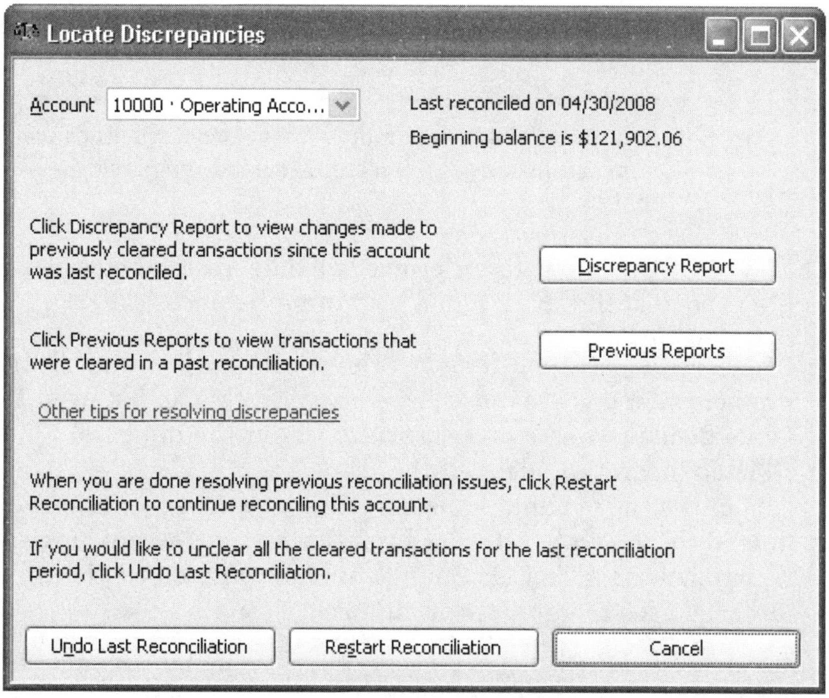

Figure 6-5: Use the tools in the Locate Discrepancies dialog to troubleshoot reconciliation problems.

If the previous reconciliation reports don't provide the answer to your problem, choose Discrepancy Report. As you can see in Figure 6-6, this report displays information about transactions that were changed after they were cleared during reconciliation.

The reconciled amount is the amount of the transaction as it was when you cleared it during reconciliation. If that amount is a positive number, the transaction was a deposit; a negative number indicates a disbursement (usually a check).

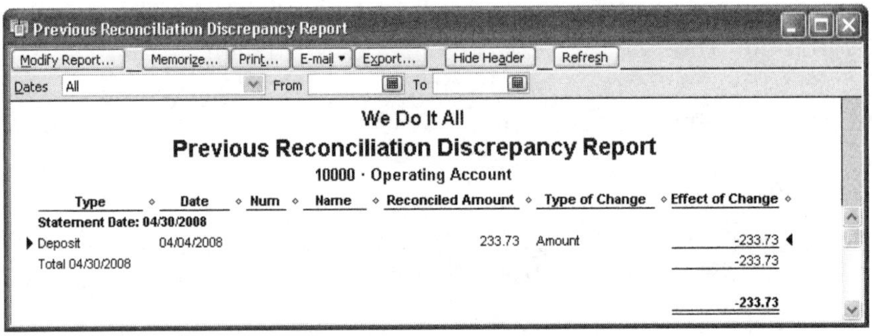

Figure 6-6: This report should be empty—if it displays any transactions, somebody manipulated a cleared transaction—that's a no no.

The Type Of Change column provides a clue about the action you must take to correct the unmatched beginning balances:

- Uncleared means you removed the check mark in the Cleared column of the register (and you persisted in this action even though QuickBooks issued a stern warning about the dangers).
- Deleted means you deleted the transaction.
- Amount is the original amount, which means you changed the amount of the transaction. Check the Reconciled amount and the amount in the Effect Of Change amount, and do the math; the difference is the amount of the change.

Unfortunately, QuickBooks doesn't offer a Type Of Change named "Void," so a voided transaction is merely marked as changed. A transaction with a changed amount equal and opposite of the original amount is usually a check that was voided after it was cleared.

To resolve the problem, open the bank account register and restore the affected transaction to its original state. This is safe because you can't justify changing a transaction after it was cleared — a transaction that cleared was not supposed to be changed, voided, deleted, or uncleared; once cleared, it must remain what it was forever.

If you don't see the problem immediately, trying comparing previous reconciliation reports to the account register. Any transaction that is listed in a reconciliation report should also be in the register, with the same amount.

- If a transaction is there, but marked VOID, re-enter it, using the data in the reconciliation report. That transaction wasn't void when you performed the last reconciliation, it had cleared. Therefore, it can't possibly meet any of the criteria for voiding a transaction.
- If a transaction appears in the reconciliation report, but is not in the register, it was deleted. Re-enter it, using the data in the reconciliation report.
- Check the amounts on the printed check reconciliation report against the data in the register to see if any amount was changed after the account was reconciled. If so, restore the original amount.

WARNING: *If you merge bank accounts, you lose the previous reconciliation reports for both accounts involved in the merge procedure.*

Chapter 7

Enhanced Sales Features

Easy invoicing for time and expenses

Sales orders

Backorders

Creating transactions automatically

Inventory assemblies

Units of measure

The QuickBooks Premier editions have features that enhance the functions available to you for sales transactions. These features aren't available in QuickBooks Pro, and in this chapter, I'll discuss the additional power you get in your Premier edition.

Easy Invoicing for Time and Expenses

In the Premier editions you can create customer invoices for time and reimbursable expenses from a single list (called Invoice for Time & Expenses) that displays all the charges waiting to be invoiced to customers. This means you can invoice customers for time and expenses in two ways:

- You can use the list of time and expenses to create invoices for these charges quickly.
- You can use the standard QuickBooks Add Time/Costs feature to invoice customers for these charges when you're creating a regular invoice for items and services.

***TIP**: You can also add "regular" charges for products and services to any invoice you create from the list of time and expenses.*

The advantage of the Time & Expenses list is that when you're creating invoices, the list eliminates the need to click the button labeled Add Time/Costs to see if there are any reimbursable costs linked to the customer.

Enabling the List of Time & Expenses

You have to enable this feature in the Time & Expenses category of the Preferences dialog. Select the Company Preferences tab (see Figure 7-1) and select the option labeled Create Invoices From a List of Time and Expenses.

Note that this feature is independent of the other options on this dialog. Even if you don't track time, or don't treat reimbursed expenses as income (instead, you post reimbursed expenses back to the expense account that received the original posting), you can enable this feature.

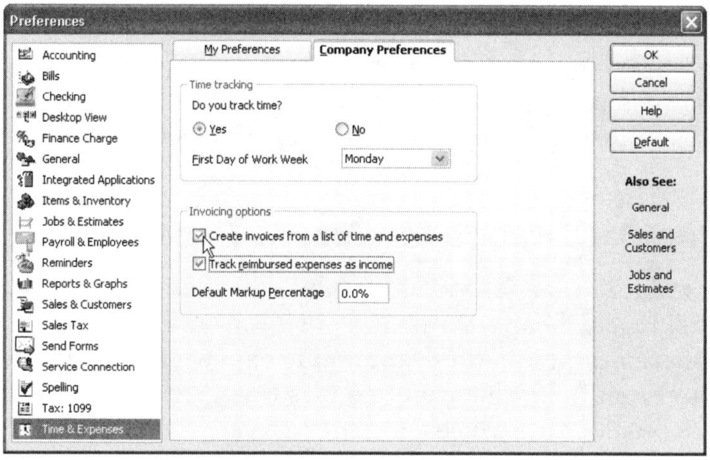

Figure 7-1: Enable this easy-to-use list for invoicing expenses to customers.

Opening the List of Time & Expenses

When this preference is enabled, QuickBooks adds the command "Invoice for Time & Expenses" to the Customers menu. Select that command to open the Invoice for Time & Expenses window seen in Figure 7-2.

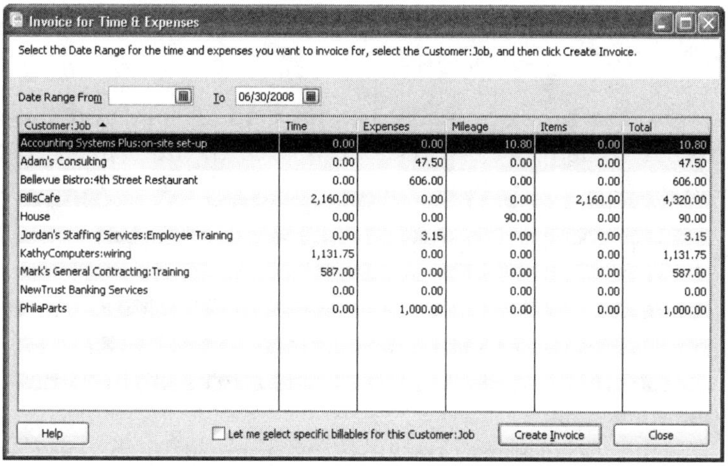

Figure 7-2: View the list of customers who have reimbursable charges waiting to be invoiced.

Changing the Columns in the Time & Expenses List

You can control the columns that appear in the window. Right-click anywhere in the listings part of the window to see the available columns (Time, Expenses, Mileage, Items) and select or deselect the columns you want to view.

Choosing the Date Range for Time & Expenses

You can select a date range for viewing unbilled expenses by filling in the From and To fields, but I can't think of a good reason to enter data in the From field. If there are unbilled reimbursable expenses before the date you enter in the From field, the system omits them. In the To field, enter the date you'll be using for invoices.

How the Time & Expenses List Calculates Amounts

The Time & Expenses List is a convenience; a way to view the list of customers for whom you assigned expenses that haven't yet been added to invoices for those customers. The amounts that appear in this list may not be the amounts you'll add to their invoices. In fact, the amounts you see on the list may confuse you.

For example, in Figure 7-2, the customer NewTrust Banking Services displays zero in every category. Obviously, some expense or other has been linked to this customer or else the customer wouldn't appear on the list. What's going on?

To understand the totals you see, you have to understand the process that builds the list. This process varies according to the type of reimbursable charge.

For Expenses and Items, the following process occurs:

1. Check transactions (usually Vendor bills or checks) to see if a customer or job is linked to the transaction.
2. If a customer or job is linked, check the status of the Billable field for the transaction.
3. If the Billable field is marked, use the amount in the calculation for this customer.

For Time charges, the following process occurs:

1. Check timesheets to see if a customer or job is entered on a timesheet charge.
2. If so, check the status of the Billable field for the charge.
3. If marked Billable, check the price of the Service item using the data in the item's record in the Item list.
4. Multiply the number of hours by the price that exists in the item's record and use the amount in the calculation for this customer.

For Mileage charges, the following process occurs:

1. Check transactions entered in the Enter Vehicle Mileage transaction form to see if a customer or job is entered on the form.
2. If so, check the status of the Billable field for the charge.
3. If marked Billable, check the price of the mileage item in the mileage item's record in the Item list.
4. Multiply the number of miles by the price that exists in the item's record and use the amount in the calculation for this customer.

The problem, or potential problem, occurs in time or mileage charges you've posted as billable to a customer. If the service item or mileage item doesn't have a price in its record, the price is considered to be zero. If the timesheet or the vehicle mileage transaction form records a quantity of X, the calculation is "X multiplied by 0", which is, of course, zero.

When you select the listing to create an invoice, you have the opportunity to enter the amount you want to use for the invoice.

***TIP**: The best way to set up items (to use this list efficiently and to make it easier to track job costing) is to configure items with both cost and price information. A price field is always available in an item record. Item dialogs for many item types include an option that says the item is used in assemblies, or is subcontracted, or purchased for a customer (the text differs depending on the type of item). Selecting that option adds fields to the dialog where you can enter costs.*

Creating Invoices from the Time & Expenses List

You have two methods for creating an invoice from the Time & Expenses list:

- Automatically create the invoice using the data displayed for the customer.
- Select the option labeled Let me select specific billables for this Customer:Job

The latter method lets you enter a different rate for expenses (necessary if the displayed expenses are zero), and also lets you choose specific expenses for the invoice you're preparing (leaving the remaining expenses for a later invoice).

Creating Invoices Automatically From the Time & Expenses List

To create an invoice automatically, select the appropriate Customer:Job listing and click Create Invoice. QuickBooks opens the Create Invoices transaction window with the customer or job, and the invoice data already entered (see Figure 7-3).

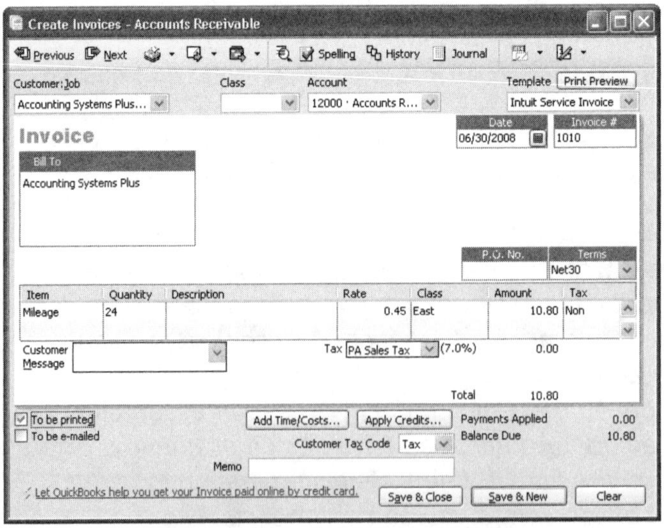

Figure 7-3: Preparing an invoice for reimbursable expenses is a one-click action.

You can add other items (services or products) to the invoice. Then click Save & Close to return to the Invoice for Time & Expenses list.

Modifying Billables From the Time & Expenses List

If you select the option labeled Let me select specific billables for this Customer:Job, selecting the listing and clicking Create Invoice opens a Create Invoices transaction window, and also opens the Choose Billable Time and Costs dialog (see Figure 7-4).

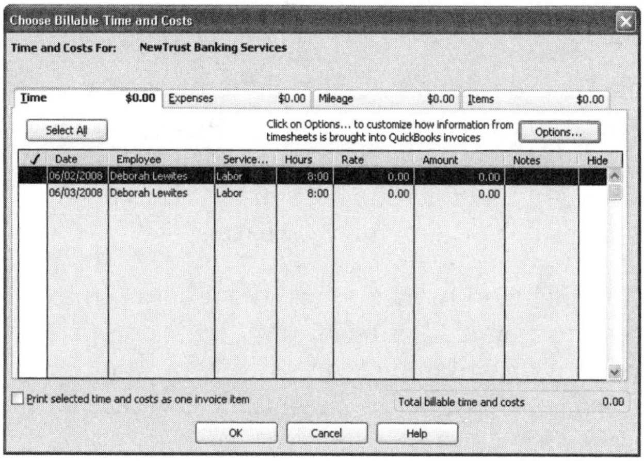

Figure 7-4: Select the reimbursable costs and/or enter the amounts you want to add to the invoice.

This is the same dialog you see when you're creating invoices and click the Add Time/Costs button on the transaction form. You can select the costs you want to include on the invoice, change the amounts of billable costs, and invoke the other options available in this dialog (enter separate lines for charges, combine charges, etc.).

In addition to the billable expenses, you can add services and products to the invoice before saving it.

Sales Orders

The QuickBooks Premier Editions include support for sales orders, and that makes life a lot easier for you if you sell products. Inherent in sales orders is the ability to track backorders – a sales order that has items waiting to be shipped and invoiced is, in effect, a backorder.

Without the additional features in QuickBooks Premier editions, you have to use complicated workarounds to track these functions. (For accountants who support clients who don't have Premier Edition, QuickBooks 2008: The Official Guide offers detailed instructions on creating and using workarounds to track backorders in QuickBooks Pro.

NOTE: Sales orders are really only useful for inventory items.

When you create sales orders, no financial accounts are affected. The transaction itself is posted to the Sales Order account in your chart of accounts, which is a non-posting account. You can open the account register (non-posting accounts are listed at the bottom of the chart of accounts) to view or manipulate the sales orders you've created.

The inventory items included in a sales order are marked to indicate the fact that they're reserved on a sales order, and the appropriate calculations are made to Quantity Available reports. However, no financial postings are made to income, COG, or the inventory asset accounts.

Enabling Sales Orders

To use sales orders, you must enable their use by choosing Edit → Preferences and selecting the Sales & Customers category. In the Company Preferences tab, make sure the option Enable Sales Orders is selected. You can also enable the following additional sales order options:

- Warn about duplicate sales order numbers. Sales orders have their own self-incrementing number system (unconnected to invoice numbering). It's a good idea to select this option to keep your sales order records accurate.
- Don't print items with zero amounts when converting to Invoice. Selecting this option removes any line item that has a zero amount in the Ordered column or in the Rate column from the printed version of the sales order (or the invoice created from the sales order). The onscreen copy of the sales order still shows all the lines.

Enabling Warnings about Inventory Stock Status

All editions of QuickBooks offer the option to warn you that the Quantity On Hand (QOH) is insufficient to ship the product you're selling, when you're creating an invoice.

In the Premier editions, you can enable warnings that are more precise. You can tell QuickBooks to examine additional data when determining whether you have sufficient inventory to turn a sales order into an invoice.

All of the options for enabling warnings about inventory stock status are in the Company Preferences tab of the Items & Inventory Preferences dialog (see Figure 7-5), which you reach by choosing Edit → Preferences.

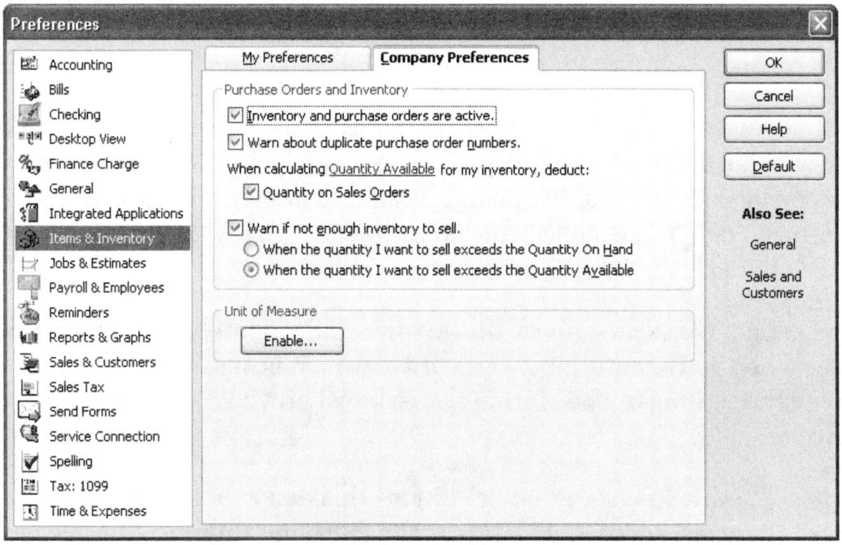

Figure 7-5: You can specify how QuickBooks reports stock status when you sell inventory items.

Quantity on Hand vs. Quantity Available

The options referring to calculating and reporting quantities while you're creating sales transactions are actually giving you a choice between tracking Quantity on Hand or Quantity Available.

- Quantity on Hand (QOH) is the number of units in the warehouse (or the garage, or wherever you store your inventory). It's a "shelf count".
- Quantity Available is a more precise figure; it's the number of those units on the shelves that are available for you to sell.

Notice the text on the dialog that reads, " When calculating quantity available for my inventory, deduct:" under which is the option labeled Quantity On Sales Orders.

If you select the option to be warned about the quantity available, QuickBooks deducts all the units of stock that are currently on sales orders that haven't yet been turned into invoices. The resulting number is the amount of stock available for you to enter in a sales order. (When sales orders are turned into invoices, the inventory comes off the shelves, which changes the QOH.)

If you don't select that option, QuickBooks doesn't deduct the number of units currently promised on sales orders, and therefore the quantity available isn't accurate.

If anyone else converts a sales order with the same product into an invoice before you do, and packs and ships the stock, you'll be surprised, because the 10 units of widgets you thought you could sell a customer are not available. That's because you didn't know about those sales orders that were entered before you created your sales order.

Don't get too excited about this feature-unfortunately the warning doesn't appear when you're entering a sales order (which is, of course, when you need to know these things). The warning appears when you convert the sales order to an invoice.

In some QuickBooks Premier editions this dialog has additional choices, because there are additional features. The following Premier editions have advanced features for tracking inventory stock status while creating sales transactions:

- Manufacturing & Wholesale Edition (see Chapter 12)
- Retail Edition (see Chapter 15)
- Accountant Edition (see Chapter 10)

These advanced features are discussed in the chapters specific to each of those editions. In all of those Premier editions, the insufficient stock level warning is displayed while you're creating the sales order.

Creating Sales Orders

After you enable sales orders in the Preferences dialog, a Sales Order icon appears on the Home page, and the Create Sales Orders command appears on the Customer menu. Use either access point to open a blank Create Sales Orders window, which looks very much like an invoice window (see Figure 7-6). Fill in the heading and line item sections, and save the sales order.

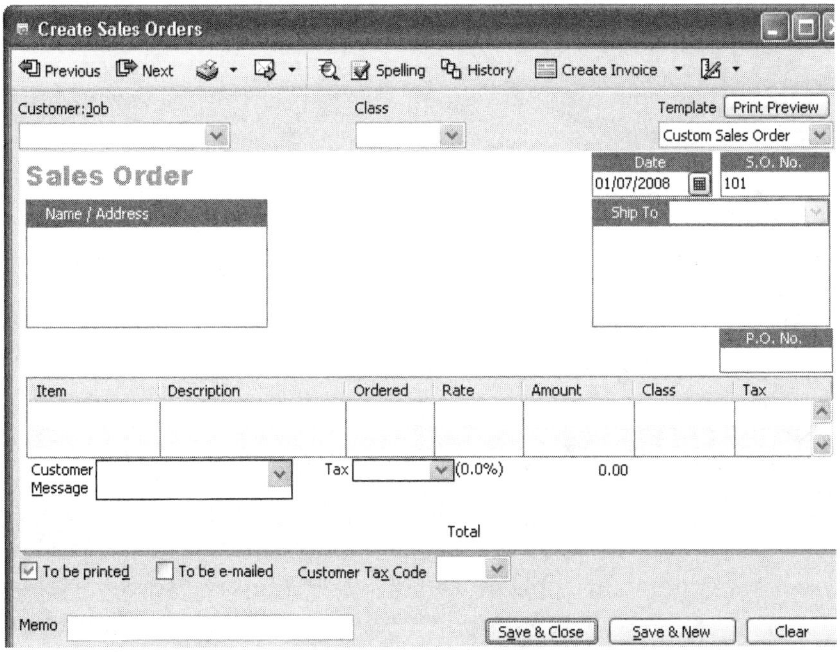

Figure 7-6: The Sales Order transaction form is similar to an invoice.

Sales Order Templates

The first time you open the sales order transaction window, the Custom Sales Order template is selected by default. QuickBooks provides several templates for sales orders, and you can select the template you prefer from the drop-down list in the Templates field.

Sales Order With Rep adds the Rep field to the Custom Sales Order template. The sales rep for the customer is automatically filled in, as long as you entered the sales rep in the customer's record. You can change the sales rep (frequently the person creating the sales order inserts his or her own name in that field), and when you save the sales order, QuickBooks displays a dialog that asks if you want to change the sales rep on the customer's record to match the new selection. Select Yes or No, depending on the circumstances and your policies about sales reps and commissions.

Work Order is the same as the Custom Sales Order, but the transaction title (above the customer's name box) is Work Order instead of Sales Order. Use this template when you're creating a custom-built product or an assembly.

Standard Work Order adds the following fields to the Work Order template: Terms, Rep, and Ship Date.

***NOTE**: QuickBooks also offers a Pick List and a Packing Slip in the Template drop-down list.*

Turning Sales Orders into Invoices

Businesses have a variety of standards and protocols upon which they base the decision to turn a sales order into an invoice. Some businesses require a sales person to obtain a manager's approval to verify the customer's credit status, or to approve a price change (usually a discount). Some businesses merely wait until the items on a sales order are picked and packed.

Regardless of the protocols you use, eventually you turn a sales order into an invoice, and you have two methods for accomplishing this task:

- Open a blank Create Invoices window, and load the sales order into the form.

- Open the original sales order, and convert it to an invoice with a click of the mouse.

Creating an Invoice by Loading a Sales Order

To create an invoice by loading an existing sales order into the Invoice, press Ctrl-I to open a blank Create Invoices window.

When you select the customer or job, QuickBooks opens the Available Sales Orders dialog seen in Figure 7-7, which lists all the current open sales orders. (If no sales orders exist for the selected customer or job, the dialog doesn't appear.)

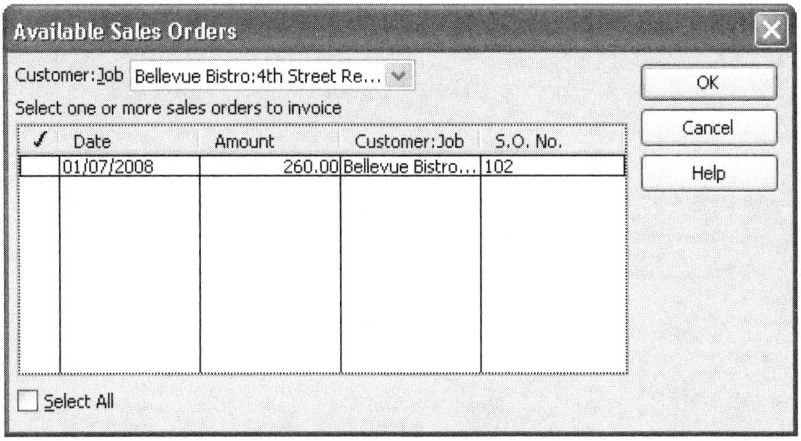

Figure 7-7: QuickBooks automatically displays all the open sales orders for the selected customer or job.

Select the appropriate sales order, and click OK. See "Creating the Invoice", later in this section to learn how to move through the rest of the processes.

Converting a Sales Order to an Invoice

You can open the original sales order to create the invoice. You have two quick ways to find the original sales order:

- Select the customer or job from the Customers & Jobs tab in the Customer Center, and select the sales order in the right pane. (If the right pane displays a long list of transactions, filter the list by selecting Sales Orders from the drop-down list in the Show field.)

- Choose Reports → Sales → Open Sales Orders by Customer.

Double-click the listing for the sales order you need, which opens the original transaction window. Then click the Button labeled Create Invoice at the top of the sales order to turn the sales order into an invoice.

Creating the Invoice

Whether you start from the Create Invoices window or the Sales Order window, creating an invoice from a sales order works the same way.

QuickBooks displays the Create Invoice Based on Sales Order dialog (see Figure 7-8), so you can decide whether to create an invoice for the entire sales order, or create an invoice for only specific items on the sales order.

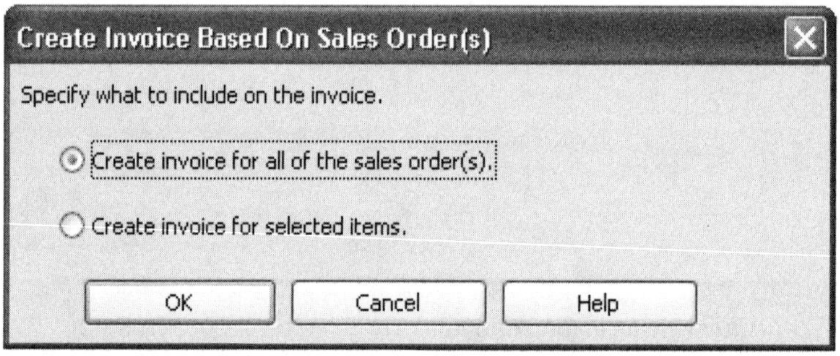

Figure 7-8: Select the appropriate option for filling the sales order.

The latter option is available in case some items aren't available (in which case they stay open on the sales order, creating a virtual backorder).

Here's an important tip (or trick): Select Create Invoice For Selected Items, even if you want to invoice the entire sales order. Remember, earlier in this chapter I pointed out that QuickBooks does not inform you of insufficient quantities when you create a sales order-you only learn about stock problems when you create an invoice. (This does not occur if you're running one of the Premier editions mentioned earlier in this chapter that have advanced sales order options).

If there's not enough stock to fill this sales order, after you select the option to create an invoice for the entire sales order, you encounter some problems.

However, I'll go over both scenarios, and I'll show you what happens if you opt to fill the entire sales order and then find out you don't have enough stock.

***NOTE**: If the sales order includes only one product, it doesn't matter which option you select.*

Invoicing the Entire Sales Order

If you selected the option to invoice the entire sales order, and you have enough stock to fill the order, the Create Invoices window opens with everything filled in from the sales order. QuickBooks automatically uses the Custom S.O. Invoice template, because it is configured to display columns that can hold the information from the sales order.

Add the shipping costs, if you charge customers for shipping. Add other items to the invoice, such as service items, or any additional products the customer has ordered. Then print and send the invoice as you usually do.

Managing Insufficient Quantities

If any items on the sales order don't have a sufficient QOH, the warning message seen in Figure 7-9 appears. Unfortunately, the warning message doesn't tell you which item is in short supply.

Figure 7-9: Uh oh

Click OK to clear the warning message and the invoice appears, automatically filled in with all the items that were on the sales order. However, you still have no indication about which item lacked sufficient QOH to ship this order. There are several methods for solving this mystery:

- If you think the inventory records are wrong, or you know you have sufficient quantity to ship because the order has been picked, you can safely ignore the message.
- If you don't use pick slips, or you don't pick and pack an order until it's invoiced, you can walk into the warehouse and count the QOH for each item on the invoice. For short counts, come back and change the quantity in the Invoiced column.
- Choose Lists → Item List on the QuickBooks menu bar, select the listing for the first item in the invoice, and press Ctrl-Q to see a status report on the QOH.

If necessary, adjust the quantity in the Invoiced column. Repeat for each item in the invoice that has insufficient quantities.

When you change the number in the Invoiced column, the invoice changes depending on the Premier edition you're using:

- In the Accountant, Manufacturing & Wholesale, and Retail Premier editions, QuickBooks automatically enters the difference between the Ordered and Invoiced columns in the Backordered column. You don't have to look up the current stock status.
- In all other Premier editions, no Backorder calculation is available. Instead, the original sales order is saved with the number of units you invoiced recorded in the sales order.

When you open the original sales order (see Figure 7-10), the products that were available were invoiced and are marked closed (a check mark appears in the Clsd column). The products that had insufficient quantity to ship are not closed, and the sales order displays the original number of units ordered as well the number of units Invoiced (and, we can assume, shipped).

The sales order remains open, and when you receive the products you can invoice the remainder of the order.

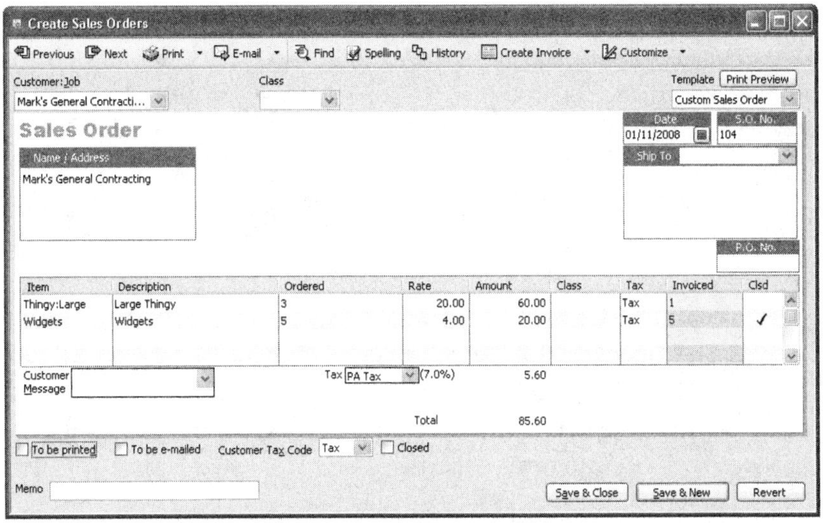

Figure 7-10: The user adjusted the invoice, so the sales order now shows which products weren't invoiced and shipped.

Invoicing Selected Items

If you chose the option Create Invoice For Selected Items, when you click OK the Specify Invoice Quantities For Items On Sales Order dialog appears (see Figure 7-11). The information available with this option for creating the invoice makes it much easier to prepare the invoice properly.

The QOH for each item is displayed, but you can't trust the numbers on this dialog unless you select the option to show the quantity available instead of the quantity on hand. The QOH does not take existing sales orders into consideration.

Selecting the option Show Quantity Available Instead Of Quantity On Hand often reveals the fact that the items on hand are already linked to one or more sales orders. If necessary, adjust the number of units in the To Invoice column of the dialog. The sales order is loaded in the Create Invoices transaction window, using the numbers you adjusted (the units to invoice).

Earlier in this chapter, I told you how to set your preferences to warn about the available quantity instead of the QOH, but that preference only kicks in when you're creating an invoice. The Specify Invoice Quantities For Items On Sales Order dialog obviously doesn't check that preference. Therefore, you have to select the option Show Quantity Available to match the preferences you set.

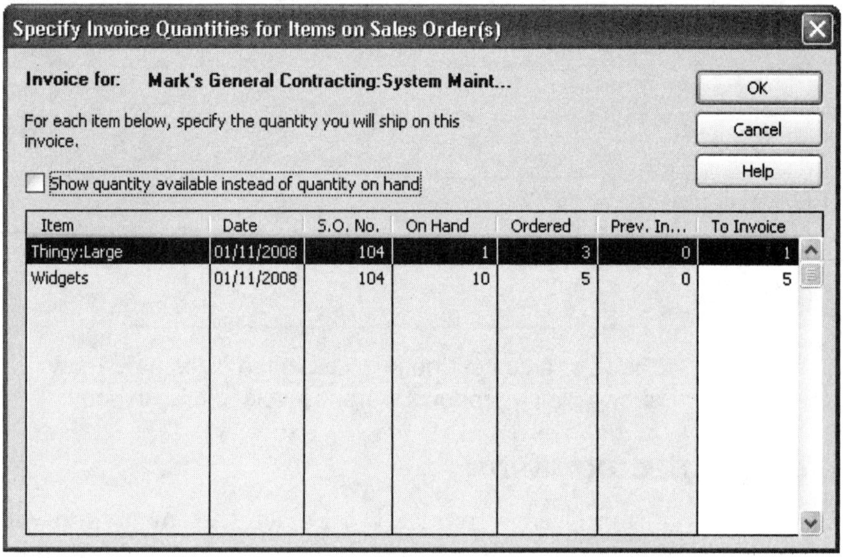

Figure 7-11: There's a shortage of one of the products on the sales order.

When the quantity that's available is less than the QOH, it means the item is on a sales order (including the sales order you're currently converting to an invoice), or on multiple sales orders. The items are still on the shelf, they're just promised.

In many companies, this kicks off any of several amusing scenarios involving sprint races and arguments. If the other sales orders aren't yet ready for invoicing, you win. But before you can claim your prize (the right to create an invoice), you have to prevent other people from doing the same thing. Someone may be ready to invoice a sales order that contains the same item. Here's how to win for real:

1. Run, don't walk, to the warehouse, and gather up the quantity you need of the items that are in short supply.

2. Take the items to the shipping desk and mark them with the invoice number you're preparing. (It doesn't hurt to add a threatening note about the consequences to anybody who thinks about appropriating these items to create an invoice from one of the other sales orders.)
3. If you think Step 2 won't work, bring the items back to your desk and hide them until you finish your invoice, and then take them to the shipping desk and stay there to supervise the packing process.

If multiple users are working on multiple computers on the network, turning sales orders into invoices, it's more difficult to declare yourself the winner. Somebody else may have already confiscated the items, or several of you may arrive in the warehouse at the same time.

Instead of a tug-of-war, you need to set shipping priorities. I've seen these discussions turn into real arguments, although there's usually an executive who declares the winner. Here's the priority list many companies use:

- The first priority is a customer who doesn't accept backorders, and wants you to ship and invoice only what's in stock.
- The second priority is a "best customer"-a customer it's important to keep happy (of course, a "best customer" is usually defined by the amount of money the customer spends with your company).
- The third priority is whatever argument the best debater in the group presents. This usually involves listening to phrases such as "this is the first order from a new customer", or "we've done this to this customer three times already".

When you can't ship all the items, you have to change the numbers in the Specify Invoice Quantities For Items On Sales Order dialog. In the To Invoice column, enter the quantity you want to invoice. Then click OK.

If any item isn't available, and you entered zero for the amount to invoice, QuickBooks issues a warning message about handling zero amount items (see Figure 7-12).

The warning is important, because if you delete the zero amount line items, you won't be able to track backorders. Setting a preference to avoid printing zero items is discussed earlier in this chapter, and you should enable it if you don't want your customer to see the zero amount line on the printed invoice.

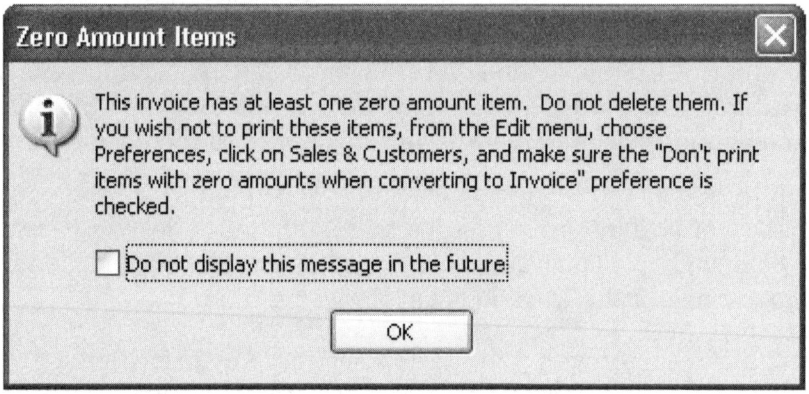

Figure 7-12: QuickBooks warns you not to delete items from the invoice.

I think it's helpful to print zero amount line items. After all, the customer certainly remembers the original order, and you're showing the customer that you, too, remember the items in the original order. However, if you choose not to print the zero-based lines, they remain on the on-screen version so you can track the items for backorders. If you're shipping and invoicing less than the number of items in the sales order (but not zero), that also qualifies as a backorder.

***TIP**: If you know this customer won't accept backorders, and has issued instructions to ship whatever is available, it's OK to delete the zero-based lines. You won't be tracking backorders for this customer.*

Save the invoice, print it, and ship the goods that are in stock. If the invoice matches the sales order (meaning everything on the sales order was shipped), the original sales order is marked Invoiced In Full when you open it to view it. All you have to do is wait for the customer's check to arrive.

If the invoice didn't match the sales order, the unshipped goods remain on the sales order. When the products arrive, open the sales order, click the Create Invoice button, and start the process again.

When you save the invoice, only the amounts on the invoice are posted to the Accounts Receivable, Income, Inventory, and Cost of Goods accounts. The amounts for backordered items are not posted to the general ledger.

Managing Backorders

When you aren't able to ship and invoice all the items in a sales order, the sales order becomes a virtual backorder, even if you're not using one of the Premier editions that tracks backorders, because the sales order maintains information about the items that were not invoiced.

Tracking Receipt of Goods

Unfortunately, as new products arrive in your warehouse, QuickBooks does not assign the products to existing unfilled sales orders (backorders) automatically. Instead, you must manually track incoming goods against the backorders in your system.

You can track incoming goods within QuickBooks, or outside of QuickBooks. In this section, I'll go over some of the techniques that are working well for my clients.

Using Stock Status Reports

You can track the status of items by viewing a stock status report, and comparing the contents to the backorders you're tracking. Get into the habit of printing your backorders, which you can do by calling up a sales order after its linked invoice has been created, and clicking the Print button.

To see a stock status report, choose Reports → Inventory → Inventory Stock Status By Item. The report that opens lists every item in inventory, along with its current status (on hand, on purchase order, on sales order).

The usefulness of this report varies, depending on the number of items you stock, and the number of backorders you're tracking. If your company has a limited number of items, it's not terribly difficult to go through the report to find the items you're looking for in order to fill your backorders. However, if you have a lot of items, or many backorders (or both), it's more efficient to design reports that give you what you need quickly.

Creating Customized Stock Status Reports

If you create customized stock status reports for backorders, you can check each customer's backorder quickly, which is handy if the customer calls and asks when you expect to ship the remaining products.

To do this, you need to customize the report on a per-customer basis, or on a per-backorder basis. Either way, start by choosing Reports → Inventory → Inventory Stock Status By Item.

Customizing the Display of a Stock Status Report

When the report opens, make it easier to read by eliminating columns that don't provide information you need. You cannot use the Modify Report feature to remove columns on this particular report, but you can close up the columns so you don't have to scroll through the report.

Use the diamond-shaped marker to the right of any column you don't need, dragging it to the left until the column disappears. The following columns can safely disappear for the purpose of tracking backorders:

- Pref Vendor
- Reorder Pt
- Order
- Sales/Wk

Customizing the Content of a Stock Status Report

To customize the report for customers or backorders, click Modify Report, and make the following customizations:

1. In the Filters tab, select Item from the Choose Filters list.
2. In the Item field, click the arrow and scroll to the top of the list, and choose Selected Items to open the Select Items dialog.

3. Select Manual, and then select the appropriate items:
   - For a customer report, select all the items a single customer is waiting for (all the customer's backorders).
   - For a backorder report, select all the item(s) attached to a particular backorder.
4. Click OK to return to the Filters tab, then click OK again to return to report window.

The report displays only those items you selected, and you can use it to compare stock status against existing backorders.

Checking Receipt of Goods Manually

It's always a good idea to keep an eye on the items you're waiting for by tracking what comes in. This works well if you enlist the help of the warehouse personnel who receive goods. In fact, it's a good idea to establish a policy that receiving personnel must check backorder lists.

Print a list of the products you're awaiting to fill backorders by choosing Reports → Sales → Open Sales Orders By Item. The report displays each item on a backorder, along with the customer's name, the sales order number, the quantity on the backorder, and the quantity already invoiced (see Figure 7-13).

The quantity you need is the difference between the quantity ordered and the quantity invoiced. Hang the list in the receiving area, and write your name and telephone extension on the document so you can receive a call when the goods arrive.

If you need to order goods from vendors to fill backorders, have the order delivered directly to the person who's tracking the backorders for these items (maybe that's you). If you use purchase orders, make sure the shipping address has your name on it. If you order by telephone, or over the Internet, be sure to indicate the shipment is to be directed to the person who's tracking the backorders for these items.

Even if you have shipments sent to your attention, or to the attention of the person who's tracking backorders, you cannot immediately fill the backorders. You must first use the Receive Items procedures to record the fact that the items came in. Then you can create invoices from the backorders to ship the items to customers. No shortcuts, please, it really messes up the accounting records.

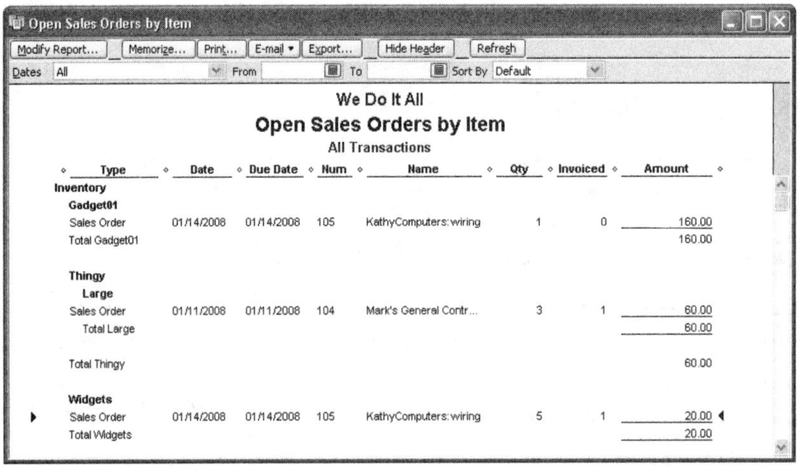

Figure 7-13: Print a report of items that are on backorder so the warehouse knows what to look for.

***TIP**: QuickBooks doesn't have a report for all sales orders, or for closed sales orders; you can only choose reports on open sales orders. Accountants tell us they want to be able to double-check sales order status by comparing the items in the original sales order to the items in the open sales order (if the open sales order is acting as a back order). We've created several useful sales order report templates in our Client Kit CD for accountants who want to provide them to clients. The CD can be purchased at www.cpa911publishing.com.*

Creating Transactions Automatically

In QuickBooks Premier editions, you can automatically create transactions from transactions, which is rather nifty. I've already explained how to create an invoice automatically from a Sales Order.

You can perform the same one-click transformation for other transactions by clicking the arrow to the right of the Create Invoice button on the transaction window and selecting the appropriate transaction type.

- Create a Purchase Order from a Sales Order
- Create a Sales Order from an Estimate
- Create an Invoice from an Estimate
- Create a Purchase Order from an Estimate
- Create a Sales Order from a Quote
- Create an Invoice from a Quote
- Create a Purchase order from a Quote
- Create an Invoice from a Proposal
- Create a Sales Order from a Proposal
- Create a Purchase Order from a Proposal
- Create an Invoice from a Work Order
- Create a Purchase order from a Work Order

***NOTE**: Quotes, Proposals, and Work Orders are transaction templates that are built into some of the industry-specific versions of QuickBooks. All of them are customized versions of estimates or sales orders.*

Automatic Purchase Orders From Sales Orders

One of the most useful of the QuickBooks automated transaction features is the ability to turn a sales order into a purchase order automatically. When you're creating a sales order that includes an item you know you're out of, a mouse click creates a purchase order.

***TIP**: This is also a useful feature for items you don't keep in stock, and purchase only when a customer places an order.*

Fill in the sales order, and then click the arrow to the right of the Create Invoice button. Select Purchase Order from the drop-down list. QuickBooks displays the Create Purchase Order Based On The Sales Transaction dialog, seen in Figure 7-14. (The word "allowed" appears in the dialog because items that are percentage based can't be automatically transferred to a purchase item.)

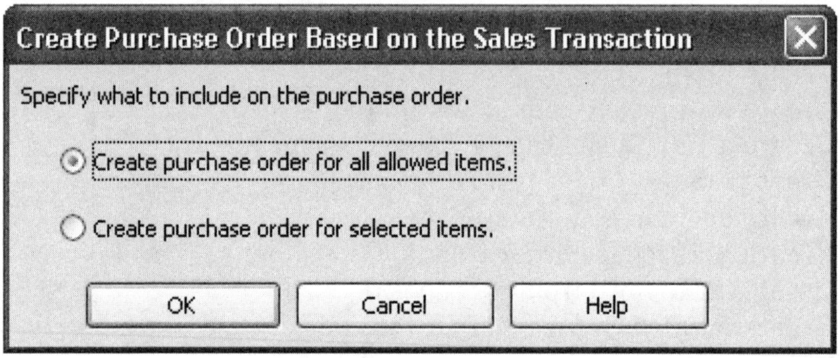

Figure 7-14: Select the appropriate option for purchasing the item(s) on this sales order.

The option to create a purchase order for all allowed items only works if all the items on the sales order are purchased from the same vendor (or if the sales order contains only one item).

Selecting this option opens a Create Purchase Orders window with the line items pre-filled with all the items on the sales order. If the items have a Preferred Vendor entry in the item record, the vendor's name is also filled in automatically.

Most of the time, the option to create a purchase order for selected items works best. Selecting that option opens the dialog seen in Figure 7-15, where you can select the item(s) you want to purchase.

Select each item you need to purchase by clicking in the leftmost column to place a checkmark in the column. QuickBooks displays the current QOH, and automatically fills in the quantity to order, using the quantity entered in the sales order. You can change the value of the Qty column if you want to order more than needed for this sales order.

Click OK to open a Create Purchase Orders window with the product information filled in (see Figure 7-16).

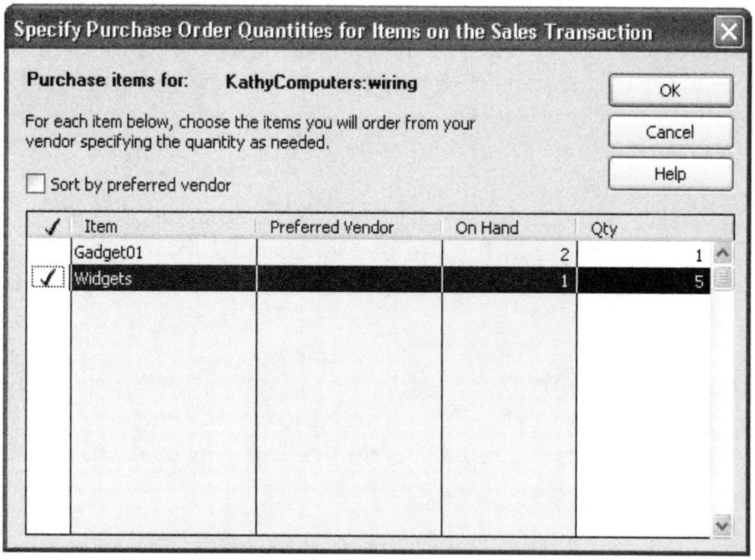

Figure 7-15: Select the items you need to purchase to fill this order.

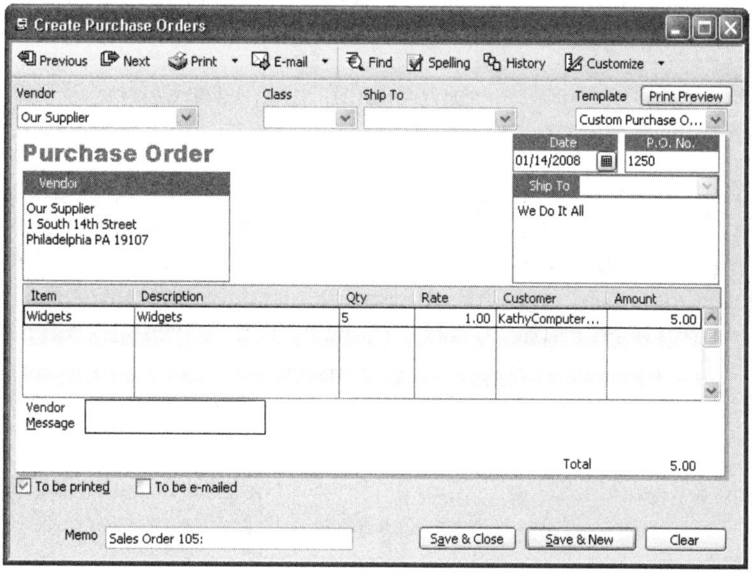

Figure 7-16: The customer's missing merchandise is automatically ordered, and linked to the customer.

Delete the customer or job name from the Customer column. The fact that the customer name (or job) is automatically inserted in the line item makes the transactions involved in the future very complicated. (The following paragraphs explain what happens if you don't take my advice to delete the customer or job name from the Customer column.)

If the customer or job is linked to the purchase order, when you receive the goods, and the bill for the goods, the fact that a customer or job name is on the transaction automatically makes this a reimbursable expense.

When you turn the sales order into an invoice, QuickBooks automatically enters the products in the sales order into the invoice. QuickBooks also automatically displays a message reminding you that this customer has outstanding billable time or costs.

When you click the Time/Costs button at the top of the invoice window, you see the purchase you linked to this customer as a reimbursable expense. If you don't transfer the amount to the invoice, you'll see the message about outstanding billable time or costs every time you create an invoice for this customer or job.

Using both the automatic conversion of a sales order to an invoice and the reimbursable costs creates two item lines.

- If you delete the item line that's connected to the reimbursable costs, the costs go back to their "uncollected" status and you will see a reminder to include them in invoices forever.
- If you delete the item line that was transferred from the sales order (and correct the amounts for the reimbursable expense line that remains on the invoice), the inventory isn't decremented and no postings are made to the COG account. The reimbursable expense isn't an inventory item.

So, remove the customer name, and save the purchase order. You're returned to the sales order, and you can save the sales order.

***NOTE**: QuickBooks enters the sales order number in the memo field of the purchase order to indicate it was created automatically, and to remind you which sales order is awaiting these products.*

Automatic Sales Orders from Estimates

If you create an estimate (or a proposal or quote) for a customer, after the customer approves your estimate you can create a sales order automatically. Then, from the sales order, you can automatically create purchase orders and invoices.

Click the arrow to the right of the Create Invoice button on the Create Estimates transaction window, and choose Sales Order. QuickBooks displays a message telling you it has transferred the items on the estimate to a sales order. Click OK to open the sales order transaction window, where you can add items, change the shipping address, and make any other needed changes.

Save the sales order, automatically create a purchase order for any needed inventory items, and when you're ready to invoice the customer, that's automatic, too.

***TIP**: You can also create a purchase order automatically from an estimate.*

Inventory Assemblies

Assemblies are products you create using existing inventory parts. Only QuickBooks Premier and Enterprise Editions offer the software features for assemblies (which are sometimes called pre-builds). In the following sections I'll go over the tasks involved in creating and managing assemblies.

***TIP**: This feature works slightly differently in the Accounting, Manufacturing & Distribution, and Retail Premier editions, because those products have additional features for creating and managing assemblies. See the respective chapters on those Premier editions for details.*

Creating an Assembly Item

An assembly is an inventory item, and you start by adding it to your Items list. Choose Lists → Item List to open the Item List window, and then press Ctrl-N to open the New Item dialog.

Select Inventory Assembly as the type of item, and the New Item dialog displays all the fields you need to create an assembly (see Figure 7-17).

Most of the fields are self-explanatory, but a few of them merit discussion, so I'll present some guidelines.

In the Bill of Materials section, select the inventory items required to build this assembly, and the quantity of each component. (You can also use items other than inventory parts; see "Using Non-Inventory Parts in an Assembly", later in this section.)

The Cost field in the middle of the dialog is optional. You can use it to create a marked-up cost for the assembly. Then you can use that marked-up cost to do cost-plus pricing (choose Customers → Change Item Prices to calculate and save cost-plus pricing). The data you enter in this field does not affect the postings to your COG account, which continues to post the real cost (the total cost of the items in the Bill of Materials list).

The Sales Price field must be filled in manually. If you configured QuickBooks for automatic markups (in the Sales & Customers Preferences dialog), that feature doesn't apply to assemblies.

The dialog has a field for entering a vendor from whom you purchase this assembly, which you probably won't use. If you subcontract the work to a vendor, you purchase the completed item the way you'd purchase any other item. That makes this an item, not an assembly.

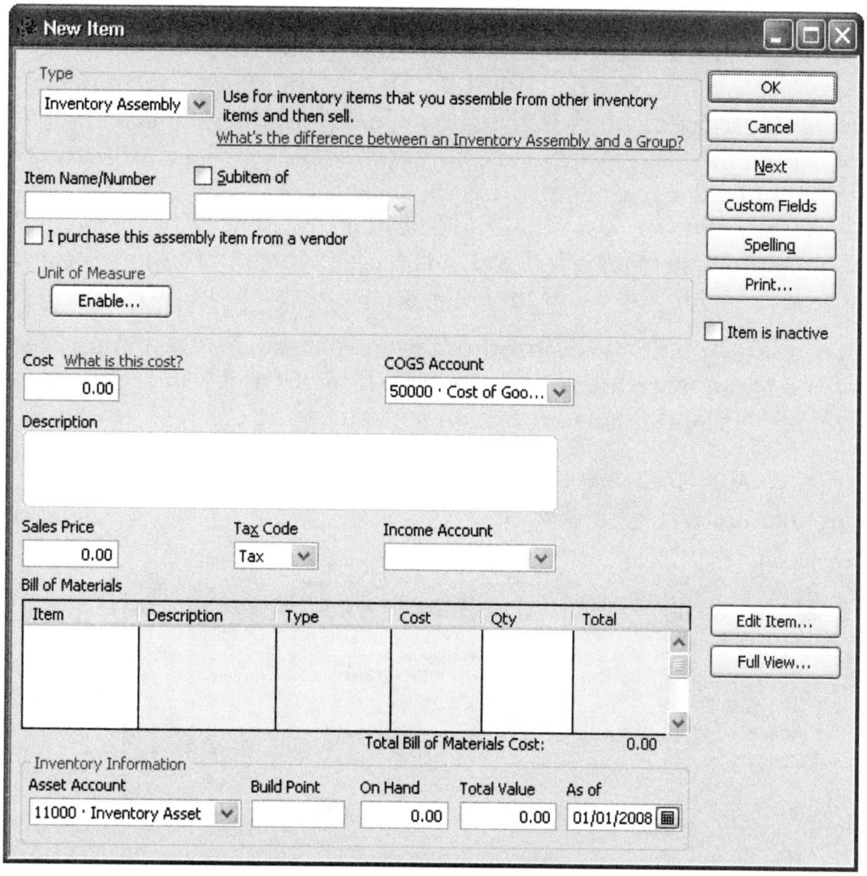

Figure 7-17: The New Item dialog holds all the information you need for assemblies.

Using Non-Inventory Items in an Assembly

By default, QuickBooks won't let you add any item that isn't an inventory part to the Bill of Materials for an assembly. That's because the items in the Bill of Materials each carry a cost, and the total cost becomes the posting to Cost of Goods when you sell the assembly.

You can edit the records of non-inventory items that you want to add to the assembly so that those items have a cost attached (or create new non-inventory items specifically for this purpose). The following item types can be used in assemblies if they're properly configured:

- Service. Useful for adding the cost of labor. Create a service item that's suitable for this if your Items list doesn't already contain one.
- Non-inventory part. Useful for adding the cost of parts that you don't track as inventory items. This could include boxes, tape, consumable goods (such as nails, screws, etc.) or other things involved in putting an assembly together.
- Other Charge. Useful for adding the cost of almost anything, but I usually use it for overhead (I calculate the approximate cost per hour to run the room in which assemblies are built).

To create or edit a non-inventory item so it can be used in an assembly, select the option with a label that begins "This item is used in assemblies..." (the remainder of the label text changes depending on the item type).

When you select that option, the item's dialog changes to include information about cost (see Figure 7-18).

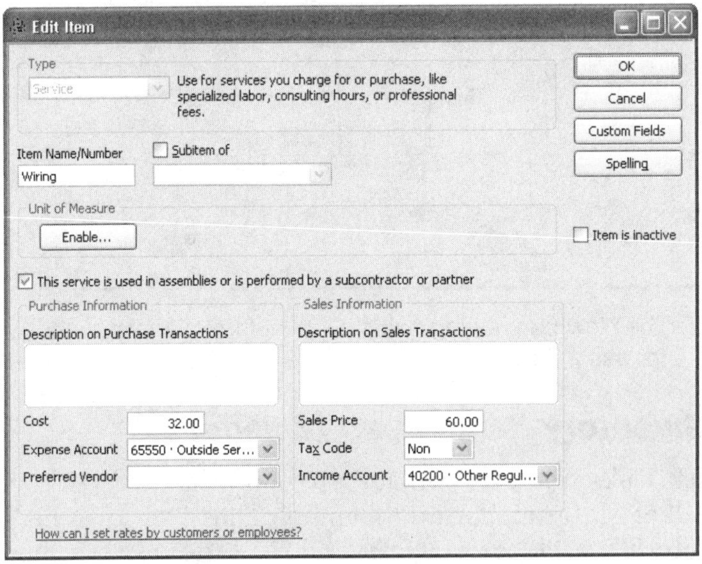

Figure 7-18: Configure a non-inventory item so it can be used in an assembly.

When you use a non-inventory item in a build, QuickBooks treats the item as if it were an inventory item. The cost is included when the build is posted to the inventory asset account, and is applied to COGS when you sell the assembly.

Editing Assemblies

You can edit an assembly in much the same way you can edit any other item. Double-click the assembly's listing in the Item list and make the required changes.

For example, you may decide to configure other item types for inclusion in assemblies, as discussed in the previous section. In the assembly's dialog, move to the next available line in the Bill of Materials section, and add the item(s). The cost of the assembly changes to reflect the new material.

Building an Assembly

After your assembly item is in your Item list, you can build it. During this process, the component inventory items are removed from inventory, and the finished assembly item is received into inventory.

Choose Vendors → Inventory Activities → Build Assemblies to open the Build Assemblies dialog. Select the assembly item (only assembly items appear in the drop-down list).

QuickBooks automatically fills in the components required for the assembly item, along with the QOH for each inventory component (see Figure 7-19).

***WARNING**: Non-inventory components aren't tracked for QOH, so if they're not service items, you must make sure you have sufficient supplies.*

The Qty Needed column remains at zero for each component until you indicate the number of builds you're creating. The dialog displays the maximum number of builds you can create with the current QOH of inventory parts.

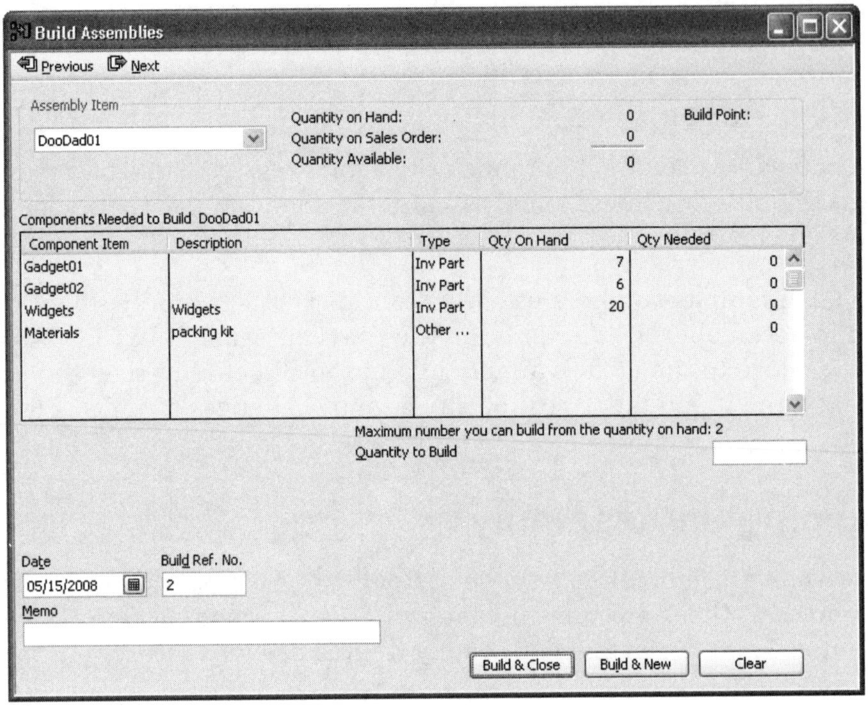

Figure 7-19: QuickBooks automatically provides QOH data for the assembly and for the inventory component parts.

***NOTE**: You can build more than the maximum number you have component parts for, but builds that are missing parts are recorded as pending builds (see the section "Managing Pending Builds").*

Enter the quantity to build, and press Tab. The component quantities are adjusted: Qty On Hand is reduced, and Qty Needed is increased to match the number of builds you indicated, as seen in Figure 7-20.

Click Build & New if you want to build another assembly, or click Build & Close if you're finished. The build is moved into inventory and you can sell it.

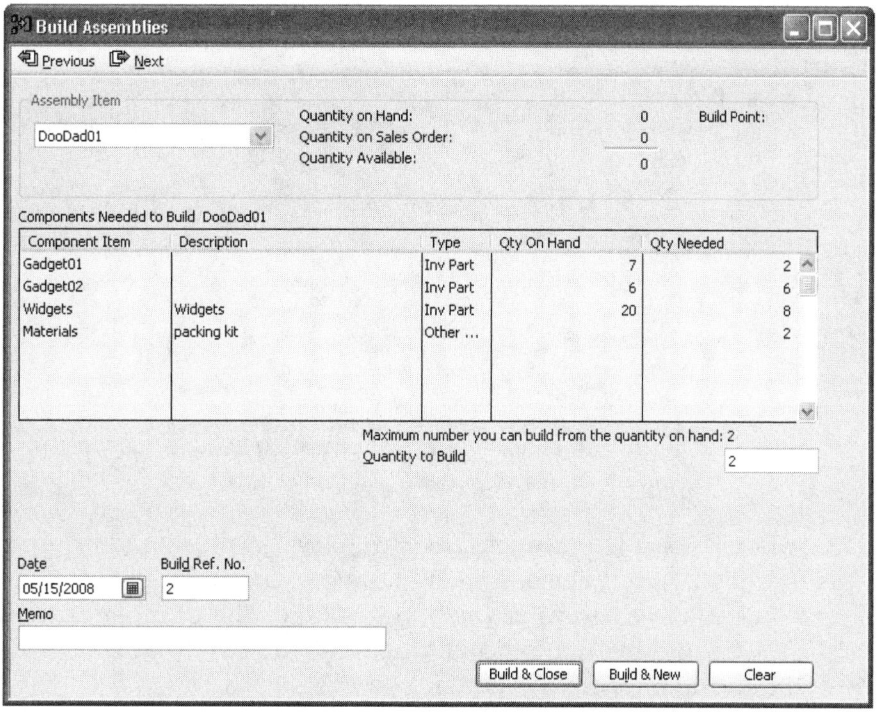

Figure 7-20: When you enter the number of builds you're creating, QuickBooks fills in the Qty Needed column.

Managing Pending Builds

If you don't have enough of the components to build the number of assemblies you need, you can continue with the build process, but the build is marked Pending. Pending builds are finalized when all the components are available.

Creating a Pending Build

When you specify a number of builds that exceeds the available quantity of components, QuickBooks displays a dialog to warn you that you don't have enough components (see Figure 7-21).

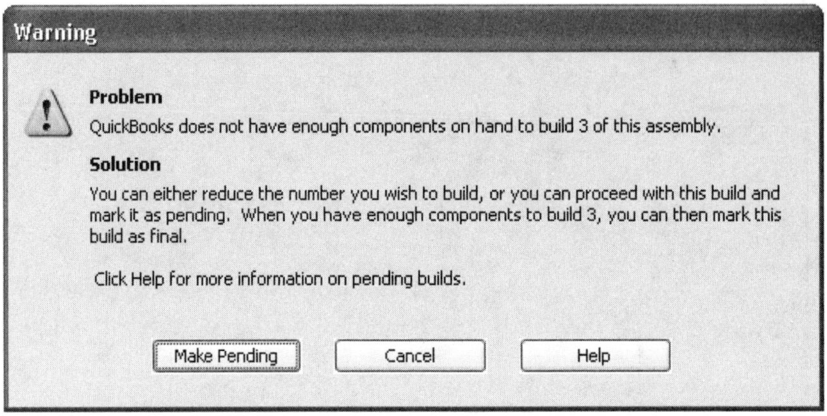

Figure 7-21: You can either make this a pending build, or cancel the build.

- Click Cancel to return to the Build Assemblies window, and reduce the number of builds to match your available components.
- Click Make Pending if you want to leave the number of builds as is. The build is marked pending, and you can finalize the build when the missing components arrive.

The entire build is marked pending. No assemblies are brought into inventory, and no components are decremented from inventory. This is true even if sufficient quantities of some of the components exist to complete a fewer number of builds.

If you have enough components to build fewer assemblies than you'd specified in the Build Assemblies window, you should click Cancel. Then start again, reducing the number of assemblies so you can get the build into inventory and generate income.

The only time you should select the Make Pending option is when all the assemblies are for the same customer, and that customer wants everything delivered together, so you have to wait until you can build all the assemblies.

If you create another build for the same assembly before additional components arrive, the Build Assemblies window displays the same QOH for the components as existed when you created the previous, pending, build.

For example, when you created the pending build for two assemblies, you may have had enough components to build one assembly, but not two. The next time you open the Build Assemblies window for this assembly product, you still have enough components to build one assembly. If you build the new assembly you use up components, and the pending build has more missing components than it did when you originally saved it.

Tracking Pending Builds

Check the pending builds frequently, so you can purchase components as you need them. To see a report on the current pending bills, choose Reports → Inventory → Pending Builds. When the report opens (see Figure 7-22), it lists all pending builds.

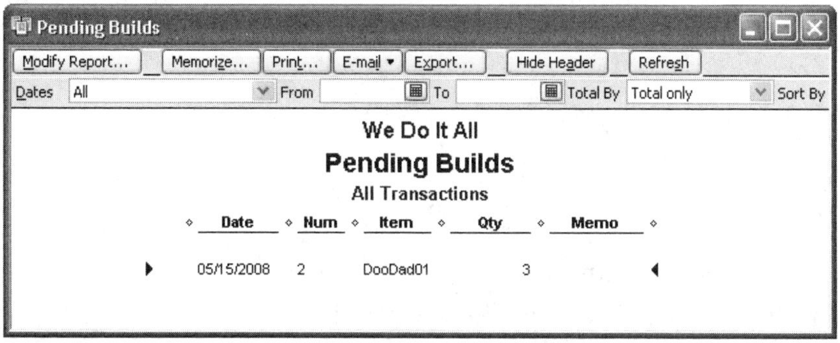

Figure 7-22: Keep an eye on pending bills to make sure you keep up with purchases.

Unfortunately, QuickBooks doesn't provide a report called "components needed for pending builds". Nor is there any way to produce a stock status report that shows items that are listed on pending bills.

Lacking those useful functions, you have to double-click each listing in the Pending Bills report to see the current stock status for components. Make notes, and then buy the components you need.

Finalizing a Pending Build

When you receive the components that are missing in a pending build, you can finalize the build and put the assembly item into your inventory. Open the pending build by opening the Pending Builds report, and double-clicking the listing for the build you're ready to finalize.

When the window opens, the current QOH of components is displayed, and the maximum number you can build is updated to match the component availability.

If you now have sufficient quantities of components to build the assemblies, the Remove Pending Status button at the bottom of the window is activated. (The button is grayed out and inaccessible if the components aren't available).

Click Remove Pending Status to finalize the build, and close the window. QuickBooks asks you to confirm that you want to save your changes. Click Yes. The assembly item is moved into your inventory, and the inventory item components are removed from inventory.

Disassembling an Assembly

You can disassemble a built assembly item, which automatically returns the inventory components to inventory.

While you could manually adjust inventory to move the components back into inventory, and remove an assembly from inventory, that's onerous. The quickest way to remove a built assembly item is to delete the transaction that built it.

Deleting the build's transaction only works if the number of builds in that transaction matches the number of built assembly items you want to disassemble. For example, if the transaction was for three builds, and you only want to remove one, you can't use this method, you must manually adjust your inventory numbers.

To delete the entire build, open the original build window, and choose Edit → Delete Build from the QuickBooks menu bar. If the build is finalized, QuickBooks readjusts your inventory appropriately. If the build is pending, no adjustments need to be made.

Units of Measure

A unit of measure (U/M) is a way to establish specific information about the basis on which you sell quantities of goods and products. For example, if you sell an inventory item named Chocolate Syrup, you can specify the U/M as a bottle, a 6-pack, or a 24-unit case. You can also use a U/M for the services you sell-perhaps you want to provide training services in units of hours or days. Don't use U/Ms for products that are bought and sold in identical units.

U/Ms are attached to items-each item has its own U/M. QuickBooks provides two ways to track and assign U/Ms:

- Single U/M per item, in which you can assign one U/M to an item.
- Multiple U/M per item, in which you can create a base U/M and then devise multiple conversions of that base U/M to permit sales of different quantities.

Table 7-1 displays the type of U/M supported by each Premier edition.

Edition	U/M Supported
Premier (not industry specific)	Single U/M only
Professional Services	Single U/M only
Nonprofit	Single U/M only
Accountant	Both Multiple and Single U/M
Contractor	Both Multiple and Single U/M
Manufacturing & Wholesale	Both Multiple and Single U/M
Retail	No U/M available

Table 7-1: Support for Units of Measure for Premier editions.

Businesses that sell goods, especially inventory items, obviously have the greatest need for the U/M feature. Before QuickBooks introduced this feature, selling inventory that you buy in large lots (perhaps a skid of 10 cases), but sell in smaller units such as single cases and single items, required the establishment of Group items. That solution is often clumsy and onerous because a group isn't automatically linked to an item, and has to be created and sold as a discrete item. U/Ms can automate the "buy it one way and sell it another way" function. (If you've already created groups, you can assign them U/M functions, which is very handy.)

Enabling Units of Measure

To enable U/Ms, choose Edit → Preferences and select the Items & Inventory category in the left pane. Move to the Company Preferences tab and click the Enable button. In the Unit of Measure dialog (see Figure 7-23), select the U/M method you want to use.

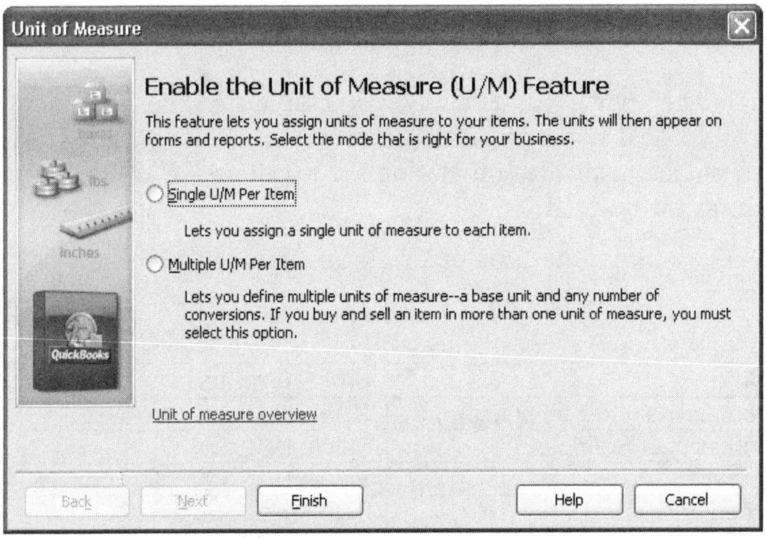

Figure 7-23: Choose the U/M you need for the products and services you sell. For your Premier edition, the Multiple U/M option may be grayed out and inaccessible.

Click Finish to return to the Preferences dialog, and then click OK. QuickBooks adds the U/M field to all the following item types so you can begin establishing U/Ms:

- Inventory Part

- Inventory Assembly
- Non-inventory Part
- Service
- Group (not Sales Tax Group)

Creating a Single Unit of Measure

If you enabled Single U/Ms, you can create one measurement type for each item. Open the Items list and double-click the item for which you want to create a single U/M.

***TIP**: It doesn't matter which item you select to create a U/M. The U/M you create is available to all items that can be sold by U/M. You need to create sufficient U/Ms to cover all the algorithms for the items you want to sell by U/M.*

In the U/M field, select <Add New> from the drop-down list to open the Unit of Measure wizard seen in Figure 7-24.

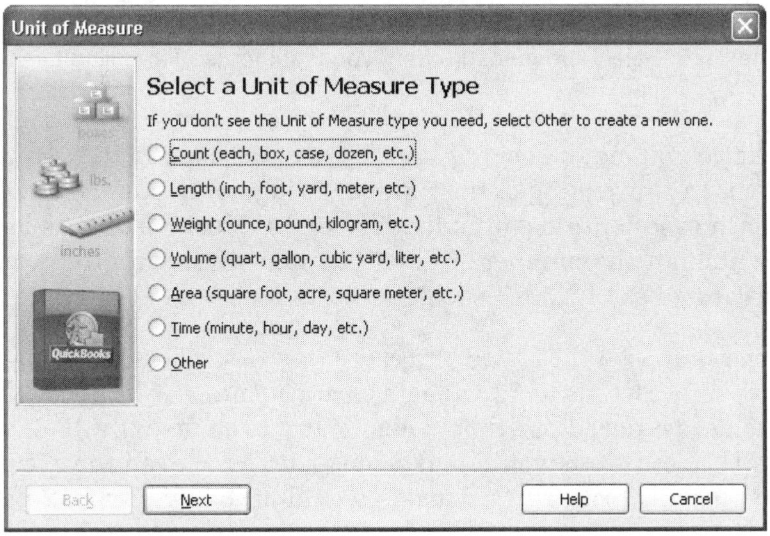

Figure 7-24: Start by selecting the type of measurement appropriate for the item you're configuring.

Select the type of measurement appropriate to this item, and click Next to select the U/M you want to use when you sell this item. Figure 7-25 shows the choices available if you selected Count in the first wizard window (different measurement types produce different U/Ms).

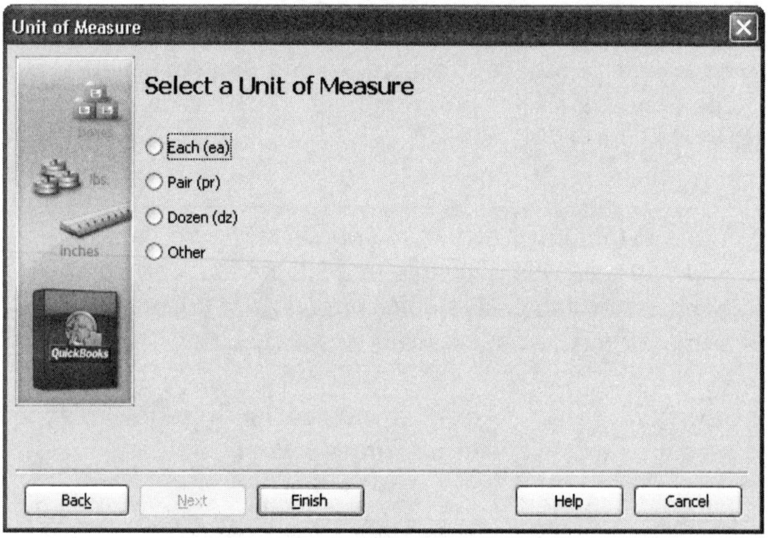

Figure 7-25: Select the measurement you want to use for selling this item.

The choice you make depends on the way you usually buy, store, and sell the item. In this example, the product (widgets) is purchased by the case and each case contains 48 individual units. Most customers buy multiple units, but the number of units per sale varies greatly. It makes sense to create a base U/M of "each".

However, suppose these widgets came in a case of 48 that was packed with four cartons of 12 widgets/carton? And, also suppose that many customers ordered multiple widgets at a time, usually 10 or 12. Creating a U/M of Dozen would make sense, because even those customers who usually ordered 10 widgets would probably buy a 12-pack carton.

In addition, creating a U/M of Each means that every case would need to be opened, and then every 12-pack carton would need to be opened, in order to store individual items. In addition, each individual item would have to be picked and packed for each sale. If many customers are already buying multiple individual units, that's extra and unneeded work, why not just offer a U/M of Dozen?

If the choices available on the Unit of Measure dialog don't include a measurement unit that fits neatly with the way you buy, store, and sell this item, click Other, and then click Next. In the window that displays (see Figure 7-26) create your own U/M. Give the U/M a name and an abbreviation. The abbreviation is what appears on forms and reports, so make sure the text you use clearly defines the U/M.

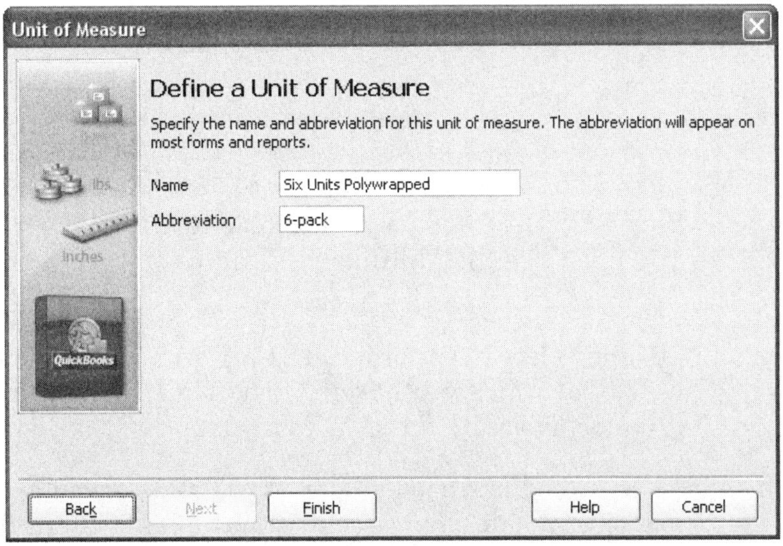

Figure 7-26: Create your own U/M if the system doesn't provide what you need.

For service items, it's common to create U/Ms based on time, because services are usually sold by the hour or by the day. Some professional services are sold in blocks of minutes, because the company has a "minimum time" rule for billing clients. For example, some professionals have a minimum 10-minute or 12-minute time block. In that case you can create a U/M for that minimum unit.

If you use timesheets and specify customers and jobs on the timesheets, and those customers are invoiced for the time, you can create a U/M for hours because that's how most timesheets are filled out by workers. However, if the service item is already configured in your Items list at an hourly price, and you're already selling the service in multiples of that price, you don't really need a U/M.

The unit of measure you create becomes available for every item that can be sold via a U/M. It's probable that not all items are able to use this U/M, so you must repeat this process to create additional U/Ms until you've designed sufficient variations to cover all the items and item types you want to sell by U/M. If you create U/Ms that are fairly generic, you probably only have to create a handful of U/Ms.

Assigning a Single Unit of Measure to Items

After you've created the Single U/Ms you need, you can assign a U/M to every item that you want to sell by U/M.

For a Single U/M, each item can only be linked to one U/M (that's why it's called a Single U/M). If you want to be able to sell an item from a choice of U/Ms you must use the Multiple U/M feature (covered later in this chapter).

Open each item and select the appropriate U/M from the drop-down list. If you find an item for which you haven't created an appropriate U/M, select <Add New> and create the U/M you need.

Not all services and products need a U/M. If you've assigned a cost/rate to a service or a product that is sold in multiples of that rate already, you don't have to encumber that item with a U/M.

If you have a service that you sell as a discrete task, for a specific amount, there's no point in assigning a U/M. For example, if you charge a flat fee for installation of a product you sell, there's no point in assigning a U/M. No customer would be asked to pay for two installations for a single product, nor for half an installation of that product.

Selling an Item with a Single Unit of Measurement

When you select an Item that has been assigned a single U/M in a sales transaction, the U/M automatically appears on the line in which you've selected the item (see Figure 7-27).

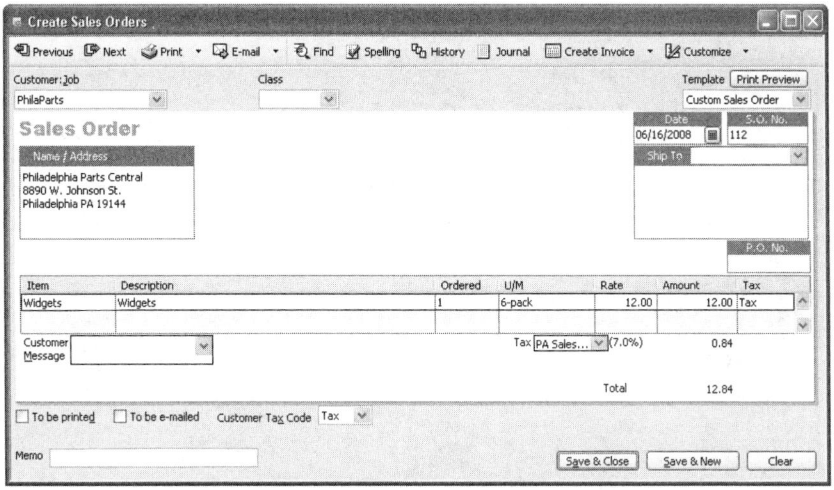

Figure 7-27: This item can only be sold in the quantity indicated by the U/M linked to it.

The U/M linked to the item is permanent; you cannot switch between it and any other U/M because this is a single U/M. You cannot remove it and return to the basic individual unit you were using for this item before you linked a single U/M to the item. The U/M column is not accessible.

Creating Multiple Units of Measure

To create a Multiple U/M, be sure you've enabled Multiple U/M Per Item in the Items & Inventory category of the Preferences dialog. Then open an item from the Items list, and select <Add New> from the drop-down list in the U/M field.

In the Select A Unit Of Measure Type window, choose the type of measurement you're setting up (see Figure 7-28). For this example, I'm using Count, because it's so common.

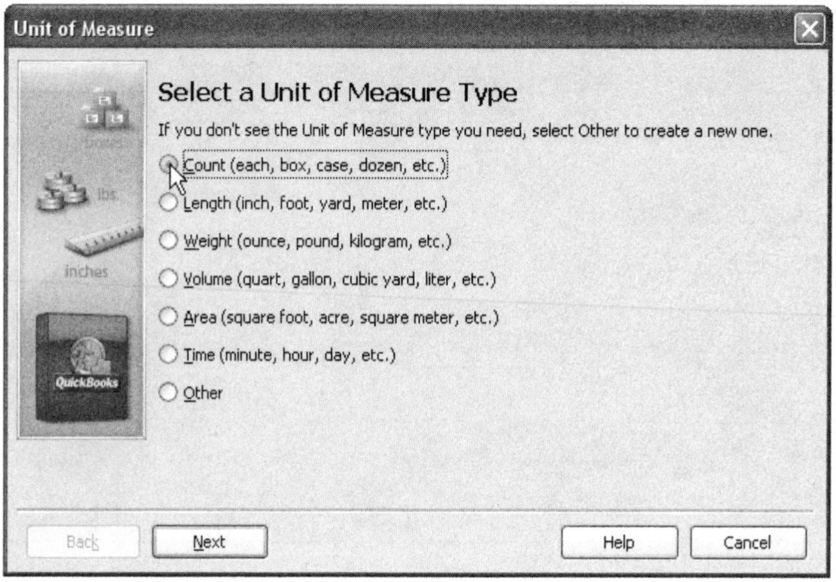

Figure 7-28: Start by selecting the type of measurement you need.

Click Next to specify the base unit of measure for this U/M. The options on this window change, depending on the choice you made for the type of measurement in the previous window. Figure 7-29 shows the base unit window choices for the measurement type Count.

The base unit you select must be the smallest unit you track. It doesn't matter how you buy the product, what matters is the smallest unit of the product you're willing to sell. For example, if you buy widgets in skids of 10 cases, and each case contains 100 boxes of 10 widgets/box, and you're unwilling to unpack a box to sell less than 10 widgets at a time, your base unit is a box of 10. If the option you need isn't available in the window, click Other and create the base unit you need (BoxOf10).

Click Next to build multiple U/Ms in the Add Related Units window seen in Figure 7-30.

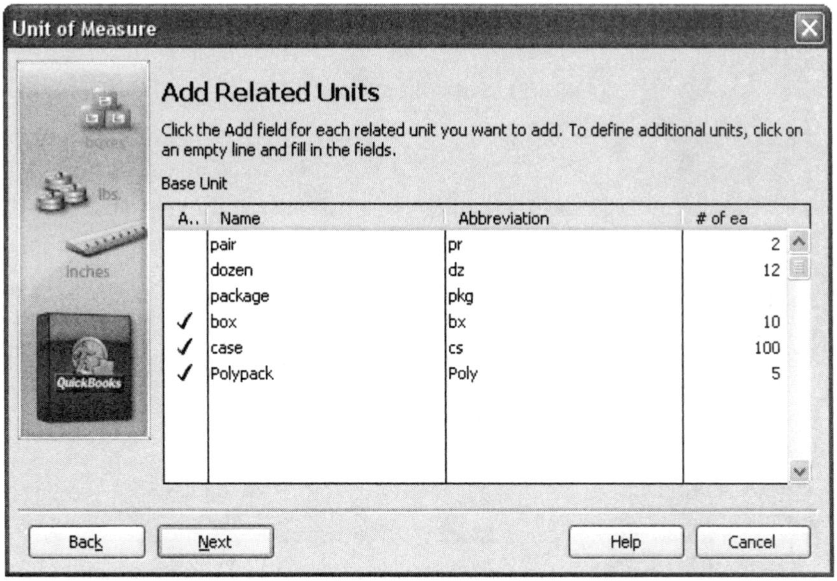

Figure 7-30: Add the units you can build and sell from your base unit.

Put a check mark next to each unit that you track, either for purchases or for sales, and indicate the number of "base units" (from the previous window) there are in each of these related units.

In this case, the system automatically offered built-in units except for Polypack, which I manually added. I checked only those units I store and sell, skipping those that I won't use.

Be sure to check the unit you use to purchase the item, even if you don't usually sell that unit. If the unit isn't available (e.g. you buy a skid or half skid), add it to the list and make sure it has a check mark. You need the purchase unit in the next window.

Click Next to select your default units of measure, as seen in Figure 7-31. Notice that the operative word is "default" – the unit of measure that will appear automatically in a purchase order or a sales transaction. When you are filling out the form, you can choose another unit from the drop-down list that contains all your added units for this U/M.

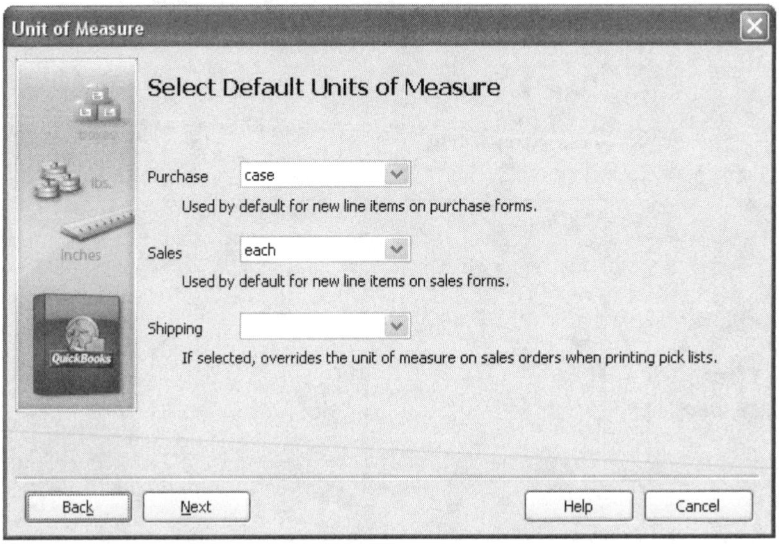

Figure 7-31: Save time when creating transactions by populating the transaction window with a default U/M.

Click Next, and give your Multiple U/M a name. QuickBooks provides a default name, but you can change it to text that you know everyone will recognize as a description for this U/M. Remember that this U/M will be available for linking to multiple items, so the name has to make sense to anyone setting up U/Ms for items.

Click Finish and then repeat these steps to create all the other Multiple U/Ms you need. QuickBooks creates a list of the U/M sets you create, on the Lists menu.

Changing or Removing the U/M for an Item

If you find that the U/M you linked to an item isn't working well, you can change the U/M function for that item. Open the item and go to the U/M field to make your changes:

- Select a different U/M for the item from the drop-down list.
- Create a new U/M that's suitable for this item by choosing <Add New> from the drop-down list.

- Highlight the current U/M and then press the Delete key to make the field blank, removing U/Ms from the item.

If you remove the U/M from the item, QuickBooks displays a message telling you that your action won't affect any transactions that were already completed using the U/M, but future transactions won't have a U/M filled out for this item. Since that's an intelligent approach, click Yes to confirm the removal.

Managing Units of Measurement

If you're using Multiple U/Ms, over the course of time, you'll need to manage the U/Ms you create. This section provides an overview of the available functions. All of the functions discussed in this section are available only for Multiple U/Ms.

Editing Units of Measurement

You can change the configuration of a U/M by editing it, and that task can be performed by clicking the Edit button next to the U/M field in the item record of any item that is using the U/M.

You can also edit a U/M by double-clicking its listing in the U/M Set List, which you open from the Lists menu. The changes you make are applied to all the items that are linked to this U/M. However, past transactions aren't changed to match your edits.

Removing Units of Measurement

QuickBooks provides no way to delete a U/M, but you can make a U/M inactive if it isn't working properly, or is no longer needed. When you make a U/M inactive, it no longer appears in drop-down lists on transaction forms or in item records. To accomplish this, right-click the U/M listing in the U/M Set List and choose Make U/M Set Inactive.

Creating Reports on Units of Measurement

QuickBooks offers three reports on your Units of Measurements, all of which are available from the Lists submenu of the Reports menu:

- Unit of Measure Set Listing, which lists the U/Ms with their Base and default U/Ms for purchasing and selling.
- Unit of Measure Sets With Related Units, which lists each U/M along with all of the related units you configured.
- Items with Units of Measure, which lists all the items that can accept U/M links and displays the U/M information for those items that have links.

All of these reports display only active U/Ms and active items, so if you're searching for something that appears to be missing, modify the report by going to the Filters tab, selecting the filter named Active Status, and then specifying All.

Chapter 8

Advanced Reporting Tools

Exporting report templates

Importing report templates

Closing date exception report

The QuickBooks Premier editions contain features for managing reports that aren't available in QuickBooks Pro. In this chapter, I'll go over some of the advanced reporting capabilities you have available in your Premier edition.

Exporting Reports as Templates

The ability to customize reports is one of the most popular features in QuickBooks. You can customize the layout, filter the content, and modify the sort order of reports. This means you can get exactly the information you want, omitting the need to wade through information you don't care about.

Adding to the power inherent in report customization is the ability to memorize a customized report. The memorization is intelligent, ignoring the actual data, and retaining only the customized settings for layout, filters, and sorted order. When a previously memorized report is opened, the data that appears is fetched from transactions, and is therefore current and correct.

QuickBooks Premier editions add a third layer of power to reports, by providing the ability to export templates of customized, memorized, reports. Here's how it works:

** Only QuickBooks Premier editions can export templates.
** All QuickBooks editions can import templates.

You can export a template when you want to move a customized report to another company file on your own system, or, if you're an accountant, you can export report templates to your clients to make sure you get exactly the reports you need.

WARNING: Report Templates are version (year) specific. As long as the template is for the same version, you can import it into any edition of QuickBooks – Pro or any Premier Edition.

Customizing Reports

A template is an exported copy of a memorized report, and it's assumed the report has been customized. However, the type and scope of the customizations you can apply are limited, because the report must be able to work with another company file.

When you click the Modify Report button in a report window, the tabs in the Modify Report dialog offer a wide range of customization options. The following sections describe the modifications you must avoid.

Selecting Display Options

When you modify a report, the Display tab of some reports has a Columns list. You can display or remove any of those columns. Generally, summary reports don't offer this list, but detail reports do.

You can customize the report by adding or removing columns, but you must be careful to avoid using any custom fields you created (see Figure 8-1).

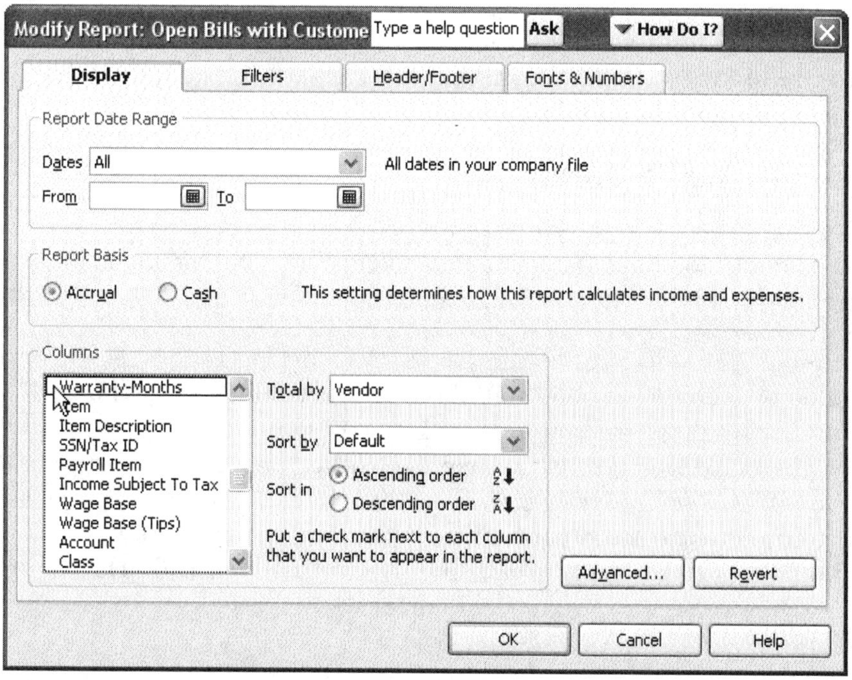

Figure 8-1: Deselect the columns for custom fields you created.

***TIP**: I frequently deselect the column labeled "left margin" (which is automatically selected), because removing that column makes it easier to fit more information on a printed page, and lessens the amount of scrolling required when you display reports on the screen.*

Selecting Filters

You cannot include filters that are unique to the company file that's open when you customize the report. Instead, as you choose the filters, you must be careful to select filters that work anywhere, anytime, for any QuickBooks company file.

For example, if you're filtering for accounts, you cannot select specific accounts. Instead, you must select account types (Income, Expense, etc.).

Most of the filters offer universal choices that allow you to customize the report to obtain the data you need. Some filters don't have lists; instead, they have simple options such as Open or Closed. You can't get into trouble with those filters, because they offer no opportunity to use data from the company file.

Memorizing Reports

After you create the customized report, heeding the warnings about omitting any specific data from your own company file, memorize it by clicking the Memorize button on the report window.

When you enter the name for the memorized report, be sure to create a name that makes its content clear to everyone. Names that are meaningful to you (because you knew what you wanted to accomplish with your customizations) may not work for other people. For example, the name "OpBillNoAge" may signify to you that the Open Bill report lacks the aging days because you removed the Age column. However, if you're planning to export the report, a name such as OpenBills-DateOnly", or "OpenBills-NoAging" might be a better report title.

Exporting a Template

QuickBooks creates templates for export by saving the report in its own proprietary format, which has a file extension .QBR. To export a memorized report as a template that can be imported into another QuickBooks company file, use the following steps:

1. Choose Reports → Memorized Reports → Memorized Report List.
2. In the Memorized Report List, select the report you want to export.
3. Click the Memorized Report button at the bottom of the window to display the command list.
4. Select Export Template to open the Specify Filename For Export dialog (which looks like a Save dialog).
5. Accept the default name for the template (which is the name of the report), or enter a different name.
6. Click Save.

Only the settings are saved in the template, not the data that appeared in the customized report. The data, of course, was specific to the QuickBooks company file that was open when you created the report.

By default, QuickBooks saves the template in the folder in which you installed QuickBooks. It's a good idea to create a different folder for your templates so you can find them easily (the QuickBooks folder is crowded). The best place to save your exported templates is in a subfolder named MyQBTemplates that you create under your My Documents folder

Sending a Template

If you're sending your report template to someone else (instead of importing into another company file on your own system), the easiest way to deliver the file is as an attachment to an e-mail message. Report templates (files with the extension .QBR) use very few bytes. You could also burn a CD and mail it.

Don't forget to send your recipient instructions for importing the template (see the section, "Importing a Report Template", later in this chapter).

Importing a Report Template

Importing a report template actually does nothing more than convert the template file into a memorized report. The report is added to the Memorized Report list of the company file that's open during the import process. To import a template, use the following steps:

1. Choose Reports → Memorized Reports → Memorized Report List.
2. Click the Memorized Report button at the bottom of the window, and select Import Template.
3. Navigate to the drive or folder that contains the template file, and double-click its listing.
4. In the Memorize Report dialog, enter a name for the report, or accept the displayed name (which is the name used by the person who exported the template).

The report is now available in the Memorized Reports list.

Creating Groups of Memorized Reports

It's a good idea to create memorized report groups, so you can quickly find the right report when you need to export its template. Create your groups to match the type of memorized reports you amass. Here's how to create a memorized report group:

1. Choose Reports → Memorized Reports → Memorized Report List, to open the Memorized Report List.
2. Click the Memorized Report button at the bottom of the window, and select New Group.
3. In the New Memorized Report Group dialog, enter a name for the group, and click OK.

If you already have some memorized reports that you want to move into the new group, use the following steps:

1. In the Memorized Report List window, select the report you want to move into a group.
2. Press Ctrl-E to edit the report listing.
3. Select the Save In Memorized Report Group check box.
4. Select the appropriate group from the drop-down list.
5. Click OK.

To add a new memorized report into an existing group, when you finish customizing the report, click Memorize. In the Memorize Report dialog, select the Save In Memorized Report Group check box, and then select the appropriate group from the drop-down list.

Exporting a Memorized Reports Group

If you've created report groups, you can export an entire group of memorized reports in one fell swoop. Use the following steps to accomplish this:

1. Choose Reports → Memorized Reports → Memorized Report List
2. In the Memorized Report List window, select the group you want to export.
3. Click the Memorized Report button, and choose Export Template from the menu.
4. In the Specify Filename For Export dialog, create a name for the file, or accept the default name that QuickBooks inserts. (QuickBooks uses the name of the group, followed by the word "Group".)
5. Click Save to create the file.

The recipient can import the group, adding this group to his or her Memorized Report List (covered next).

Importing a Memorized Reports Group

For the recipient, importing a report template file that is a group of memorized reports is the same as importing a single report template. When the template is imported, the recipient gains the new group, along with its contents (multiple memorized reports). The group name appears in the Memorized Report List window, and the individual reports are listed.

Closing Date Exception Report

The Closing Date Exception report, available only in QuickBooks Premier editions, tells you whether closed transactions were modified or created. To understand the importance of the Closing Date Exception report, you have to understand what closing the books means in QuickBooks.

QuickBooks doesn't "close" the books the way most other accounting software applications do. For businesses that use most other accounting software, closing a period is a definitive action, and can't be undone. Once closed, a period is locked, and no transactions in that period can be added, removed, or changed.

Those "real" closings have some important advantages. The biggest benefit to a closing process that's a true lock-down is that all the reports that were produced about the locked period remain accurate and valid forever, as are any tax returns that were filed using that data. There is no chance that anything can change.

Another benefit is the fact that someone bent on illegal activities (such as embezzling) cannot get into a prior period to hide an illegal transaction. This is a temptation that is based on the usually correct assumption that business owners (and even accountants) rarely look closely at prior period transactions.

On the other hand, a real closing procedure can be a frazzling experience, because you can't close the books until you're sure you've recorded everything that needs to be entered. I have many clients with accounting departments that fall behind on the day-to-day work for a few days each month, because they're closing the previous month.

The same thing happens, with even more intensity, every January or February, when it's time to close the year. Even with all that effort and pressure, it's not unusual to hear "uh oh" after the books are closed. The bookkeeper, controller, or accountant has found a transaction that should have been recorded in the prior year. It's too late!

QuickBooks Closing Date Procedures

When you close a year in QuickBooks, the lock you put into place isn't impenetrable. It's a combination lock (remember the lock on your high school locker?) and anyone can enter who knows, or can guess, the combination.

***TIP:** You can use the QuickBooks closing process every month, to close the previous month, if you wish. This is not a feature that is locked into a year-end only function.*

Setting a Closing Date

In QuickBooks, you close a year by setting a closing date in the Accounting category of the Preferences dialog. Choose Edit → Preferences, select the Accounting category in the left pane, move to the Company Preferences tab, and click Set Date/Password. Only the Admin user can gain access to this dialog.

Enter the date that signifies the end of the period in which users shouldn't change or add transactions (see Figure 8-2).

In addition to entering the date, you should specify a password to allow users (including yourself) to add or modify transactions on or before the closing date. The password is not required, but if it's omitted, any user can continue to record, edit, void, or delete transactions in the previous year.

If you don't create a password, when a user creates, modifies or deletes a transaction that carries a date falling in the closed year, QuickBooks issues the warning seen in Figure 8-3.

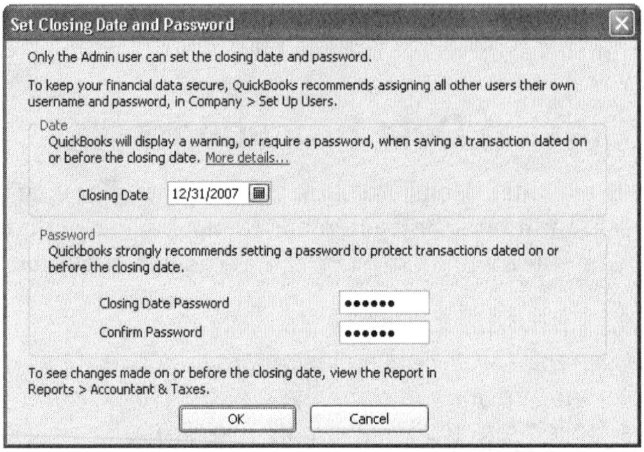

Figure 8-2: Enter your closing date to specify that all transactions on or before this date are closed.

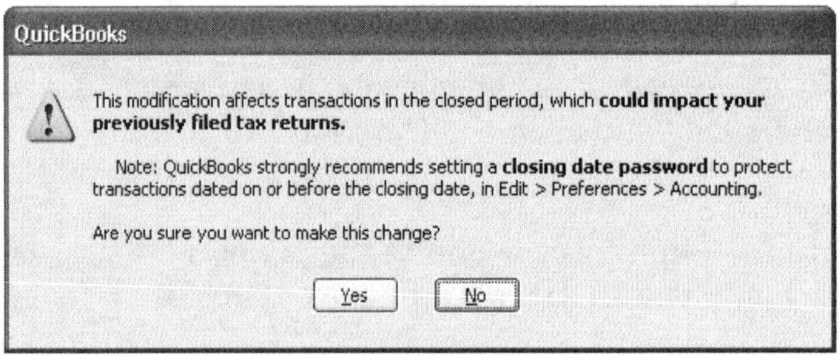

Figure 8-3: Clicking Yes lets any user add, remove, or change a transaction in a closed period.

If you specified a password when you set your closing date, QuickBooks asks the user for the password (see Figure 8-4). If the user enters the correct password, QuickBooks permits the user to add, remove, or modify transactions in the prior year.

Locking Users Out of the Prior Period

You can keep users out of the prior period by setting user permissions appropriately. This means that even if a user has discovered the password for entering prior period transactions, he or she can't perform the task.

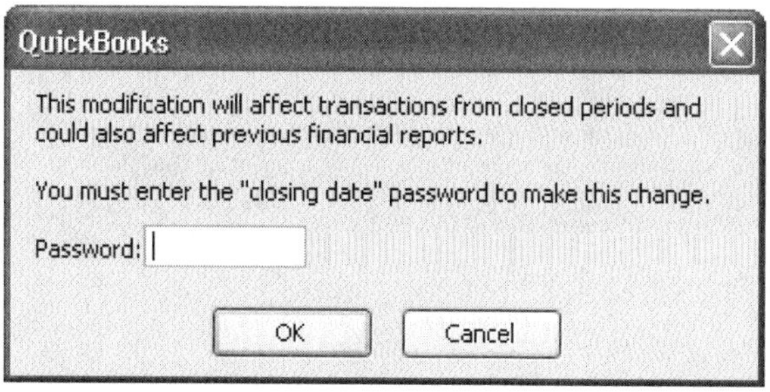

Figure 8-4: Anyone who knows the password can change the balances on which you based your tax return.

Even if you want to give a user full access to all the accounting functions, QuickBooks provides a way to stop that user from creating, changing, or deleting transactions in the closed period. In the last permissions window (see Figure 8-5), select No as the answer to the question about working in a closed period.

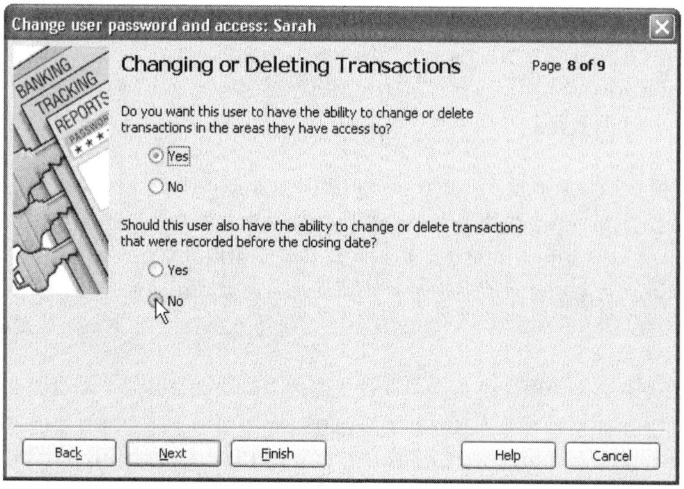

Figure 8-5: An ounce of prevention is worth a pound of cure.

Users with this permission denied can't work with a transaction that's dated on or before the closing date. When they try to save the transaction, QuickBooks stops the action with the message seen in Figure 8-6.

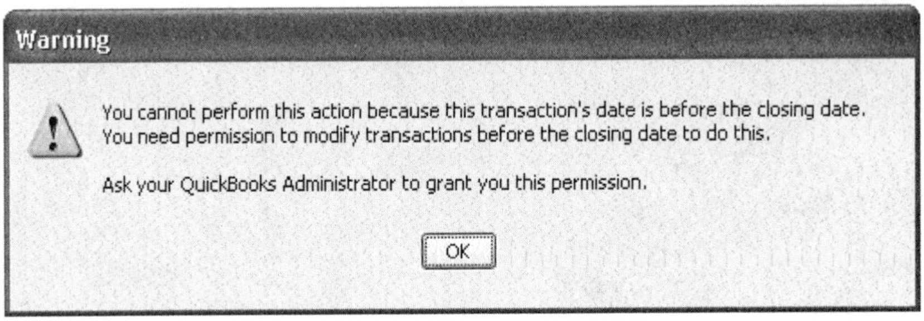

Figure 8-6: Even if this user has learned the password, the closing date is absolute.

***NOTE**: You can re-open your books after you've closed them. Just delete the Closing Date and click OK.*

Password Protection Doesn't Always Work

If a password is linked to the closing date, only users who know the password can work in the previous year. I've seen this paradigm fail many times, as I've worked with clients to uncover problems that turned out to be embezzlement activities.

I've encountered situations where a business owner trusted a user enough to give that person the password, and the trust was misplaced. Sadly, in a number of those cases, the nefarious user was a family member. (Business owners tend to entrust passwords to members of their family who work in the business, and that's not always a wise decision.)

I've also had clients who discovered illegal activities in a closed period that were eventually traced to employees who hadn't been given the password. In every case, the closing date password was easily available—a note in an unlocked drawer, an easy-to-guess password (the owner's birth date, nickname, dog's name, or other easy deduction), and even notes affixed to monitors.

I've found orders that were shipped with a date previous to the closing date, and the neer-do-well employee happily enjoyed the ill-gotten goods that were delivered. The shipment was often sent to an accomplice who was the customer on the transaction. The shipment didn't appear on reports that were generated as a matter of course, because the transactions didn't fall in the date range of the report (which is almost always a date range in the current fiscal year). Eventually, the accountant, or a sharp bookkeeper, may notice the problem, and the hunt for a solution sometimes (but not always) uncovers the crime.

Other problems I've encountered were inventory adjustments (to cover pilfering), and even the deletion of a check made out to cash that somehow made it through the reconciliation process without raising questions. However, to ensure long-term secrecy, the check was deleted *after* the books were closed. Because the changed balances don't show up on current reports, they frequently escape notice. If they *are* noticed, they're often difficult to track.

Sometimes, discovery occurs because of a disparity between the closing balances of the year-end reports, and the opening balances of current reports. Another clue is an out-of-sequence number, or a missing number. For example, if the first invoice in the current year is number 501, and you find that Invoice 506 is dated in the prior year, be suspicious.

If the transaction has been deleted (a missing transaction number), detection can be quite difficult. If the transaction wasn't deleted, it's easy to find the problem if the customer name attached to the transaction isn't familiar. However, a smart embezzler merges that customer into an existing customer, making the investigation more difficult.

Lest you think I dwell only on the darkest side of the world, let me hasten to tell you that the majority of incidents that involve messing around with transactions in the closed period aren't nefarious.

Innocent changes to transactions are frequently made by users who are honestly trying to correct a problem. These users think it's faster and more efficient to change a transaction that was entered erroneously last December than it is to create a journal entry in January to correct balances. For perfectly harmless reasons, users delete or void transactions in the previous year, or add transactions by dating them in the previous year.

Changes to previous periods drive accountants crazy, because the notion that a closing balance must equal the next opening balance is a basic rule of accounting. Incorrect opening balances can also affect your tax returns. And, of course, unexplained changes between a closing balance in one year and the opening balance in the next year can present difficult challenges if you're undergoing an audit.

Generating the Closing Date Exception Report

To view the Closing Date Exception Report, choose Reports → Accountant & Taxes → Closing Date Exception Report. The report lists all transactions that were added or changed to the closed year after the closing date was set. Figure 8-7 is an example of the report.

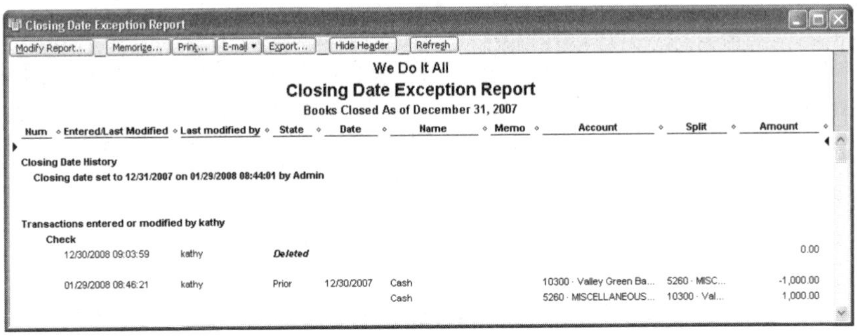

Figure 8-7: A user wrote a check to cash in the closed period, and then deleted it.

(Only users with permission to view sensitive accounting reports can open the report.)

Interpreting the Closing Date Exception Report

I think it's important to understand how to read and interpret the Closing Date Exception Report, which can be confusing.

The top of the report has the Closing Date History. If the closing date was set, then removed (the books were re-opened), and then the closing date was set again, the report shows that fact.

The section below the closing date information displays the details of each exception (change). A description of the type of transaction appears above each entry.

The columns display additional information about each transaction, and the important data is the following:

- Entered/Last Modified Date is the date on which the transaction was changed (or entered, if the transaction is new). This date is after the closing date, or the entry wouldn't exist in this report.
- Last Modified By is the name of the user who performed the task. If you're not using logins, you still know what was changed (which is the important financial information) but you won't know for sure who did it.
- State is the current state of this transaction (significant if there were multiple actions on a transaction).
- The Date column displays the date on which the transaction occurred.
- The columns on the right display the financial information (posting accounts, amount)

***TIP**: User logins don't work unless you enforce security rules. To make sure users bent on nefarious actions can't gain entry via another user's login, insist that all users close the company file when they leave their desks.*

Chapter 9

Planning and Forecasting

QuickBooks Premier editions include tools you can use to plan and predict your growth: Business Planner, and the Forecasting tool.

The Business Planner is a powerful software application that lets you project your business finances for the next three years. The business plan it produces is detailed and professional.

The forecasting tool lets you predict revenue and cash flow for a year. You can manipulate the data in your forecast to create "what if" scenarios that help you make decisions about the course and speed of your growth.

Business Planner

Business Planner is a robust application that walks you through the process of creating a comprehensive business plan, which is a detailed prediction of your company's future. The tool's user interface is wizard-like, and it works very much like the EasyStep Interview you use to set up a QuickBooks company file. A series of sections, each of which has multiple windows to go through, cover the categories involved in building a plan.

NOTE*: The business plan you produce is based on the format recommended by the U.S. Small Business Administration for loan applications or a bank line of credit.*

Creating a comprehensive business plan isn't a cakewalk, and you should plan on devoting quite a bit of time to complete yours, if you want a truly comprehensive plan. You can create a business plan for your own business, or, if you're an accounting professional, for a client's business.

Launch the Business Planner by choosing Company → Planning & Budgeting → Use Business Plan Tool. The program opens to the Welcome screen, which explains the processes involved in creating the business plan (see Figure 9-1). Click Next to move through the windows and the sections that follow.

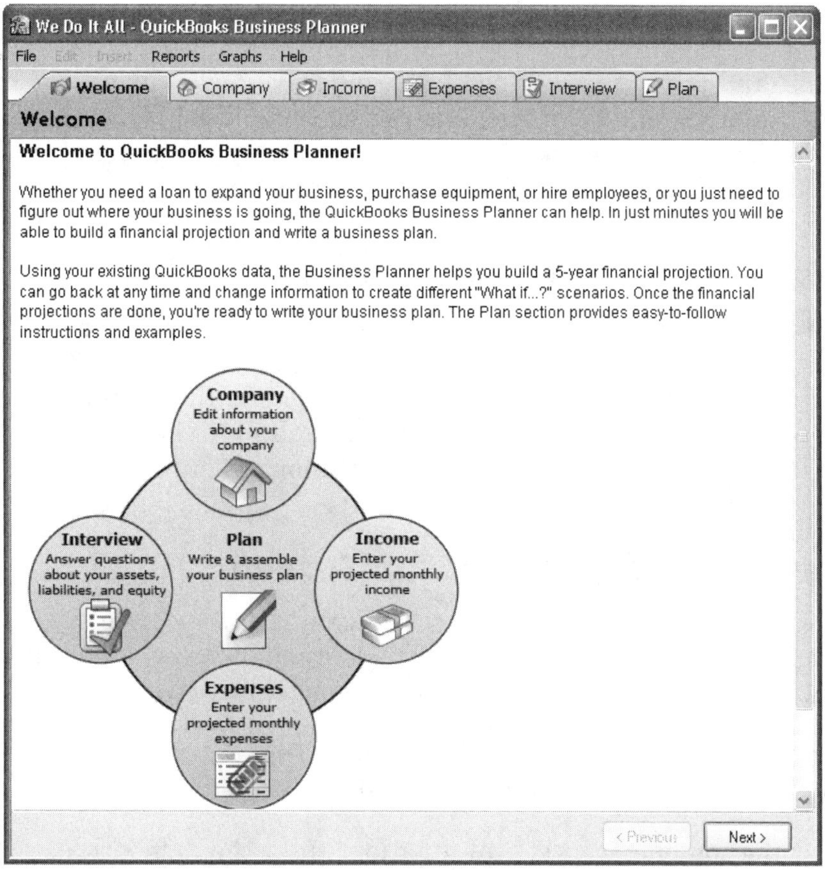

Figure 9-1: The Business Planner window has tabs for each section of the process.

***WARNING**: You must have a copy of Acrobat Reader to use Business Planner. If you don't have Acrobat Reader (or you have a very old copy of the software), QuickBooks issues a message that includes a link to the download page, and you can download the software (it's free). After you install the software launch the Business Planner again.*

Every time you close the Business Planner, QuickBooks automatically saves it in the folder in which your company file is stored, with the filename <*CompanyFileName*>.BPW. This means that each time you open the Business Planner, the information you've already entered remains, and you're taken to the last window you were using. To make changes to any information you entered earlier, click Previous to back up. You can take your time creating your plan without worrying about starting from scratch every time you open the software.

Entering Company Information

The first set of wizard windows is part of the Company Section, where you enter basic information about your business. Depending on the information you enter in each window, the questions in the ensuing windows differ. The following sections offer some guidelines to help you understand the questions you may see, and the information you're asked to enter.

General Company Information Section

A series of wizard windows appears, and you click Next to move through the windows. The data you enter in this section of the wizard appears on the cover of your printed plan, so enter information with that in mind.

For the company name, enter the name you do business as (if your business has both a legal name and a DBA name).

For the company contact information, enter the name, title, and telephone number of the person who will be the contact for the recipient of your plan. For example, if you're planning to give the business plan to a bank, use the name of the person who has the answers to any questions the bank's officers may ask. On the other hand, you may want to list the person who has the best relationship with the bank's officers.

Income Tax Information

Enter the income tax form you use. Only C Corporations (and some LLCs) pay taxes (using Form 1120), so if your business is organized as any other type of entity, no company tax information is calculated. Businesses other than C Corps (and LLCs that report as corporations) pay no income taxes (profits or losses are transferred to your personal tax return).

***TIP**: I've found that many small business owners have a problem finding the appropriate tax form if they're operating as a proprietorship. They look for Schedule C, which isn't listed in the drop-down list of tax forms. Instead, select Tax Form 1040, which is where proprietors file their business income. Schedule C is merely an attachment to that form.*

If your company files Tax Form 1120 (a C corp), the business planner calculates your estimated tax payments. After you select Tax Form 1120, and click Next, you're asked to estimate your corporate tax rate. Remember that you probably have a combined tax rate, because you have to consider both federal and state corporate taxes. For your convenience, the wizard displays a federal tax table you can consult.

Incidentally, even if you remit your estimated corporate taxes quarterly, the business planner calculates the payments on a monthly basis, using the profits for that month. If a month shows a loss, the planner carries over the loss to the next month in order to calculate income taxes.

If your business uses any other tax form, the software doesn't factor in business income tax payments. When you click next, the wizard asks you to fill in the estimated monthly amount for owner distributions.

***TIP**: If your company is an S Corporation, owner distributions don't include salaries paid to the owners (those amounts are treated as expenses).*

Customer Credit Information

In the next window, enter the approximate percentage of your sales that are credit-based. If you don't extend credit to your customers, enter zero, and you won't see the ensuing windows that deal with receivables.

Except for over-the-counter retail sales businesses, most businesses provide credit to their customers. Using agreed upon terms of credit, you send invoices, which means you probably have current (or even overdue) receivables.

NOTE: *Credit card sales are cash sales, and accepting credit cards from customers is not the same as extending credit.*

If you entered any figure except zero for the question about the percentage of sales that involve credit, the next window asks about terms. Select the payment terms you offer customers from the drop-down list. If you offer multiple terms, enter the terms you apply most frequently.

The drop-down list doesn't offer any terms that imply discounts for timely payment (e.g. 2%10 Net 30), because the business planner doesn't factor in those discounts. The terms drop-down list includes the common terms: Less than 30, Net 30, Net 60, Net 90, Net 120.

In the next window, enter the percentage of your credit sales that you think could qualify as bad debt. Bad debt means money owed to you that you're fairly sure you'll never collect.

Business Plan Start Date

Enter the start date for the business plan, which doesn't necessarily have to coincide with the start date of your fiscal year. By default, the selection is the first month of your next fiscal year.

Enter a start date that seems appropriate for the purpose of your business plan, and for the recipient of your business plan documentation.

For example, you may have a specific project in mind (physical office expansion, product line expansion, and so on), for which you're presenting the business plan to banks or investors. Use a business plan start date that matches, or comes close to, the date on which you plan to begin this new financial project.

Income Projection

In the Income section, you face several chores. You must set up income categories (you can have up to twenty), and project the income for each category for the next three years.

A Projection Wizard is available to help you enter figures based on data the Projection Wizard pulls from your QuickBooks company file. The Projection Wizard saves you a lot of work, and you can always change any of the figures that are automatically entered if you want to create "what if" scenarios.

However, if you've just started using QuickBooks, you won't have sufficient data in your company file to extract anything meaningful, so you must enter the information manually.

Even if you have sufficient data in your QuickBooks company file, you may prefer to enter the income information manually, especially if you're about to embark on a new product or service, or you've just found a new customer base. In that case, you probably want to project income that reflects your new, expanded, business expectations.

If you're an accounting professional who is creating the business plan and projections for a client, you can manually enter the figures you obtained from your client. Or, you can ask the client for a copy of the company file, load it in QuickBooks, and launch the business plan software. Then you can let the wizard fetch data from the file.

Open the Projection Wizard by clicking its toolbar icon, which isn't at the top of the Business Planner window; instead, it's atop the income category table (see Figure 9-2).

In the following sections, I'll cover both scenarios, starting with the Projection Wizard, and then explaining how to enter projections manually.

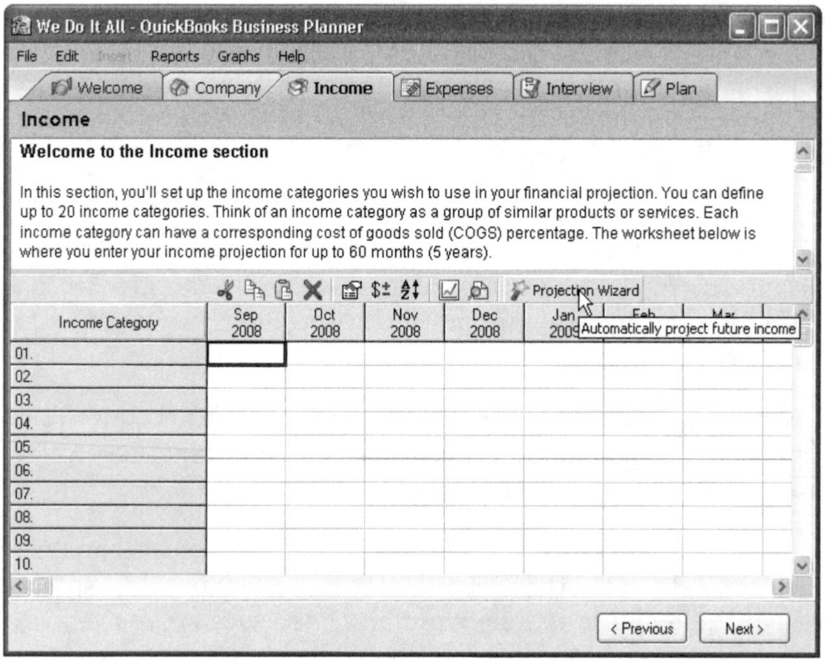

Figure 9-2: You can launch the Projection Wizard whenever you wish.

Using the Projection Wizard

The Projection Wizard opens with an introductory window. Click Next to begin the real work. Enter the beginning date for your business plan. By default, the wizard enters the month and year you earlier specified as the beginning of your business plan, but you can change that date.

Choose the Projection Basis

When you click Next, the wizard examines the company data, and then asks how to proceed (see Figure 9-3).

The method you choose depends on the amount of data in your QuickBooks company file, and the financial differences among the months of data. The Business Planner uses monthly data to project a percentage of increase (or decrease).

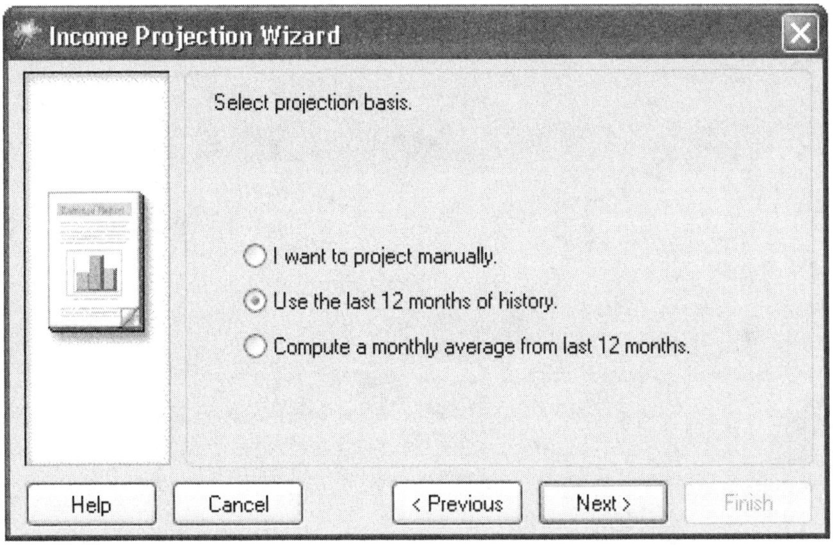

Figure 9-3: Select the method you want to use to project future income.

If you select the option I Want To Project Manually, the wizard closes and you're returned to the Business Planner. In the ensuing sections I'll assume you didn't choose that option.

If you select the option Use The Last 12 Months Of History, the algorithm is rather complicated, and is adjusted to take into consideration the current month, and the interval between your first month and the current month. The algorithm also attaches more weight to recent months than it does to earlier months.

If your recent months have shown a substantial upturn or downturn in performance, and the cause of that inconsistency isn't permanent, those monthly figures might influence the projections, and make them less reliable. In that case, tell the wizard Compute A Monthly Average From Last 12 Months.

Apply a Growth Factor

When you click Next, you're offered the opportunity to apply a yearly growth factor (see Figure 9-4). Select a number from the drop-down list, or enter a number directly into the field. The number is interpreted as a percentage.

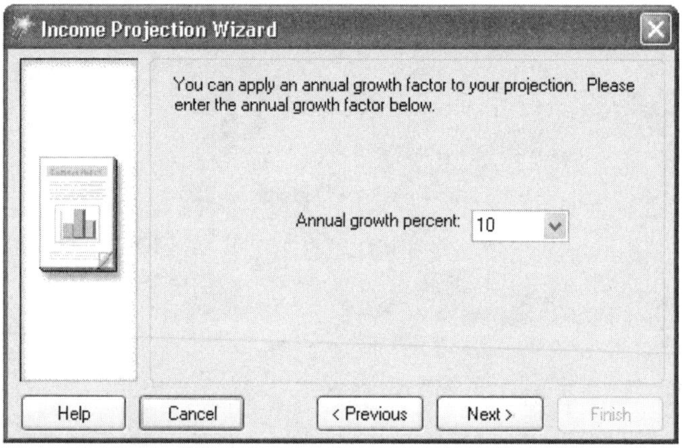

Figure 9-4: Apply the annual growth to be considered in your projection.

Select the Income Categories to Project

Click Next to see a list of the income accounts the wizard found in your chart of accounts. Each account is pre-selected for inclusion in the wizard's calculations (see Figure 9-5).

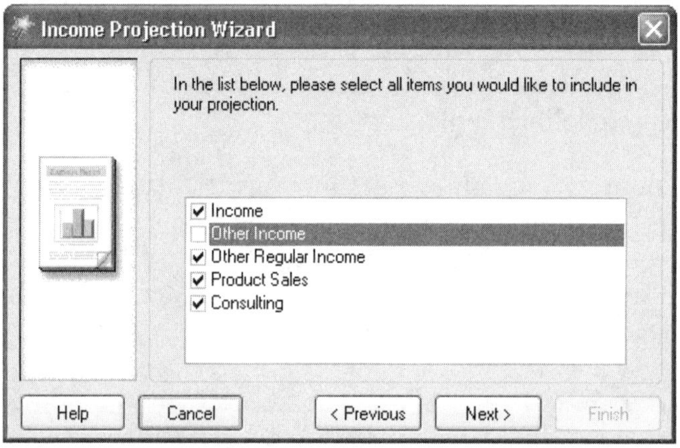

Figure 9-5: Deselect any income type that doesn't belong in your projection.

You can deselect any income account you don't want to use by clicking the check box to remove the check mark. For example, it's common to exclude an interest income account, or a miscellaneous income account that doesn't reflect ongoing revenue. Click Finish to start the calculations.

The wizard only selects active accounts. If you've made an account inactive and you want to use it for your projection, close the Projection Wizard (you don't have to close the Business Planner) and activate that account.

View the Results

The wizard performs its calculations and fills in the monthly figures, as seen in Figure 9-6. You may see an informational message first, telling you that the wizard used a percentage of gross revenue to calculate cost of goods. The message also explains that you can change the wizard's mathematical assumptions by editing the properties of any income category (see the section "Editing the Properties Behind the Data").

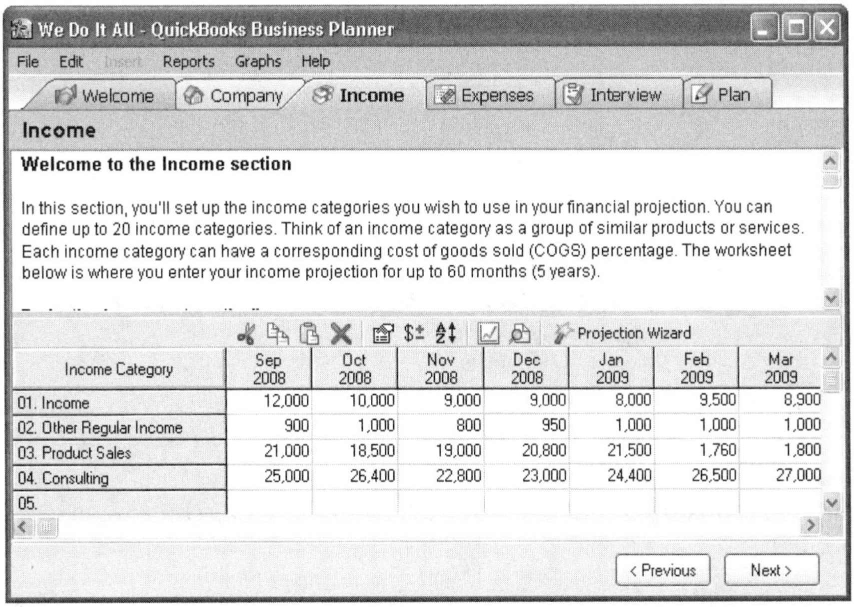

Figure 9-6: The wizard enters monthly figures for a 36-month projection.

Editing the Wizard's Data

You can edit the data the wizard automatically inserts. It's important to note that the wizard automatically adjusts income figures by subtracting a percentage of the gross to cover cost of goods. You can clean up those numbers, either because the wizard's percentage for cost of goods is radically different from your real costs, or because you don't have any cost of goods deductions since you only sell services.

To change the contents of a cell, select it. Then enter a number to replace the existing number. If you want to change the number by a specific percentage, after you select the cell, press Ctrl-F (or click the Function icon on the toolbar) to open the Functions dialog for the cell, seen in Figure 9-7. Then specify the percentage by which you want to raise or lower the figure.

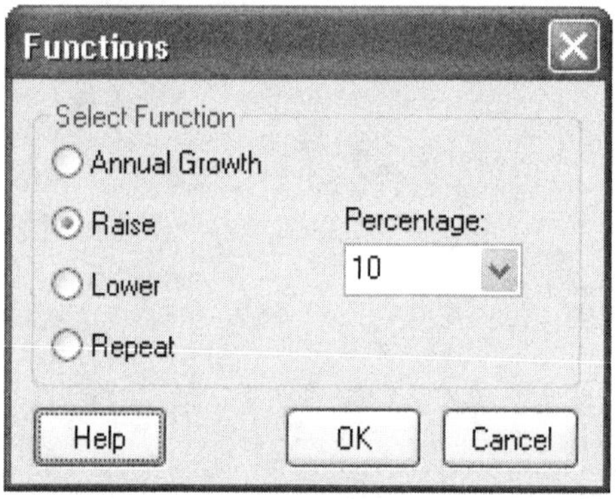

Figure 9-7: Use the Functions dialog to change the value of a cell by a percentage.

You can also edit the calculation basis for an entire row by clicking the row heading (the title on the left edge of the row) to select the entire row. Then press Ctrl-F (or click the Function icon on the toolbar). The same Functions dialog appears, but its impact is on the row instead of a single cell.

Here are the guidelines for using the Functions dialog for a row:

- Select Annual Growth, and then enter a percentage figure, to change the annual growth projection you'd previously entered for the selected row. This is a good way to project your company's future income by revenue type, instead of using a single percentage for the entire business.
- Select Raise or Lower, and then enter a percentage, to change all the figures in the row by that percentage.
- Select Repeat to copy the contents of the first cell in the row to all the other cells in the row.

Editing the Properties Behind the Data

You can change the basic properties of a row (an income account), including its title, and the way Business Planner calculates Cost of Sales. Double-click a row heading to open its Properties dialog, seen in Figure 9-8.

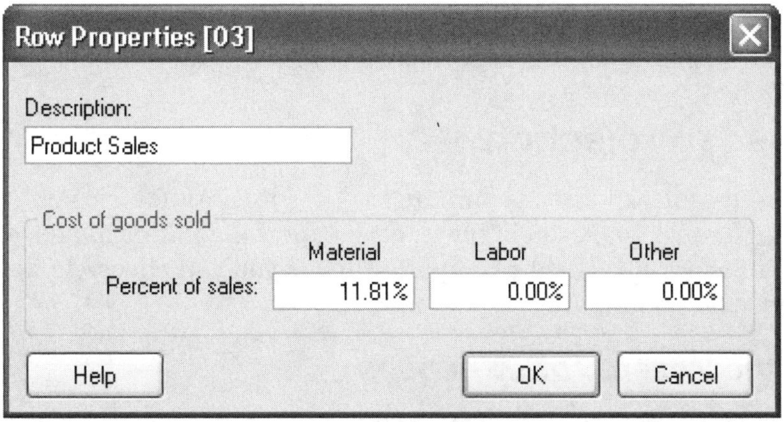

Figure 9-8: Changing the properties for an income category changes the way the data is calculated.

If the selected income category has labor or other costs in addition to, or instead of, standard cost of goods, adjust the data in the dialog to gain a more realistic projection. If no costs of goods are involved for this type of income, change all the fields to zero.

Entering Income Data Manually

If you opt to skip the Projection Wizard, or if the wizard tells you there isn't enough data in your company file to proceed, you can enter the numbers for your income manually. Click Next, and then click Finish in the next wizard window to close the Projection Wizard. The bottom of the program window resembles a blank spreadsheet, with rows for categories and columns for months.

Double-click the row header for the first category to open its Properties dialog (refer back to Figure 9-8), and enter the title (an income category). If the category involves a product, also enter the information for costs of goods (in percentages). If the category is a service, you can omit the cost of goods figures.

After you set up all your categories, you can begin entering figures. Move horizontally through the months by pressing the Tab key. If you want to fine tune your figures by raising or lowering amounts by a percentage, click the Functions icon to perform the task.

Expenses Projection

Entering data for expenses is similar to entering data for income. The Projection Wizard is available for finding expense account names and amounts in your QuickBooks company file, or you can choose to design the expenses section manually.

Using the Wizard for Expenses

You can click the Projection Wizard icon to automate your expenses projections, which involves almost exactly the same steps involved in using the wizard for projecting income. Click Next to move through the windows.

As with income projections, you can apply an annual growth percentage to the expense data in your business plan.

The Projection Wizard selects and displays the expense accounts it will use for the projection, selecting both parent accounts and subaccounts. The Projection Wizard usually skips the following expenses:

- Interest
- Depreciation
- Amortization
- Bad debt expenses

If any of those expenses are checked, uncheck them. Business Planner automatically calculates the appropriate amounts for the expense types it skips, using information from answers you provide as you go through the interview.

You can manipulate the data the Projection Wizard enters. Use the instructions in the previous section on Income Projections to define expense categories, enter financial data, and set the calculation methods.

Entering Expenses Manually

As with the income section, you can enter the numbers for your expenses manually, and use that data for your projections.

Double-click the row header for the first category to open its Properties dialog and enter the title (an expense category). After you set up all your categories, you can begin entering figures. Move horizontally through the months by pressing the Tab key. If you want to fine tune your figures by raising or lowering amounts by a percentage, click the Functions icon to use the utilities it offers.

Interview Section

The next part of the Business Planner is the Interview section. Most of the information you enter in this section is connected to your balance sheet accounts (assets, liabilities, and equity).

Assets

The wizard displays the current balances in your asset accounts, including cash, fixed assets, accumulated depreciation for fixed assets, accounts receivable, and any other asset accounts (see Figure 9-9). These figures are taken from your company file.

The current balances are considered opening balances for the business plan. If you expect significant changes in any of these accounts before the first day of your business plan, make an adjustment to the appropriate account(s) in the Balance column.

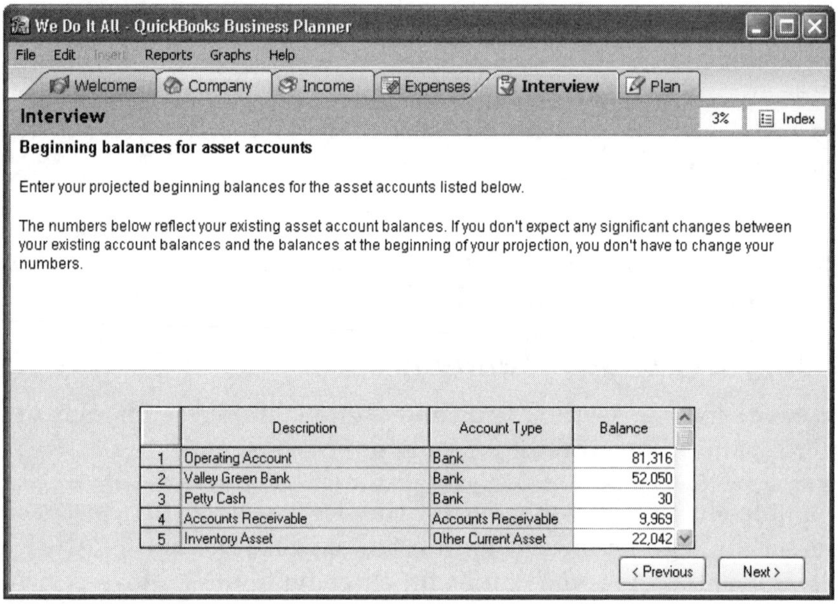

Figure 9-9: The Business Planner transfers data from your general ledger.

Minimum Bank Balances

The next window asks for the minimum bank balance your company must have available at all times. (The window also displays the current balance in each of your bank accounts.) Enter an amount that represents the total cash on hand you believe to be a minimum for sustaining your business.

To define the minimum balance, you must consider your monthly expenses, the number of times you have unexpected expenses (and their average amounts), and any other bank balance considerations you must meet. There are no rules or percentages for you to follow, this is a figure that is closely related to your type of business, and the way you do business. Ask your accountant for advice if you're having difficulty ascertaining a number.

Inventory

The next window asks if you maintain inventory, and if you answer affirmatively, the ensuing windows ask for information related to inventory issues, including the following:

- Inventory related accounts (assets, cost of goods sold, and expenses).
- Terms you have with vendors that supply inventory items. Only net terms are offered in the drop-down list, the Business Planner ignores discounts for timely payment.
- Inventory levels. Specify fixed or variable. Companies with fixed levels usually have regular, predictable, sales of products (especially common with retail businesses). Companies with variable levels usually have irregular sales, and commonly respond to special orders, seasonal sales, or other variable patterns.
- Inventory values. If you select a fixed inventory level, you need to specify the amount of inventory you maintain, in dollars. If you select a variable inventory level, you must specify the number of days of inventory you like to keep on hand.

New Asset Purchases

The Business Planner needs to know whether you plan to purchase additional assets at the beginning of the business plan projection. The assets can be anything except inventory, such as the following:

- Land
- Buildings
- Building improvements
- Equipment (business, manufacturing, vehicles, furniture, fixtures, etc.)
- Deposits

If you select No, the Business Planner moves on to the next category (Liabilities). If you select Yes, you have additional information to enter. Start by providing information about the category and cost of your upcoming asset purchase.

The Business Planner asks if you'll be financing any of the asset purchases. If you respond in the affirmative, enter the loan information.

Specify whether the loan is a standard loan (fixed monthly payments covering interest and principal), or a one-pay loan (interest only, with a single payment for principal at the end of the loan). The Business Planner can calculate the monthly payment, term, interest rate, or total amount of the loan, as long as you enter data in three of those four categories.

Liabilities

The next part of the Interview section is about your company's liabilities. The Business Planner displays the liability accounts it finds in your chart of accounts, along with the current balance for each of those accounts.

Set Beginning Balances for Liability Accounts

The Business Planner needs to establish beginning balances for the three years of the projection. You can change the amount of any displayed balance to reflect a more accurate amount for projecting your company's financial position.

Enter Line of Credit Information

All of the accounts of the type Credit Card are displayed, along with their current balances. In addition, the Business Planner displays the names of your accounts of the type Current Liability, and asks if any of these accounts are line of credit accounts.

The current balances of the accounts you select as line of credit accounts are added to the total balances of your credit cards, and the grand total is treated as your current line of credit obligation.

In the next window, enter the total credit limit for the aggregate line of credit accounts. If you don't know the limit for any credit card, try to find a copy of a bill—the limit is displayed on every statement you receive. In the next window, enter the average interest rate for all your line of credit accounts.

Long Term Loans

In the Long Term Loans section, the Business Planner displays the name and current balance of all the accounts in your chart of accounts that are of the type Long Term Liabilities.

Enter the description, type of loan, APR, interest rate, and other financial information for each long-term loan.

Investing in Your Business

As you entered data in each of the Business Planner windows, the software performed calculations in the background. The calculations took into consideration your income, the status of your receivables, your debt, and other financial factors. The results of the calculations are displayed in the next window.

If no additional capital is deemed to be required to meet your financial goals and obligations, you're asked if you'd like to invest capital anyway. If you're planning to infuse your business with capital, enter the amount; otherwise leave the amount at zero, and click Next.

However, as a result of the calculations, you may be advised to provide additional capital to meet your monthly expenses over the course of the three years of the projection. For example, if you'd indicated you were planning to purchase an automobile, and didn't indicate an auto loan, you're probably going to be short of cash. Or, perhaps you entered a figure for a minimum bank balance that is larger than your current capital can handle.

The Business Planner displays the amount you need to invest to cover the shortage. Enter the amount you're planning to put towards the shortage, and click Next. If you didn't enter an amount sufficient to cover the shortage, the next window asks about the loans you're planning to cover your shortage.

The next two windows ask about financial transactions you may be considering during the three years of the projection. Enter the amounts for any additional assets you think you may purchase, and the amounts of any loans you think you may incur.

Writing Your Business Plan

Now that all the information about your company's finances has been recorded in the Business Planner, you can begin writing your business plan.

Business plans include detailed written sections that cover a wide range of topics. You must explain the figures, your plans for growth, your marketing goals, and so on. The terminology you use should be chosen with the reader in mind (a bank, a venture capitalist, a potential partner, etc.).

As seen in Figure 9-10, the Business Planner provides assistance by displaying the components of the written plan in the left pane. Expand each section by clicking the plus sign, which reveals the subsections. Move through the components by clicking Next.

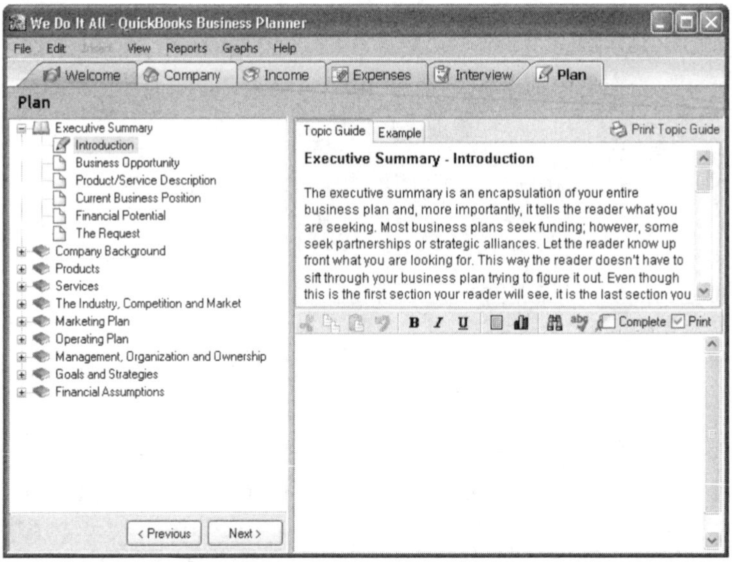

Figure 9-10: Step through each section in the left pane to complete the written plan

---

***TIP**: Click the Example tab to see sample text for each component.*

The writing area offers standard formatting tools so you can make the written plan look professional. In addition, the toolbar has icons for inserting data and graphs (linked to the data) from the Income and Expenses sections you completed in the Business Planner.

***TIP**: Click the Print Topic Guide button above the writing area to print helpful guidelines about the current topic, or about all topics. You can opt to include the sample text in your printout.*

You may find that some of the subsections in the left pane are irrelevant to your business, and if so, just skip them. You can rename the section titles you're using in your plan, except for "Introduction".

There's no hard and fast rule that you have to write your plan using the order in which the categories are presented in the left pane. You're perfectly free to organize your writing in a way that makes sense for your company.

Previewing Your Business Plan

To see a preview of the layout of your plan, choose File → Preview Business Plan from the Business Planner menu bar. The Preview Business Plan window displays a summary of your plan's contents (see Figure 9-11). Notice that the financial projections have been placed in the appendixes for the reader's reference.

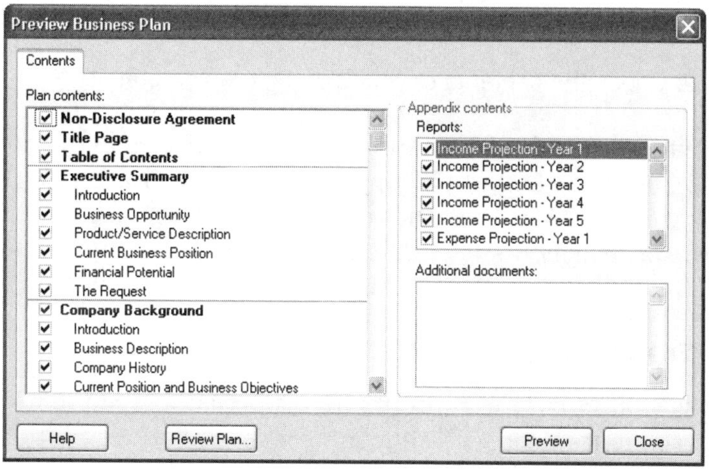

Figure 9-11: Check the Table of Contents to make sure everything you wanted to cover is there.

To view your plan, click the Preview button on the Preview Business Plan window. The document is a PDF file, so you must have Acrobat Reader installed to view it. Your plan opens in the Preview window as a formatted document (see Figure 9-12).

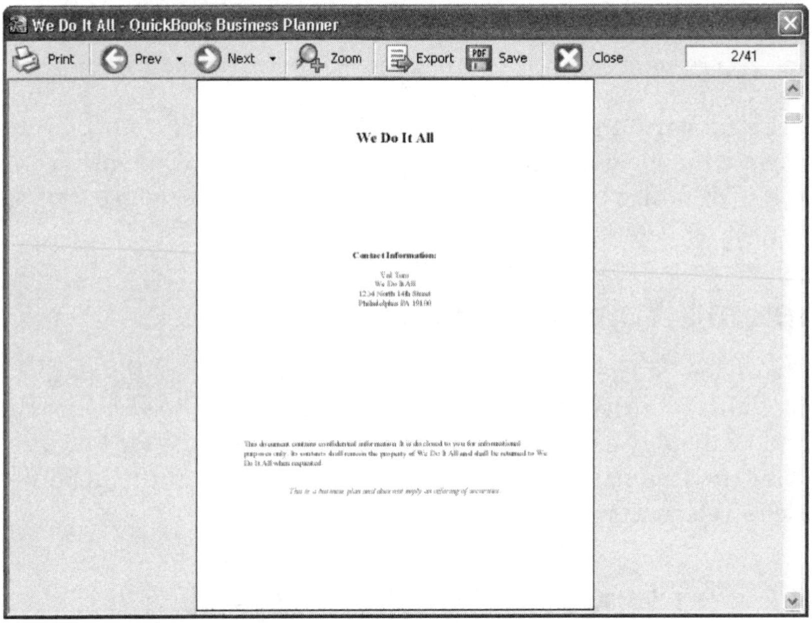

Figure 9-12: Check the contents of your plan before you print it.

Use the Next and Previous buttons on the toolbar to move through the pages of the plan. The box in the upper right corner indicates the current page being viewed, as well as the total number of pages. Click Zoom to zoom in on the currently displayed page so you can see the contents clearly.

Customize the Plan Contents

You may want to customize the contents for a particular recipient—different types of recipients need different information. You can deselect parts of the plan before you preview and print it. Deselecting a component does not remove it, or its contents, from your business plan, it merely omits the component from the preview document and the printed document you produce at this time.

- To remove an entire section from the preview/printed document, remove the check mark from the section title.
- To exclude specific topics, remove the check mark from the appropriate topic title.
- Deselect an Appendix document by removing the check mark from the listing.
- Deselect any unnecessary additional documents you added to your plan.

After you select and deselect content, click Preview to preview the plan in its current state.

***NOTE**: It's best to preview the entire plan to make sure it contains no mistakes before you customize it for any particular recipient.*

Print the Business Plan

To print the plan as previewed, click the Print icon on the toolbar. Specify the number of copies to print, and select the page range:

- All
- Current Page
- Pages From X to Y (substitute starting and ending page numbers for X and Y)

Click OK to begin printing your plan. If you have multiple printers, and the selected printer isn't the one you want to use, close the Preview window and return to the main QuickBooks Business Planner window.

Save the Business Plan as a PDF File

You can save the plan as a PDF file instead of printing it if you want to send it to the recipient via e-mail, or on a CD. To accomplish this, click the Save icon on the toolbar.

In the Save Plan As PDF dialog, name the document, and save it in any folder you choose. By default, the Save As PDF dialog selects the folder in which your company files are stored, but you can change the folder.

Export the Business Plan

Click Export to send the file to your word processor. If you have Microsoft Excel installed on your computer, the Export dialog includes an option to export the financial projections (your appendixes) to a Microsoft Excel spreadsheet.

The text part of your business plan is loaded in Word, and you can format, edit, and otherwise manipulate the document as you wish. The file is exported to Word as an RTF (Rich Text Format) file, which means it can be opened in any word processor without changing the formatting or graphics. To save the document, choose File → Save As from the Word menu bar and choose Microsoft Word Document as the File Type, and specify a location and filename.

The non-text part of the plan (the spreadsheet-type information about accounts and amounts and the projections) is loaded in Excel, with a separate worksheet for each year's income and expense projection.

The Word document does not contain the information that was exported to Excel; instead, the document contains links to the Excel document. Clicking a link opens Excel with the linked worksheet displayed.

If you print the business plan from the Word and Excel files, it doesn't have the same layout as printing the plan from the Business Plan Tool. You must collate the pages manually, and the Table of Contents in the Word Document won't be accurate.

Backing Up the Business Plan

QuickBooks backs up your business plan file as part of the standard QuickBooks backup process. However, if you have to restore your company file, the business plan file (with the extension .BPW) is not restored directly to the folder you choose to restore your file. Instead, the .BPW file, in addition to other restored auxiliary files, resides in a folder named

Miscellaneous Files, which is a subfolder of a folder named Restored_<*CompanyFileName*>_Files. This folder structure is created by QuickBooks when you restore a company file backup. Copy the .BPW file from the Miscellaneous Files subfolder to the parent folder in which your restored company file resides.

You can make a separate backup of your business plan while you're working in the Business Plan Tool by choosing choose File → Backup on the Business Planner window. In the Back Up dialog, choose a location for the backup file (My Documents is a good choice).

Then, if something happens to your business plan file (not the same as losing your company file and needing to restore it), you can restore the business plan file from within the tool. Choose File → Restore on the QuickBooks Business Planner window and locate the backup file. Select the file's listing and click Open, then follow the prompts to restore your plan.

Forecasting

You can create a forecast to help you predict your future revenue and cash flow, and then use the data in the forecast to create "what if" scenarios that help you plan and control the growth of your business.

> ***TIP****: A forecast is sometimes called a Cash Flow Budget.*

A good forecast doesn't have to be terribly complicated; it just has to provide the information you need to plan for survival, or for expansion (depending on the current state of your business and your reason for creating the forecast).

The forecasting tool in QuickBooks works on a one-year basis, which is the common duration for a forecast. The forecast is based on income and expense accounts, although you can further narrow it by focusing on a customer or a class.

When you create a forecast, you're bound to notice that the user interface, as well as the processes, is very similar to the QuickBooks budget feature. In fact, everything about a forecast smells a lot like a budget.

I couldn't find an official set of definitions that spelled out the differences between a forecast and a budget, but most accountants think of these two documents as entirely different from each other. Of course, if you ask an accountant, "What's the difference?" you get a rather broad answer. My own accountant tells me that in his mind, a forecast is a set of projections you make based on both history and any logical assumptions you care to make about the future, while a budget is based on the "knowns", and excludes assumptions.

Creating a Forecast

To create a forecast, choose Company → Planning & Budgeting → Set Up Forecast. If this is the first forecast you're creating, you see the Create New Forecast window. If this is not the first forecast you're creating, the last forecast you created opens. Click Create New Forecast if you want to create a new forecast.

Enter the year for this forecast. By default, QuickBooks fills in the forecast year field with next year, but if it's early in the current year, you may prefer to create a forecast for this year. Click Next.

Setting the Criteria for a Forecast

In the next window, you can select the criteria for this forecast. The criteria for accounts are set in stone; you must use Profit & Loss accounts for your forecast. However, you can set additional criteria, such as basing the forecast on a customer, a job, or a class.

In this discussion, I'm going to assume you aren't setting additional criteria, and QuickBooks also assumes you aren't setting additional criteria, because the No Additional Criteria option is selected by default. Click Next to move on.

Choosing the Method for Obtaining Data

In the next window, specify whether you want to create your forecast with data you enter manually, or with data from your QuickBooks company file. Then click Finish.

Of course, if you just started using QuickBooks, you have no data for last year, so you'll have to enter the data manually. If you opt to use existing QuickBooks data, monthly data from the prior year is transferred to the forecast window (see Figure 9-13). If you chose manual data entry, the forecast window has no data.

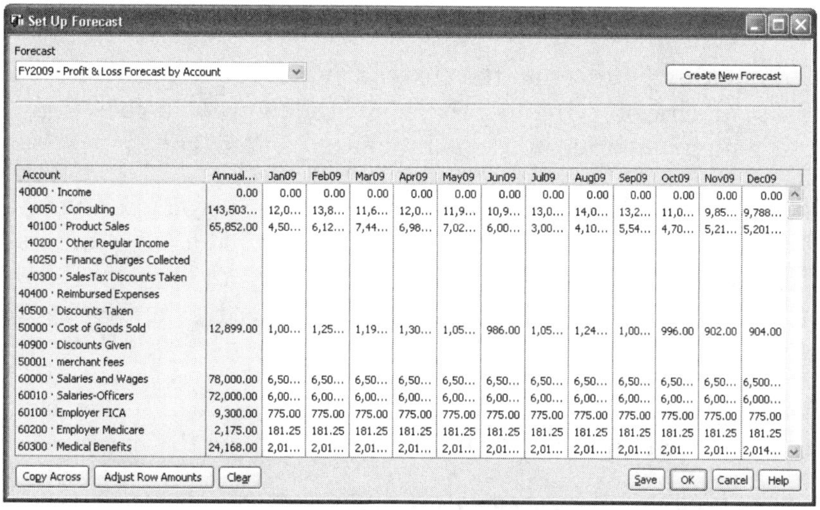

Figure 9-13: This forecast is for next year, so this year's monthly totals are loaded to serve as a base.

Entering Data Manually

If you want to enter the data manually, you can run a Profit & Loss report to get an idea of the actual numbers (choose Reports → Company & Financial → Profit & Loss Standard).

If you're creating a forecast because you're expecting to change the way you do business, the existing numbers may not be the figures you want to insert in your forecast. Use the numbers in the Profit & Loss report as a base, enlarging or reducing totals to match what you think your plan for the next year will produce.

Data Entry Shortcuts

To save you time (and extraordinary levels of boredom), QuickBooks provides some shortcuts for entering forecast figures. You can use these tools if you're entering your data manually, or if you're changing existing data to create a new scenario.

Copy a Number across the Months

To copy a monthly figure from the current month (the month where your cursor is) to all the following months, enter the figure and click Copy Across. The numbers are copied to all months to the right.

This is handier than it seems. It's obvious that if you enter your rent in the first month, and choose Copy Across, you've saved a lot of manual data entry. However, if your rent is raised in June, you can increase the rent figure from June to December by selecting June, entering the new figure, and clicking Copy Across.

The Copy Across button is also the quick way to clear a row. Delete the data in the first month and click Copy Across to make the entire row blank.

Automatically Increase or Decrease Monthly Figures

You may want to raise an income account by an amount or a percentage starting in a certain month, because you expect to offer new products and services, or increase your customer base.

On the other hand, you may want to raise an expense account because you're expecting to spend more on supplies, personnel, or other costs as the year proceeds.

Select the first month that needs the adjustment and click Adjust Row Amounts to open the Adjust Row Amounts dialog seen in Figure 9-14.

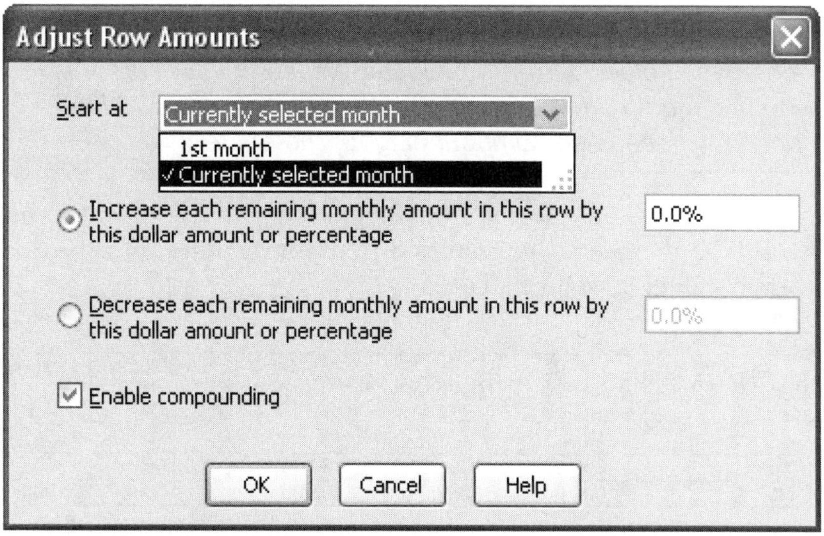

Figure 9-14: Automatically increase or decrease amounts across the months.

Choose 1st Month or Currently Selected Month as the starting point for the calculations. You can choose 1st Month no matter where your cursor is on the account's row. You must click in the column for the appropriate month if you want to choose Currently Selected Month.

- To increase or decrease the selected month, and all the months following, by a specific amount, enter the amount.
- To increase or decrease the selected month and all the months following, by a percentage, enter the percentage rate and the percentage sign.

Compounding Automatic Changes

If you select Currently Selected Month, the Adjust Row Amounts dialog adds an additional option named Enable Compounding. When you enable compounding, the calculations for each month are increased or decreased based on a formula starting with the currently selected month and taking into consideration the resulting change in the previous month.

***TIP**: Although the Enable Compounding option appears only when you select Currently Selected Month, if your cursor is in the first month and you select the Currently Selected Month option, you can use compounding for the entire year.*

For example, if you entered $1000.00 in the current month and indicated a $100.00 increase, the results differ from amounts that are not being compounded, as seen in Table 9-1.

Compounding Enabled?	Current Month Original Figure	Current Month New Figure	Next Month	Next Month	Next Month
Yes	1000.00	1000.00	1100.00	1200.00	1300.00
No	1000.00	1100.00	1100.00	1100.00	1100.00

Table 9-1: Compounded vs. non-compounded changes.

Forecast Window Buttons

The Set Up Forecast window has the following buttons:

- **Clear** deletes all figures in the forecast window—you cannot use this button to clear a row or column.
- **Save** saves the current figures and leaves the window open so you can continue to work.
- **OK** saves the current figures and closes the window.
- **Cancel** closes the window without any offer to record the figures.
- **Create New Forecast** starts the whole process again.
  If you've entered any data, QuickBooks asks if you want to record your data before closing the window. If you record your data (or have previously recorded your data with the Save button), when you start again, the forecast window opens with the saved data. You have to clear all the figures to create a new forecast.

No Delete button exists in the forecast window. To delete a forecast, load it in the forecast window, and choose Edit → Delete Forecast.

Editing the Forecast

After you save the forecast, you can modify it as needed. To make changes, choose Company → Planning & Budgeting → Set Up Forecast.

If you only created one forecast, it opens in the Set Up Forecast window. If you've created multiple forecasts (for customers, jobs, or classes), select the forecast you want to modify from the drop-down list in the Forecast field (at the top of the window).

Use the instructions in the previous section to change the data, and then save the forecast.

Creating Reports on Forecasts

You can view your forecast, or compare its data to real figures, by choosing Reports → Budgets & Forecasts, and then selecting either Forecast Overview or Forecast vs. Actual. Selecting either report launches the Forecast Report wizard.

Forecast Overview Report

To view the forecast, select it from the drop-down list in the first wizard window, and click Next. (If you only created one forecast, you don't have any choices, of course.)

In the next wizard window, select the layout for the report. If the forecast you're viewing is a Profit & Loss Accounts forecast, your only choice is Account By Month, which is the spreadsheet-type layout you used when you created the forecast.

If the forecast you're viewing is a Customer:Job or Class forecast, choose Account By Customer:Job, or Customer:Job By Month (substitute Class for Customer:Job if you created class forecasts).

The name of the layout choice holds the description: the first word in the choice represents the rows, and the word after the word "by" represents the columns.

Forecast vs. Actual

This report lets you see how the forecast matches up against actual figures. The wizard offers the same display options as described for the Overview Report. The report displays the forecast, the actuals, the difference between them in dollars and the difference in percentage.

Chapter 10

Accountant Edition Features

The Premier Accountant Edition differs from all the other Premier editions. It contains features, tools, add-on programs, and third-party offers that aren't included in the other Premier editions. The Premier Accountant Edition is designed to serve two purposes:

- Provide a robust accounting application for running an accounting practice.
- Provide tools and features that make it easy to support QuickBooks clients.

In this chapter I'll go over some of the most important and most useful features in the Premier Accountant Edition.

All QuickBooks Editions Included

The best part of purchasing QuickBooks Premier Accountant Edition is that you've really bought all the QuickBooks editions. In addition to the Premier Accountant Edition, you can also run QuickBooks Pro, QuickBooks Simple Start, QuickBooks Premier (not industry specific), and all of the QuickBooks Premier industry specific editions (Contractor, Manufacturing & Wholesale, Nonprofit, Professional Services, and Retail). To switch among QuickBooks editions:

1. Choose File → Toggle To Another Edition to open the Select QuickBooks Edition dialog.
2. Select the edition you want to use, and click Next. QuickBooks displays a window confirming the edition you've selected.
3. Click Toggle to close the currently loaded edition and open the selected edition.

***NOTE**: The company file that is open at the time you toggle is loaded in the new edition.*

Running Your Practice

In this section, I'll go over some of the features in Premier Accountant Edition that you'll find helpful for running your own practice in QuickBooks. Most of the information will also help you work with client files.

Company Data File

QuickBooks provides a wide range of options for tracking clients, projects, and income. The flexibility built into QuickBooks lets you set up your company data file in the way that best meets your needs.

Proving the old legend of the shoemaker's children, I've found many accounting firms that spent years operating without full-featured accounting software. They have a time and billing program for receivables and payments, and they use write-up software to record revenue totals and disbursements.

Fixed assets and liabilities are tracked in spreadsheets, and a variety of other software documents keep track of other financial details. They have an outside payroll service, but they don't track the weekly payroll (at the end of a quarter or year, they enter the totals provided by the payroll service). Preparing the firm's tax return must be a real joy!

Many of these firms, especially those who support clients using QuickBooks, have begun installing QuickBooks for their own use—and I find the Premier Accountant Edition in use at many accounting practices. When I visit these firms to help them tweak their QuickBooks software, I often find configuration options that aren't helping accountants make QuickBooks truly useful.

As a result, a lot of after-the-fact work (especially the calculation of subtotals and the process of analyzing revenue) continues to be performed in spreadsheet applications. Very little of the work done outside of QuickBooks would be required if the configuration options were more carefully considered. I guess old habits are hard to break.

Creating a New Company File

If you're new to QuickBooks, after you launch the software for the first time, you're offered an opportunity to create a new file. You can create a company file by using the EasyStep Interview (a wizard), or by creating the file manually, by selecting Skip Interview on the first wizard window.

Using either method, QuickBooks presents a list of industries for you to choose from, and because you're using the Premier Accountant Edition, the listing titled Accounting or Bookkeeping is preselected. This file is predefined with lists and features that are useful for running your practice.

Configuring the Chart of Accounts

QuickBooks creates a partial chart of accounts for accounting firms, but it's missing many accounts. In addition, the accounts are not numbered by default (and I've met very few accountants who didn't prefer numbered accounts).

To number your accounts, choose Edit → Preferences and select the Accounting category in the left pane of the Preferences dialog. In the Company Preferences tab, select the option Use Account Numbers, and also select the option Show Lowest Subaccount Only (to avoid having to scroll through parent and subaccount names when you're selecting an account in a drop-down list).

If you added any accounts to the chart of accounts that was installed automatically by QuickBooks, they will not be automatically numbered, and selecting the "Show Lowest Subaccount Only" option produces an error message that tells you that you must create numbers for all accounts before you can enable this option.

After you enter account numbers for the accounts you added manually, return to the Accounting category of the Preferences dialog to enable the Show Lowest Subaccount Only option.

Incidentally, the reason selecting Use Account Numbers works automatically is that QuickBooks actually provides account numbers for the chart of accounts it establishes automatically during company setup. Even though numbers are attached to every account, QuickBooks sets the default configuration for the chart of accounts so it doesn't display those numbers. I have never figured out why—the numbers are there, most accountants prefer account numbers, why not display them?

When you've enabled account numbers, check the number scheme to make sure it matches your own preferences. QuickBooks uses the standard numbering paradigm for an Accountant/CPA chart of accounts:

- 10000 starts the asset accounts
- 20000 starts the liability accounts
- 30000 starts the equity accounts
- 40000 starts the income accounts
- 50000 starts the cost of goods sold accounts
- 60000 starts the expense accounts
- 70000 starts the "other" income accounts
- 80000 starts the "other" expense accounts

Configuring Customers and Jobs

Many accountants track only customer names, omitting jobs from the configuration of their company data files. Specific types of work for clients are tracked by items, or by posting revenue to specific income accounts.

Using Jobs

If you use service items or revenue accounts to track types of services, analyzing any individual client's history requires quite a bit of work. You have to customize a report so it filters items and/or revenue accounts.

All of the information is available, without customization, on a job report. If you want to view individual client histories to analyze your work and income stream, you should consider tracking clients by jobs.

Incidentally, jobs are not restricted to projects with a start and end date; a job can be defined as a definition of work. For example, you might decide to create the following jobs for clients:

- Business tax preparation
- Personal tax preparation
- Audits (performing or attending)
- Planning (preparing pro formas, business plans, and so on)

Using Customer Types

If you choose Accounting as the industry type during company file setup, QuickBooks prepopulates the Customer Types list for specific business types. You can view and manipulate those customer types by choosing Lists → Customer & Vendor Profile Lists → Customer Type List. Figure

10-1 shows the customer types that QuickBooks automatically adds to your data file.

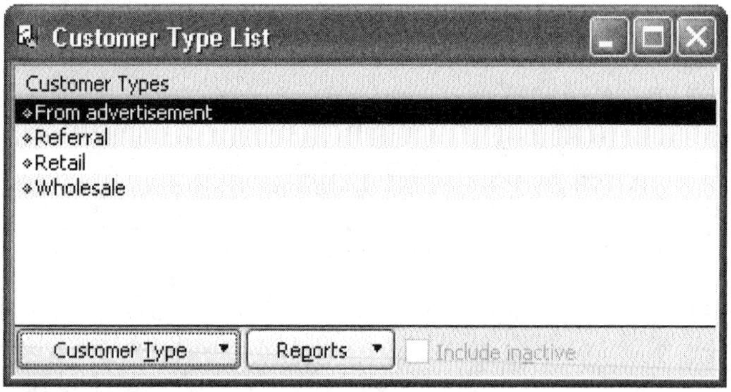

Figure 10-1: The prepopulated customer types may not suit your practice.

If these types work for you, assign a type to each customer. However, many accountants find that these customer types don't work, because this isn't the type of information that's useful for creating the reports they need.

At many accounting firms, I install what my clients think is an extremely useful design for customer types—the month of the fiscal year end for business clients. Create twelve customer types, from January to December. Then assign the appropriate type to each customer record. Every month, run a report for the customer type two months hence, and begin the steps for year-end work, which could encompass any of the following:

- Use the Write Letters feature in QuickBooks to send a note reminding clients of the things they must do to close their books and produce reports. Include a request to call the office to make an appointment.
- If you use pretax preparation worksheets (a copy of last years figures and a line for clients to enter the current totals), use the Print Labels feature to send the packages to the appropriate customer type.

- Print a Customer listing of only the appropriate type, and have a staff member set up the appointments.

Add your own end of year protocols to this list of chores, and you'll find that it's easy to identify the right clients because almost all QuickBooks reports let you filter for a customer type.

Managing Items

Items are the services and products a company sells. As an accountant, you sell services, and your item list can be as simple or as complex as your client services and invoicing standards require.

Most accounting firms need service items such as tax preparation (both personal and business), audits, tax planning, business planning, write-up or other bookkeeping services, and special services such as preparing business plans or projections. Create an item for each service you provide.

You can create subitems to refine your items list. For example, if your tax preparation processes involve partners, associates, bookkeepers, or other multiple types of personnel, you may charge a different rate for each type. Create a subitem for each parent item service that involves multiple billing rates. Don't assign a rate to the parent item; assign rates only to the subitems.

Using Price Levels

Price levels provide a way to fine-tune your pricing in situations where you want to pass along a discount (or a higher rate) on an item. QuickBooks Premier editions offer two types of price levels:

- Fixed percentage price levels
- Per item price levels (not available in QuickBooks Basic and Pro editions)

To use price levels, you must first set up your items. If your items have no assigned rates, you can use price levels to set all rates for the item. If your items have been assigned a rate, you can create price levels based on that rate. (Chapter 3 contains the information you need to create and apply price levels.)

Using Billing Rate Levels

The Billing Rate Level List lets you assign a billing rate to a person performing a specific service. This list is only available in the following Premier Editions:

- Accountant Edition
- Contractor Edition
- Professional Services Edition

After you create billing rate levels, and associate them with service providers, invoicing for services becomes almost automated. Every time you create an invoice with billable time, QuickBooks automatically fills in the correct rate for the service, based on the person who performed the work.

For instance, you can have one rate for audit activities that are performed by a senior partner, and another rate for audit activities performed by a junior partner. The senior partner rate for audits may be different from the senior partner rate for creating business plans. The permutations and combinations are almost endless, which makes this a very powerful feature. Learn how to create and apply billing rate levels in Chapter 3.

Supporting QuickBooks Clients

The Premier Accountant Edition is built from the ground up to help you support QuickBooks clients. You can create report templates that provide the information you need, export them, and send them to clients (see Chapter 8).

In addition, the Premier Accountant Edition has preconfigured data files for specific industries. These are the same preconfigured company files that are available in the other industry-specific versions of Premier editions. If you have clients using industry-specific Premier editions, you can duplicate their environments in your own copy of Premier Accountant Edition. More important, you can use the industry-specific company files to prepare company files for all your QuickBooks clients.

Predefined Company Files

Many of the industry-specific Premier editions offer predefined company files for businesses in that industry. When a Premier edition user starts the process to create a company file, at the point of selecting an industry QuickBooks automatically select the industry type that's linked to the Premier edition. For example, Premier Contractor Edition automatically selects construction as the industry type.

These company files contain more than just the appropriate chart of accounts; in addition, many of the lists are prepopulated, and the appropriate features have been enabled. These predefined company files for the entire range of Premier editions are also available in the Premier Accountant edition.

You can use the predefined files for your QuickBooks clients when they need to create or tweak their company data files. The client does not have to be running the Premier edition for that industry. In fact, the client does not have to be running any Premier edition. If you have a client in the construction industry running QuickBooks Pro, use the contractor's predefined company file, and give it to your client. As long as the QuickBooks edition is the same version (the same year), the client can use the file.

These features provide a value added service for your clients that is very easy to administer. The workload at your office isn't onerous, and you save the client the long, often confusing, process of creating or tweaking a company file. That's worth something!

Components of Predefined Files

The predefined industry-specific company data files usually (but not always) contain the following components:

- A start-up chart of accounts configured for the industry.
- An items list reflecting common products and services for the industry.
- Preferences configured for the industry.
- Classes configured for the industry.
- Customer and Vendor Type lists configured for the industry.
- Sales transaction templates configured for the industry.

The chart of accounts for most of the predefined company files contains income and expense accounts that are suitable for the specific industry. However, you'll have to add some asset and liability accounts. The following balance sheet accounts may be missing:

- Bank accounts
- Fixed assets
- Current liabilities (although a Payroll Liabilities account always exists)

Most of the industry-specific predefined files have the account number preference disabled. Open the Preferences dialog, go to the Accounting category, and enable account numbers. Take this step before you add any accounts, because QuickBooks only automatically adds numbers to predefined accounts, and won't add a number to an account that was created manually. After you enable account numbers, the account number field is available in the New Account dialog.

Using the Predefined Company Files

There are two ways to make use of the predefined industry-specific company files, and each method has a specific advantage for the various scenarios you may encounter with your clients.

- Create the file, give it a generic company name (e.g. Contractor), tweak it, and give it to your client. This works best for clients who are just starting with QuickBooks.
- Create the file, give it a generic company name, tweak it, and export the components to an .IIF file. Give the export file to your client with instructions on importing the file. This is useful for

clients who have set up their basic QuickBooks company file and need to refine the chart of accounts, and add components such as items, customer types, and so on.

I've found that I can improve the efficiency of these processes by preparing folders on my hard drive that help me store files appropriately. I created the following folders:

- GenericQBWFiles. This folder holds the industry-specific company files I created and tweaked.
- ClientQBWFiles. This folder holds the client-specific files I prepare.
- Client Export Files. This folder holds the .IIF export files I prepare for clients.

Here are the steps to take when you want to turn a generic .QBW file into a client file:

1. In Windows Explorer or My Computer, open the folder that holds the generic company files (GenericQBWFiles in the above example).
2. Copy the appropriate generic file to the folder you use to store company files for specific clients (ClientQBWFiles in the above example).
3. Rename the copied file (the file in the ClientQBWFiles folder) to match the client name.
4. Open QuickBooks and load the client-named file. When the company file opens, the title bar still uses the generic company name you applied when you created the file.
5. Choose Company → Company Information and change the company name from the generic name to the client's company name.
6. Enter the income tax form used by this client.
7. Enter the EIN or SSN for the client.
8. Click OK.

The QuickBooks title bar now displays a company name that matches the client's name, and is related to the name you gave the file. (The filename doesn't have to be an exact match for the company name.)

If the income tax form the client uses is different from the income tax form you used when you created the generic file, QuickBooks issues a message that warns you that tax related information will be removed from the accounts. That's fine, you don't mind if the tax information disappears. The tax information is established for each account so that users can do their own taxes. Because this company is a client, you'll be doing the taxes.

Creating Generic Client Files

To create an industry-specific generic file, choose File → New Company. In the EasyStep Interview window, click Skip Interview. Fill out the company information using a generic company name that reflects the industry type you're creating. Click Next and select the industry type for this client. Tweak the file, paying attention to the following:

- Enable account numbers.
- Set other preferences to suit the majority of your clients in this industry. For example, enable sales tax if the industry for which you're creating the file usually collects sales tax.
- If most of your clients use outside payroll services, be sure payroll isn't enabled.
- Add missing accounts to the chart of accounts.
- Go through the all the lists to add, remove, and change entries to match the needs of the majority of your clients in this industry.

***TIP**: If you've exported memorized reports as report templates, import them into this company file.*

The file is now ready to be sent to your clients who are just starting to use QuickBooks. The client must have installed QuickBooks 2008, but it doesn't matter if it's Pro or Premier edition.

Instruct the client to copy the file to the folder that holds QuickBooks data. To use the file, the client chooses File → Open Or Restore Company, and follows the prompts to open a company file, then selects the file you sent.

If you're e-mailing the file to the client, and either you or the client lacks a fast Internet connection, you can reduce the size of the attachment by sending a portable file (see "Using Portable Files", later in this chapter).

Creating IIF Import Files

If your client is already using QuickBooks, and you want to tweak the company file, you can create an import file. To accomplish this, you must first export all or some of the contents of the generic file you prepared. Choose File → Utilities → Export → Lists To IIF Files. In the Export dialog (see Figure 10-2), select the components you want to include in the client's import file.

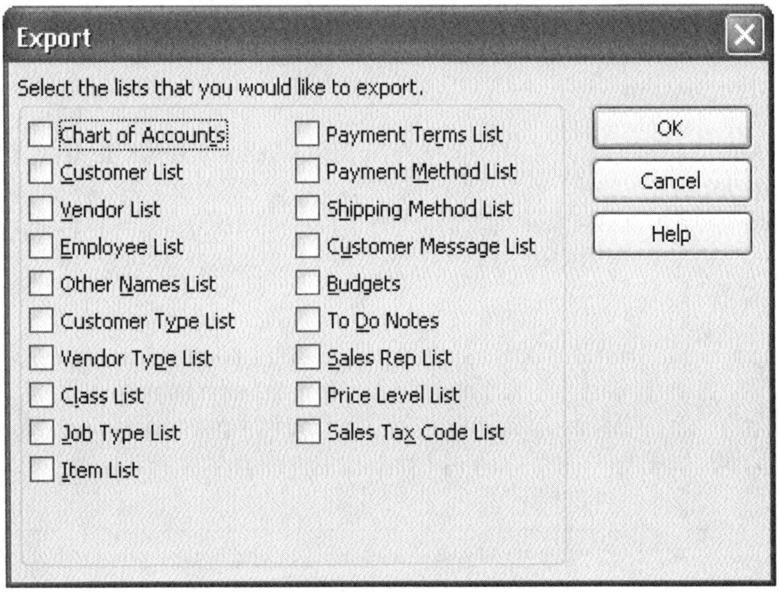

Figure 10-2: Export the components you want your clients to import.

Click OK and save the file with a name that reminds you of its contents. For example, if you exported all the lists from your generic file for contractors, name the file ContractorAll.IIF. If you exported only the Items list, name the file ContractorItems.IIF.

Creating IIF Files for QuickBooks 2008

If the clients to whom you send import files have installed QuickBooks 2008 (any edition), you don't have to do anything more to the export file. It's automatically an import file that will work.

Send the file to the client, and instruct the client to import the file by choosing File → Import → IIF Files

Creating IIF Files for Earlier Versions of QuickBooks

If you want to send the import file to clients who are using an earlier version of QuickBooks, you must make some changes to the export file in order to create an import file that will work. Open the file in Excel (or another spreadsheet application).

The first two rows of the exported file contain version-specific information for QuickBooks 2008. Delete those rows by selecting the row numbers and choosing Edit → Delete.

Choose File → Save As, and save the file with a filename that indicates you've adapted the file for earlier versions of QuickBooks. For example, you can name the file ContractorListsAll-Pre2008.IIF. Be sure the Save As Type field in the Save As dialog specifies Text (Tab delimited).

When you click Save, Excel issues a message to remind you that text files lack Excel features. Click Yes to continue to save the file as a text file. When you close Excel, you're given another opportunity to save the file as an Excel file, but don't accept the invitation.

***TIP**: An IIF import file designed for pre-2008 versions works in QuickBooks 2008, too. You can make these changes in your main import file, and send the file to all clients, regardless of the version of QuickBooks they've installed. This way, you don't have to maintain two IIF files.*

IIF Files for Specific Business Types

Some of the preconfigured files need more work than others. For example, the contractor predefined company has a long list of items. Many of the items may not be useful to certain types of contractors, and the Item List may lack items needed for some types of contractors.

To create useful company files for plumbers, electricians, carpenters, and so on, it's better (and less confusing to the client) to have only the items related to the specific client type. You could create multiple generic company files, each containing the right settings, but that's too much trouble. Instead, create import files. For example, to create customized Items Lists for specific types of contractors, follow these steps:

1. Export the Items List from the Contractor predefined company file.
2. Open the file in Excel, and remove, change, and add items for a specific type of contractor (for instance, a plumber).
3. Save the file with an appropriate filename (e.g., PlumberItems.IIF).
4. Close the file, and open the original export file.
5. Repeat steps 2 and 3, modifying the list for a different type of contractor.

You can use this approach for any type of specialized import file, including the chart of accounts as well as lists. After a while, you'll have an enviable collection of import files that will help your clients use QuickBooks more efficiently without the need to create components manually. Don't forget to delete the two rows of version information, or you won't be able to give the file to pre-2008 users.

***TIP**: You can use import files to perform mass updates of fields to existing data in QuickBooks lists. See Appendix C for more information.*

Industry Specific Reports

Each industry-specific version of QuickBooks Premier has a group of reports that are useful for the industry type in which the reports are installed. The reports are built in to the industry-specific editions of QuickBooks Premier software.

QuickBooks Premier Accountant Edition contains many of the industry-specific reports that are included in industry specific Premier editions. Choose Reports → Industry Specific to see the list.

***TIP**: For a more comprehensive list of industry-specific reports, use the Toggle feature to switch to each of the Premier industry specific editions, and examine the reports installed in the edition.*

Being able to access reports that are available in the other Premier editions is valuable for supporting your QuickBooks Premier edition clients. You can open a report and discuss its settings with your clients, or customize one or more of these reports for a client with particular needs. After you customize the report, export it so you can send the report template to the client (see Chapter 8 to learn about exporting report templates).

Another great value in these reports is your ability to use them to provide report templates that are specifically designed for clients who are not using Premier editions. It's a worthwhile added value service to provide customized reports that are industry specific for client businesses running QuickBooks Pro. You can even export a template group that contains the entire range of the industry-specific reports for any industry type.

This works because you don't have to customize a report to turn it into a memorized report. Just open any built-in report and click the Memorize button. Then you can export it and send the file to your clients.

Working Trial Balance

The Working Trial Balance is a spreadsheet-like display of general ledger activity over a specified period (see Figure 10-3). You can use it with a client's company file, or with the Accountant's Copy of a client's file. To access this tool, choose Accountant → Working Trial Balance.

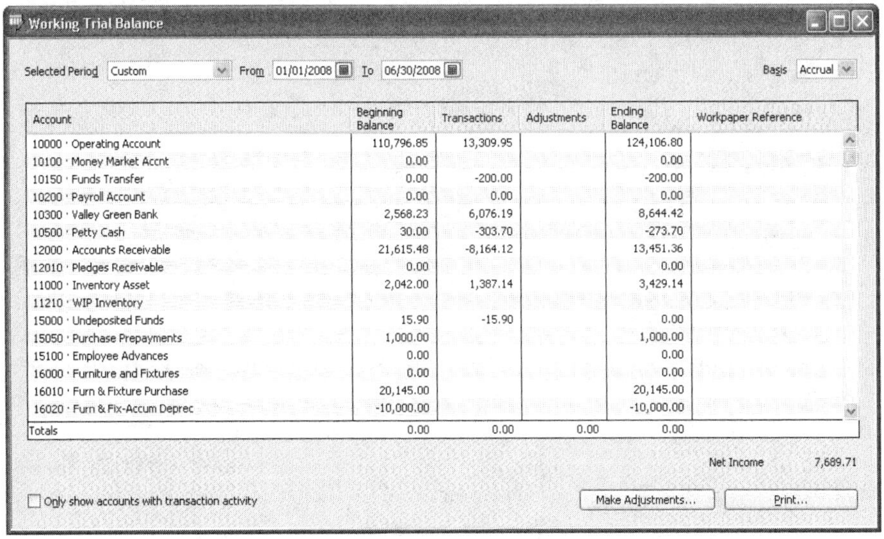

Account	Beginning Balance	Transactions	Adjustments	Ending Balance	Workpaper Reference
10000 · Operating Account	110,796.85	13,309.95		124,106.80	
10100 · Money Market Accnt	0.00			0.00	
10150 · Funds Transfer	0.00	-200.00		-200.00	
10200 · Payroll Account	0.00	0.00		0.00	
10300 · Valley Green Bank	2,568.23	6,076.19		8,644.42	
10500 · Petty Cash	30.00	-303.70		-273.70	
12000 · Accounts Receivable	21,615.48	-8,164.12		13,451.36	
12010 · Pledges Receivable	0.00			0.00	
11000 · Inventory Asset	2,042.00	1,387.14		3,429.14	
11210 · WIP Inventory					
15000 · Undeposited Funds	15.90	-15.90		0.00	
15050 · Purchase Prepayments	1,000.00			1,000.00	
15100 · Employee Advances	0.00			0.00	
16000 · Furniture and Fixtures	0.00			0.00	
16010 · Furn & Fixture Purchase	20,145.00			20,145.00	
16020 · Furn & Fix-Accum Deprec	-10,000.00			-10,000.00	
Totals	0.00	0.00	0.00	0.00	

Figure 10-3: Use the Working Trial Balance to view and manipulate account activity.

For each account, the report displays the opening balance, the closing balance, and the total about of transactions (using QuickBooks transaction windows and adjustments made with journal entries) that created the closing balance. In addition, this tool has the following powerful options:

- You can hide the display of accounts that have no activity.
- Double-clicking an account listing opens the account's record so you can view or edit it.
- Double-clicking the amount in a column opens a detailed report on the transactions that created the amount that's displayed.
- You can create a journal entry for any account by selecting the account and clicking the Make Adjustments button.
- You can use the Workpaper Reference column for notes if you make any changes.

Accountant's Copy

An accountant's copy is a copy of a company file that's sent from the client to the accountant. The Accountant's Copy feature is designed to let the client continue to work in the company file at the same time the accountant is working in the Accountant's Copy, although there are limitations on the type of work that both the client and the accountant can perform.

When the accountant is finished working in the Accountant's Copy, the file is returned to the client. The Accountant's Changes can be merged into the client's company file.

Following is the process in chronological order:

1. The client creates an Accountant's Copy of the company file and sets the dividing date (see the next section, Accountant's Copy Dividing Date). This file is the Accountant's Copy Transfer File, which has a file extension .QBX).
2. The client sends the file to the accountant, either on removable media or by uploading the file to a secure server that QuickBooks provides (see "Sending an Accountant's Copy", later in this section).
3. The accountant opens the transfer file (.QBX) which turns the file into an Accountant's Copy Working File, which has a file extension .QBA.
4. When the accountant finishes working on the file, the changes are exported in the Accountant's Copy Changes File, which has a file extension .QBY, and the file is sent to the client.
5. The client opens the file and reviews the changes (and can choose to import or reject the changes).

Accountant's Copy Dividing Date

The dividing date, selected by the client when the Accountant's Copy is created, determines who can do what:

- The accountant can work on existing transactions that are dated on or before the dividing date, and can create transactions on both sides of the dividing date.

- The client can work on transactions (editing existing transactions or creating new transactions) that are dated the day after the dividing date, or later.

***TIP**: To see (and download) a task-by-task table in a PDF file that explains what the client can do and what the accountant can do, go to the QuickBooks Tips section of www.cpa911.com and select the article titled Accountant's Copy Rules for QuickBooks 2008.*

Even though the client selects the dividing date, that date should be determined by the accountant. The dividing date should match the period for which you need to examine your client's records and make needed changes. The period could be a previous year, quarter, or month. Some clients need an income statement and/or balance sheet, covering a specific period, for a bank because of an existing or potential line of credit. Other clients may need an "accountant approved" report for the company's partners or a nonprofit association's board.

To give yourself a period in which to insert changes such as adjusting journal entries or reversing journal entries, have your client set the dividing date about two weeks after the end date you need. For example, if the report you need is as of the end of the last fiscal year, set the dividing date for two or three weeks after that date.

Creating an Accountant's Copy - Instructions for Clients

The way you create an accountant's copy depends on the method you want to use to send it to the accountant:

- Save the file to removable media and send or deliver it to the accountant.
- Upload the file to a secure server that QuickBooks maintains for this purpose, and automatically send e-mail to the accountant to provide instructions for downloading the file.

Technically, you can save a file and attach it to an e-mail message, but the file is quite large and many ISPs may refuse to handle it.

Therefore, I'm covering this topic assuming the file will be saved on removable media or uploaded to the QuickBooks server.

Saving the Accountant's Copy on Removable Media

To create an accountant's copy and save it on removable media, use either of the following commands:

- Choose File → Accountant's Copy → Save File, which opens the Create Accountant's Copy dialog. Be sure the option labeled Accountant's Copy is selected.
- Choose File → Save Copy Or Backup, which opens the Save Copy or Backup dialog. Select the option labeled Accountant's Copy.

In either dialog, click Next to move to the window in which you set the dividing date for this accountant's copy. When the dividing date is set, click Next to save the file in the Save Accountant's Copy dialog.

By default QuickBooks saves the accountant's copy to the desktop, using a filename that has the format <*CompanyFileName*> (Acct Transfer *Month Day, Year Time*).QBX.

If you're sending the file on a flash drive, change the location by choosing the flash drive in the Save In field at the top of the dialog. If you're planning to send the file on a CD or DVD, save the file to your hard drive and then transfer the file to the CD/DVD.

Send or deliver the file to your accountant.

Sending an Accountant's Copy to the QuickBooks Server

To create an accountant's copy that is uploaded to a secure server maintained by QuickBooks, from which your accountant can download the file, choose File → Accountant's Copy → Send to Accountant, which opens the Send Accountant's Copy dialog that explains the process. Step through the wizard as follows:

1. Select the dividing date.
2. In the next window, enter your accountant's e-mail address, your name, and your e-mail address.

3. In the next window, enter a password for the upload/download of this file. This is *not* the password your accountant needs to open the company file; it's a password required to download the file from the server, to prevent anyone else from downloading the file. It must be a *strong password*, which means it contains at least eight characters, mixes letters and numbers, and at least one letter must be in a different case from the other letters (usually this means one letter is uppercase).
4. Optionally, enter a message for your accountant that will appear in the body of the e-mail message notifying your accountant that you've uploaded the file. E-mail text is not encrypted, so don't give your accountant the password in this message.
5. Click Send to upload the file to the server. QuickBooks displays a message telling you it must close all windows to create an accountant's copy; click OK to continue.

QuickBooks sends e-mail to your accountant (see Figure 10-4), and also sends a confirming message to you.

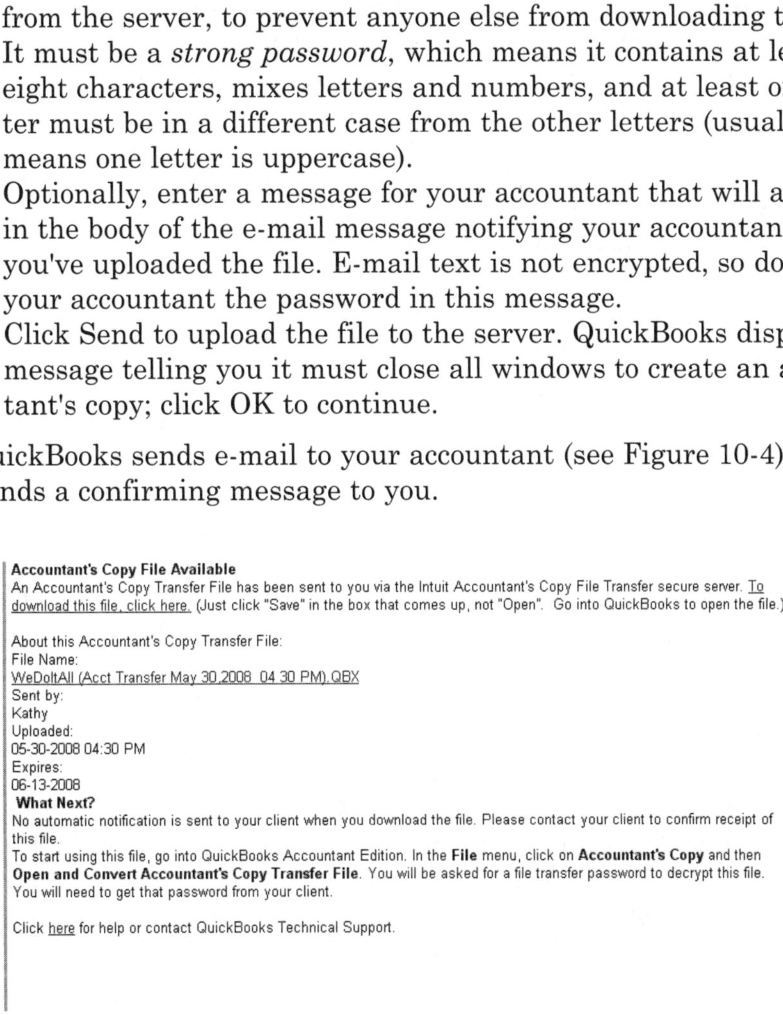
Accountant's Copy File Available
An Accountant's Copy Transfer File has been sent to you via the Intuit Accountant's Copy File Transfer secure server. To download this file, click here. (Just click "Save" in the box that comes up, not "Open". Go into QuickBooks to open the file.)

About this Accountant's Copy Transfer File:
File Name:
WeDoItAll (Acct Transfer May 30,2008 04 30 PM).QBX
Sent by:
Kathy
Uploaded:
05-30-2008 04:30 PM
Expires:
06-13-2008
What Next?
No automatic notification is sent to your client when you download the file. Please contact your client to confirm receipt of this file.
To start using this file, go into QuickBooks Accountant Edition. In the **File** menu, click on **Accountant's Copy** and then **Open and Convert Accountant's Copy Transfer File**. You will be asked for a file transfer password to decrypt this file. You will need to get that password from your client.

Click here for help or contact QuickBooks Technical Support.

Figure 10-4: An e-mail message notifies your accountant that the file is available, and explains how to get it.

If you've password-protected your QuickBooks data file, you must give your accountant the Admin password in addition to the password needed to download the file.

Working in an Accountant's Copy

An Accountant's Copy can only be opened in the Premier Accountant Edition. The file has to be opened (as a transfer file) and then saved (as a working file). The working file is loaded in the QuickBooks window so you can begin using it. Use the following steps to accomplish these tasks:

1. Choose File → Accountant's Copy → Open & Convert Accountant's Copy Transfer File. QuickBooks displays a window that provides an overview of the way the Accountant's copy works.
2. Click Next to see an explanation of the permitted transactions. The message includes the statement that if you want to do more than the Accountant's Copy permits, you can convert the Transfer File to a full company file and do anything you wish (see Creating a Company File from a Transfer File, later in this section).
3. Click Next and navigate to the folder that contains the file you received from the client.
4. Double-click the file's listing. QuickBooks displays a message explaining that the file is about to be converted to an Accountant's Copy Working File. Click OK.
5. The Save As Accountant's Copy dialog opens, displaying the same folder you selected to retrieve the file. By default QuickBooks retains the filename, changing the extension to .QBA. Unless you have some reason to change the folder, click Save.
6. QuickBooks converts the file, which takes a few minutes, and then opens the file.
   (If the file contains users and passwords, the Login dialog appears with the Admin user entered in the User Name field. You must enter the Admin password to continue.)
7. QuickBooks displays another message reminding you that this is an Accountant's Copy. Click OK to begin working.

The title bar of the QuickBooks window displays the company filename along with the parenthetical text "Acct Copy, Div Date DD/MM/YYYY". You can begin data entry according to the "can do/cannot do" rules. When you begin working in the file, QuickBooks displays a message explaining how the transaction windows appear in order to let you know what you can and cannot do (see Figure 10-5).

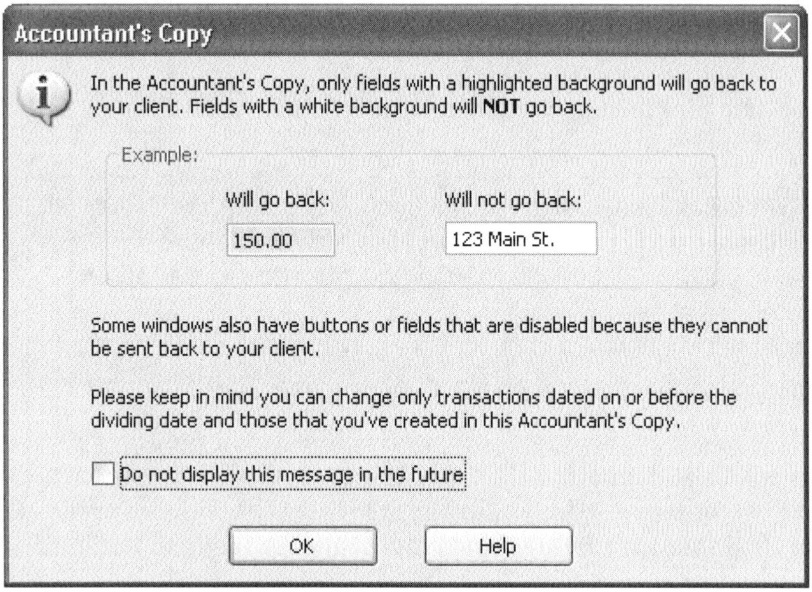

Figure 10-5: It's easy to tell which part of a transaction window can accept data that "takes", and will be merged into your client's file.

Once the file is converted to an Accountant's Copy working file, you can close and open it as needed. To open the file choose File → Open or Restore Company, and click Next. Navigate to the folder that contains the file and open it.

Creating the Accountant's Copy Change File

While you're working in the Accountant's Copy you can review the work you've done by choosing File → Accountant's Copy → View/Export Changes for Client.

When you've completed your work, and you're ready to send the file back to your client, open this window and click Create Change File For Client.

The Save Accountant Changes dialog opens, and displays the folder that stored the working file (you can change the location). The file is renamed with the format <*CompanyFileName*> (Acct Changes).QBY. QuickBooks issues a success message when you save the file.

Send the file to your client via e-mail (it's a small file), or on a CD.

***TIP**: Save the working file until you make sure the client has received and successfully imported the file. If there's a problem, you can work with the file and re-send the corrected merge file.*

Merging the Accountant's Copy Changes

Meanwhile, back at the client site, here's how to merge the accountant's changes with the company file. Only the QuickBooks administrator can merge an Accountant's Copy into the company file; moreover, the file must be in single-user mode. Take the following steps to begin the merge process:

1. Open the company file if it isn't already open.
2. Choose File → Accountant's Copy → Import Accountant's Changes.
3. In the Import Accountant's Changes dialog, navigate to the folder that holds the file you received from your accountant, and double-click the file (which has an extension .QBY).
4. QuickBooks displays a listing of the changes your accountant made, along with any notes your accountant wrote.

You can expand any listing to see all the details by clicking the plus sign to the left of the listing (or click Expand All to see everything). If you want a permanent record of these changes, click the Print button in the lower right corner of the window to print a copy of the changes (QuickBooks expands the listings so all the details are printed).

When you've examined the changes, you can accept or reject them. Your acceptance or rejection is wholesale; that is, you cannot accept some changes and reject others.

To merge the accountant's work into your company file, click Incorporate Accountant's Changes. Then follow the prompts as QuickBooks displays messages about this task, backs up your company file, imports the transactions, and displays a list of the transactions that were imported which has the same content as the original window that listed the accountant's changes.

If any transaction had a problem, or caused a problem, its listing displays a yellow triangle. If you see any yellow triangles, click the print button to have a record of the errant transaction so you can fix it later.

Click Close to close the Import Results window. QuickBooks displays a message urging you to set or update your closing date to make sure that the accountant's changes that affected the earlier period are not changed in the future. You can proceed as you think best.

If problems were noted in the Import Results window, locate the appropriate transaction in your company file and fix it, or delete it.

You're no longer limited in what you can do in your company file, and the titlebar text referring to the fact that an Accountant's Copy exists is gone.

Rejecting the Accountant's Changes

If you don't want to merge the transactions into your company file, click Close. Then cancel the accountant's copy by choosing File → Accountant's Copy → Remove Restrictions. After you confirm your decision in the dialog that appears, your company file is fully operational, and there are no limitations on the tasks you can perform.

Creating a Company File from a Transfer File

QuickBooks provides a command that lets you convert the transfer file you received from a client into a full-blown company file. The explanation for providing this function is "If the restrictions on using Accountant's Copy won't accommodate your situation, you can convert an Accountant's Copy to a regular company file".

This isn't a good reason to convert the file. Your client sends you an Accountant's Copy because it's a way for you to work on the file while he continues to run his business with QuickBooks. If you convert the file, your file overwrites his file when you return it, and all the work he did is lost.

If you want to do full-scope data entry on a client's file, either go on site, or ask the client for the full file and explain that the client must stop working until you complete your work and return the file. One good way to obtain a full company file is to ask the client for a portable company file (covered in the next section, "Using Portable Files").

A valid reason to convert an Accountant's Copy to a company file is to replace the client's file if the client doesn't back up regularly and suffers a computer crash while the Accountant's Copy exists. Give the converted file to the client, along with a lecture about daily backups.

Using a Portable Company File

A portable company file is a copy of a QuickBooks company file that has been condensed to save disk space. Portable files not only take up less room on a disk, they also save upload and download time if you send the file as an attachment to an e-mail message.

Generally, the process of creating and using portable company files proceeds as follows:

1. A company file is saved as a portable file (with the extension QBM).
2. The portable file is sent to a recipient (e.g. client sends to accountant).
3. The portable file is opened in QuickBooks at the recipient's computer, and the process of opening the file expands it to its original size and adds the QBW extension (making it a regular company file).
4. After the file has been changed, updated, fixed, etc., the process is repeated in the other direction.

The significant process is the fact that the file is saved as a .QBW file, and therefore overwrites the existing <*CompanyFileName*>.QBW file in the same folder.

When an accountant receives the file from a client, that's usually not a problem, because even if the same company file exists in the accountant's folder, it's an older version of the file, dating back to the last time the client sent the file.

On the client side, however, overwriting the existing company file can be a major problem. If the client works in the company file, when the returned file is opened, it overwrites the existing company file and all the work that was done since the portable file was created is gone.

This differs from the use of an accountant's copy, which has two properties that the portable company file lacks:

- The changes made in an accountant's copy can be merged back into the company file from which it came.
- The accountant's copy has limited functions available.

Because the changes an accountant makes to an accountant's copy can be merged into the client's company file, the client can continue to work in the company file while the accountant is working in the accountant's copy.

You must explain to your clients who send you a portable file that they cannot work in their company files until they've replaced the existing file with the portable file you return. You must also realize that data entry tasks are piling up at the client's office, so you must work on the file in a timely fashion and return the file to the client quickly.

***NOTE**: Portable files can also be used by clients to move data between the office and home, so they can work at home, and then bring the updated file back to the office.*

Creating a Portable Company File

Both sides of the exchange have to use the same steps to create a portable company file, so be sure to give your clients these instructions:

1. Choose File → Save Copy or Backup.

2. In the dialog that opens, select Portable Company File and click Next.
3. Save the file. QuickBooks displays a message telling you it has to close the company file in order to create the portable company file. Click OK.

By default, QuickBooks names the file in the format <*CompanyFileName*> (Portable).QBM and saves it to the Desktop of the computer on which the user is working.

If you're taking the file to the recipient location (office, client site, or home), select a USB flash drive if you have one (if you don't, you should). If you're going to copy the file to a CD or e-mail it to the client, save it in a convenient folder.

It takes a while to create the file (the amount of time depends on the size of the file, but even a new, small file takes several minutes to convert to a portable company file). When the file is saved, QuickBooks issues a success message. Your company file is reopened, and you can go back to work.

Installing a Portable Company File

On the client side, where installing a portable company file means overwriting the current company file with the portable file, back up the company file first. In fact, my advice is to make a backup to removable media, and then also copy the original company file (the one with the .QBW extension) to another folder on the hard drive or to removable media. The copy of the QBW file can be copied back to its own folder if something happens during the conversion of the portable company file to a regular company file.

To install a portable company file on your computer, follow these steps (provide these instructions to your client when you return the file):

1. Choose File → Open Or Restore Company.
2. In the dialog that appears, select Restore A Portable File and click Next.
3. In the Open Portable Company File dialog, navigate to the folder or drive that holds the portable file.

4. Double-click the file's listing to open the wizard-like window that explains your next step is to decide on the location for saving the file.
5. Click Next to open the Save dialog.
   - Accountants should save the file in a folder designed to hold files from clients.
   - Clients must replace their existing company file with this file, so they must select the folder in which their company file resides.

For clients, since the company file already exists, and since portable files are restored with a .QBW extension, QuickBooks issues a warning that you are about to overwrite an existing file. Click Yes to confirm the replacement (because the new company file that's created from the portable file is up-to-date and the existing file isn't).

Then, QuickBooks issues another warning, telling you that you're going to delete the existing company file. As long as the client made a backup and/or copied the original .QBW file to another location as a safety measure, type **YES**, and click OK, to confirm replacing the existing file with the contents of the portable company file.

After the portable company file is uncompressed and saved, it's loaded in the software window, ready to be used.

Fixed Asset Manager

All versions of QuickBooks have a Fixed Asset Item list, which you can use to store information about fixed assets. This list is meant to track data about the assets you depreciate. Except when it's opened in QuickBooks Premier Accountant Edition, this is merely a list, and it doesn't provide any method for calculating depreciation, nor does it link to any depreciation software. It's designed only to keep a list of assets.

QuickBooks Premier Accountant Edition has a nifty tool, Fixed Asset Manager that can synchronize data with the Fixed Asset Item list.

Fixed Asset Manager doesn't require the presence of the Fixed Asset Item list, so if your client hasn't used the list, you can still manage fixed asset depreciation.

Fixed Asset Manager calculates depreciation for fixed assets, and lets you create journal entries using the calculated amounts. It works with the currently open QuickBooks company data file, which is usually a client's company file.

***TIP**: Fixed Asset Manager integrates with Intuit's ProSeries Tax products, so you can automatically pass asset data from QuickBooks to ProSeries Tax.*

In the following sections, I'll provide an overview of the Premier Accountant Edition Fixed Asset Manager. The program is complex and powerful, and it's beyond the scope of this book to go over all its functions. You can use the Help files in the Fixed Asset Manager to learn the step-by-step procedures for all the functions.

***NOTE**: You can also use Fixed Asset Manager with an Accountant's Copy provided by your QuickBooks client, but you might lose some of the functionality of Fixed Asset Manager. Details are available in the Help files.*

Creating a Fixed Asset Manager Client File

Fixed Asset Manager must know the type of tax form a business files. Before you open Fixed Asset Manager, make sure the right tax form is configured for the company file that's open. In fact, make sure the tax form information isn't blank, which is often the case. To see the tax form information, in the company file choose Company → Company Information.

With the QuickBooks company file (the client file) open, choose Accountant → Manage Fixed Assets. When the Fixed Asset Manager software opens for the first time, it looks for an existing Fixed Asset

Manager client data file for the currently open company. If no previous client data file exists you must create one.

In the opening software window, select the option Create A New Fixed Asset Manager Client, and click OK. The Fixed Asset Manager New Client wizard launches. As with all wizards, you must click Next to go through all the windows.

Configuring Company Information

The wizard takes information from the QuickBooks file that's open, displays the company information, and then queries the accountant about the following data:

- Current fiscal year
- Prior short years
- Qualification for the "small corporation" exemption from AMT
- Depreciation bases
- Default depreciation method for each selected basis

The wizard also asks how you want to synchronize fixed asset data between the company file and the Fixed Asset Manager client file it's creating. The first question asks how you want to bring data from QuickBooks into Fixed Asset Manager. The following window asks how you want to move data from Fixed Asset Manager into QuickBooks. What all of this is doing is setting up synchronization options between the company file and Fixed Asset Manager. In the future the files will synchronize so you stay on top of the client's fixed asset purchases and depreciation.

The last wizard window is a summary of the QuickBooks company information. If any information is incorrect, use the Back button to return to the appropriate wizard window and make changes. When all the information is correct, click Finish.

Importing the Fixed Assets

Fixed Asset Manager finds the Fixed Asset Item List, and displays a log report. Fixed Asset Manager identifies the assets using the text in the Purchase Description field of the QuickBooks Fixed Asset Item list—not the name assigned to the asset.

***NOTE**: If an asset isn't transferred to Fixed Asset Manager, the log report indicates that fact. Usually, the reason is a date of purchase that is later than the end date of the fiscal year you indicated in the wizard. For example, if you're setting up Fixed Asset Manager in 2008 for 2007 depreciation, assets purchased in 2008 are not transferred.*

Click OK to close the log report and open the Fixed Asset Manager software window, seen in Figure 10-6. A robust set of functions is available on the menu system, and in the various tabs.

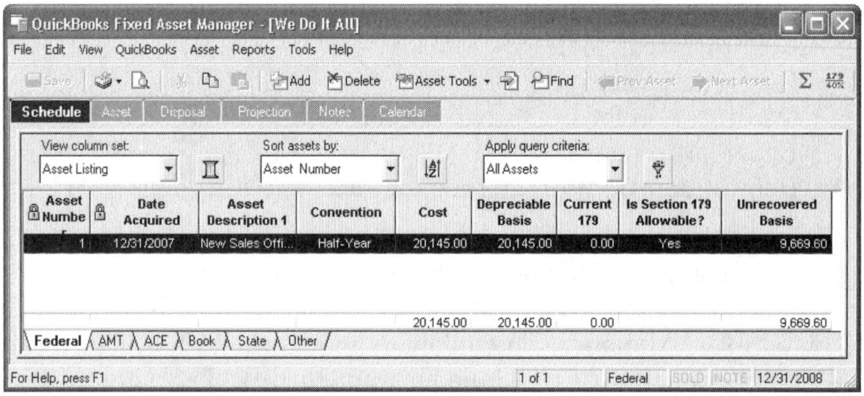

Figure 10-6: The QuickBooks Fixed Asset Manager client file is loaded and you can begin your work.

Entering Fixed Assets Manually

If the client's company file has no entries in the Fixed Asset Item List, but has maintained information about the purchase of fixed assets, you can enter the data manually. Click the Add icon on the toolbar, and enter the appropriate data by scrolling through both sections of the window.

Importing Data from Other Software

If asset and depreciation records are tracked in another software application, you can import the data to Fixed Asset Manager. In the Fixed Asset Manager window, choose File → Import. The only import file format on the submenu is Comma Separated Value (CSV) file.

If the other program can't export data to a CSV file, but can save data in a file format that is readable by Microsoft Excel, open the file in Excel, and then save the file in CSV format.

***NOTE**: You must map the fields in the import file to the fields in Fixed Asset Manager. Fixed Asset Manager provides help for this task during the import.*

If you've been managing fixed assets for the client in ProSeries tax software, you can import data directly from that software to Fixed Asset Manager. If ProSeries is available (installed on the computer), the File → Import submenu includes the listing ProSeries Tax.

Viewing and Editing Assets

As I said earlier in this section, I'm not going over all the features and functions of Fixed Asset Manager (because it would fill a separate book), but I'll present a few guidelines that should help you get started.

Schedule Tab

In the Schedule tab, Fixed Asset Manager identifies the assets using the text in the Purchase Description field of the QuickBooks Fixed Asset Item list—not the text in the Name field. In fact, Fixed Asset Manager doesn't even import the name field from the QuickBooks Fixed Asset Item list.

Fixed Asset Manager assigns a number to each asset, and that number becomes the asset's name (you can think of it as a code) in the Fixed Asset Manager client file. If the assets were obtained automatically from a QuickBooks Fixed Asset Item list, the numbers represent the order of assets in that list.

The asset that's currently selected in the Schedule tab is the asset used when you visit any of the other tabs at the top of the software window.

Asset Tab

Use the Asset tab to enter information about tax forms, posting accounts, and other data about the selected asset.

The upper section of the tab is the place to enter general information for the selected asset, including any classification fields. The bottom section of the Asset tab is the Basis Detail section. Enter the cost, date acquired, tax system, depreciation basis, recovery period, and other information needed to calculate the asset's depreciation. You can also configure Section 179 deductions here, if appropriate for this asset.

Disposal Tab

Use the Disposal tab to dispose of assets. Fixed Asset Manager displays the cost basis, and any Section 179 deductions. Enter the sales price, the expense of sale, and any other relevant information about the disposal.

For ProSeries client file exports, select a property type from the drop-down list to determine where the disposal information will appear on Form 4797, Sales of Business Property.

Projection Tab

Use the Projection tab to determine the best depreciation method for the selected asset by reviewing its projected depreciation. Use the Bases tabs at the bottom of the window to see the projections.

__TIP__: You can change information in the Asset tab to alter the projections available in the Projection tab.

The other tabs on the Fixed Asset Manager window are informational. The Notes tab is a blank window where you can write notes and reminders. The Calendar tab displays information about an asset on the selected date (select date acquired, date of disposal, or both).

Configuring Depreciation

Use the Tools menu to set up depreciation, using the following tools:

- **Prepare For Next Year**. This process removes disposed assets from the asset list, adds the current year depreciation to each asset's record, updates unrecovered basis fields for each asset, and calculates depreciation for next year. Be sure to print reports on the current status of each asset before using this tool.

- **Recalculate All Assets**. This process recalculates the current depreciation for each asset. Prior depreciation is calculated and posted according to the rules you configure in the dialog.
- **179/40% Test**. This process applies the Section 179/40% test to the appropriate assets. You can select the convention you want to use for the test.

Using the Section 179/40% test

To determine whether the Section 179 deductions claimed for the current year are within allowed limits, or to calculate the percentage of assets acquired in the last three months of the year, use the Section 179/40% test.

Perform these diagnostics after you enter client asset information and before you print reports or link the file to the client's tax return. To perform these tests, choose Tools → 179/40% Test. Review the Section 179 test, then click the 40% test tab to review mid-quarter totals.

Reviewing Section 179 limitations

The Section 179 test determines the total cost of all eligible Section 179 property, the total Section 179 expense deduction made, and how much of the deduction exceeds federal limits for the active year

Reviewing the Mid-Quarter 40% test

Fixed Asset Manager totals the cost of all assets purchased in the active year and all assets purchased in the last quarter of the active year. If the percentage of assets purchased in the last quarter is greater than 40%, you can convert these assets to the mid-quarter convention.

Using the Client Totals Summary

Use the Client Totals Summary to review the accumulated cost and depreciation before and after current-year calculations for each basis supported in a client file. To see the Client Totals Summary, choose View → Client Totals.

Calculating Depreciation

When the selected asset is properly configured, go to the Asset tab and choose Asset → Calculate Asset. If the command is grayed out, Fixed Asset Manager does not have all the information it needs to perform the calculation. Check all the fields to make sure you've entered the required information about this asset.

***TIP**: You can configure Fixed Asset Manager to automatically calculate assets after making modifications. To select this setting, choose Tools → Program Options. Select the Automatically Calculate Assets option, and click OK to save the change.*

Posting a Journal Entry to QuickBooks

Fixed Asset Manager automates the process of creating a journal entry for depreciation expense and/or accumulated depreciation. Choose QuickBooks → Post Journal Entry To QuickBooks, and then enter the appropriate information.

Creating Reports

Fixed Asset Manager provides a variety of report options, including preconfigured report templates. Choose Reports → Display Reports to view the available reports.

To organize a report list, choose Reports → Report List Organizer. Select the reports you want to associate with this client file (you're creating a custom report list). You can also opt to print reports in batches.

Select a report list from the drop-down list (or create a new report list by clicking New). Then select and deselect the reports you want to include.

Exporting Depreciation Data

Fixed Asset Manager has built in tools for exporting depreciation data, and then importing the data to another software application. The following file formats are supported:

- ProSeries
- Microsoft Word
- Microsoft Excel

- ASCII (text) file
- CSV file
- Tax Worksheets

Creating Tax Worksheets

Fixed Asset Manager automatically creates tax worksheets, using the information in the client file. Choose Reports → Display Tax Worksheet to open the Print Preview dialog. Select the worksheets you want, and click OK to preview them, and then print them. The following tax worksheets are available:

- Form 4562 Part I — Section 179 Summary Copy
- Form 4562 Part II & III— Lines 15, 16 and 17
- Form 4562 Part III — Lines 19 and 20
- Form 4562 Part IV — Summary
- Form 4562 Part V — Listed Property
- Form 4562 Part VI — Amortization
- Form 4797 Part I — Property Held More Than One Year
- Form 4797 Part II — Ordinary Gains and Losses
- Form 4797 Part III — Gains from Disposition of Depreciable Property
- Form 4626— Depreciation Adjustments and Tax Preferences
- Form 4626— ACE Worksheet
- Form 4626— Gain/Loss Adjustments

Understanding Fixed Asset Manager Synchronization

When you open and close Fixed Asset Manager, data is synchronized between the software and the QuickBooks company file (and a log is displayed). You can also manually update the asset information between QuickBooks and Fixed Asset Manager. The commands, and the default settings for automatic synchronization, are on the QuickBooks menu.

Before you synchronize, be sure to print reports about the asset list from both software applications, so you have a way to track changes. Remember, if you dispose of an asset in Fixed Asset Manager, the synchronization process removes the asset from the QuickBooks Fixed Asset Item list.

Financial Statement Designer

The Financial Statement Designer (FSD) gives you the power to customize financial statements that are directly linked to a client's QuickBooks data. This means you don't have to export financial data to other programs when you want to create a customized statement. This is a powerful and robust program, and in the following sections, I'll give you an overview of the program.

As a built-in program, FSD opens from within QuickBooks, and uses the data in the currently open QuickBooks company file (usually a client's file). To open the program, choose Accountant → Financial Statement Designer (the program is also listed on the Reports menu).

When the Financial Statement Designer opens, the program window offers two options:

- Create A New Financial Statement Designer Client, which creates a file for the current company.
- Reconnect To An Existing Financial Statement Designer Client, which opens a client file you previously created.

For this discussion, I'm assuming you selected a new client file, and I'll go over some of the tools and features you'll find as you create that file.

Financial Statement Designer Components

The FSD has three components:

- Financial Statement Organizer
- Financial Statement Editor
- Supporting Document Editor.

Financial Statement Organizer

The Financial Statement Organizer is the "front end" of the FSD. It's the component you see when you start using the FSD. This is where you select the options for the financial statement(s) you're building.

All of the following tasks are performed in the Financial Statement Organizer:

- Creating a new set of financial statements and supporting documents.
- Setting the date range for the statement.
- Setting the statement basis.
- Selecting a template for the new financial statement.
- Printing financial statements and supporting documents.
- Saving statements and supporting documents as PDF files.
- Editing saved financial statements and supporting documents.
- Viewing the list of saved financial statements and supporting documents.
- Creating folders to organize your statements and documents.

Financial Statement Editor

The Financial Statement Editor is the component you use when you're designing a financial statement. When you double-click a financial statement in the Financial Statement Organizer window, QuickBooks fetches the data from the company file, and displays the statement in the Financial Statement Editor.

The Editor uses a spreadsheet paradigm. You can insert rows and columns, add accounts and formulas, attach supporting schedules, and change the formatting of your financial statements.

Editor Toolbars

The Financial Statement Editor includes three toolbars that are similar to the toolbars you use in Excel.

The **Standard Toolbar** provides the normal file operation functions, such as New, Open, Cut, Copy, Paste, Save, Print, Print Preview, Undo, and Redo. In addition to these familiar icons, the Standard toolbar offers a Refresh icon (to refresh the data in the statement), and a Statement Date icon (to set a different date range).

The **Format Toolbar** contains icons to apply fonts, font color, indentations, alignments, cell underlines, formats (for decimals, percentage, and currency), and AutoSum functions.

The **Formula Bar** identifies the current location of the cursor, and provides a text box for entering formulas.

Design Grid

The Design Grid is the area that displays the account descriptions, balances, report headers and footers, column headers, and the results of the formulas you've entered.

You can customize statements by inserting columns or rows to show prior year balances, percentages, and variances between other columns and sub-totals. You can also insert rows for sub-totals to group accounts, or add blank rows for spacing between account types.

To enhance the appearance of the document, or add information, click the Insert menu and select one of the following commands:

- Page Break inserts a page break at the location of the cursor.
- Page Number prints the page number.
- Current Date and Time prints the date and time of printing (actually two separate fields; you must insert both fields to print both on the report).
- Statement Date prints the statement ending date.
- Statement Basis prints the statement basis (cash or accrual).
- Client Information prints a selected field from the Client Information window (such as company name, e-mail address, URL for the company's web site, etc.).
- Accountant Information prints a selected field from the Accountant Information window (such as firm name, e-mail address, URL for the accounting firm's web site, etc.).

Properties Panel

The Properties panel is on the left side of the Editor window. This panel consists of four sections: Column Properties, Row Properties, Cell Properties, and Statement Properties. You can use the Properties panel to view or change the properties for a particular area of the financial statement.

Use the Column Properties to set the date range for account balances in a specific column. For example, you can configure one column for prior period balances, and another column for current period balances.

Row Properties affect a variety of settings, depending on the element you select in the Design Grid. You can use the Row Properties to do the following:

- Repeat column headers on every page
- Change the account description that appears on the financial statement
- Add or remove accounts for a combined account row
- Reverse the sign of an account balance
- Print an account row even if the account balance is zero.

The Cell Properties let you set a date range that overrides the column's date range for account balances. The change affects only the selected cell.

The Statement Properties allow you to set the column spacing.

Attaching Supporting Schedules

Supporting schedules are used to report the details for major account categories (such as inventory, or operating expenses) in a condensed financial statement. To attach a supporting schedule, choose Tools → Attach Supporting Schedules.

When you attach a supporting schedule to a financial statement, both the financial statement and the selected supporting schedule(s) are printed. You can choose the order of printing on the General tab of the Print window.

Previewing and Printing Financial Statements and Documents

You can preview and print a complete set of financials statements and supporting documents. You can export and e-mail the documents, and even save them as PDF files. Previewing financial statements and documents lets you see how they will look when they're printed, giving you a chance to make sure they're formatted correctly.

- To preview the financial statement, choose File → Print Preview.
- To print the financial statement, choose File → Print.

The Options tab on the Print dialog includes selections that apply to financial statements. You can configure the way account balances appear on the financial statements, as follows:

- Divided by 1000.
- Use whole numbers (numbers are rounded to the nearest dollar). Select the account to which rounding errors are posted from the drop-down list on the Options tab of the Print dialog.

You can suppress the printing of accounts with a zero balance, and you can replace the zeros with another character (enter the character in the box).

***TIP**: The settings on the Options tab of the Print window can also be set in the Options window of the Financial Statement Editor (choose Tools → Options).*

Exporting FSD Files

You can export your financial statements to an FST file format, which is the format used by the Financial Statement Editor. You can then import the FST files into another client's company so statements provided by your firm use the same organization and appearance.

You can export the financial statements to the following file formats:

- ASCII and tab-delimited text files (.txt)
- Comma-delimited files (.csv)
- Excel files (.xls).

You can export your supporting documents to the following file formats:

- RTF (.rtf)
- ASCII and tab-delimited text (.txt)
- Comma-delimited files (.csv)

Saving FSD Files as PDF Files

You can save your financial statements and supporting documents to PDF files. These files preserve the text formatting of your financial statements and can be viewed using Acrobat Reader (which can be downloaded from the Adobe Web site at http://www.adobe.com).

Of course, like all PDF files, they print beautifully, maintaining the formatting, design, and layout you want. In addition, you can e-mail the files to any user, regardless of the operating system that user runs.

Chapter 11

Contractor Edition

- Contractor company files
- Managing the sale of materials
- Handling customer deposits
- Job costing
- Estimates
- Handling change orders
- Managing retainage
- Payroll issues
- Customized reports

QuickBooks Premier Contractor Edition includes features and functions designed for businesses in the construction and contracting industries. My experience with contractor clients includes generals, subs, and independent trade businesses (plumbers, electricians, and so on). QuickBooks Contractor edition has features for all of those construction types. In this chapter, I cover the issues that arise most frequently.

Contractor Company Files

If you're just starting with QuickBooks, you have to create a company file. QuickBooks Premier Contractor Edition has a predefined company file for contractors that works extremely well.

The predefined company file for contractors isn't marked as such when you create a new company file. It's merely listed as an industry type, with no indication that it contains a suitable chart of accounts, and some prepopulated entries in lists. (This is what we call an "undocumented feature".)

You can create a company file using the predefined file either with the EasyStep Interview, or by clicking Skip Interview on the opening window of the EasyStep Interview, and creating the file manually. In the wizard window for selecting your industry, choose the Construction Trades listing.

Because this is a preconfigured company file, many of your preferences are already set up appropriately, and quite a few of the lists are populated with entries. Open the lists so you can delete the entries that aren't specific to your business, and rename the entries you need if the names aren't appropriate. In this chapter I discuss some of the prepopulated lists and make suggestions about changing those list entries to make them more useful.

If you're upgrading a previous version of QuickBooks to the Premier Contractor edition, you already have a company file, lists, and configuration settings. However, you should consider creating a new file using the predefined file, just to gain ideas for tweaking your chart of accounts, your settings, and your lists. Create the file and name it Test or Training or something similar.

Creating a second company file is a great way to experiment with complicated transactions—it becomes a "test file". If you're not sure how you want to handle a transaction in your real company file, open the test file and create transactions, then look at the reports.

Classes for Contractors

The predefined company file for contractors contains classes that are deemed desirable for contractors. As you can see in Figure 11-1, these classes track job related revenue and costs.

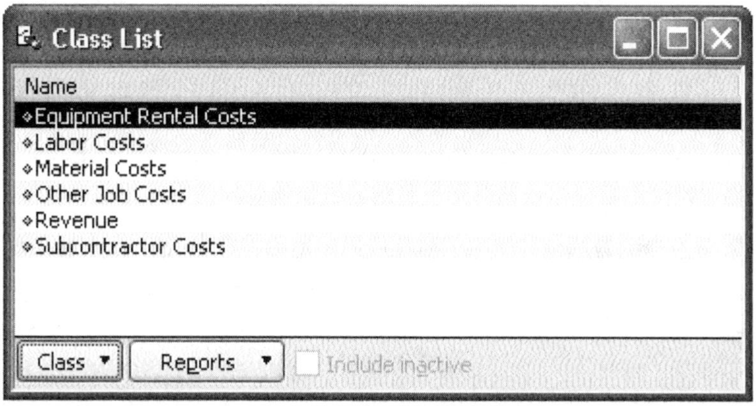

Figure 11-1: The predefined classes may not suit your needs.

The best use of classes (actually, the whole purpose of classes) is to produce a separate Profit & Loss statement for each class. Large corporations use this type of record keeping to track the Profit & Loss of each division or department. Some businesses use classes to track the Profit & Loss of each branch office.

I've never had a construction client where the classes created automatically by QuickBooks were useful. These predefined classes are for tracking costs, and there are two things wrong with that approach:

- The best use of classes is to provide separate Profit & Loss Statements for each class. I've never met a business owner or an accountant who wanted to see a Profit & Loss Statement based on equipment rental costs.
- You already track costs by posting transactions to expense accounts in the chart of accounts. If your chart of accounts is well designed, you can learn everything you need about your costs from standard QuickBooks reports.

In the following paragraphs, I discuss some of the scenarios I've encountered with contractor clients, and the way we set up classes to meet their reporting needs.

Creating Virtual Branch Offices with Classes

If you perform work in more than one city, town, county, or state, you probably have expenses (usually tax, permit, and licensing expenses) for each location. For example, you may have to pay taxes based on gross receipts or net profits earned in that locality, as well as payroll taxes for employees (including yourself) who perform work in that locality.

If the local income taxes are based on gross receipts or net profits, you need to track the income you generated in each location, and also track the costs you incurred for work in that location. Those are the numbers you need in order to create a P & L. In addition, many local authorities impose yearly or per-job fees for permits, licenses, and other specific costs of doing business in those localities. Some have license rules and you must pay for courses and tests to obtain a license to work in the locality.

Some accountants take the total gross or profit for the company, and then report these local earnings by applying a percentage. For example, if you have a net income of $100,000, and you tell your accountant you do 15% of your work in East Overcoat Township, your accountant files a tax return with the East Overcoat tax authority that assumes a tax liability based on $15,000.

I've had calls for help from contractors who couldn't defend the numbers that approach produced when they were called in for an audit by a local taxing authority. Besides, suppose the work you do in East Overcoat isn't as profitable as the work you do in Hollow Spoon Township, but the East Overcoat tax rate is much higher? You might want to raise your prices for work in East Overcoat, or charge customers an additional flat fee to cover the increased tax rate.

If you treat each local authority as a branch office (by using a class), you can produce Profit & Loss reports for each class. Furthermore, you can assign a percentage of your overhead expenses to each class, using a formula that's based on the real numbers produced by your P & L By Class reports.

Here are some guidelines for using classes for this purpose:

- Create a class for every location/taxing authority, and also create a class named Administration (for general overhead expenses that aren't specific to any job).
- Post every income transaction to the appropriate class.
- Post every expense that is specific to the local authority to the appropriate class (such as permits, licenses, and taxes).
- Assign classes to expenses that are job related. For example, if you write a check to a supplier for something you purchased for a specific job, link the expense to the appropriate class for that job.
- Split expense postings when you write a check that covers costs for multiple jobs. Each line of the vendor bill or check should be assigned to a class, and the line items must total the payment to the vendor.
- Create payroll items to match your classes, and track the hours your employees spend in each locality. If you use a payroll service, ask them to help you set up a way to track employee time by locality. Remember to post your employer payroll costs to classes, too.

Tracking the Source of Work with Classes

If P & L reports by locality aren't an issue, you might want to know the profit margins of work that you obtain in different ways. You can use classes to track the source. Then, your P & L By Class reports provide a way for you to analyze where the best profits are.

For example, perhaps you get customers who call you directly (usually referred by one of your happy customers or because they saw your sign in the lawn of a customer), and customers who are referred by hardware stores or do-it-yourself chain stores with whom you've registered your services (or you put a sign on a corkboard). And then, of course, there's advertising such as the local yellow pages, or ads in the community newspaper.

If you track your net profits by source for a while, you may discover a pattern, and you can adjust the way you look for work to match the pattern. If you learn that referrals from the local hardware stores turn out to provide more profit than referrals from any other place, visit more hardware stores to arrange for referrals.

If you learn that the least profitable jobs come from paid advertising (don't forget to post the advertising costs to this class), you can save some money by cutting back your advertising budget.

Using classes for this purpose only lets you track profits (and assign overhead intelligently) by broad general categories. If you want to track the profit by each referring entity (specific hardware stores, or specific advertising contracts), you need to track customers and jobs by type (covered later in this chapter).

Tracking the Type of Work with Classes

Depending on your specific type of business, you might want to track the profitability of different types of jobs. For example, you may have some jobs that fit into rather easy-to-define categories, such as:

- New construction (includes new rooms in existing houses)
- Restoration of historical properties
- Rehab of rundown properties
- General repair work

To track profits and losses for each type of work create the appropriate classes. The particular categories I mention here are used by local contractors I've worked with. Restoration is a big issue where I live, and generally contractors charge more because they need to do research about the original plans for the house, and historical societies keep an eye on the finished work they produce. Often, rehabs are government subsidized and require additional expenses, such as filling out complicated RFPs (Request For Proposal), and obtaining professional certification. Your own professional categories may vary, but this list gives you some ideas for determining how different types of work can be classified.

The class-based reports you create can provide more than just the P & L figures you need for tax forms. These reports give you insight on the financial advantage (or disadvantage) of each division of your business. If you learn that your bottom line for rehab work is much better than your bottom line for new construction, perhaps it's time to turn your company into a rehab specialty business.

Tracking General vs. Subcontractor Profits with Classes

If you act as a general contractor for some jobs, and as a subcontractor for other jobs, you can track the profitability over the year(s). To report net profits from your general contractor work separately from your subcontractor work, create classes for each type of work.

Customer Types for Contractors

You should create entries representing the customer types you want to track, and then apply the appropriate type to each customer. The predefined customer types in the QuickBooks contractor company file are:

- From Advertisement
- Referral
- Retail
- Wholesale

This list doesn't work properly because it isn't consistent. Customer Types should separate a specific piece of information into categories, and should be designed to avoid confusion or overlapping. In this case, the first two listings have nothing to do with the next two listings; in fact, most of your customers could be typed as "one of the first two listings and also one of the last two listings". This is not going to work!

The first two customer types provide an excellent method of tracking the way you obtain jobs. You can easily use the information you gain to increase business. Of course, these customer type entries don't work unless you specifically ask each customer how they learned about your business.

The Retail and Wholesale types are more suited to businesses that sell products to both retailers and wholesalers. You can delete those types and add other types that reflect other methods that bring you business.

If tracking referrals shows you get more business in one particular way, or the least amount of business in one way, test the referrals paradigm. Do something to increase referrals (besides the obvious ploy of doing a good job and making your customers happy), and then track the results.

For instance, when you send your final invoice, enclose a flyer that offers something for every referral that turns into a job. Buy merchandising gifts that fit your business, and send a gift to each customer that refers a new customer. Depending on the type of contractor business you have, a suitable gift may be a tape measure, a stud-finder, polish for plumbing fixtures, a flashlight, or any other inexpensive and useful gift. Print small labels with your name, logo, and telephone number, and affix one to the gift.

If referral business increases, continue to reward referring customers. If referral business doesn't grow, and advertisements continue to be more effective, increase your advertising budget. Test one new medium at a time, and track the results.

You can also use these predefined customer types as the basis of more complex, and more meaningful, customer types. For example, you could have the following customer types:

- Ad-yellow pages
- Ad-local paper
- Ad-cable TV
- Ad-broadcast TV
- Refer-Joe's hardware
- Refer-Bob's hardware
- Refer-customer

***NOTE**: You can use up to 31 characters for a Customer Type entry.*

Sometimes, the source of business isn't important to you. Perhaps you don't feel you need to spend money on advertising, or you don't need to track the source of business because all your business comes from a store or a general contractor. In that case, use customer types that provide another quantifying description for customers, and track those descriptions in reports.

For example, you may find it useful to sort customers by the type of work. Depending on your type of contractor business, you could use New and Rehab as customer types. Alternatively, examine the list of suggestions for using classes earlier in this section, and use one that isn't suitable for your own class list, but may work nicely as your customer type list.

Job Types for Contractors

Use the Job Type list to sort jobs in some manner that's useful for analyzing the work you do, creating profit reports for job types, or creating job-costing reports for each type of work. The QuickBooks predefined company file for contractors contains several job type entries, seen in Figure 11-2.

Figure 11-2: The pre-loaded job types are useful for some types of construction businesses.

If any of the predefined job types don't work for you, delete the useless ones and create your own descriptive types, based on the types of jobs you take on.

Vendor Types for Contractors

You can track vendors by type, to analyze the categories in which you spend your money, and to contact vendors appropriately. The QuickBooks predefined company file contains some built-in vendor types, but I usually advise clients not to use them. Most of the categories they represent can be tracked automatically in QuickBooks. For example, expense accounts in the chart of accounts provide the same information.

I prefer to use vendor types to quantify vendors in a way that makes it easier to contact them for specific reasons. For example, vendors who are your subcontractors need to be contacted when you need bids for a potential job. In that case, I use vendor types that sort appropriately when my client needs to send an RFP. The following examples illustrate the possible vendor types for a plumber:

- Demolition
- Digging/back hoes
- Gas line install
- Wiring
- High tech controls

My clients then create a vendor report filtered by type, displaying the vendor contact name, address, phone number, fax number, and e-mail address. This makes it easy to send out an RFP.

Items for Contractors

The entries you put into the Items list should be well thought out, because you use them constantly. You need an item for every category of sale you make, but not for every single individual product or service—the word "category" is the important keyword to consider.

The predefined company file for contractors has an Items list you should examine. This list almost certainly doesn't match your exact needs (it's a wide-ranging list covering all types of contractor businesses), but you can get a sense of the way an Items list can be put together. Delete the items you don't need, and add any items you need that are missing.

***TIP**: You can edit the Items you keep from the predefined list to get rid of the numbers at the beginning of the item name. Most people find it easier to use the items in alphabetical order when they're selecting an item in a drop-down list of a transaction window.*

Managing the Sale of Materials and Parts

Most contractors don't need to track inventory formally, because they don't buy parts for resale, the way a retail store does. Instead, they keep parts in stock for use in jobs (which is a form of resale, but not the same as running a retail parts store).

I find that many independent contractors have a long list of parts, both inventory and non-inventory, in their Item lists. Frequently, the list contains multiple entries of the same item.

For example, I've seen item lists in electrician's files that included Plate Covers-2hole, Plate-Covers-4hole, and so on. Plumbers have listings such as PVC-4', PVC-8', and so on. Plumbers who do this probably add a new inventory item every time they buy a different length of PVC. This is almost always totally needless, and makes the time you spend on record keeping longer than necessary.

It's much better to keep a short list of items. For example, use an item named Pipe in your invoices. If your customer cares about the number of feet of pipe you used, enter that information in the Description column of the invoice (I'll bet most customers don't care). Even better, use an item named Materials in your invoices, and then use the Description column to inform your customer that it was pipe.

When you create your items for materials, use the Non-inventory Part item type, and select the option This Item Is Purchased For And

Sold To A Specific Customer:Job. Fill out the cost and the price, along with the posting accounts.

When appropriate, use a per-unit cost and price. For example, you can have an item named Wood and enter the per-running-foot cost and price. Then, when you use 25 feet of that wood on a job, enter the item, enter a quantity of 25, and let QuickBooks do the math.

Applying Units of Measure to Materials

The best way to manage the sale of materials without creating a mile-long list of different sizes, lengths, and amounts is the Units of Measure feature. Details about setting up and using this nifty feature are in Chapter 7.

The Premier Contractor Edition supports multiple units of measure (U/M), which means you can create a base U/M and then devise multiple conversions of that base U/M to permit sales of different quantities of the same item. Multiple U/Ms support the following types of measurements:

- Count (e.g. single, dozen, package, case, etc.)
- Length
- Weight
- Volume
- Area
- Time
- Self-configured (invent your own)

This list contains every possible useful measurement calculation for contractors.

***NOTE**: To create a Multiple U/M, be sure you've enabled Multiple U/M Per Item in the Items & Inventory category of the Preferences dialog. Then open an item from the Items list, and in the U/M field, select <Add New> from the drop-down list to create a U/M.*

Handling Customer Deposits

When you receive a deposit from a customer, you cannot record the money as income. You haven't yet earned the money; it still belongs to the customer. You can turn it into income by completing the work (or a portion of the work, as agreed to with the customer). Until that time, that money is a liability to your company.

Elements for Tracking Customer Deposits

To track the money you receive as deposits separately from money you earn as income, you need to set up an account to track the deposits. When you earn the revenue, it's posted to an income account. In order to create the transaction that moves the deposit/liability into income, you need to create an item that you can use in the transaction. I cover both these elements in the following sections.

Creating a Liability Account for Customer Deposits

You need a liability account to track customer deposits, and you use this account when you receive a deposit from a customer. If you used the pre-defined company file for contractors, the account already exists as Customer Deposits Received.

If you have to create this account, open the chart of accounts and press Ctrl-N to create a new account. Select the account type Other Account Types and then select Other Current Liability from the drop-down list. Click Continue, and name the account Customer Deposits, or something similar.

When you earn the money by doing the work, you credit the customer's invoice for the amount of the deposit (or a portion of it), and that action moves the funds from the liability account to the income account you use to track revenue.

Creating an Item for Customer Deposits

You need an item for customer deposits, which you use when you create transactions involving those deposits. To create the item, open the Items list, and press Ctrl-N to open the New Item dialog. Then create the item using the following guidelines:

- The type of item is Service.
- The rate is zero, because it's customer-specific, and is therefore entered at the time you create the transaction.
- The account to which it's linked is the liability account you created to track customer deposits.

Receiving a Customer Deposit

When a customer gives you a deposit you have to record it. The transaction is a Sales Receipt (this is not an invoice, it's a direct exchange of money between you and your customer). Use the following steps to record the deposit:

1. Choose Customers → Enter Sales Receipts
2. Select the customer or job.
3. Enter the payment method; if the customer gave you a check, enter the check number.
4. Select the item you created for deposits.
5. Enter the amount of the deposit.

The transaction window should resemble Figure 11-3.

Here's what happens in your company file when you record the deposit:

- The deposit account attached to the Deposit item (the current liability you created to track deposits) is credited for the amount of the deposit.
- The bank account (or undeposited funds, which gets moved to the bank account when you actually deposit the funds) is debited for the amount of the deposit.
- The customer's record is updated to record the transaction.

Applying the Customer Deposit to an Invoice

When you're ready to send an invoice to a customer who gave you a deposit, you have to apply the deposit against the invoice total. You can do this at the end of the job, with a total invoice, or partway through the job, if you send invoices periodically.

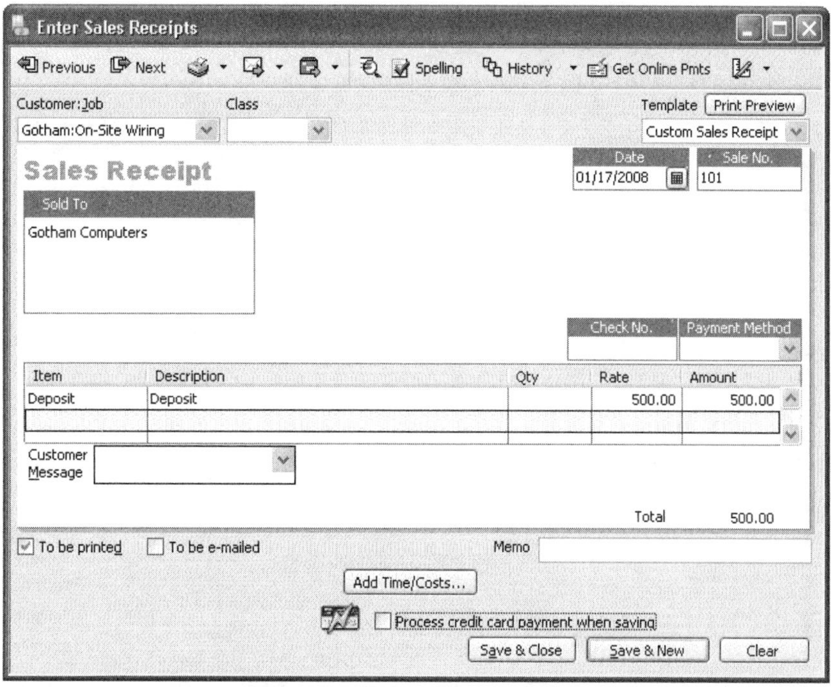

Figure 11-3: Record a deposit from the customer in the Sales Receipt form.

To create the invoice, press Ctrl-I to open the Create Invoices transaction window. Fill out the invoice with all the services and materials you've sold the customer. For the last item, use the customer deposit item you created, and enter the amount of the deposit with a minus sign (see Figure 11-4).

QuickBooks posts the invoice in the following manner:

- The income account(s) attached to the item(s) on the invoice are credited.
- The Deposit account (the liability account) attached to the customer deposit item is debited (this "washes" the credit you posted

when you used the Sales Receipt transaction to record the deposit).

- The A/R account is debited for the balance due.

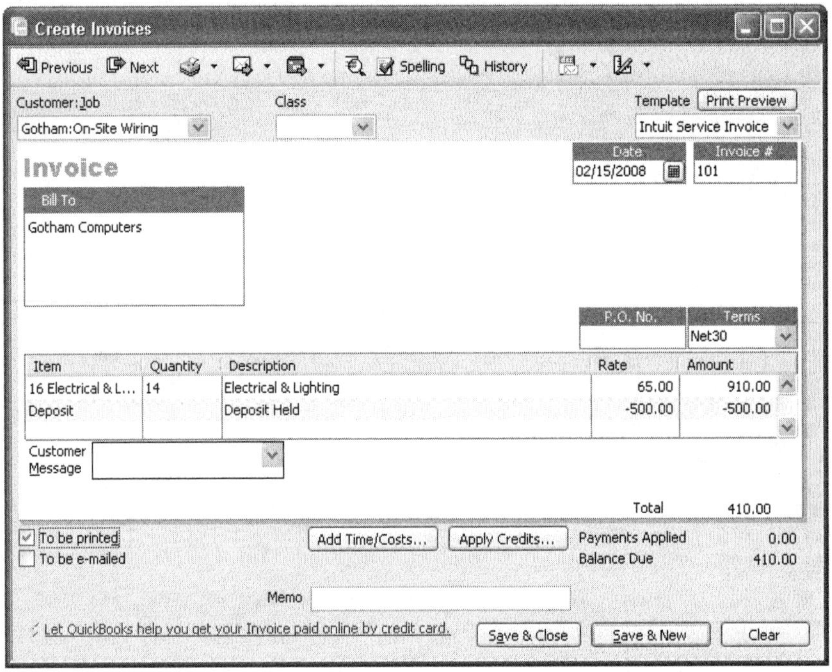

Figure 11-4: Apply the deposit against the total of the services or products you sold.

(When the customer pays the bill, the A/R account is credited, and your bank account is debited).

Reporting on Customer Deposits

You need to keep track of the customer deposits you've collected, so you know which customers have given you deposits, the amount of each deposit, and which deposits have already been applied to invoices.

You need this information when you prepare invoices for each customer, so you can enter the correct amount in the invoice item in which you're applying the deposit.

QuickBooks does not have a report that gives you this information, so you have to build it. The process takes a few minutes, so after you've created this report you must memorize it to avoid doing the work again. Use the following steps to build a report that tracks the current state of customer deposits:

1. Choose Reports → Custom Transaction Detail Report.
2. Click Modify Report to open the Display Tab of the Modify Report dialog.
3. In the Date field, select All from the drop-down list.
4. In the Columns field, select and deselect column names to end up with the following columns:
    - Type
    - Date
    - Source Name
    - Amount
5. In the Total By field, select Customer from the drop-down list.
6. Move to the Filters tab.
7. In the Filter list, select Item.
8. In the Item field, select the item you created for customer deposits.
9. Move to the Header/Footer tab.
10. In the Report Title field, replace the title with a title that matches this report, such as Customer Deposit Status.
11. Click OK to return to the report, which should now list all the information about customer deposits (see Figure 11-5).
12. Click Memorize and name the report, using the name you entered as the report title.

Notice that the report is sorted and subtotaled by customer. Each job attached to the customer is listed, along with its own total. Invoices on which you've applied deposits are listed, along with the amount of the deposit that was applied and the balance due of the deposit.

To generate this report whenever you need it, choose Reports → Memorized Reports, and select the name you gave this report when you memorized it.

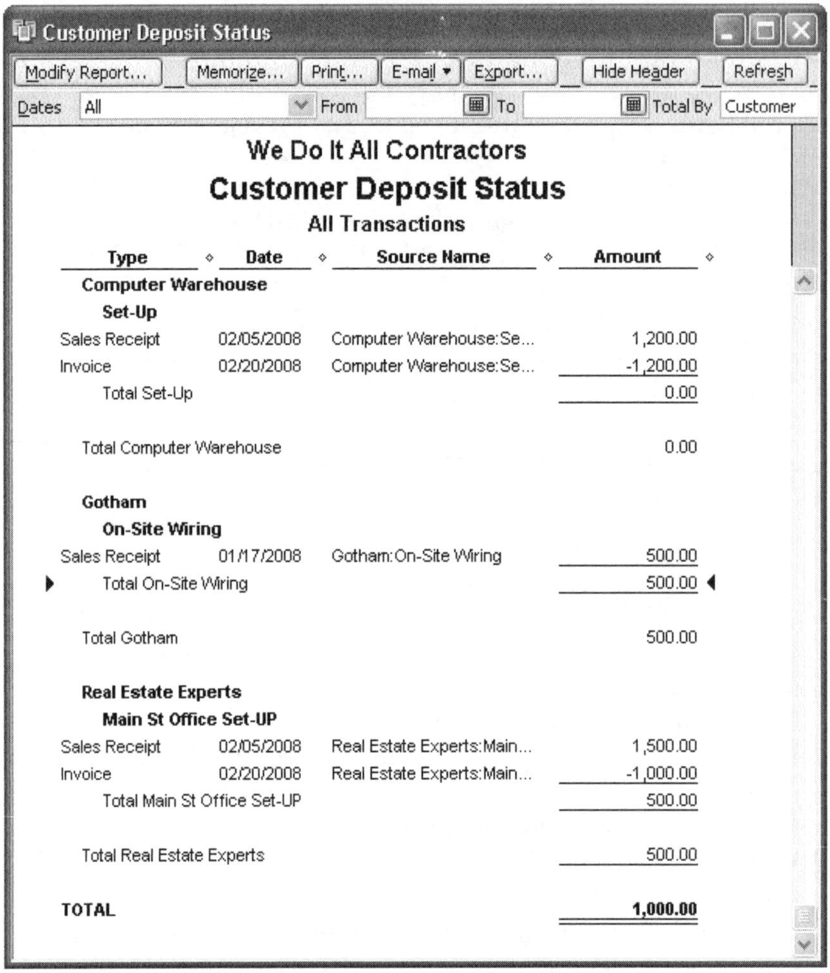

We Do It All Contractors
Customer Deposit Status
All Transactions

Type	Date	Source Name	Amount
Computer Warehouse			
Set-Up			
Sales Receipt	02/05/2008	Computer Warehouse:Se...	1,200.00
Invoice	02/20/2008	Computer Warehouse:Se...	-1,200.00
Total Set-Up			0.00
Total Computer Warehouse			0.00
Gotham			
On-Site Wiring			
Sales Receipt	01/17/2008	Gotham:On-Site Wiring	500.00
Total On-Site Wiring			500.00
Total Gotham			500.00
Real Estate Experts			
Main St Office Set-UP			
Sales Receipt	02/05/2008	Real Estate Experts:Main...	1,500.00
Invoice	02/20/2008	Real Estate Experts:Main...	-1,000.00
Total Main St Office Set-UP			500.00
Total Real Estate Experts			500.00
TOTAL			**1,000.00**

Figure 11-5: Keep track of customer deposits.

Deposits that are Just Payments in Advance

Sometimes, a customer deposit is nothing more than an advance payment. This usually means that the job is completed in a short time—usually a couple of hours or a single day.

In this circumstance, you create an invoice upfront (before beginning the job), apply the advance payment, and then leave the balance unpaid until you finish the job and ask for the balance. You don't have to treat the advance payment as a liability.

It's best to do everything in advance, during your initial conversation with the customer. Give the customer the price for the job, and tell the customer how much you need as an advance. Then, back at the office, create the invoice, apply the deposit, and print the invoice. Take the printed invoice to the job, and get the advance check/cash. When you've completed the work, hand the invoice to the customer and wait for a check (or a promise to mail the check).

Creating an Advance Payment Item

To use an advance payment, you must create an item for it. In the New Item dialog, select Payment as the Item type, and name the item Advance Payment or Payment in Advance. As you can see in Figure 11-6, items of the type Payment don't have a lot of fields to fill out.

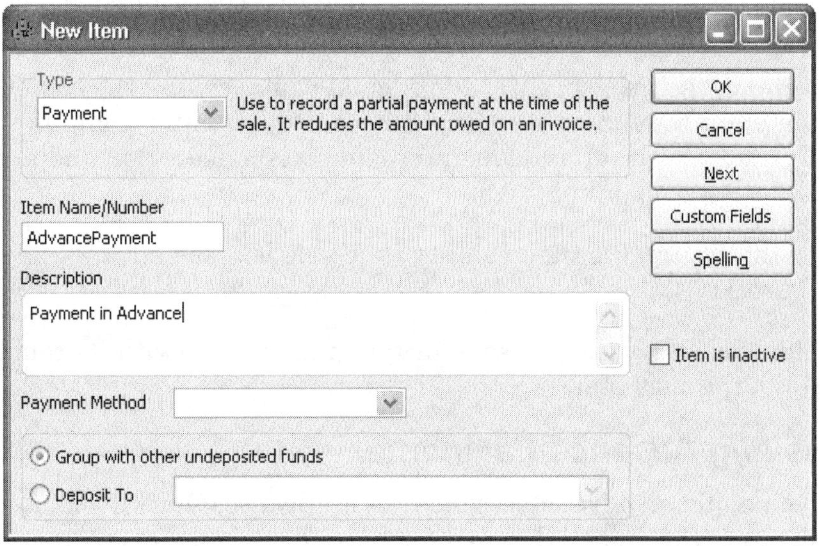

Figure 11-6: Set up an item to handle payments in advance on an invoice.

The description field is optional, but you should enter the text you want to appear in the invoice, to make it clear to the customer that the advance has been applied to the invoice. The payment type is also optional.

Select the Undeposited Funds account as the account that receives the deposit. If you don't use the Undeposited Funds account, select Deposit To and choose your operating account from the drop-down list.

Applying an Advance Payment to an Invoice

In QuickBooks, you receive an advance payment and create an invoice at the same time. The advance is not treated separately as a sales receipt or a payment against an existing invoice. You can create the scenario for the advance payment in any of several ways:

- Create the invoice, including the advance payment, and take it to the customer. Get the advance check at the same time. (This assumes you've made these arrangements with the customer.)
- Ask the customer to send you the advance, and when it arrives don't use a Sales Receipt transaction to record it. Instead, create the invoice with the advance payment included.

To create the invoice, enter the item(s) you're selling the customer, and then enter the Advance Payment item. Do ***not*** enter a minus sign; QuickBooks knows that a Payment type item is a deduction and automatically enters the minus sign.

The invoice total is the amount of the sale less the advance payment (see Figure 11-7).

When you finish the job, send or take the invoice (with its remaining balance) to the customer.

Depositing Advance Payments

When you apply an advance payment to an invoice, QuickBooks automatically deposits the money the way you specified when you created the payment item.

If you linked the advance payment item to the Undeposited Funds account, the next time you use the Payments to Deposit window, the advance payment is there. The payment is differentiated by the code INV in the Type column.

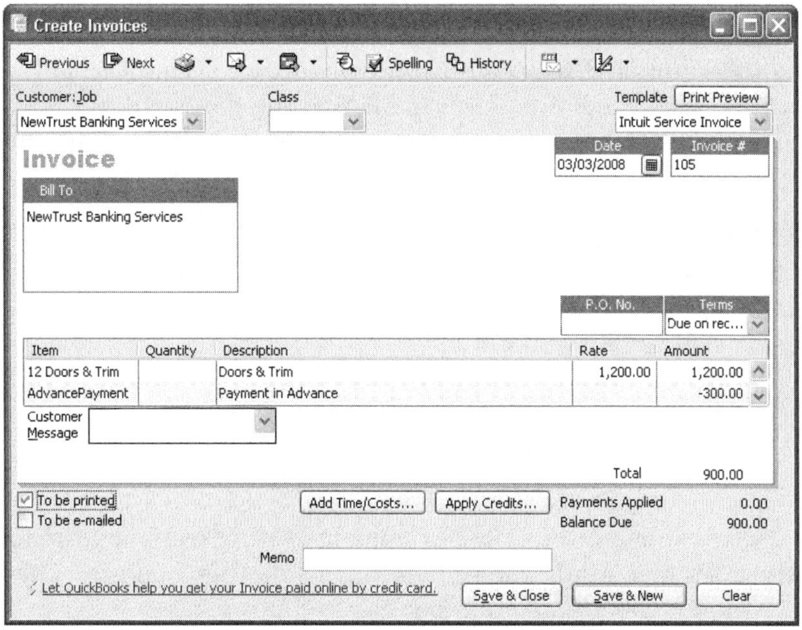

Figure 11-7: Create an invoice and apply the advance payment.

Creating a Virtual Bank Account for Customer Deposits

You don't need to open a separate bank account to hold customer deposits (only businesses that keep escrow funds, such as lawyers, are required to do that). However, if most of your jobs are long-term, and you're holding on to customer deposits for an extended period of time, you might want to think about opening a money market account (or another type of business bank account that pays interest).

If you deposit customer deposits into your regular business bank account, you must make sure you don't spend down into the deposit money. You can keep a post-it note that tracks the total of customer deposits you're holding, and maintain that balance in the bank. Or, you can configure your bank account so that it tracks two sets of totals; the total funds for customer deposits, and the total funds for the money you can spend.

If your customer deposits and regular funds are co-mingled in a single account, you can use virtual bank accounts to separate deposit funds from operating funds. When you use the operating account to pay your business expenses, the balance won't include the deposit amounts you're holding. This makes it easier to avoid spending the money you're holding as customer deposits.

In addition, having a bank account for customer deposits (whether real or virtual) provides a quick way to check the status of those funds. The amount in the bank account should always equal the amount in the customer deposit liability account.

Virtual bank accounts are subaccounts of your business bank account. The bank account you've already created in your chart of accounts is the *parent account.*

Create two subaccounts: one for your operating (regular) funds, and one for the customer funds you're holding. To do this, open the chart of accounts window and create subaccounts as follows:

1. Press Ctrl-N to open the New Account dialog.
2. Select Bank as the account type and click Continue.
3. Enter a number for the virtual operating account (if you're using account numbers). Use a number one digit higher than the number of your bank account. For example, if your bank account number is 10100, make the new account 10101.
4. Enter a name for the new account, such as Operating Funds.
5. Select the option Subaccount Of, and select your bank account from the drop-down list in the text box.
6. Optionally, enter a description of this account.
7. Click Save & New to open a blank New Account dialog, which has Bank selected as the account type.

8. Enter the next number as the account number (if you're using numbered accounts).
9. Enter a name, such as Customer Deposit Funds.
10. Select the option Subaccount Of, and select your bank account from the drop-down list in the text box.
11. Optionally, enter a description.
12. Click OK.

In the chart of accounts window, your new subaccounts are listed (and indented) under your bank account. Now you have two tasks to complete your new, more efficient, setup:

- Transfer funds out of the parent account into the subaccounts.
- Transfer any customer deposits you already have, which were posted to income when you received them, to the liability account you created to track deposits.

Transferring Funds to Subaccounts

After your bank subaccounts are created, you need to transfer the appropriate amounts into each subaccount. When you finish, the main bank account has a zero balance, although it displays the total of the balances of the subaccounts when you view the chart of accounts.

You need to figure out how much money in your bank account belongs to your customers as deposits. When you know that amount, you know how much to move from your bank account to the virtual customer deposit account.

Create a journal entry to transfer the funds by choosing Company → Make General Journal Entries. Enter the entire current balance of the bank account in the Credit column (you're emptying the account virtually, not for real).

In the next rows, debit the appropriate amounts for each subaccount (see Figure 11-8). The debit for the virtual customer funds account is the total of customer deposits you're holding. The debit for the virtual operating funds account is everything that's left in the bank account.

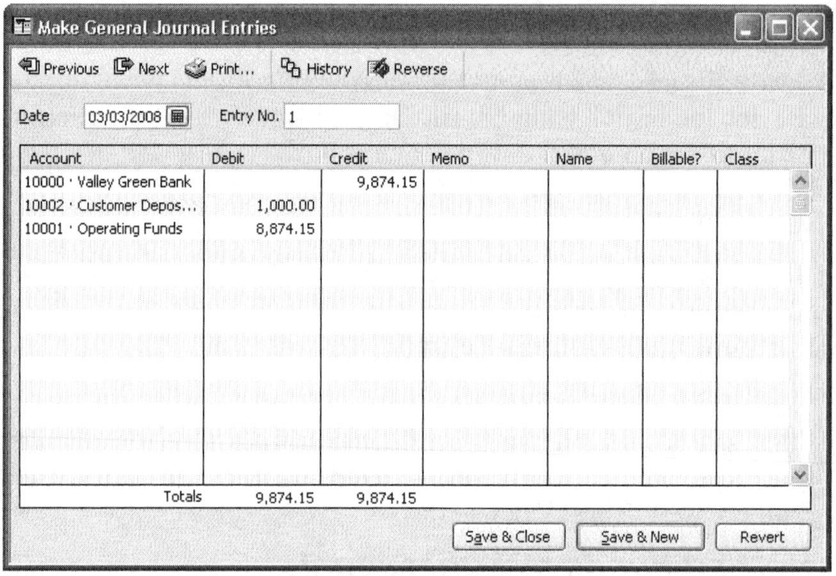

Figure 11-8: Empty the parent bank account, and fill the subaccounts.

***TIP**: If you enter the debit for the customer deposit total after you credit the entire balance of the real bank account, QuickBooks does the math and automatically enters the correct amount for the debit to the virtual operating funds account.*

When you open the Chart of Accounts List window, the balance displayed for the main bank account is the total of the balances in the subaccounts.

When you create reports that include the bank account (such as a Balance Sheet), QuickBooks displays the totals for each bank subaccount, and the grand total for the bank account.

Depositing Funds to Subaccounts

Your QuickBooks company file configuration probably enables the Undeposited Funds account. This means when you create transactions for received funds (customer payments of invoices, or cash receipts), the money is deposited into the Undeposited Funds account. (If you haven't configured your company file to use Undeposited Funds, you should, because it makes reconciling your bank account much easier.)

When you deposit the funds in the bank, you use the Make Deposits feature to transfer the funds into a bank account. This is the best way to manage bank deposits, because it matches the way your bank statement reports deposits. However, if you're using virtual bank accounts via sub-accounts, it means you have to be careful about the way you deposit money into your new virtual bank accounts.

When you move revenue from the Undeposited Funds account into the appropriate bank account, you have to separate regular income from customer deposit income. Select all the regular income, and deposit that in the operating funds subaccount. Select all the customer deposit receipts, and deposit them in the customer deposit subaccount.

Often, this isn't an easy task, because you can't tell which income is for regular earned income, and which is for customer deposit payments.

The way to resolve this dilemma is to come up with a solution that announces itself in the Payments to Deposit window. Using the Memo field in a customer payment transaction window doesn't work, because memo text isn't displayed in this window.

For my clients, I solved the problem with a new payment method, named CustomerDeposit, with a payment type of Other. To create a new payment method, use the following steps:

1. Choose Lists → Customer & Vendor Profile Lists → Payment Method List.
2. Press Ctrl-N to open the New Payment Method dialog.
3. Name the new method CustomerDeposit.
4. Select the Payment Type "Other" (see Figure 11-9).

When customer deposits arrive, either as a payment against an invoice, or as a cash receipt, the sales transaction window has a field for the Customer Deposit Payment type. The transaction window also provides a field to accept the customer's check number (always important to record in case of any disputes with the customer).

- In the Receive Payments transaction window, when you select Customer Deposit (or any other payment method classified as Other), the Check # field changes its name to Reference #.
- In the Enter Sales Receipts transaction window, when you select Customer Deposit (or any other payment method classified as Other), the Check No. field doesn't change its label.

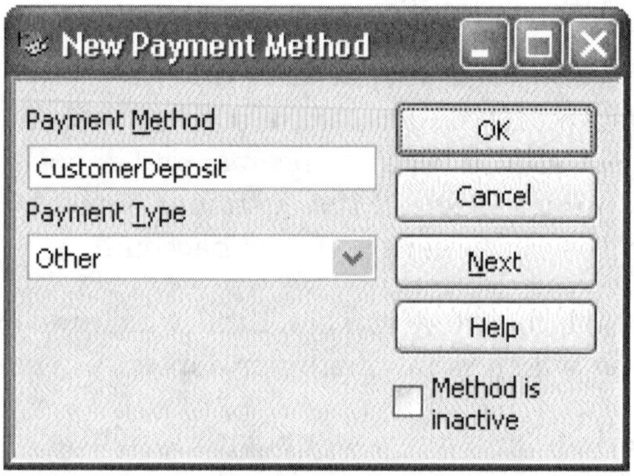

Figure 11-9: Payment methods help you identify which bank account should get the deposits.

When you use the new Customer Deposit payment method in transactions, the Payments to Deposit window is much easier to work with. As you can see in Figure 11-10, customer deposits are clearly discernable.

It's easy to deposit different payment types into different bank accounts, and QuickBooks provides two methods: one works if you only have a few listings in the Make Deposits window; the other works best if you have a lot of listings in the window.

If you only have a few deposits listed in the Payments to Deposit window, use the following steps to separate your deposits by bank account:

1. Put a check mark next to each deposit of the type CustomerDeposit.
2. Click OK to open the Make Deposits window.
3. Select the Customer Deposit bank account from the drop-down list in the Deposit To field at the top of the window.
4. Click Save & New to return to the Payments to Deposit window.
5. Click Select All to select all the remaining deposits.
6. Click OK, and in the Make Deposits window select the Operating Funds subaccount.
7. Click Save & Close.

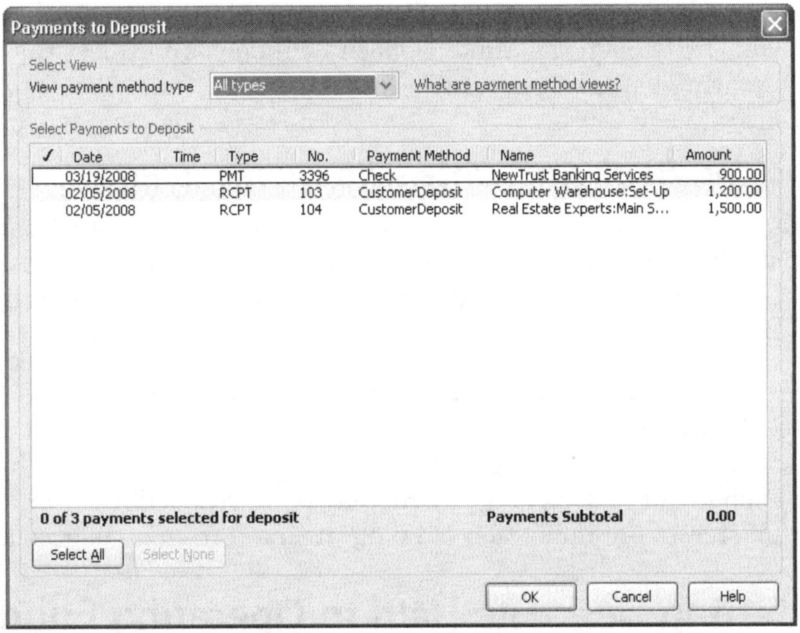

Figure 11-10: You can separate payments by type when depositing funds into a bank account.

If you have a great many deposits listed in the Payments to Deposit window (perhaps you've been storing checks in your desk and haven't been to the bank for a long time), or if you use other Payment Methods such as credit cards, cash, electronic transfers, etc. use the following steps:

1. Click the arrow next to the View Payment Method Type field at the top of the Payments to Deposit window, and choose Selected Types from the drop-down list.
2. In the Select Payment Types dialog, choose Other.
3. Click OK to return to the Payments to Deposit window, where only your customer deposit payments are displayed.
4. Click Select All to select all your customer deposit funds, and then click OK to open the Make Deposits window.
5. Select the Customer Deposit bank subaccount, and then click Save & New to return to the Payments to Deposit window.
6. Make sure All Types is selected in the field at the top of the window, and click Select All to select the remaining payments.
7. Click OK to open the Make Deposits window, and select the Operating bank subaccount.
8. Click Save & Close.

Reconciling Bank Accounts with Subaccounts

When you reconcile the bank account, use the parent account. Because your subaccounts are virtual bank accounts, instead of real separate bank accounts, the parent account actually maintains all the activity in the bank register.

After you fill out the Begin Reconciliation window and click Continue, the Reconcile dialog displays all the transactions for both accounts. QuickBooks doesn't pay any attention at all to the fact that there are subaccounts; this is just a regular bank reconciliation and no transaction shows any indication of being initiated from a subaccount.

Transferring Deposits Held to Operating Funds

When you earn the money, it's not a customer deposit any more, it's not a liability any more, it's income, and it's yours to spend.

When you create the invoice and give the customer the credit for the deposit, as described earlier in this chapter, in the section, " Applying the Customer Deposit to an Invoice", that action turns the deposit into income.

Now that it's income, and you can spend it, you have to move the funds into the operating funds subaccount. The easiest way to do that is to transfer funds between accounts, as follows:

1. Choose Banking → Transfer Funds to open the Transfer Funds Between Accounts transaction window.
2. In the Transfer Funds From field, select the Customer Deposits Held subaccount.
3. In the Transfer Funds To field, select the Operating Funds subaccount.
4. In the Transfer Amount field, enter the total of the customer deposits that are now operating funds (see Figure 11-11).

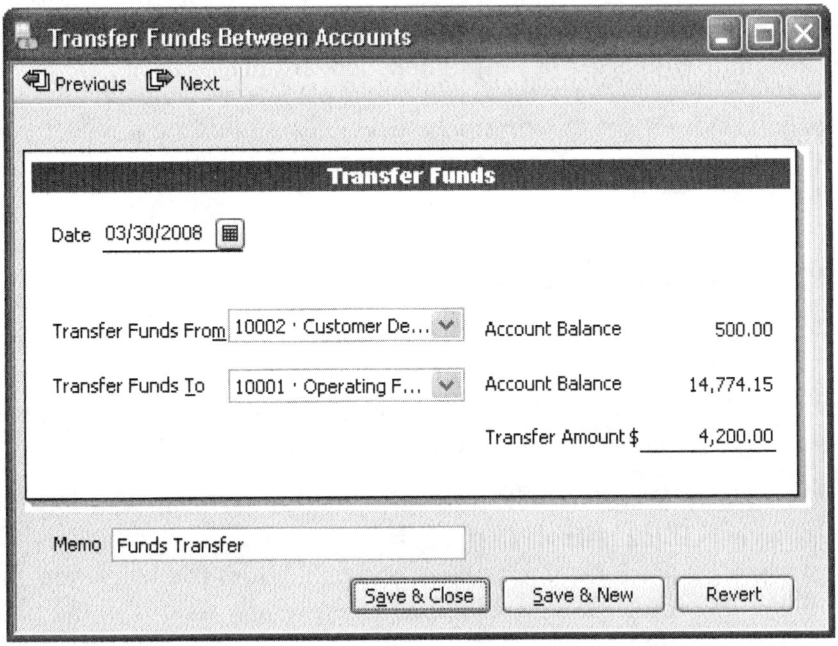

Figure 11-11: Transfer funds between subaccounts.

The balance remaining in the Customer Deposits Held subaccount matches the balance in the Customer Deposits liability account (those totals must always match).

Job Costing

Job costing is tracking the costs of each job so you can keep an eye on your costs and your profits. In QuickBooks, if you use estimates, you can also use job costing to track your estimated costs against your real costs (see the section "Estimates", later in this chapter).

Going over all the processes involved in setting up and implementing job costing involves far more information than I could present here. Each type of construction business has different needs, and you'll find that as you continue to use QuickBooks, and create reports, you'll think of other job-costing details you want to track. As a result, you'll be continuously tweaking your company file and creating new rules for entering transactions. In the following sections I'll present an overview of some of the things to think about as you implement job costing.

For job costing to work properly, every job should be a job. If you have a customer that you believe is a one-time-only customer, create a discrete job anyway.

Items and Job Costing

To track job costs effectively, you need to make sure you have all the items you need in your Items list. That means items that describe the materials and services you provide, as well as the materials and services you purchase. Use the following guidelines when you set up items:

- Create an item for each type of work you perform, and for materials you sell as part of that work.
- Create an item for each phase of work, when the work you perform has multiple phases. (This is especially useful if one phase is subcontracted.)
- Use subitems to refine both your invoicing and job costing activities. For example, if you have an item for Permits & Licenses, create subitems for the specific types of permits and licenses you need to perform your work.
- All the items you create should be of the Service type (even if the item covers materials).

- Items for materials should be generic; use lumber as an item instead of creating multiple items for different types or sizes of lumber.
- Don't enter cost and sales prices for items unless it's an item or a subcontracted service that you always buy and resell at a specific cost and price.

When you create your service items, select the check box labeled "This service is performed by a subcontractor, owner, or partner" (even if the item doesn't seem to fit that definition). Selecting this option changes the New Item (or Edit Item) dialog by adding fields for tracking both costs and sales (see Figure 11-12).

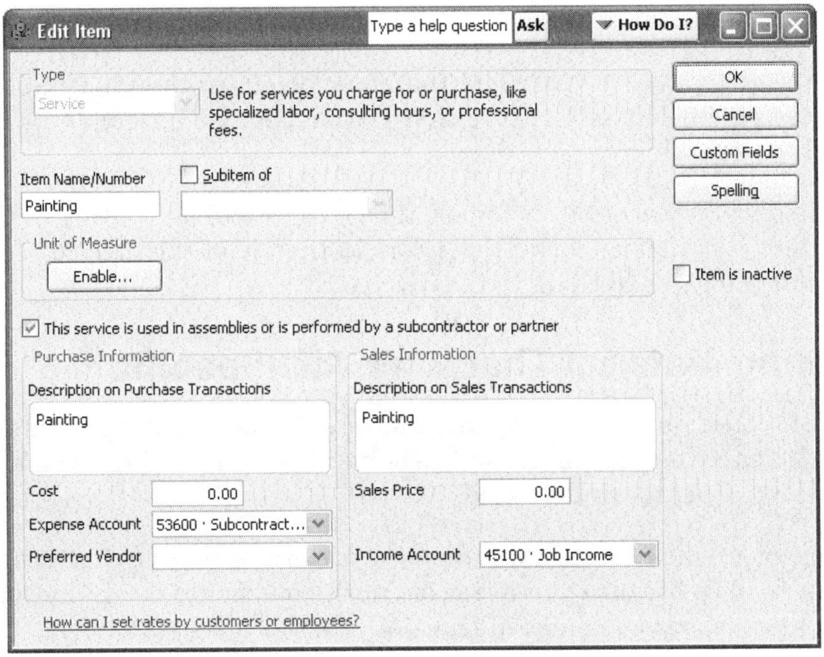

Figure 11-12: Set up your item to track both costs and sales.

In the Expense Account field, select the account to which you post job-related costs. This account should be of the type Cost of Goods—it might be an account named Materials, or an account named Subcontracted Work (if this item is something you usually job out). In the

Income Account field, select the income account to which you post job revenue.

Linking Expenses to Jobs

When you pay a vendor for materials or subcontracting work that's related to a job, link the expense to both an item and a job. You do this whether you're entering the vendor's bill in the Enter Bills transaction window, or you're using the Write Checks window to pay a vendor for whom you didn't enter a bill.

To do this, you use the Items tab, instead of entering accounts in the Expenses tab. Enter the item connected to the expense, the amount of the expense, and the job for which you incurred this expense.

If the vendor bill covers more than one job, enter the information over multiple lines, to make sure that postings for each item and job are applied to each job properly

When you invoice the customer, the charges will be waiting in the Time and Costs dialog (click Time/Costs at the top of the invoice window), and you can add them to the invoice.

Tracking Material That Isn't Job-Specific

If you purchase materials or services for a job, you link the purchase to the job by entering the job in the Customer:Job column of the vendor bill or the Write Checks window.

However, when you use warehoused materials on a job (the stuff you buy just to keep because you use it on jobs), you should track that usage in QuickBooks, so you can keep track of your job costs.

To track these generic parts and materials, you can use a system I call "paying yourself back for the consumed parts". As you pay yourself (which doesn't involve any real payments), you assign a previously purchased product to a job.

Let's say you purchased $1000.00 worth of materials, posting the purchases to an item named Materials. As you use the materials, you want to track them against a job, and bill the customer. To accomplish this, create a new account in your chart of accounts named Adjustment Register. The account type is Bank. If you're using numbered accounts, use a number that falls at the end of the number range for your other (real) bank accounts.

You'll use this account to record a zero amount check by creating two entries—one positive entry and one negative entry, which washes the total. During the entry process, you allocate the cost to a customer or job, and to a class (if you're tracking classes). Here are the steps:

1. Choose Banking → Write Checks to open the Write Checks window.
2. In the Bank Account field, select the Adjustment account.
3. In the Date field, enter the date you used the material.
4. Don't enter anything in the payee field.
5. In the Items tab at the bottom of the window, select the item you used when you purchased these supplies.
6. In the Description column, optionally enter a description of the material you used.
7. Skip the Qty and Cost columns and enter the Amount in the Amount column.
8. Select the Customer:Job (and select a Class if you're using classes). Make sure the Billable column has a check mark.
9. On the next line, fill in the exact same information for all columns except the Customer:Job and Class columns, using a negative quantity
   (If you filled out the Customer:Job and Class columns, you'd be setting the charge to the customer and class to zero, which you don't want to do).
10. Click Recalculate. The amount of the check changes to zero.
11. Click Save & Close.

When you invoice the customer, the charges will be waiting in the Time and Costs dialog, and you can add them to the invoice.

Estimates

Estimates are a necessity for contractors, and creating an estimate in QuickBooks is a straightforward process. Choose Customers → Create Estimates to open the Create Estimates transaction window.

Enter the customer, item, and financial information, including a markup if you're using markups. QuickBooks calculates the total. When you print the estimate for your customer, only the total amounts appear; any cost and markup rates you entered are not printed.

If the job has phases (for instance a demolition phase, then a building phase, then a finishing carpentry phase, and finally a cleanup phase), you should think about creating separate estimates for each phase. This makes progress billing less complicated, and also provides a way to track estimated-to-final costs on a phase-by-phase basis (which is valuable information to have when you create an estimate for another job with the same work load).

***NOTE**: QuickBooks 2008: The Official Guide has a full discussion that covers all the basics of creating estimates and using progress billing.*

Change Orders

Change orders are a common fact of life for both general and sub contractors. QuickBooks Premier Contractors Edition supports this feature, which makes your business life easier. If you're using QuickBooks Pro, you can always change an estimate, but you end up with a changed estimate. With the change order feature, you see all your change order items on the estimate form

Unfortunately, many independent contractors don't bother to create or track change orders, and sometimes this leads to misunderstandings (and occasionally, serious disputes) with customers.

It only takes a few seconds to create a change order, and you should get into the habit of using this feature for any changes to the original estimate. In fact, if you're not bothering to create estimates for every job, you should change that habit, too.

Creating a Change Order

To create a change order, you must have saved an estimate. Change orders don't exist by themselves; they're linked to estimates. To create a change order, follow these steps:

1. Open the original estimate.
2. Make changes to the quantity, price, or other line item components.
3. Click Save & Close.
4. QuickBooks displays a message asking if you want to record your changes. Click Yes.
5. QuickBooks displays the Add Change Order dialog (see Figure 11-13) asking if you want to add this change order to the estimate. Click Add.

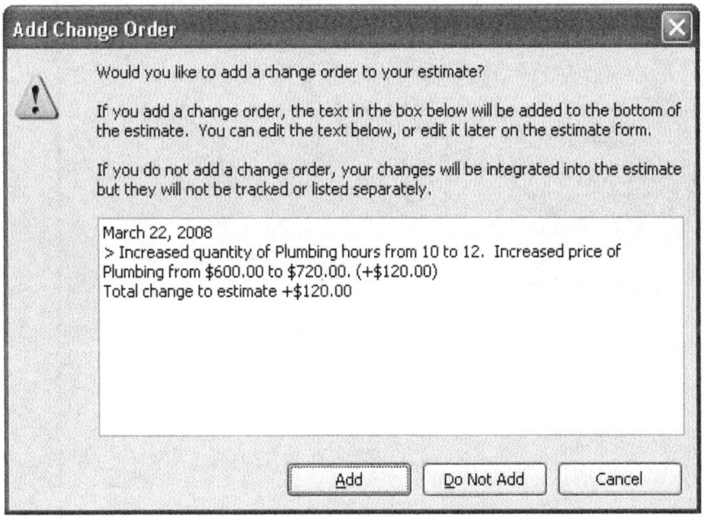

Figure 11-13: Track your changes by adding them to the estimate.

Making Additional Changes to an Estimate

It's not uncommon to require multiple changes to an estimate, especially if the estimate has many entries. Frequently, you may have to add services or items, due to some unexpected event as you complete the job.

You can continue to add or remove items in the original estimate, creating an audit trail of the job's changes. However, you have to be careful about the way you add further items.

When you view the original estimate, the change order(s) appear below the line items. A blank line sits between the line items and the change order(s), as seen in Figure 11-14.

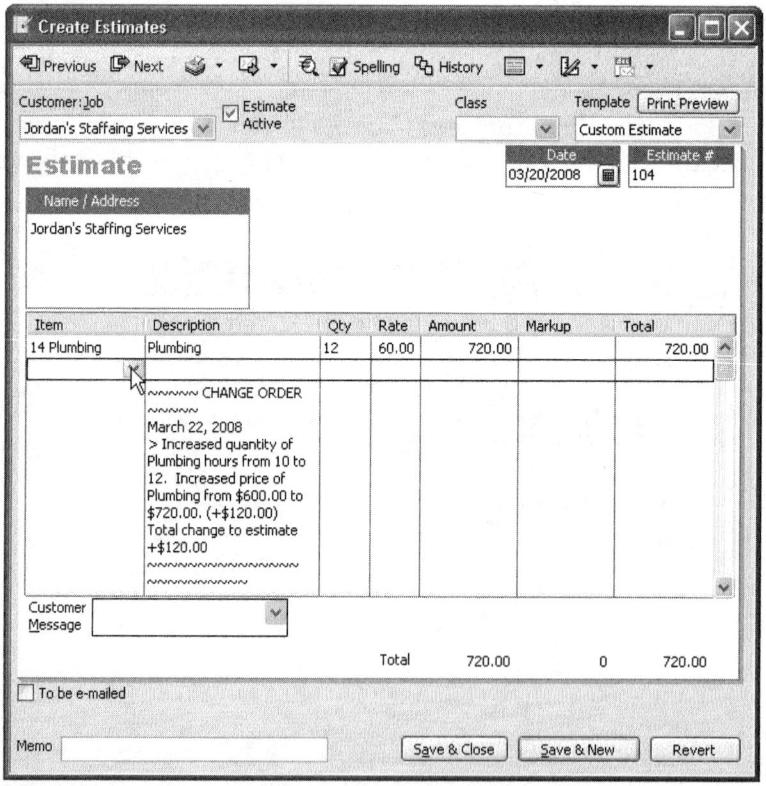

Figure 11-14: Add items in the blank line above the change order.

You should use the blank line above the change order to add items (or to remove items by entering them with a minus sign), because you want your change orders to remain below the items list. If you click the Item column in the same line that contains the change order to use that row, the change order is deleted.

If you need more than one new line, right-click the Item column of the existing new line, or the line in which the change order appears, and choose Insert Line. A new blank line appears above the line your cursor is in.

Managing Retainage

Construction contracts frequently contain a *retainage* clause (sometimes called a *retention* clause). This clause specifies that a certain percentage of the total price of the job will not be invoiced to the customer until all parties agree that the job is completed satisfactorily.

The retainage percentage is usually ten percent, and it means that you can only invoice ninety percent of the job until the terms governing retainage are met. If you use progress invoicing (invoicing a percentage of the contract price as the appropriate percentage of the work is completed), you must deduct the retainage percentage from the total of each invoice.

> ***NOTE:*** *Some contractors negotiate retainage so that progress invoices don't deduct retainage, and the entire ten percent of the total is deducted from the last invoice. This provides a better cash flow for covering costs of the work. This method only works if the progress invoicing structure results in the last invoice being large enough to cover the entire retainage amount.*

If your business encounters a retainage clause, you have to configure QuickBooks to track and report the retainage figures. This means creating accounts and items, and then entering the appropriate transactions.

Configuring QuickBooks for Retainage

The money involved in retainage is part of the contract you signed, and is your money. It's yours contractually, and it's yours because there's an expectation that you'll earn it. That makes the retainage amount an asset, so you need an asset account in your chart of accounts to track retainage.

Creating a Retainage Account

You need to create an account to track retainage. The common account type is Other Current Asset, and you can name the account Retainage, Retentions, or anything similar.

Creating Retainage Items

You need several items to include on your sales forms to implement retainage. You need an item to deduct the percentage, an item to subtotal the sales form before deducting the percentage, and an item to use when it's time to collect the retainage due to you.

Retainage Deduction Item

To create the retainage deduction item, follow these steps:

1. Choose Lists → Item List to open the Item List window.
2. Press Ctrl-N to open the New Item dialog.
3. Select Other Charge from the drop-down list in the Type field.
4. Name the item Retainage Deduction (or Retention Deduction).
5. Enter Deduction for Retainage (or something similar) in the Description field.
6. Enter -10% in the Amount Or % field – note the minus sign and the percent sign. (If you have multiple retainage rates, create an item for each, such as Retainage10, Retainage15).
   If your retainage percentage is not 10%, substitute the correct amount. If you have multiple retainage rates, create an item for each rate, naming them Retainage10%, Retainage15%, etc.
7. Enter a non-taxable tax code in the Tax Code field (which only exists if you've enabled Sales Tax).

8. In the Account field, select your retainage asset account.
9. Click OK.

Retainage Subtotal Item

The retainage item is a percentage, and QuickBooks calculates percentages against the line immediately above the percentage item on the sales form. Therefore, you must subtotal all the items on your sales form before you enter an item that calculates a percentage. This requires a discrete subtotal item in your items list.

Create a new item, using the following configuration settings:

- The item type is Subtotal.
- Name the item Subtotal (or something similar).
- Optionally, enter a description that will appear on your sales forms ("Subtotal works fine).

Retainage Collection Item

After the job is approved, you bill the customer for the retained amount, so you need an item to include on your invoice form. Use the general instructions described earlier to create the retainage deduction item. However, use the following configuration settings:

- The item type is either Service or Other Charge. I prefer Other Charge because it keeps the listing near the retainage deduction charge.
- Name the item Retainage Collection (or something similar).
- Optionally, enter a description to appear on your sales forms.
- Do not enter a rate or amount—you'll fill that in when you create the sales form.
- In the Account field, select the retainage asset account.

Using the Retainage Item in Sales Forms

You must use your retainage items whenever you create a sales form for a customer that has a retainage clause in the contract.

During the course of the job, create invoices as usual. After all the applicable line items are entered for each invoice, insert the subtotal item in the next line. Then, insert the retainage deduction item in the line after the subtotal item. QuickBooks will use the percentage figure and calculate the invoice correctly.

When the job is finished, and the contractual terms for collecting the retainage amount are met, the retainage can be released to you. Create an invoice, and use the retainage collection item to bill the customer for the withheld funds. Enter the amount due in the Amount column of the invoice.

Of course, to enter the amount due, you have to discover the correct amount. No built-in QuickBooks report exists to provide this amount, so you must create a report for this purpose. Use the following steps to determine the retainage amount you've deducted for a specific customer or job:

1. Choose Reports → Customers & Receivables → Customer Balance Summary.
2. Click Modify Report.
3. Go to the Filters tab.
4. Select Account in the Filter list.
5. In the Account list, scroll down the list to find and select your retainage asset account.
6. Click OK.
7. In the report window, locate the customer or job, and note the amount (which is the total amount you deducted over the course of all invoicing for this customer or job).

Memorize this report to avoid the need to set the filters next time you need this information for a customer. Click the Memorize button and name the report Retainage Totals (or something similar).

Depositing Checks with Two Payees

If you're in the construction business, and you're a subcontractor, the checks from the general contractor frequently arrive with two payees.) This scenario often occurs when you're working in a "time and materials" environment. You sell a customer (usually a general contractor) a product or a service you sub out to a vendor. The vendor charges you $1000.00. You enter the vendor's bill and send the sub or the product to the job.

You send the customer (the general) an invoice for $1000.00. The check arrives from the customer, and there are two payees: you and the vendor.

You can't deposit the check into your bank account, and then write a check to the vendor, because your bank won't take a check that isn't endorsed by both payees. Here's the solution:

1. Create a fake bank account named "Passthrough Payments" (or something similar).
2. Open a Receive Payments window and pay off the customer's invoice with the check. Be sure to note the check number for later reference.
3. Deposit the check to the fake bank account.
4. Select Pay Bills, and choose the fake bank account in the Payment Account field. Select the appropriate vendor bill and use the same check number to pay the bill.
5. Endorse the check and send it to the vendor with a copy of the vendor's bill.

The transactions you entered "wash" the fake bank account, so it has a zero balance. If that account shows a balance, you've forgotten to take one of the steps:

- If the account has a positive (debit) balance, you received payment for the customer invoice, but you didn't pay the vendor's bill.
- If the account has a negative balance, you paid the vendor's bill, but you didn't pay off the customer's invoice.

When you open the register for the fake bank account, you can see a history of every check you treated in this manner.

Payroll Issues for Contractors

If you do your own payroll, you have to make sure you set up your company file to manage all the payroll issues. All the information you need to set up in-house payroll is in *QuickBooks 2008: The Official Guide*.

Timesheets

QuickBooks has a built-in program for tracking time. You can track employee hours by customer:job, and by class. To learn how to use timesheets, read *QuickBooks 2008: The Official Guide.*

Workers Comp

If you sign up for QuickBooks Enhanced Payroll, QuickBooks can manage workers comp automatically. The setup options are available in the Payroll & Employees category of the Preferences dialog. Click the Set Preferences button to open the Workers Comp dialog. Select Track Workers Comp to enable the feature.

When workers comp is enabled, you can also opt to see reminder messages to assign workers comp codes when you create paychecks or timesheets. In addition, you can select the option to exclude an overtime premium from your workers comp calculations (check your workers comp insurance policy to see if you can calculate overtime amounts as regular pay).

To set up the workers comp calculations, choose Employees → Workers Compensation → Set Up Workers Comp. Follow the prompts to set up your workers comp expenses.

Certified Payroll

Most construction projects funded by public funds require certified payroll reports. Occasionally, privately funded projects require certified payrolls. You can manage payroll certification within QuickBooks by performing the tasks described in this section.

Creating a Prevailing Wage Rate Payroll Item

You must create payroll items for the prevailing wage rates. Open the Payroll Items list and press Ctrl-N to create a new item, and then follow these steps to move through the wizard, clicking Next as you enter data in each wizard window:

1. Select Custom Setup in the Add New Payroll Item Wizard.

2. Select Wage as the payroll item type.
3. Select Hourly Wages as the wage type.
4. Select Regular Pay as the hourly wage type.
5. Name the item Prevailing Wage Rate.
6. Enter the account for posting these wages.
7. Click Finish.

If you don't have an exclusion from overtime calculations, repeat this process to create an Overtime Prevailing Wage Rate.

Applying the Prevailing Wage Rate Payroll Item

When you create a timesheet and/or paycheck for an employee's work on a certified job, use the Prevailing Wage Rate payroll item you created. If all your work requires certified payroll, or if certain employees only work on certified payroll jobs, edit the Payroll & Compensation data in the employee records. Enter the Prevailing Wage Rate item instead of the generic hourly item.

Creating Certified Payroll Reports

You can view the application of certified payroll rates by selecting the payroll item and pressing Ctrl-Q. Change the date range of the QuickReport that opens to meet your needs.

QuickBooks Premier Contractor Edition includes a report that provides all the information you need to fill in Box 1 of a Certified Payroll Form for employees. Choose Reports → Contractor Reports → Certified Payroll - Box 1 Employee Information.

***NOTE**: QuickBooks has included a great many preconfigured reports of use to contractors. You can view the list by choosing Reports → Contractor Reports. The list of reports is quite comprehensive (and the report names are self-explanatory).*

Chapter 12

Manufacturing and Wholesale Edition

Advanced inventory and sales order features

Customer RMAs

Returning products to a vendor

Tracking damaged and missing inventory

Customized reports

Like most computer consultants who specialize in accounting software installations, I spend the majority of my time with manufacturing and wholesale clients. When I started consulting, a million years ago, these were the first business types to install computerized accounting systems.

Many companies purchased software systems designed specifically for their type of business. The systems are called "vertical applications" and they're written specifically for certain types of manufacturing or distribution businesses. The software packages are extremely expensive, because they're designed for businesses that gross millions of dollars a year, and have extremely complicated process that the software tracks.

For smaller businesses, it's certainly possible to track the same accounting processes with QuickBooks, and the Premier Manufacturing and Wholesale Edition includes features to help you do just that.

If you think about it, the paradigm is always the same. You buy stuff at a certain price, and you sell it at a higher price (distribution), or you buy stuff to build stuff you sell (manufacturing). Many businesses do both; they resell products, and they assemble their own products for resale.

This is all very straightforward, and small manufacturing and wholesale business can easily manage their finances with QuickBooks.

***TIP**: Chapter 7 has instructions for using the Premier editions features that help you run your business, such as automatic generation of purchase orders, managing back orders, and so on.*

Stock Status Information for Sales Orders

The QuickBooks Premier Manufacturing & Wholesale Edition offers advanced functions for tracking sales orders. Two important and useful advanced features are built into this edition of QuickBooks Premier:

- Stock shortage warnings during the creation of a sales order.
- One-click access to stock status reports in the Create Sales Orders transaction window.

These features are only available in the Premier Manufacturing & Wholesale, Retail, and Accountant editions. The other Premier editions don't advise you about stock shortages until you convert a sales order to an invoice.

Stock Status Configuration Options

By default, QuickBooks warns you about inventory stock shortages when the Quantity on Hand (QOH) is less than the quantity you enter on a sales order. However, when you're creating a sales order, the QOH isn't necessarily the only time you need to be warned about shortages.

If the QOH of a product is 10, and you want to sell 5, the math isn't as simple as it seems. If existing sales orders include that product, and those sales orders add up to 6 units, you don't really have 5 units available when you're creating a new sales order, you only have 4 units available.

Similarly, if the QOH is 10, and the people in the warehouse have begun assembling products that use that inventory part, a substantial number of the QOH may be in the process of going into an inventory assembly.

You need to configure QuickBooks to track the quantity available, not the quantity on hand.

To access this configuration option, choose Edit → Preferences, and select the Items & Inventory category in the left pane. Move to the Company Preferences tab, and make the appropriate adjustments to the configuration options (see Figure 12-1).

Control the way QuickBooks calculates available stock by selecting either or both of the options in the dialog:

- Quantity reserved for Pending Builds means QuickBooks checks the list of pending builds to see if the item you're entering in a sales form is included; if so, it deducts the total number of units of the item involved in the pending builds from the QOH.

- Quantity on Sales Orders means QuickBooks checks all existing sales orders and deducts the total units of the item you're selling from the QOH.

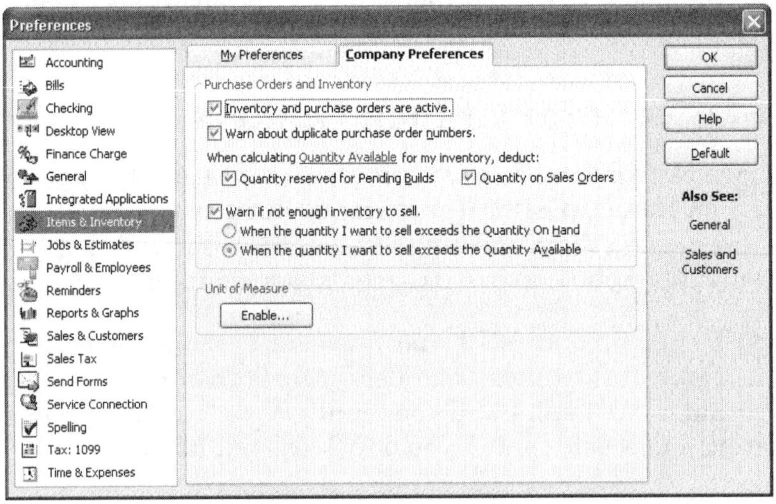

Figure 12-1: Configure the stock status algorithms that help you manage sales of inventory efficiently.

Specify the conditions under which a Warning about insufficient inventory is displayed. You can choose QOH or Quantity Available.

Out of Stock Warnings

If an item is out of stock (QOH is zero), QuickBooks issues a warning as soon as you select the item in the sales order, even before you enter the quantity (see Figure 12-2). You can continue with the sales order, and wait until stock is available before converting the sales order to an invoice.

If you configured stock status warnings to occur when Quantity Available (instead of QOH) is insufficient, the definition of "out of stock" includes inventory that is still on the shelves, but sales orders exist for the item. (If the sales orders had been turned into invoices, the stock would have been removed from the shelves, and therefore from the QOH.)

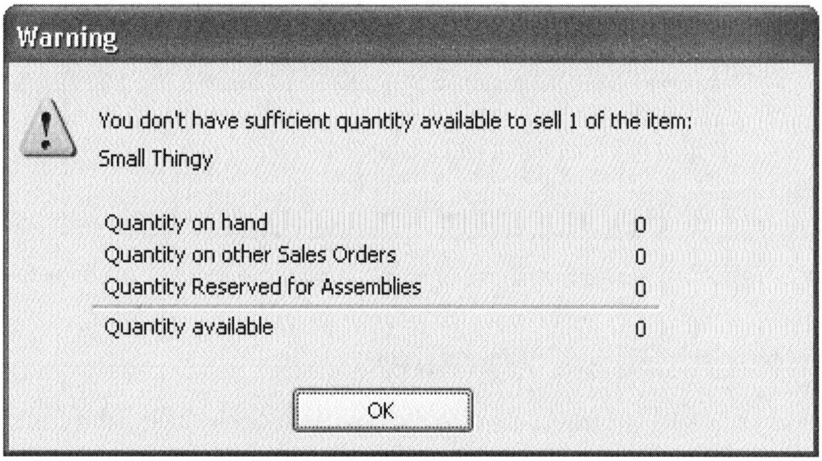

Figure 12-2: When there's no stock left, QuickBooks tells you as soon as you enter the item in the sales order.

As you can see in Figure 12-3, the warning message explains clearly that no quantity is available, so the item is deemed "out of stock". Because insufficient stock is available, the warning is displayed as soon as you enter the item in the sales order (before entering a quantity).

You can continue with the sales order and wait until stock is available before converting the sales order to an invoice, or negotiate an exchange of stock with the person who created the other sales orders. This is one of those times when you need to consider whether one customer should take priority over another customer.

You can free up stock that's available, but promised, to make sure your best customers receive their orders quickly. See "Modifying Sales Orders to Obtain Promised Stock", later in this section.

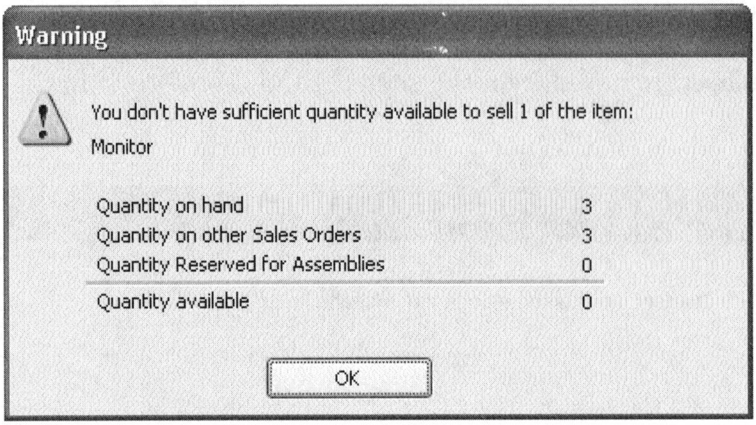

Figure 12-3: This item isn't out of stock, but all the stock is promised.

Insufficient Stock Warnings

If stock is on hand, when you enter the item in the sales order, you may not have sufficient stock available to fill the quantity the customer ordered. When you enter the number of units in the Ordered column, if there isn't sufficient stock to fill this order, QuickBooks displays a message explaining the stock status (see Figure 12-4).

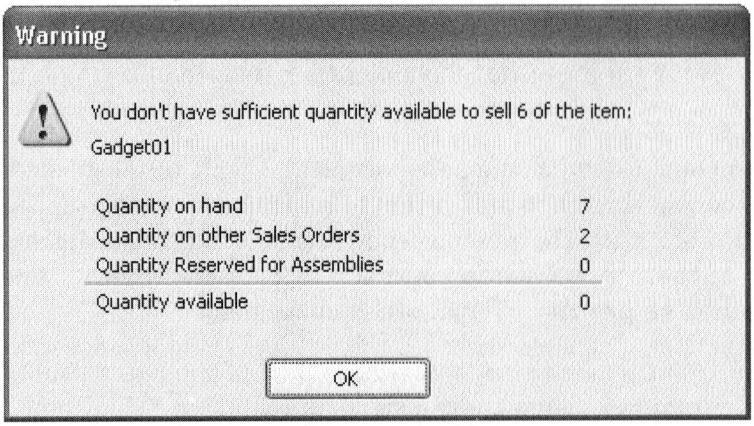

Figure 12-4: This item's stock status is less than the quantity ordered, so you can't invoice this order in full.

The math on the dialog is wrong; do the math yourself so you can enter the real amount available on the sales order and then create an invoice to ship the available stock. Depending on your customer's preferences, you can create a backorder for the remaining items, or hold the invoice until sufficient stock is available to fill the entire order.

Checking Stock Status Details

One of the nifty enhanced functions in the Premier Manufacturing & Wholesale Edition is the ability to check stock status, in detail, right from the sales order transaction window. After you enter the item in the sales order, whether you receive a stock status warning or not, click the icon that appears on the right side of the Ordered column.

QuickBooks calls this icon and resulting report "Available to Promise". This is a report on the current status of this item. As you can see in Figure 12-5, this report has more information than the stock status warnings QuickBooks displays.

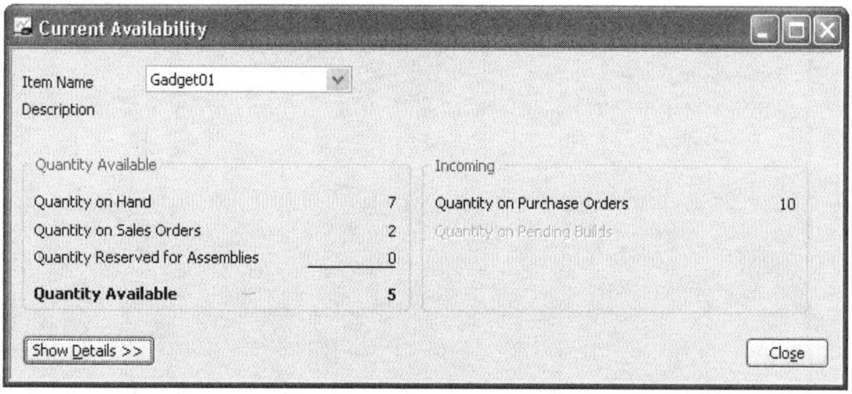

Figure 12-5: There's not enough stock, but a purchase order exists, which means stock should arrive soon.

You can learn even more about the stock status of this item by clicking the Show Details button. Then choose the type of information you want to see by selecting one of the following topics from the drop-down list:

- **Sales Orders**. This choice displays all the current sales orders that contain this item. See "Modifying Sales Orders to Obtain Promised Stock" to remove items from one of those sales orders so you can invoice and ship the current sales order.
- **Pending Builds**. This choice displays all the pending bills that include this item.
- **Purchase Orders**. This choice displays all the current purchase orders for this item, including the expected date of arrival (see Figure 12-6).

The Purchase Order due date is probably not accurate. The default PO in QuickBooks uses the date the PO is created as the delivery date. See the section "Customizing Purchase Orders" to learn how to make POs more efficient.

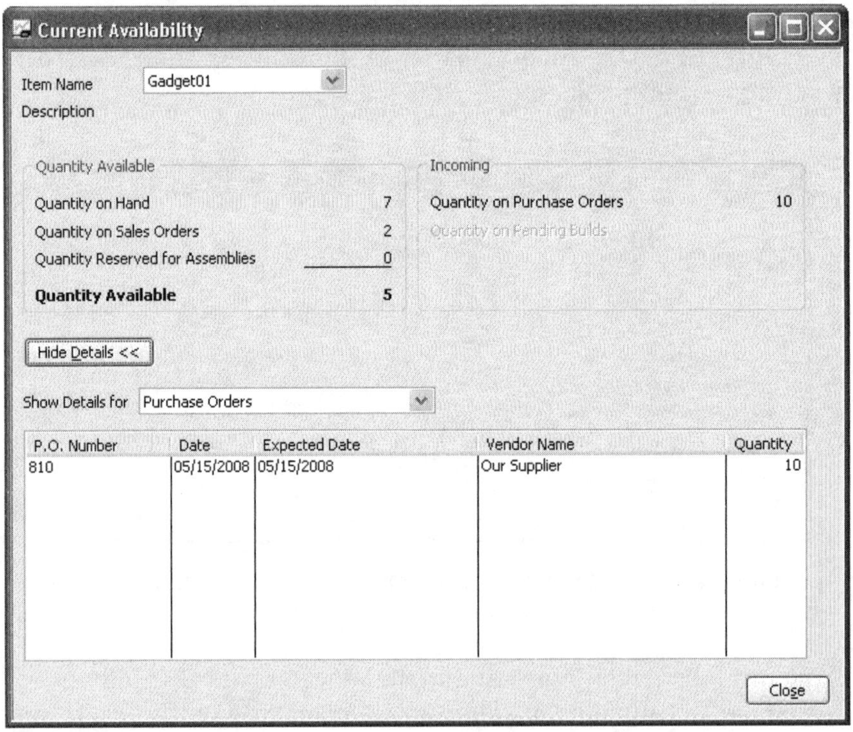

Figure 12-6: If more stock is due to arrive soon; don't convert the sales order to an invoice until that date.

Modifying Sales Orders to Obtain Promised Stock

When you click the Show Details button, and select Sales Orders, QuickBooks displays a listing of the sales orders that include the item you want to include in the sales order you're creating.

If the sales order you're creating is for a customer you think should be shipped product faster than the customers on the existing sales orders, you can modify any of the displayed sales orders to reduce the item's quantity.

Double-click the listing for the sales order you want to change. However, since you have a sales order in process in the Create Sales Orders window, and QuickBooks can neither open a second sales order in the window, nor open another instance of the Create Sales Orders window, you have to decide how to remove the current sales order from the window. QuickBooks displays a message that offers three choices for handling the current sales order:

- **Save Changes**. Save the current sales order with its current items and quantities, and open the selected existing sales order in the Create Sales Orders window. You can return to the sales order you saved to adjust the quantity, after you finish modifying the older sales order.
- **Discard Changes**. Close the current sales order without saving it, and open the selected existing sales order. You can create the new sales order after you've adjusted the quantities in the existing sales order.
- **Continue Editing**. Forget about opening an existing sales order, and return to the sales order you're currently working on.

Unless the sales order you're trying to create is for an important customer who doesn't accept back orders, and no additional stock is expected in the near future, it's best to continue working on the current sales order.

When stock arrives, you can ship to this customer first by converting this sales order to an invoice before the earlier sales orders are converted. See the next section, "Sales Order Fulfillment Worksheet", to learn how to allocate stock to sales orders.

Sales Order Fulfillment Worksheet

The QuickBooks Premier Manufacturing & Wholesale Edition has a Sales Order Fulfillment Worksheet that you can use to decide how to fill sales orders if there is insufficient stock to fill all sales orders.

To open the worksheet, choose Customers → Sales Order Fulfillment Worksheet. When the worksheet opens (see Figure 12-7), its appearance is determined by the availability of the stock entered in sales orders, and the way you sort the data. You can sort the display of sales orders by selecting a sort order from the drop-down list.

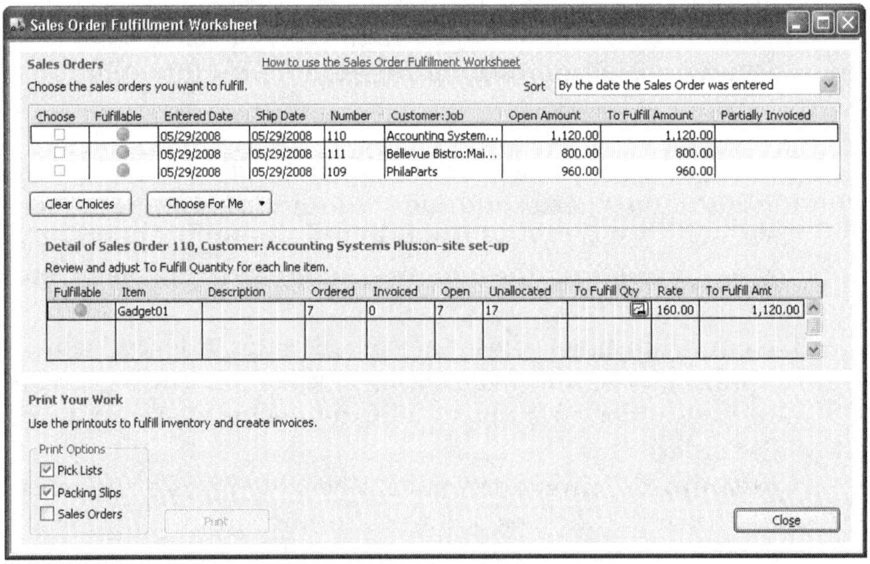

Figure 12-7: A worksheet is available to help you decide which sales orders to fill when stock is limited.

In the sales order listing at the top of the window, QuickBooks uses symbols to indicate the fulfillment status of each sales order:

- A solid green circle means there is sufficient stock to fill the order.

- A half filled amber circle means there is sufficient stock to ship a partial order. This could mean that less stock than ordered is available for the items in the sales order, or one (or more) items on the sales order is out of stock (even though there is sufficient stock to fill the order on another item.
- An empty square with a red X means there is no stock available to fill the order.

Select any order to display stock status details for that order in the bottom of the window. QuickBooks uses the same symbols to indicate the fulfillment capabilities of each item in the sales order.

The fact that more than one sales order has a green circle doesn't mean you can fulfill all the "green circle" sales orders. Depending on stock availability, it could mean that you can fulfill one order, and when you do, the stock is used and the other sales orders won't be able to ship (and their symbols will change).

Click the button labeled Choose For Me to display a variety of choices you can select to have QuickBooks automatically select the sales order to fill (see Figure 12-8).

To choose sales orders manually, select a listing and click the check box in the first column. The bottom of the window inserts the number of items required to fill the order (or partially fill the order if the sales order does not have a green circle) in the Fulfill Qty column. If this action uses up the available stock, the symbols for other sales orders that include this stock change to an empty square with a red X.

Selecting a sales order does not turn it in to an invoice, nor does it lock the available stock so that it belongs to this sales order. This is a worksheet, an informational window. However, you can begin the process of converting a sales order to an invoice from the worksheet window.

The first step is to make sure that the reported availability numbers match what's actually on the shelves. Select the sales order you want to fill, and click the Print button at the bottom of the window. Select Print Pick Lists and then send the printed pick list to the warehouse to make sure the sales order can be filled to match the quantity in the Fulfill Qty column.

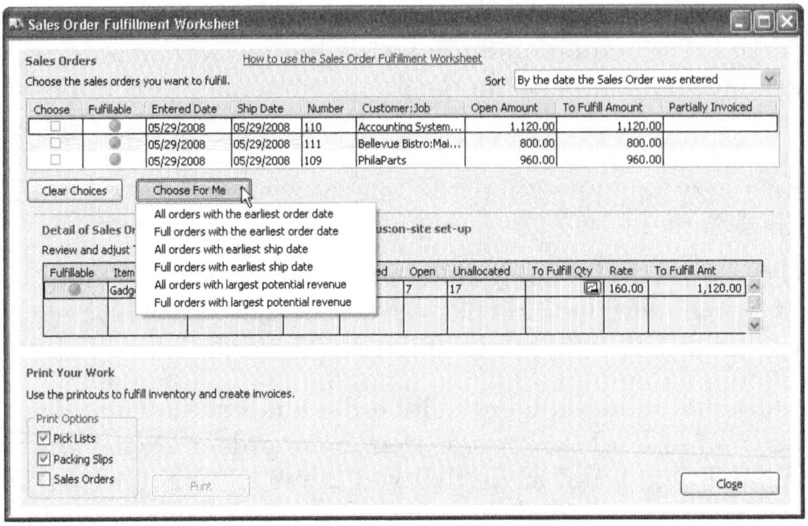

Figure 12-8: Select the stance you want to take about filling sales orders.

***TIP**: If you're on a network, install a printer near the stock shelves, and select that printer when you print pick slips.*

If enough stock is available to fill the order, double-click the sales order listing to open the original sales order. Then click the Create Invoice button at the top of the Create Sales Orders window and follow the prompts to turn the sales order into an invoice.

When you return to the worksheet, the symbols on the worksheet change to indicate the new status of order fulfillment, now that you've actually removed product from inventory.

You could also close the worksheet window, convert the appropriate sales orders to invoices, and then check the worksheet stats again when new product arrives. This worksheet is an ad-hoc document, which means that any information you entered in the window wasn't saved, and each time you open the worksheet the data in the window displays real time information as of the moment you open it.

Customizing Purchase Orders

The default Purchase Order template (named Custom Purchase Order) is selected by default when you create POs. It lacks some fields that I consider important. However, it's quite easy to customize the template to make sure all the information you need appears on the PO. QuickBooks provides two ways to customize this template:

- Customize the Custom Purchase Order template.
- Create a new customized template, with a different name, based on this Custom Purchase Order template.

I prefer the latter approach, just because I don't like changing a basic template—instead I can keep the basic template available for other, different, customizations.

This is a two-step process: First, duplicate the default PO template and give it a new name, then customize the new template.

Duplicating a Template

Use the following steps to duplicate the default PO template (or any other built-in template):

1. Choose Lists → Templates to open the Templates List window.
2. Right-click the listing for Custom Purchase Order and select Duplicate.
3. In the Select Template Type dialog, select Purchase Order and click OK.
4. The Templates List window displays a listing named Copy Of: Custom Purchase Order.
5. Double-click that listing to open the Basic Customization dialog.
6. Click Manage Templates and in the right pane of the Manage Templates dialog, change the name of the template. Use a name that describes your customization—in this case I used the name PO With Due Date.
7. Click OK to return to the Basic Customization dialog.

In this dialog you can make minor changes to the template, such as changing fonts, colors, the company information that prints on the transaction document, and so on.

However, in this case you want to make major changes to the template, to add fields or columns to the document.

Customizing the Purchase Order Template

With your new template displayed in the Basic Customization dialog, click the Additional Customization button at the bottom of the dialog. This action opens the Additional Customization dialog seen in Figure 12-9.

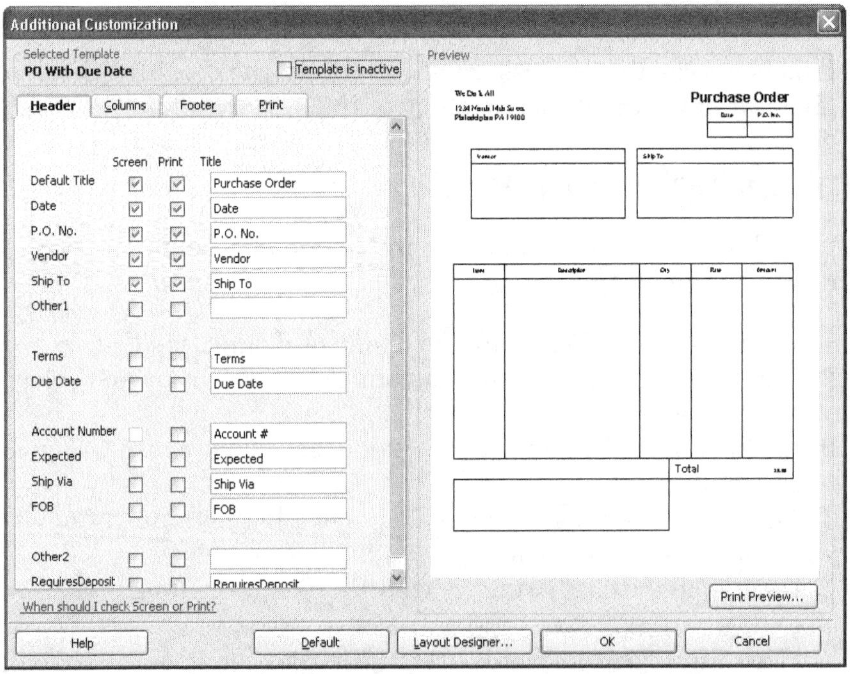

Figure 12-9: Customize the template to make sure all the information you require is included.

On the Header tab you can include or exclude fields for the on-screen version, the printed version, or both. For example, if you've created custom fields for vendors and you want to include the data in the custom field for the vendor receiving the PO, that might be data only needed on the screen as you prepare the PO.

***NOTE**: Many businesses don't mail purchase orders; instead, they phone the information in and only create the PO to have a record of its existence.*

The most important change for POs is to include a field for the expected delivery date on the PO. Click both the check boxes next to the field named Expected. You can also change the text that appears above the field—perhaps you'd prefer to have Delivery Date instead of Expected.

***NOTE**: As you make changes, QuickBooks may display a message about using the Layout Designer to make sure all the elements you're changing fit properly in the template. Most of the changes you make don't require a complete overhaul of the layout, so you can select the option to stop displaying the message. Keep an eye on the preview panel in the right pane, or click Print Preview to see if changes you're making cause fields or columns to overlap. If so, you can use the Layout Designer to move fields and columns (it's easy to use because it's visually logical). The Layout Designer is discussed in detail in QuickBooks 2008: The Official Guide.*

Examine the other fields in the Header tab to see if you want to make any other changes (such as including the Ship Via field in the template).

Move to the Columns tab (see Figure 12-10) to see if there are any columns you want to select or deselect.

If you don't usually order items specifically for a customer and use the job costing or automatic billing of customers, you can remove the Customer & Job columns.

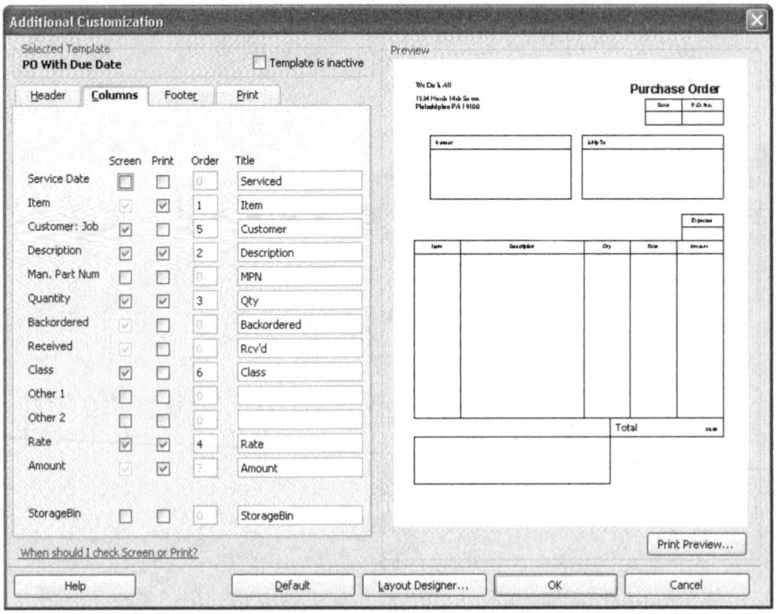

Figure 12-10: Customize columns for your purchase orders.

If you're tracking the Manufacturer's Part Number in your inventory item records, add that column to your P.O. template.

Click OK when you finish customizing fields and columns, and then click OK in the Basic Customization dialog to save the new template and add it to the Template drop-down list when you create POs.

Adding Purchase Order Info to the Items List

One of the quickest ways to ascertain the current availability level of an item is to open the Items list, which displays information about availability. However, by default the list does not include information about the number of items currently on order via POs.

To add PO information to the Items list click the Item button in the lower left corner of the list window and choose Customize Columns. Select Quantity On Purchase Order in the left pane of the Customize Columns dialog, and then click Add to add this column to the list window.

To make the list even easier to work with, select the Quantity On Purchase Order listing in the Chosen Columns list and click Move Up to put the new column next to the Quantity on Sales Order column.

Units of Measure

A unit of measure (U/M) is a way to establish specific information about the basis on which you sell quantities of goods and products. For example, if you sell an inventory item named Chocolate Syrup, you can specify the U/M as a bottle, a 6-pack, or a 24-unit case.

U/Ms are attached to items—each item has its own U/M. QuickBooks provides two ways to track and assign U/Ms:

- Single U/M per item, in which you can assign one U/M to an item.
- Multiple U/M per item, in which you can create a base U/M and then devise multiple conversions of that base U/M to permit sales of different quantities.

The Premier Manufacturing and Wholesale Edition supports both types of U/Ms, and you can learn how to set up and configure them in Chapter 7.

Customer RMAs

RMAs (sometimes called RAs) are a fact of life in your business. You have to deal with customer returns, but you can, and should, impose rules and protocols; otherwise, tracking the financial consequences becomes extremely difficult.

One rule that most distributors impose is that no merchandise can be returned unless an RMA number that you provide is on the packing slip and/or the shipping label.

Creating RMAs

When a customer wants to return an item, QuickBooks has a way for you to assign an RMA number, and track it, using a Microsoft Word document. Of course, you must have Word installed on your computer to take advantage of this feature.

Choose Mfg & Whsle → Inventory Activities → Customer Return Materials Authorization Form. Microsoft Word opens with the form loaded in the software window (see Figure 12-11).

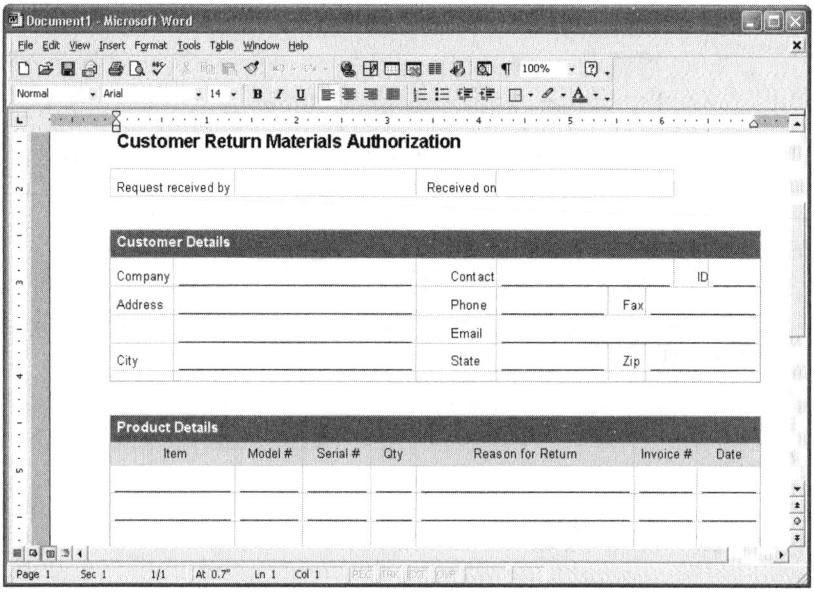

Figure 12-11: QuickBooks provides a form for tracking RMAs.

The document doesn't really exist as a discrete file (you can see that the title bar lacks a file name), so the first thing to do is save this document so you can access it from Word.

Choose File → Save As, and name the document. By default, Word saves the document in your My Documents folder. You could create a folder for your QuickBooks documents and forms, either directly on the root of your hard drive (e.g. C:\QBForms), or as a subfolder in your My Documents folder.

Save the document before you fill anything out, so you have a boilerplate you can open directly in Word. This means the person managing

RMA forms doesn't have to be a QuickBooks user, nor does it matter if he has QuickBooks software installed on his computer (see "Manipulating the RMA Form", later in this section).

You can use this form whenever you need a customer RMA. The form is configured as a Word table, so you can enter data into all the appropriate cells. Every time you fill out the form, use the Save As command to save the document, using a new filename.

Print a copy of the form for your bookkeeper, who can issue a credit in QuickBooks when the material comes back from the customer. You should also print a copy for your warehouse personnel, so they know the material is due.

***TIP**: If you name each RMA document with the format XXXX-<CustomerName> (where XXXX is the RMA number), when you open the folder in which you're storing RMAs, you can automatically determine the next RMA number.*

This form is inert, which means it has no automatic functions connected to QuickBooks or your QuickBooks company file. You have to track RMA numbers manually, outside of QuickBooks.

Additionally, the form provides fields that make it easy for you to create a credit memo for the customer when the products are returned. However, the data in your QuickBooks file, such as Item Name and Invoice #, don't automatically appear—no drop-down lists exist of course, because you're not working in QuickBooks.

Manipulating the RMA Form

The RMA form that QuickBooks installs and uses is a Word template file, which means its file extension is .DOT instead of .DOC (the extension for Word documents).

If you're comfortable editing Word templates, you can open it directly in Word, make changes to it, and then save it using a different filename. It's best to copy the file to the My Documents folder of the person in your organization who tracks RMAs. You can find the file in \<*QuickBooks Installation Folder*>\Components\Vertical Forms. Substitute the folder into which you installed QuickBooks for <*QuickBooks Installation Folder*>. The file name is CustomerReturnMaterialsAuthorizationForm.dot.

In fact, even if you're not going to change the form, you should copy it to the My Documents folder of the person who manages RMAs. Have that person open the file, and use File → Save As on the Word menu bar to save the document as a Word document file (a file ending in the extension .DOC).

Processing Customer Returns of Inventory

When a customer returns inventory, you have to track the inventory return and the customer's financial information in a way that fits the scenario. For example, the customer may have already paid for the inventory and is returning it because it's damaged. Or the customer may not have paid for the inventory, and is returning it "just because".

The condition of the inventory (whether it is damaged, or is fine and can be resold), and the state of the customer's indebtedness to you are the factors that determine the type of transaction you create.

Providing Credits for Damaged Inventory

If the inventory being returned by your customer is damaged, you cannot put it back into your warehouse. However, you need to credit the customer's account, which automatically puts the inventory back into stock. To accomplish this, credit the customer's account, and then create an inventory adjustment, as explained in the following sections.

Creating a Credit for a Paid Invoice

If the customer paid the invoice that covers the damaged returns, you must enter a credit memo, or issue a refund check. The credit memo/refund should cover only the returned items, not the entire invoice (unless the only item on that invoice was this product).

When you create the credit memo, enter the returned item(s) in the line item section of the transaction window. You should also credit any shipping charges (proportionately, if the credit memo is for an invoice that included more items than those being returned).

When you save the credit memo, QuickBooks asks if you want to save the credit for future use by the customer, create a refund check, or apply the credit to an existing invoice.

If you opt to save the credit or apply it to an existing invoice, QuickBooks makes the following postings:

- Debits the Inventory Asset account (puts the product back into inventory).
- Credits the COG account (removes the cost expense).
- Debits the sales account connected to the item (lowers your income).
- Credits the A/R account (lowers the total receivables).

In addition, appropriate changes are made to your sales tax liability account (if the item and the customer are both taxable), and to any shipping charges you included in the credit.

If you create a refund check, QuickBooks makes the following additional postings:

- Debits Accounts Receivable (reversing the action taken when you saved the credit memo)
- Credits the bank account (removes the money from the bank).

After the customer's record is updated, you must adjust your inventory to remove the damaged goods that QuickBooks put back into inventory. See the section "Adjusting Inventory for Damaged Goods".

Voiding an Unpaid Invoice

If the customer has not yet paid the invoice, and the invoice only contains the product being returned, void the invoice. QuickBooks makes the following postings:

- Debits the Inventory Asset account (puts the product back into inventory).
- Credits the COG account (removes the cost expense).
- Debits the sales account connected to the item (lowers your income).
- Credits the A/R account (lowers the total receivables).

If the invoice contains additional items, do not void it. Instead, issue a credit for the returned item, and when you save the credit choose the option to apply the credit to a specific invoice, and then choose the invoice that contains the damaged inventory.

Adjusting Inventory for Damaged Goods

You must remove the damaged inventory that QuickBooks put back into your system when you created the customer's credit memo. To do this, choose Vendor → Inventory Activities → Adjust Quantity/Value on hand to open the Inventory Adjustment transaction form seen in Figure 12-12.

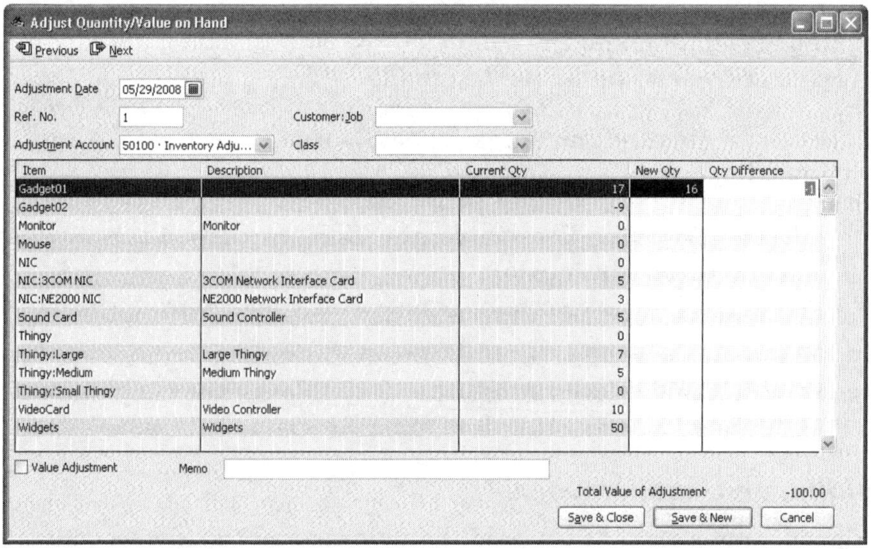

Figure 12-12: Adjust your inventory to remove damaged products.

In the Adjustment Account field, select the inventory adjustment account. Locate the item in the listings and adjust the number of units by the number of returned damaged units. You can either enter data in the Net Qty column (mentally subtracting the returned number from the displayed Current Qty number), or enter the number of returned items in the Qty Difference column (don't forget the minus sign). It's a good idea to use the memo field for details, so when you see this transaction in reports (or your accountant sees it) you can explain it.

In addition, if you purchased this inventory, you must return it to your vendor (usually the manufacturer), and you can also track the details by using the Damaged Goods Log. These functions are discussed in the next section.

Returning Products to a Vendor

When you return products to a vendor you have to enter the appropriate transaction in QuickBooks. The actions you take differ, depending on the scenario:

- You have a P.O. in the system, but haven't entered the receipt of goods or bill (because you noticed damage when the product arrived).
- You have a receipt of goods in the system, but have not yet entered the bill (because it didn't arrive with the package).
- You have entered both a receipt of goods and a bill into the system.

Voiding or Modifying a Purchase Order

If you haven't yet created the receipt of goods/bill transaction for the P.O. that covers the damaged products, you can void the purchase order. This only works if the P.O. contains only the damaged products, and all of the products were damaged (which would be an unusual occurrence).

If the P.O. contains a quantity larger than 1 of the item, and some of the items aren't damaged, you can void the P.O. and create a new one with the correct data. Be sure to notify the vendor about this action, telling them to ignore the original P.O. and look for a new P.O number.

You can also modify the P.O. by reducing the quantity to reflect the number of items you're returning. Notify the vendor that you've changed the P.O. and ask them to adjust their records.

Voiding or Modifying a Receipt of Items

If you received the items into inventory (without the bill), you can void or modify the Receipt of Goods transaction. The quickest way to locate the original Item Receipt is to open the Vendor Center, select the vendor, and select Item Receipts in the Show field.

If the receipt covers only this item, and if the entire quantity of items is damaged, void the receipt. If the receipt covers multiple items, and/or only some of the quantity received of a single item is damaged, adjust the data in the Qty column, and click Recalculate to adjust the total.

Voiding or Modifying a Receipt of Items and Bill

If you received the items into inventory and also entered the vendor's bill, adjust your transactions according to the contents of the receipt and bill. If everything covered in the receipt of items/bill is damaged, void the transaction.

If you only need to adjust the quantity of an item to reflect the damaged goods you're returning, adjust the data in the Qty column, and click Recalculate to adjust the total.

Entering a Vendor Credit for a Paid Bill

If you paid the vendor before returning damaged goods, you need to create a credit with this vendor. Use the following steps to accomplish this:

1. Choose Vendors → Enter Bills
2. Select the Credit option at the top of the Enter Bills window.
3. Select the vendor.
4. Use the Items tab in the line item section of the window to enter the item and the amount of the credit (don't use a minus sign, QuickBooks knows what a credit is).

5. If appropriate (meaning if you and the vendor agree), use the Expenses tab to enter a credit for any shipping costs you incurred for the delivery or will incur for the return of goods.

You can use the credit against existing bills or future bills from this vendor.

Entering a Vendor Refund

If the vendor agreed to send you a refund check, enter a credit as described in the previous section. The credit applies the appropriate postings to your inventory and A/P accounts. When the check arrives, use the following steps to enter it into your QuickBooks system:

1. Choose Banking → Make Deposits to open the Payments to Deposit window.
2. If there are deposits listed that you want to make, select them.
3. Click OK (even if you haven't selected any deposits) to open the Make Deposits window.
4. In the first blank line make the following entries:
   - Enter the Vendor in the Received From column.
   - Enter Accounts Payable in the From Account column (this washes the A/P posting you entered when you created the vendor credit memo).
   - Optionally, enter a note in the Memo column, enter a check number, and select the payment method in the appropriate columns.
   - Enter the amount of the check in the Amount column.
5. Save the deposit.

Saving the credit memo and depositing the check into the bank created all the right postings to your general ledger. However, the postings did not specifically affect this vendor.

To take care of this last step (matching the vendor credit to the vendor's check), choose VendorPay Bills to open the Pay Bills window. When the window opens, in addition to any bills that are currently due, you see a bill for this vendor, and the Amt Due column has the amount of the check you deposited.

It's easy to spot this transaction since unlike the other listings in the Pay Bill window, this bill has no due date. That's because it's not really a bill, it's a credit waiting to be assigned to itself. Select the bill for payment by clicking in the leftmost column to insert a check mark in the check box. QuickBooks immediately displays the message seen in Figure 12-13.

Figure 12-13: QuickBooks pays this ersatz bill by crediting it against itself.

Click OK, and then click Pay Selected Bills in the Pay Bills window. QuickBooks displays the Payment Summary window, showing a zero amount paid.

Creating a Non-Conforming Material Report

After you have an RMA number from your vendor, you can track detailed information about the return of damaged goods with the Non-conforming Material Report, which is a Word document QuickBooks installs for this purpose.

Choose Mfg & Whsle → Inventory Activities → Non-conforming Material Report to open the document in Word (see Figure 12-14). Fill out the appropriate cells, and use Word's Save As command to save the document with an appropriate name for this return. Print a copy to use as a packing slip.

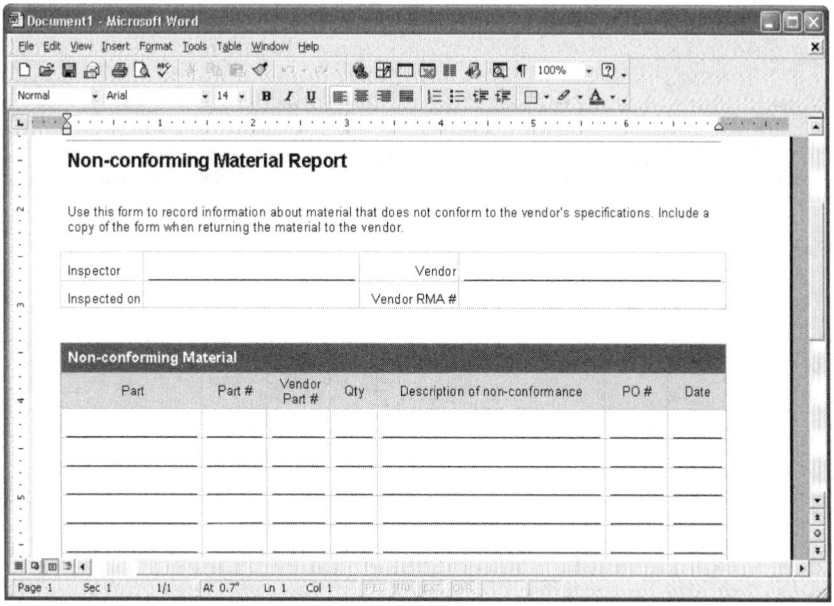

Figure 12-14: Track details for merchandise you return to the vendor.

You can copy this template to the My Documents folder of the person in charge of handling vendor returns, and access it directly from Word, instead of working through QuickBooks. Save the document as a Word document, instead of a Word template, as described in the preceding section on the Customer Return Materials Authorization Form.

Tracking Damaged and Missing Products

If you want to keep a log on inventory products that are damaged internally (or go missing) you can use the Damaged Goods Log that QuickBooks installs. This is a Word template that you open in Word, as explained in the previous sections on other Word documents.

To open the log from within QuickBooks, choose Mfg & Whsle → Inventory Activities → Damaged Goods Log. When the Word document opens (see Figure 12-15), you can fill it in.

Use the instructions presented earlier to copy this Word template to the My Documents folder of the person who tracks damaged and missing inventory. You should create a second document, changing the name to Missing Goods Log, so you can track damaged and missing goods separately.

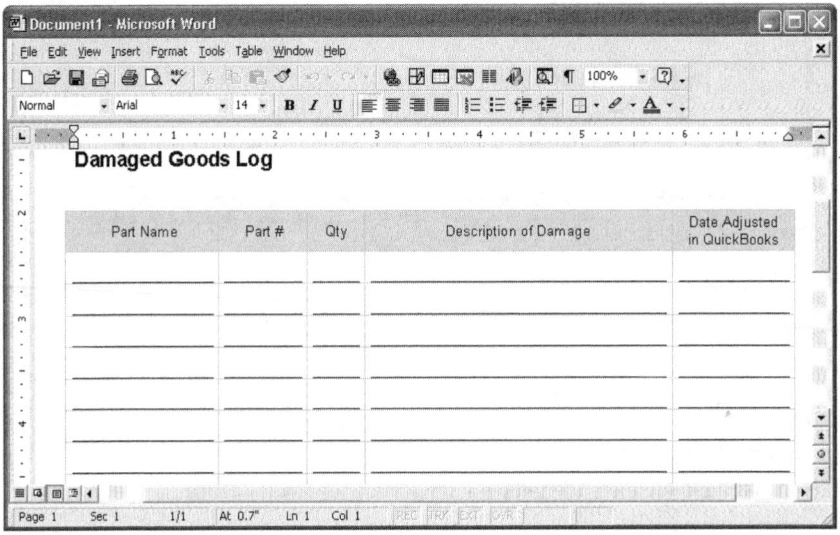

Figure 12-15: Track details about damaged or missing inventory items.

***NOTE**: Damaged inventory that isn't returned to vendors should be physically removed from inventory so it's not accidentally counted the next time you do a physical count.*

When inventory is damaged, or disappears, you must adjust your inventory, using the following steps:

1. Choose Vendors → Inventory Activities → Adjust Quantity/Value On Hand.
2. In the Adjust Quantity/Value On Hand dialog, select the Adjustment Account from the drop-down list.
3. Select the listing for the missing or damaged item.

4. In the Qty Difference column, enter the number of missing or damaged units of this item with a minus sign. QuickBooks automatically calculates the New Qty column.

If inventory is missing, it could be the result of a miscount or an item being placed on the wrong shelf, or in the wrong room. However, if this happens more than a couple of times, you need to look for another reason. I've found two common scenarios to explain missing inventory items:

- Sales personnel take inventory and hide it in their own offices to make sure they can service their customers. This is common for inventory items that have high turnover and are frequently out of stock before the next order arrives from the vendor.
- Employees are helping themselves to inventory items (yes, I mean stealing). Employee theft of inventory items is a common occurrence, and the jargon for this is *shrinkage*.

No software can solve either problem, although it's been my experience that when accounting software is installed, and inventory tracking is part of the software, shrinkage slows down. To accomplish the change in attitude (I mean the existing attitude, " nobody will notice if you steal"), you need to make an announcement that when there's a difference between the software's inventory numbers and the physical count, you're going to believe the software's numbers.

Manufacturing and Wholesale Reports

QuickBooks includes many customized and memorized reports that are designed to be useful to your type of business. To view the list of reports choose Reports → Manufacturing and Wholesale Reports. The report titles are self-explanatory.

You can customize any of these reports to suit your own needs, and memorize them for frequent use.

Chapter 13

Nonprofit Edition

Unified chart of accounts for nonprofits

Using Classes

Equity accounts

Customized templates for transactions

Memorized reports for nonprofits

The Premier Nonprofit Edition isn't really designed for optimum nonprofit use. However, the Premier Nonprofit Edition includes the Unified Chart of Accounts for nonprofits, customized templates you can use to record specific types of income, and some useful customized reports.

You have to adapt your use of QuickBooks to use it successfully for nonprofits. In this chapter, I provide an overview of some of the basic issues involved in using QuickBooks for nonprofit transactions.

NOTE: *Adapting QuickBooks for nonprofit accounting is a rather complicated endeavor; more than can be covered in a chapter. Because of the demand for this information, we've published a book on the topic. Look for Running QuickBooks in Nonprofits from CPA911 Publishing at your favorite bookstore.*

Unified Chart of Accounts (UCOA)

Most nonprofits have to file a great many detailed reports about their financial activities. Federal and state governments have filing requirements, and grant-givers frequently require financial information. Except for the Form 990 model on the federal level, there's no particular across-the-board standard you can take for granted (although most states will accept the Federal Form 990).

The Unified Chart of Accounts (UCOA) is an attempt to standardize the way nonprofits keep financial records, and report them. The UCOA is based on Form 990, but it's useful and efficient even for nonprofit organizations that don't file Form 990.

Developed by the California Association of Nonprofits and the National Center for Charitable Statistics (NCCS), UCOA provides a way to unite all of your reporting needs into one set of accounting records. By using UCOA as a model for your own chart of accounts, you'll find it easier to produce reports for all who demand them.

When you create a new company file and select Nonprofit as your type of business, QuickBooks offers to install a chart of accounts suitable for nonprofit organizations. The file that's installed is the UCOA.

Renaming Accounts

Some of the accounts have generic names, and you should go through the account list to rename the accounts to fit your circumstances. Select each account you want to rename, and press Ctrl-E. The account record opens in Edit Mode, and you can change the name.

Importing the UCOA

If you updated an existing QuickBooks company file (that did not have the UCOA) to QuickBooks 2007 Premier Nonprofit Edition, you can import the UCOA. Then you can edit and merge accounts to make sure your current balances are properly transferred to the UCOA accounts you want to use.

When you installed QuickBooks Premier Nonprofit Edition, the UCOA file was installed on your computer. To import it, follow these steps:

1. Choose File → Utilities → Import → IIF Files.
2. In the Import dialog, if the folder in which QuickBooks is installed isn't selected, navigate to that folder.
3. Select UCOA.IFF and click Open.

When the file is imported, QuickBooks issues a success message. Open the chart of accounts and see if you have duplicate, or nearly duplicate, accounts (your original chart of accounts may have the same, or similar, accounts as the UCOA). If so, delete unneeded duplicate accounts, or merge your original accounts with the new accounts that were installed with the UCOA. (See Chapter 2 for instructions on merging accounts).

Accounts Receivable

For nonprofits, tracking income source and income type is far more complex than it is in the for-profit business world. Tracking accounts receivable means creating transactions and reports about money owed or expected. That money has to be categorized by the type of income.

Using Multiple A/R Accounts

If you're using the UCOA, you have multiple A/R accounts, so you can track receivables by type. Depending on the type of income you generate, you may need to add more A/R accounts to your chart of account (and remove those you don't need).

If you're not using the UCOA, you can manually add the A/R accounts you need. Following are some of the A/R accounts I've entered in client files. These may not mirror your needs, but they should stimulate your thinking as you plan the A/R section of your chart of accounts.

- Accounts Receivable: Used for invoices for services or goods you sell.
- Grants Receivable: Used for invoices entered to track expected grants.
- Contracts Receivable: Used for invoices entered to track expected service contracts (commonly from government agencies).
- Tuition Fees Receivable: Used for invoices for tuition (if you are a school, or if you offer classes).
- Pledges Receivable: Used for invoices for pledges from individual donors.
- Dues Receivable: Used for invoices for membership dues.

Using A/R Accounts in Invoice Transactions

If you have multiple A/R accounts, all invoice transaction windows have a field named Account at the top of the window. You have to remember to enter the appropriate A/R account for the invoice you're creating.

NOTE: *As a nonprofit organization, many of your invoices are really internal records of pledges from donors, or of expected grants or contracts. They're not mailed; instead, you post them so you can track future revenue.*

Entering the A/R account does more than post the transaction to the right account—it affects the invoice numbering system. Invoice numbers are automatically incremented, using the last invoice number in the A/R account being used for the invoice transaction. This means each set of invoice types has its own, discrete, numbering system, which is quite handy.

Reporting on Receivables

Maintaining multiple A/R accounts means you can create reports on the money you're expecting (called an *aging report*), and display the information by category. This lets you determine how much money you're expecting, and the source of that money.

You can see how much money is due from grants, contracts, membership fees, pledged donations from individuals, and so on by choosing Reports → Customers & Receivables → A/R Aging Summary. The aging report displays the monies you're expecting, including the age of each receivable.

You can also customize an aging report for a particular category by filtering the report for a specific A/R account, using these steps:

1. Choose Reports → Customers & Receivables → A/R Aging Summary.
2. Click the Modify Report button at the top of the report window.
3. Move to the Filters tab, where the Account field displays All Accounts Receivable.
4. Click the arrow in the Account field, and select the specific A/R account you need for this report.
5. Click OK.

The report displays the aging for the A/R account you selected.

Using Classes

Nonprofit organizations can't use QuickBooks without using classes to track transactions. Without classes, getting the reports you need for funding agencies, government agencies, and your board of directors is extremely difficult. You either have to spend many hours (or days) analyzing each transaction and creating tallies outside of QuickBooks, or spend a lot of money to have your accountant perform tasks that wouldn't be necessary if you'd used classes.

You can think of a class as a division, or department. In the for-profit world, a business that has a main office in Philadelphia, and a branch office in Camden, would create classes named Phila and Camden to track the respective profits (or loss). Every transaction is assigned to a class, so the business owner can determine the income and expenses for each location. Because that business owner tracks income and expenses by class, she can create a Profit & Loss Statement (also called an *Income Statement*) for each class.

In the nonprofit world, we do the same thing, using classes to break down income and expenses by the categories we need to track. We can produce a Statement of Activities (the nonprofit term for an income statement) for each class.

At the very least, when you create reports or tax returns, you must provide the total amount for expenses in each of the following three categories:

- Program services
- Management (administration)
- Fundraising

In addition to preparing reports and tax returns with these categories, these are the expense breakdowns that funding agencies want to see when they consider your organization for grants. And, your board of directors probably wants to see expenses broken down by these categories.

Therefore, these are the classes to start with. You can create any additional classes and subclasses you need. For example, many nonprofit organizations create a class for special events (a subclass for each individual event), and for capital improvement projects.

In addition, you should create classes to track the status of funds that are linked to programs or have some time of restriction on the way those funds can be spent.

Create classes named Restricted, Temporarily Restricted, and Unrestricted so you can track income properly. As the restricted and temporarily restricted funds are moved to unrestricted use, you can track the movement by program (using the program classes).

"Program services" is a generic category that applies to the programs you run (the services you provide). You should have a specific class for each program, and you can accomplish that either by creating subclasses, or by using a discrete class for each program.

Having a class for each program lets you create a Statement of Activities for each class, and present the appropriate report to the funding agencies for programs. Figure 13-1 is a sample Class List for a community organization.

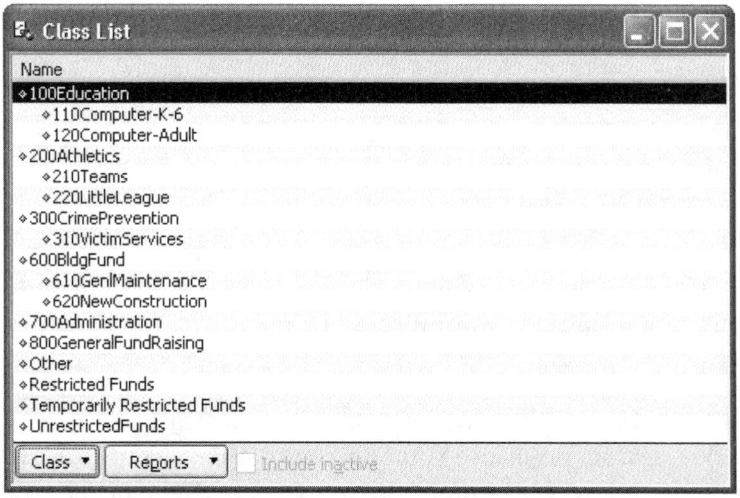

Figure 13-1: This community organization can track income and expenses for each funded program.

Customers and Jobs

QuickBooks didn't bother to change any component names or field names for the Premier Nonprofit Edition, so you have to live with the terms “customers” and “jobs”.

- A customer is a donor, and a donor is any entity (individual or organization) from whom you receive revenue.
- A job is a grant or a contract (from a donor). Each grant/contract that requires reporting must be entered as a discrete job.

Customers that don't require reports don't need jobs. This definition fits any entity that provides unrestricted funds, such as individual donors, tuition-payers, or membership fees for activities not connected with a specific program.

Equity Accounts

QuickBooks provides two equity accounts automatically: Retained Earnings, and Opening Bal Equity. These equity accounts don't work properly for nonprofits.

A nonprofit organization requires multiple equity accounts (called *net asset* accounts), to wit:

- Permanently Restricted Net Assets
- Temporarily Restricted Net Assets
- Unrestricted Net Assets

If you're using the Unified Chart of Accounts, these equity accounts are available. If you're creating your own chart of accounts, or updating an existing chart of accounts, you must add the equity accounts required for nonprofits.

The built-in Retained Earnings account is technically the Unrestricted Net Assets account. You can rename Retained Earnings, and then move the appropriate amounts out of it into the other Net Asset accounts via Journal Entry. On the other hand, you can create the Unrestricted Net Assets account and move everything out of Retained Earnings into the proper accounts.

Many organizations add subaccounts to these equity accounts, in order to track details. As you post transactions to the subaccounts, you can link the transactions to programs or donors. The subtotals of the subaccounts are displayed as the total for the parent account when you create reports.

For example, you might want a structure similar to the following set of equity accounts:

- The Permanently Restricted Net Assets parent account could have subaccounts for endowments or restricted gifts.
- The Temporarily Restricted Net Assets parent account could have subaccounts named Restricted By Type and Restricted by Time.
- The Unrestricted Net Assets parent account could have a subaccount for Transfers.
  The Transfers account receives postings as you use transaction forms to bring funds in and out. Using transaction windows (invoices, sales receipts, vendor bills, direct disbursements, or journal entries) lets you assign classes and customers to the postings.

Even after you create all the net asset accounts you need, QuickBooks won't post transaction amounts to them. You have to create journal entries to move money from the Retained Earnings account to the appropriate net asset accounts.

Customized Templates for Transactions

QuickBooks Premier Nonprofit Edition includes some templates you can use for tracking income. Both of these templates are for donations from individuals, not for grants.

Pledges

Many donations start out as pledges, and nonprofit organizations have a number of creative methods for obtaining pledges from friends of the organization. You may have a pledge form that you hand out, a sign-up sheet that's passed around at an event, or even a website that contains a form to make a pledge.

Whatever you do to get pledges, when a pledge is promised you should record it in QuickBooks to make sure your financial reports are complete (a pledge, like an invoice in the for-profit world, is part of your accounts receivable assets).

QuickBooks Premier Nonprofit edition provides a template for a pledge, which is really a standard QuickBooks invoice that's been customized. To open a blank pledge transaction window, use one of the following actions:

- Choose Nonprofit → Enter Pledges from the menu bar.
- Press Ctrl-I to open a blank invoice form and choose Intuit Standard Pledge from the drop-down list in the Template field (in the upper right corner of the window).

When the Pledge form opens, it looks like Figure 13-2. If you're using the UCOA, select the Pledges Receivable account in the Account field at the top of the form. If you're not using the UCOA, you should add a Pledges Receivable account to your system. Notice that the title bar of the Pledge window contains the name of the A/R account you've assigned to the transaction.

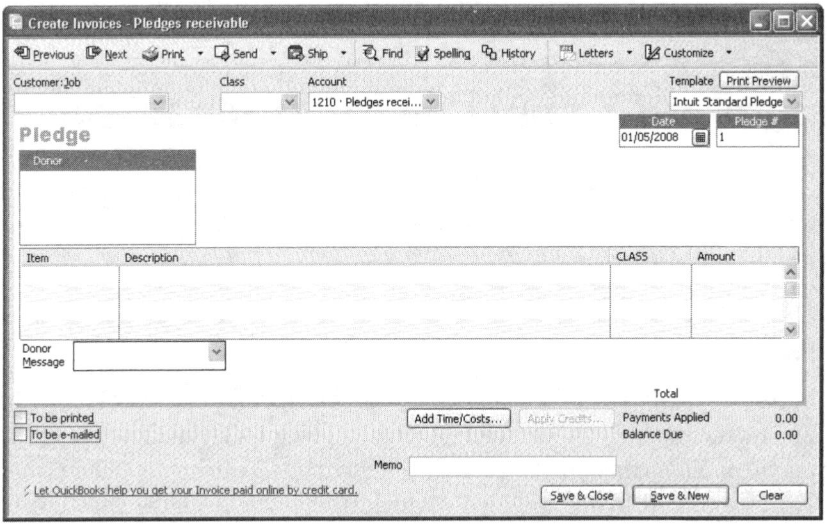

Figure 13-2: A Pledge is an accounts receivable transaction.

Using Pledges Efficiently

Unlike high-end (expensive) accounting software, QuickBooks isn't designed to provide an unlimited amount of data in its files. As

QuickBooks files get large, the software operates more slowly, but what's really important is that there's a limit to the number of names (such as customers/donors) you can store.

***TIP**: Chapter 3 has information about the maximum number of entries in QuickBooks lists.*

Many organizations receive pledges from hundreds, or thousands, of donors. Some of these donors are one-time givers; others give periodically (especially if you stay in touch with them).

If you receive a great many pledges, you don't have to track customer information for donors who pledge money within QuickBooks. You can track the names and other important information in another software application, such as a spreadsheet or database program. Then use the data in that software to correspond with to the people who made pledges.

The work you do in QuickBooks is designed to get the financial totals into the system, and it's not a good idea to try to keep customer records on a great many individuals. You probably have no reporting requirements that insist on listing every individual who pledges money (but if you are required to report individual names and amounts, you can generate the report you need from the software you're using to track donations).

Creating a Generic Pledge Customer

Create a generic customer for pledges and name it appropriately (Donor is a good choice for the name). Enter the generic name you want to use (e.g. Donor) in the Customer Name field in the New Customer dialog. Don't enter any other information in the customer record.

Recording a Pledge for a Generic Customer

Most of the time, people who fill out pledge forms don't expect to receive an invoice from you. You need to record the pledge, however, to indicate the fact that you're expecting the money. Open a Pledge (Invoice) transaction window and use the following steps to record the pledge:

1. Select the generic customer.
2. Do not enter data in the Bill To section of the form.
3. Fill out the line detail with the appropriate item.
   If the donor indicated a pledge for a specific program, enter the program in the Class column; otherwise, assign the pledge to unrestricted funds.
4. Click Save & New to create another pledge, or click Save & Close if you're finished.

Printing and Sending Pledges

Occasionally you might want to print and send a pledge form to a donor. To personalize the form (and to make it look professional), you should have the donor's name and address in the Bill To box of the invoice.

You can do this without creating a new customer; use the generic customer instead. Open the Pledge form you use for generic customers and follow these steps:

1. Select the generic customer.
2. In the Bill To section of the form, enter the donor's name and address.
3. Fill out the line detail with the appropriate item.
   If the donor indicated a pledge for a specific program, enter the program in the Class column; otherwise, assign the pledge to unrestricted funds.
4. Click the Print icon on the form window to print the pledge form.
5. Click Save & New to create another pledge, or click Save & Close if you're finished.
6. When QuickBooks displays the message asking you if you want to change the customer record to include the address you typed in the form, click No to prevent any changes in the generic customer record.

Entering Pledges in Batches

If you use a generic customer for pledges, you don't have to enter each pledge individually in QuickBooks, as long as you've recorded the names and amounts pledged elsewhere. Instead you can enter all the pledges for a day (or a week, or a month) in a single transaction.

Separate the groups of pledges by class. For example, if you received twenty pledges on a given day, and half of them were earmarked for a specific program, while the other half were general donations, you can enter two line items on a single pledge form (see Figure 13-3).

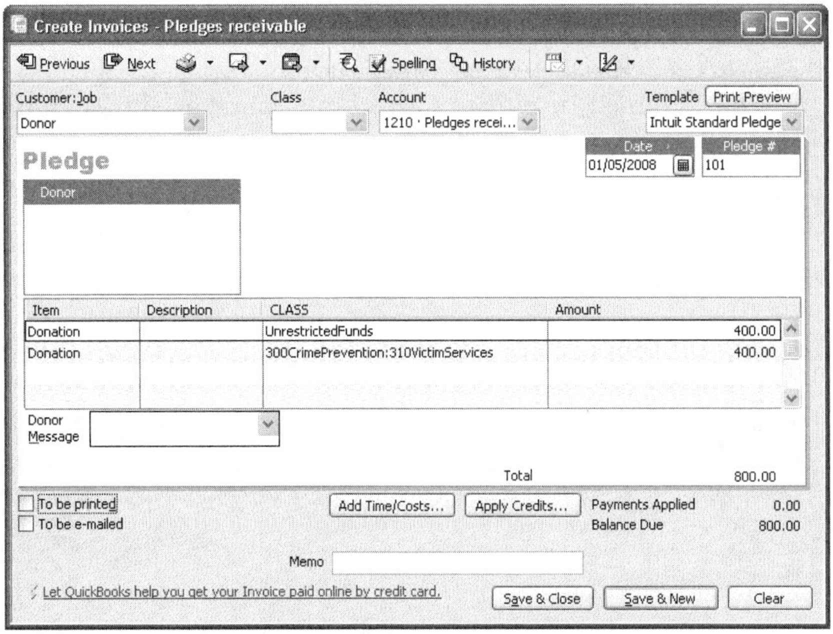

Figure 13-3: You can record pledges in batches, if you're not tracking information about each donor in QuickBooks.

If the pledge form says the money is dedicated to a program, assign the appropriate class. If the donation is for your organization, and not earmarked for any specific program, assign the amount to the Unrestricted Funds class.

Donations

Donations differ from pledges because a donation is money received "spontaneously". There's no invoice recorded in your QuickBooks file. A donation is cash, a check, or a credit card number (if you take credit cards). There's no receivable; you just put the money in the bank.

When you want to record a donation, QuickBooks Premier Nonprofit Edition has a template named Intuit Standard Donation, which is better suited to this situation than the regular sales receipt template (which is named Custom Sales Receipt). To open this template, take one of the following actions:

- Choose Nonprofit → Enter Donations (Sales Receipts).
- Choose Customers → Enter Sales Receipts, and select the transaction form named Intuit Standard Donation from the Template field at the top of the window.

The Intuit Standard Donation template looks like the Custom Sales Receipt template, but it differs in two ways (see Figure 13-4):

- The word Donation appears at the top of the form, instead of Sales Receipt.
- The address block is labeled Donor instead of Sold To.

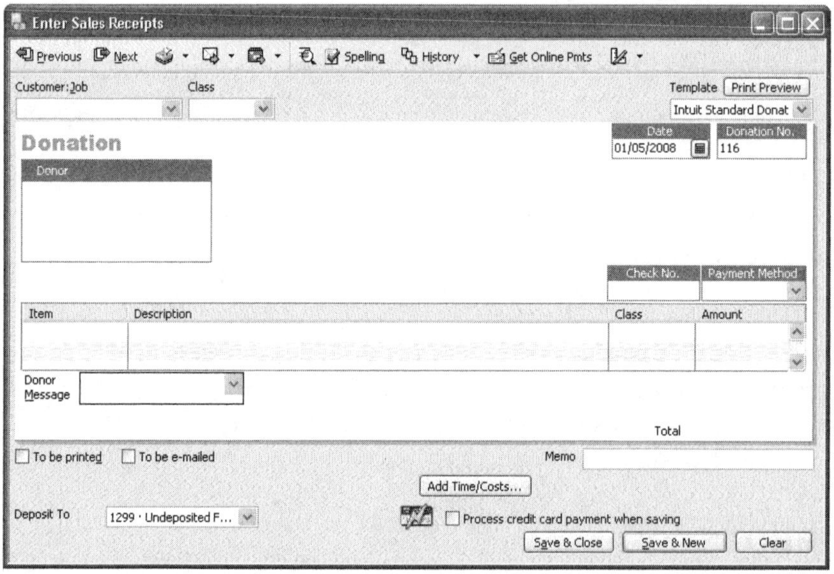

Figure 13-4: The Standard Donation Template works perfectly for receiving donations.

You don't have to add each donor to your QuickBooks file. You can keep those names in another software application. Create a generic customer name (you can use the same Donor customer name you use for generic pledges), and post all donations to that customer.

If you want to print and mail a receipt to a particular donor, enter the name and address of the donor in the Donor address box. Then, print the form by clicking the Print icon on the form's window. When you save the transaction, QuickBooks asks you if the Donor record should be updated with this new address. Select No, because you don't want to add the address to the customer record of your generic donor.

***NOTE**: You can enter donations in batches, as described earlier for pledges.*

Memorized Reports for Nonprofits

The Premier Nonprofit Edition provides useful reports that have been customized and memorized for this QuickBooks edition. Choose Reports → Memorized Reports → Nonprofit, and select one of the following memorized reports:

- Biggest Donors/Grants
- Budget vs. Actual by Donors/Grants
- Donors/Grants Report
- Budget vs. Actual by Program/Projects
- Programs/Projects Report
- Statement of Financial Income and Expense
- Statement of Financial Position
- Statement of Functional Expenses (990)

The best explanations of the content of each report are in the Report Center, which you reach by choosing Reports → Report Center. When the Report Center opens, select the Nonprofit listing in the left pane (see Figure 13-5).

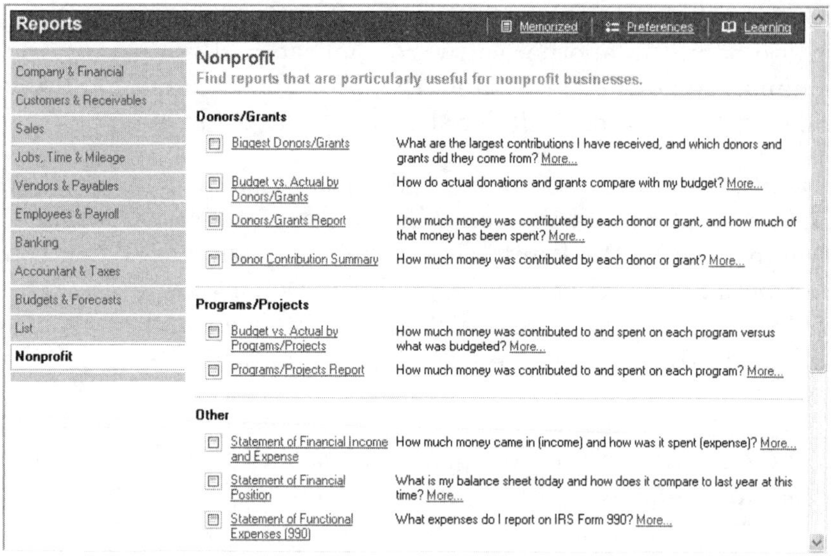

Figure 13-5: The Nonprofit Report Center is filled with information and explanations.

You can further customize any of these reports to meet your own needs, and then memorize them. Chapter 8 has information about customizing and memorizing reports.

Chapter 14

Professional Services Edition

Configuring your company file

Managing retainers

Managing customer deposits

Managing escrow

Customized templates

Customized reports

QuickBooks is extremely well suited for service businesses, and the Premier Professional Services Edition extends that innate strength. In this edition you have built in transaction templates, customized reports, and other features that are designed with professional service providers in mind.

Company File

If you're just starting with QuickBooks, you have to create a company file. QuickBooks Premier Professional Services Edition has a predefined company file that works extremely well.

The predefined company file for professional services isn't marked as such when you create a new company file. It's merely listed as an industry type, with no indication that it contains a suitable chart of accounts, and some prepopulated entries in lists. (This is what we call an "undocumented feature".)

You can create a company file using the predefined file either with the EasyStep Interview, or by clicking Skip Interview on the opening window of the EasyStep Interview, and creating the file manually. In the wizard window for selecting your industry, choose the Professional Consulting listing.

Because this is a preconfigured company file, many of your preferences are already set up appropriately, and quite a few of the lists are populated with entries. Open the lists so you can delete the entries that aren't specific to your business, and rename the entries you need if the names aren't appropriate. In this chapter I discuss some of the prepopulated lists and make suggestions about changing those list entries to make them more useful.

Lists

Most of the industry choices for Professional Services result in a company file that has been pre-populated with elements in some lists (such as the Customer & Vendor Profile Lists). In this section I discuss some of the concepts you should consider for developing lists in a service business.

Customers and Jobs List

Most professional service businesses should track jobs for customers. Even if the work you do for a customer doesn't seem to fit the description of a "job", it's best to set up a job, so you can later track additional work for the customer with additional jobs.

Even if some customers don't want reports and invoices on a job basis, tracking jobs gives you internal information about your business finances. You can track job costs and profitability, and analyze the types of jobs or projects that generate the most income.

***TIP**: Lawyers who have personal injury practices often provide advance money for doctors and other expenses before a case is settled. A job cost report works well as a settlement sheet when the insurance check arrives.*

Items

Most of the items you create for a professional service company are of the item type Service. You should plan your items to make sure you can track each type of service for job costing, and for profitability reports.

If you have services that are provided by non-employees, be sure to set up service items for that scenario. Create a service item for this circumstance, and select the option This Service Is Performed By A Subcontractor, Owner, Or Partner. Selecting that option changes the New Item dialog to include fields for tracking both costs and revenue. This means you can track profitability for the item.

If you're going to track time, remember to set up service items for unbillable time, so you can track those totals. Create a parent item named unbillable time, and then create subitems to cover meetings, proposal writing, sales calls, general administrative tasks, and so on. Using those services with the QuickBooks Timesheet feature lets you track your expenses, including overhead, quite closely.

***NOTE**: Most professional service businesses bill for time, and it's beyond the scope of this book to explain all the basics. To learn how to use all the timekeeping features in QuickBooks, read QuickBooks 2008: The Official Guide.*

Customer and Vendor Types

Create Customer Types and Vendor Types to match the way you want to separate customers and vendors when you produce reports. In addition, bear in mind the types you need for analyzing your business—where your business comes from, and where you spend money. For example, you may want to track customers by referral type, which lets you analyze the effects of your advertising and marketing expenditures.

On the other hand, you may prefer to use business types as your customer types, separating lawyers, doctors, engineers, and so on. Then, you can contact customer types if you expand your service offerings to match a need of a specific business type. You can create reports on profitability and receivables by type, and if you discover that some types of customers don't pay well, or aren't profitable, you can adjust the way you plan sales calls.

If you selected a predefined company file during setup, your file may already have entries in the Customer Type and Vendor Type lists. Some of these preloaded entries may not suit your purposes, so you can remove them and create your own.

Billing Rate Levels

The Premier Professional Services Edition includes the Billing Rate Level List, which lets you assign billing rates and automatically enter the appropriate rate in a sales transaction.

For example, you can have a partner's rate for a specific type of work, and a lower rate for the same type of work if that work is performed by a supervisor. You can apply these rates to employees and subcontractors.

If a manager sometimes acts as a senior associate, or performs some task that involves more responsibility, you can assign a higher billing rate to that different job, for that same person.

This feature provides a great deal of flexibility, so you can make sure you're billing time at a rate higher than the cost of that rate. All the instructions you need to create, assign, and apply billing rate levels are in Chapter 3. After you create billing rate levels, and associate them with service providers, invoicing for services becomes automatic. Every time you create an invoice with billable time, you can select the correct rate for the service, linked to the person who performed the work.

Classes

Classes let you track your business in a divisional manner, and then produce divisional Profit & Loss Reports. The way you use classes depends on the organization of your business. Here are a few of the common class tracking scenarios for service businesses (to stimulate your thinking):

- Tracking multiple offices. In addition to the traditional branch office structure, in recent years I've even seen this class structure applied in companies that run virtual offices (everybody works from home and the company pays some of the home office expenses).
- Tracking partners.
- Tracking service divisions. A law firm may have a domestic relations division and a personal injury division. An advertising agency may have a creative division, and a media buying division.

Income is linked to the appropriate class when creating invoices or sales receipt transactions. Expenses that are specific to a class are linked to that class during vendor transactions (bills, checks, or credit card purchases).

Allocating Overhead with Classes

Create a class for general administration, so you can allocate overhead among the divisions you're tracking with classes. Allocations are performed with a journal entry at a regular interval. You can allocate expenses monthly, quarterly, or at the end of your fiscal year.

General office expenses are posted through normal transaction entries (vendor bills, checks, or credit card purchases). All of these transactions are posted to the Administration class. These expenses can include rent, payroll (including employer payroll expenses), utilities, insurance, web hosting, online services, and so on. At some regular interval, some of these overhead expenses are allocated to each class.

Creating Allocation Journal Entries

To allocate overhead expenses, create a journal entry that moves the funds from the Administration class to the divisions you're tracking by class. For example, Figure 14-1 shows a portion of a typical allocation journal entry (the portion that allocates the monthly $900.00 rent). Originally, a check for $900.00 was sent to the landlord, and the transaction was linked to the Administration class. The allocating journal entry has two parts:

- It credits (removes) the expense and links that action to the Administration class (the original posting class).
- It proportionally debits the expense for each class, and the total of those debits equals the amount of the credit.

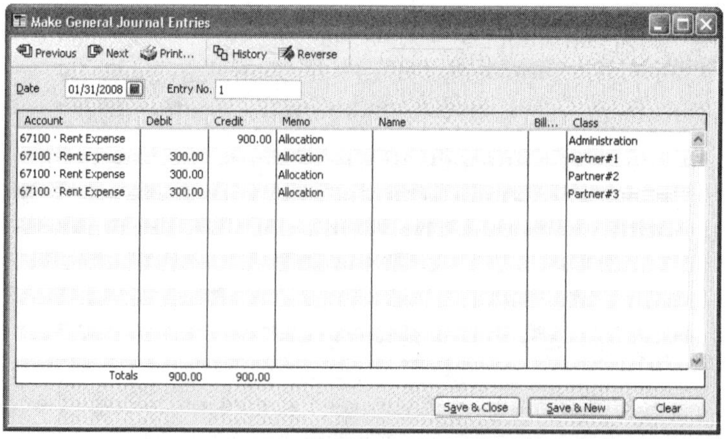

Figure 14-1: Allocate administrative costs among classes.

You don't have to allocate 100% of an overhead expense; you can allocate some of the expense and leave the remaining amount in the Administrative class. Some companies allocate different amounts to each class, using a formula that reflects a logical allocation. For example, I have clients who first determine the percentage of income each class provided to the business for the month, and then allocate overhead by a percentage that is calculated to match the percentage of income the class contributed.

Memorizing Allocation Journal Entries

If you have a sizeable list of overhead expenses, building your journal entry from scratch every month is too onerous. Instead, create a journal entry for this purpose and memorize it, using the following steps:

1. Enter each expense account as many times as needed (the number of classes including the administrative class).
2. In the Debit and Credit columns, enter the amounts that are constant (such as rent), and leave the amounts that vary blank (you fill them in each month).
3. In the Class column, enter the class name for each row.
4. After all the accounts and classes are entered, memorize the journal entry by pressing Ctrl-M.
5. Enter a name for this memorized transaction, such as Overhead Allocations.
6. Specify whether you want QuickBooks to remind you to create the journal entry, and if so, set the reminder.
7. Click OK to return to the Make General Journal Entries window.
8. Close the window by clicking the X in the upper right corner—do not click Save & Close, do not click Save & New.
9. When QuickBooks asks if you want to record the transaction, click No (you're building a template, you're not entering a transaction, and you don't have to save a journal entry to memorize it).

When it's time to allocate overhead, press Ctrl-T to open the Memorized Transaction list. Select this allocation journal entry, enter the appropriate data, and save it.

Managing Retainers

Many professional service providers work with some, or all, customers on a retainer basis. The customer sends a certain amount of money that is held as a deposit against future invoices.

When you receive a payment for a retainer, it isn't income. It becomes income when you earn it, at which point you create an invoice or a cash receipt to turn it into revenue.

To manage retainers, you need to set up the following components in your company file:

- A liability account to track retainer funds.
- A retainer item.

Ideally, you should also create a QuickBooks bank account to hold retainer funds. I don't mean a real, separate, bank account; instead, you can use a virtual bank account to make sure you keep retainers (unearned funds) separate from regular operating funds.

A virtual bank account for retainers not only ensures you don't spend down into retainer funds before they're earned, it provides a way to track a balance that can be checked against the balance in the liability account you use to post retainer funds—the two numbers must be identical.

Lawyers are required to maintain separate bank accounts for client funds (escrow accounts), but in most states, that rule doesn't cover retainers. Many professions besides lawyers work with retainer agreements for some or all clients, such as advertising agencies, technical support companies, and others.

***NOTE**: Escrow funds for clients have to be deposited into a separate escrow bank account. Other service businesses, such as real estate professionals, agents, and other professions that temporarily hold money for clients, also maintain escrow accounts. See the section "Managing Escrow", later in this chapter.*

GCLS Mullica Hill Branch

Customer ID: **********5415

Items that you checked out

Title: Running QuickBooks 2008 premier editions
ID: 32928100566086
Due: Monday, April 02, 2018

Title: To die for
ID: 32918025672986
Due: Monday, April 02, 2018

Total items: 2
Account balance: $0.00
Sunday, March 18, 2018 3:18 PM
Checked out: 2
Overdue: 0
Hold requests: 0
Ready for pickup: 0

All GCLS Libraries
will be closed
January 15, 2018
****

www.gcls.org
856-223-6060

Liability Accounts for Retainers

To track retainers, you need a liability account of the type Other Current Liability (named Retainers or Retainers Held). You may also need a liability account to track other client funds that you're holding, such as upfront deposits that are connected to a job or project.

Some businesses prefer to separate retainers from other types of upfront deposits by creating multiple liability accounts. Or, you can create an Other Current Liability account named Client Funds Held, and then create subaccounts for deposits and retainers. Only use the subaccounts in transactions. When you view the chart of accounts, or create reports that include your liability accounts, the parent account reports the total of the amounts in the subaccounts.

Moving Funds from Income to Retainers

If you haven't been tracking retainers in a liability account, you've been bringing those funds into your bookkeeping as income, and probably tracking the amount of income that's really retainer funds separately (in a spreadsheet or a piece of paper).

Now it's time to move those funds out of an income account and into the liability account you created to track retainers. The current total of the funds you're holding as retainers has to be moved from the income account into the liability account.

Choose Company → Make General Journal Entries to open the Make General Journal Entries transaction window. If you have one income account in your chart of accounts, this is an easy task:

- Debit the income account for the total amount of retainer funds you're currently holding.
- Credit the Retainers (current liability) account for the same amount.

If you've been tracking income by category and have multiple income accounts, you have to figure out how much of each income account is really retainer income that you're still holding as retainers. Then debit each income account for the appropriate amount and credit the Retainers liability account with the total.

Retainer Items

You need an item for retainers, which you use when you create transactions involving retainers. Retainers are usually Service items. If you manage both retainers and upfront deposits, you should have two items, so you can track them (and create reports about them) separately.

To create an item for retainers, use the following guidelines:

- The type of item is Service.
- The rate is zero, because it's customer-specific, and is therefore entered at the time you create the transaction.
- The account to which it's linked is the liability account you use to track retainers.

Virtual Bank Accounts for Retainers

Most companies put retainer funds into the regular business bank account. If your retainer and regular funds are co-mingled in a single account, you should consider using virtual bank accounts to separate retainer funds from operating funds. When you use the operating account to pay your business expenses, the balance won't include the retainer amounts you're holding. This makes it easier to avoid spending retainer money.

In addition, having a bank account for retainer funds (whether real or virtual) provides a quick way to check the status of retainer funds. The amount in the bank account should always equal the amount in the retainer liability account.

Creating Subaccounts as Virtual Accounts

Virtual bank accounts are subaccounts of your business bank account. I'm assuming you've already created a bank account in your chart of accounts, and this becomes the parent account.

You must create two subaccounts under the parent account: an operating account and a retainer account. The operating account assumes the same role as a single bank account—it holds your operating funds. The retainer subaccount is where you deposit retainer fees, and then move the appropriate amounts to the operating subaccount as the retainers are earned and turned into income. Use the following steps to create the subaccounts:

1. Open the Chart of Accounts List window.
2. Press Ctrl-N to open the Add New Account dialog.
3. Select Bank as the account type, and click Continue.
4. Enter a number for the virtual operating account (if you're using account numbers). Use a number ten digits higher than the number of your bank account. For example, if your bank account number is 10000, make the new account 10010.
5. Enter a name for the new subaccount, such as Operating Funds.
6. Select the option Subaccount Of, and select your bank account from the drop-down list in the text box.
7. Optionally, enter a description of this account.
8. Click Next to open a blank New Account dialog, which has Bank selected as the account type.
9. Enter the account number (e.g. 10011).
10. Enter a name, such as Retainer Funds.
11. Select the option Subaccount Of, and select your bank account from the drop-down list in the text box.
12. Optionally, enter a description.
13. Click OK.

In the chart of accounts window, your subaccounts are listed (and indented) under your bank account.

Transferring Funds to Subaccounts

After your bank subaccounts are created, you need to transfer the appropriate amounts into each subaccount. When you complete this task, the parent bank account should have a zero balance, although it displays the total of the balances of the subaccounts when you view the chart of accounts.

You must know the amount you're holding as retainer funds, as of the date you adjust the real bank account. Often these records are kept outside of QuickBooks, in spreadsheets or on paper. When you have the total, you're ready to begin transferring money to your subaccounts.

Create a journal entry to transfer the funds by choosing Company → Make General Journal Entries. In the Make General Journal Entries transaction window, credit the entire current balance of the bank account, and debit the appropriate amounts for each subaccount (see Figure 14-2). Remember that this is a virtual exercise; the money really *is* in your real bank account.

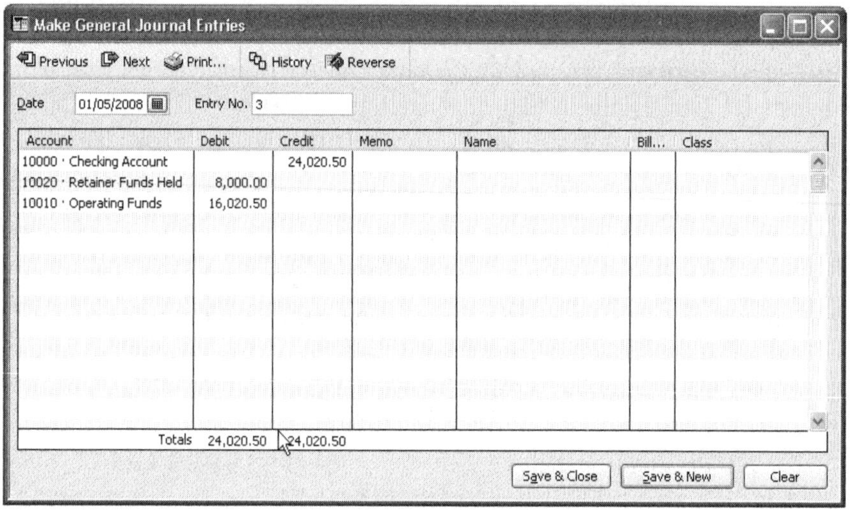

Figure 14-2: Empty the parent bank account, and fill the subaccounts.

When you open the chart of accounts window, the balance displayed for the main bank account is the total of the balances in the subaccounts. Balance sheet reports and trial balance reports display the balances of the subaccounts and the total for the parent account.

Making Deposits into Subaccounts

Your QuickBooks company file configuration probably enables the Undeposited Funds account. This means when you create transactions for received funds (customer payments of invoices, or cash receipts), the money is deposited into the Undeposited Funds account.

When you deposit the funds in the bank, you use the Make Deposits feature to transfer the funds into a bank account. This is the best way to manage bank deposits, because it matches the way your bank statement reports deposits. However, if you're using subaccounts, you have to separate regular income from retainer income. Select all the regular income, and deposit that in the operating funds subaccount. Select all the retainer receipts, and deposit them in the retainer funds subaccount.

Often, this isn't an easy task, because you can't tell which income is for regular earned income, and which is for retainer payments. As you can see in Figure 14-3, nothing in the Payments to Deposit transaction window tells you which receipts are for retainers, and which are for regular income.

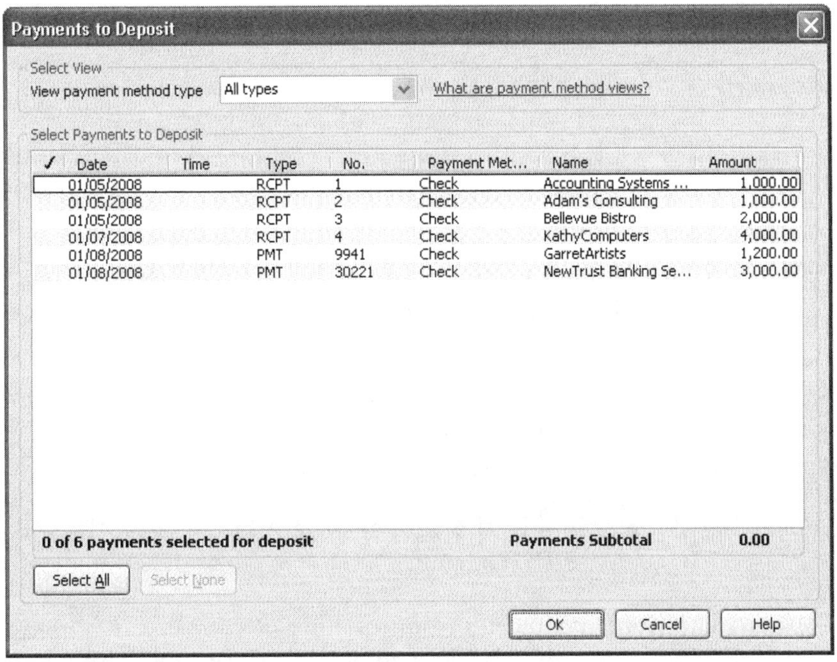

Figure 14-3: How do you deposit these receipts into the appropriate bank?

The way to resolve this dilemma is to come up with a solution that announces itself in the Payments to Deposit window. Using the Memo field in a customer payment transaction window doesn't work, because memo text isn't displayed in this window.

For my clients, I solved the problem with a new payment method. I created a payment method named Retainer, with a payment type of Other, using the following steps:

1. Choose Lists → Customer & Vendor Profile Lists → Payment Method List.
2. Press Ctrl-N to open the New Payment Method dialog.
3. Name the new payment method Retainer.
4. Select the Payment Type Other.
5. Click OK to save the new payment method.

When retainers arrive, either as a payment against an invoice, or as a sales receipt, be sure the transaction window is marked with the Retainer payment type. The transaction window has a field for entering the customer's check number (always important to record in case of any disputes with the customer).

- In the Receive Payment transaction window, when you select Retainer (or any other payment method classified as Other), the Check # field changes its name to Reference #.
- In the Enter Sales Receipts transaction window, when you select Retainer (or any other payment method classified as Other), the Check No. field doesn't change its label.

When you use the new Retainer payment method in transactions, the Payments to Deposit window is much easier to work with. As you can see in Figure 14-4, retainers are clearly discernable.

Depositing the receipts in the proper accounts requires the following steps:

1. Select the Retainer payments and click OK.
2. In the Make Deposits window select the Retainer Funds bank subaccount.
3. Select the date on which you took the receipts to the bank.
4. Click Save & New to return to the Payments to Deposit window.
5. Click Select All to select the remaining (non retainer) receipts.
6. Click OK.
7. In the Make Deposits window select the Operating Funds bank subaccount.

8. Click Save & Close.

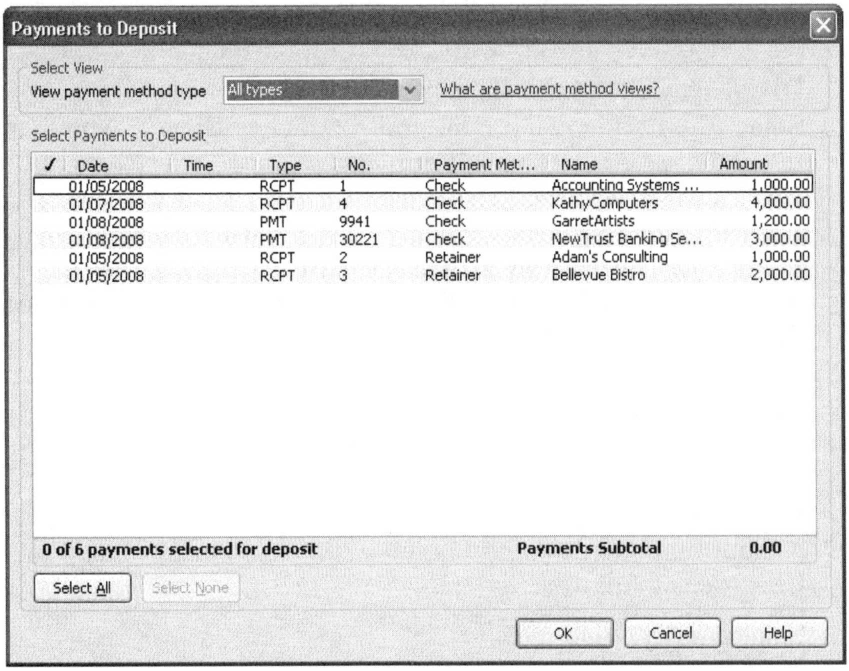

Figure 14-4: You can separate payments by type when depositing funds into a bank account.

You can automate the way you select payment types in the Payments to Deposit window, which is important in either of the following scenarios:

- You have a very large list of receipts in the window and you don't want to click off the retainer methods one at a time.
- You have other types of payment methods that have to be deposited separately (such as credit card payments which your bank handles separately on your statement).

To deposit different payment types in groups, use the following steps:

1. Click the arrow next to the View Payment Method Type field at the top of the Payments to Deposit window, and choose Selected Types from the drop-down list.

2. In the Selected Types dialog, choose Other.
3. Click OK to return to the Payments to Deposit window, where only your retainer payments are displayed.
4. Click Select All to select all your retainer deposits, and then click OK to open the Make Deposits window.
5. Select the Retainer bank account, and click Save & New to return to the Payments to Deposit window.
6. If you have credit card receipts to deposit, repeat Steps 1 and 2, selecting the appropriate credit card type in Step 2. Then repeat Steps 3 through 5 (unless a credit card receipt was for a retainer, in which case it has to be handled separately and deposited in the Retainer Funds account).
7. Click OK to open the Make Deposits window, and select the Operating bank account.
8. Click Save & New to return to the Payments to Deposit window.
9. In the Selected Types dialog, choose All Types, because all the remaining receipts should be standard income receipts.
10. Click Select All, and click OK.
11. Choose the Operating Funds bank account.
12. Click Save & Close.

Reconciling Bank Accounts with Subaccounts

When you reconcile the bank account, use the parent account. Because your subaccounts are virtual bank accounts, instead of real separate bank accounts, the parent account actually maintains all the activity in the bank register.

After you fill out the Bank Reconciliation window displays all the transactions for both accounts. In fact, the parent account doesn't pay any attention at all to the fact that there are subaccounts; this is just a regular bank reconciliation and no transaction shows any indication of being initiated from a subaccount.

Applying Retainers to Invoices

The retainers you hold aren't your funds; they belong to your customers. They become your funds when you earn them, at which point they become revenue. When you invoice your customer for services performed, you transfer retainer funds to income.

To invoice a retainer customer and apply retainer funds, create an invoice as usual, using the following guidelines:

- Enter the appropriate items in the line item section of the invoice.
- The last line item in the invoice is the retainer item, which you enter with a minus sign.
- If the retainer balance is larger than the invoice amount, apply a retainer amount equal to the invoice amount.
- If the retainer balance is smaller than the invoice amount, apply the entire retainer balance.
- In the Memo field, enter text to indicate retainer funds were applied to the invoice.
- Save the invoice.

You can print and send the invoice to the client, but many businesses don't bother sending individual invoices to retainer customers (especially because the invoices almost always have a zero total). Instead, they periodically send a report on the retainer balance.

There's a big problem with the scenario I just described. The invoice window doesn't tell you the client's retainer balance. You must ascertain that information before you create invoices. To do that, you have to create a report on retainer balances (covered next).

Tracking Retainer Balances

You need to keep an eye on customer retainer balances, so when you create invoices you know whether there are sufficient funds to apply against an invoice. To do this, you must create a Retainer Report, using the following steps:

1. Choose Reports → Customers & Receivables → Customer Balance Detail.
2. In the report window, click Modify Report.
3. In the Display tab, deselect the Class and Balance columns in the Columns list (this makes the report easier to read).

3. In the Filters tab, select Account in the Filters List.
4. In the Account field, select the Customer Retainers liability account.
5. Click OK to return to the report window (see Figure 14-5).
6. Click Memorize and name the report (e.g. Retainer Balances).

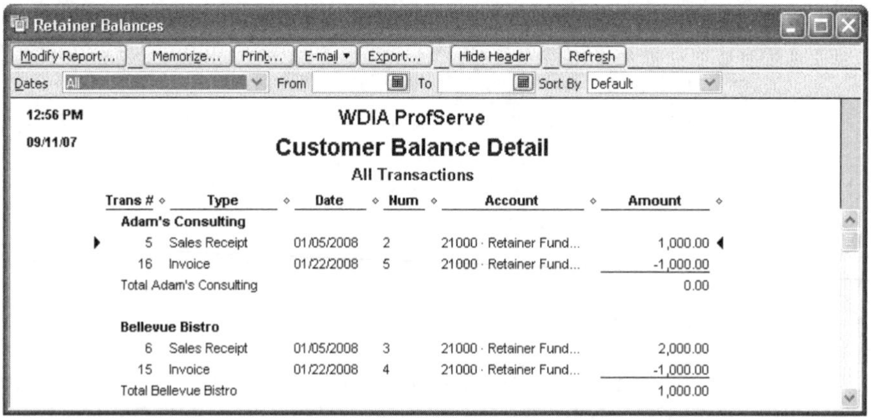

Figure 14-5: Track the use and current balance of retainer funds.

To open the memorized report in the future, choose Reports → Memorized Reports List, and select this report.

Postings for Applying Retainer Funds

When you create an invoice and apply retainer funds to the invoice, QuickBooks posts the amounts as follows:

- The income account(s) attached to the items in the invoice are credited, and Accounts Receivable is debited.
- The Customer Retainers liability account is debited, and Accounts Receivable is credited (because the line item is a negative amount).

This means your general ledger tracks the full amount of the income in the invoice, and reduces the customer's receivable by the application of the retainer amount. Your Profit & Loss report, and reports on the customer's activity, all show the full amount of the income you invoiced.

***NOTE**: If the amount of the retainer applied equals the invoice total, the invoice is a zero amount invoice. If you view the invoice, you'll see the PAID stamp in the transaction window.*

Moving Retainer Funds

After you invoice retainer customers, the retainer amounts you applied to the invoices are no longer the customers' funds, they're your funds, and you can spend them. In addition your retainer liability account balance no longer matches the retainer bank subaccount balance.

Both of these circumstances are resolved by transferring the funds in the retainer funds bank subaccount to the operating funds subaccount.

The easy way to accomplish this is to use the transfer funds transaction feature (on the Banking menu), as seen in Figure 14-6.

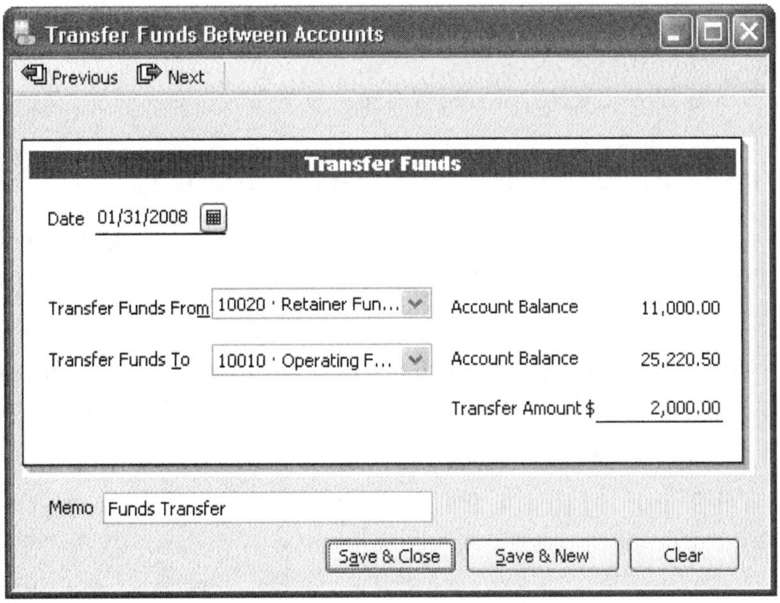

Figure 14-6: Move funds from the retainer account into your operating account.

***NOTE**: If you're keeping retainer funds in a separate bank account instead of using subaccounts, write a check or use an online transfer function to move the funds to your operating account.*

Managing Upfront Deposits

Under certain circumstances, you may ask a customer for an upfront deposit against a job. This is particularly important if the job requires you to lay out substantial funds, perhaps to hire a subcontractor, or purchase a product. This is not the same as a retainer, it's a job-based advance payment, and shouldn't be treated as a retainer.

***NOTE**: Some companies collect a certain percentage of the estimated cost of a job up front as a standard policy.*

When you receive a deposit, you cannot record the receipt as income. You haven't yet earned the money; it still belongs to the customer. Therefore, it's a liability to your company.

Creating Accounts for Upfront Deposits

You need a liability account to track customer deposits, of the type Other Current Liability. Name the account Customer Deposits, or something similar.

If you also collect retainers from clients, you can use a single account for both types of funds. However, I tend to be a purist about these things, so I prefer separate liability accounts.

If you have both retainers and upfront deposits to track, you can also set up another virtual bank subaccount for upfront deposits. See the discussion on creating virtual bank accounts with subaccounts in the previous section on tracking retainers. However, most upfront deposits are already earmarked for spending, and the outlay of the upfront funds usually occurs rather rapidly, so it's usually fine to deposit the money into your operating funds bank account.

TIP: Another way to handle a mixture of retainers and upfront deposits is to create a liability account named Customer Funds, and then create subaccounts for retainers and upfront deposits.

Creating Items for Upfront Deposits

You need to create an item for upfront deposits, so you can record the deposit activities in sales forms. The type of item you create depends on the circumstances under which you ask customers for deposits.

- For upfront deposits on services, create a Service item.
- If you only ask for upfront deposits when you have to purchase products, create an Other Charge item.
- If you collect deposits under both circumstances, choose either type of item—flip a coin.

Link the item to the liability account you created for customer upfront deposits.

Receiving Upfront Deposits

Often, the receipt of an upfront deposit is the result of a conversation or a written proposal. You may not create an invoice for the deposit, so when the customer's check arrives it's a sales receipt.

Whether you use an invoice or a sales receipt, the way you fill out the transaction window remains the same. Enter the upfront deposit item, and enter the amount.

If you use an invoice, QuickBooks posts the transaction as follows:

- Debits Accounts Receivable
- Credits the Upfront Deposit liability account.

If you use a sales receipt, QuickBooks creates the following postings:

- Debits the Undeposited Funds account.
- Credits the Upfront Deposit liability account.

If you don't use the Undeposited Funds account, and instead you deposit the funds to a bank account, that bank account receives the debit posting.

If you use the Undeposited Funds account, and you want to deposit the funds into the Customer Deposits subaccount of your bank account, use the instructions earlier in this chapter for separating the funds in the Payments to Deposit window. Create a new Payment Method named Upfront Deposit and make it a type Other, and use the drop-down list in the Payments to Deposit window to display only the type Other.

However, the display of payment methods of the Other type includes both retainers and upfront deposits (if you happen to have both types of customer receipts on the same day). This doesn't work well if you have two separate subaccounts to track these customer advance payments. There are two solutions:

- Keep notes about each cash receipt, select only the retainers, and deposit them to the retainers bank subaccount. Then select the upfront deposits, and deposit them to the upfront deposits bank account.
- When you enter the customer's check number in the original transaction window (either a Sales Receipt or a Receive Payments transaction), put a letter in front of the check number: R for retainer, U for upfront deposit. Because the check number appears in the Payments to Deposit window, this makes it easier to select the right listings in that window.

Applying an Upfront Deposit to an Invoice

To create the invoice against which you need to apply the upfront deposit, open the Create Invoices transaction window. Fill out the invoice with the items you've sold the customer. For the last item, use the upfront deposit item you created, and enter the amount of the deposit that you're applying to the invoice, with a minus sign.

QuickBooks posts the invoice in the following manner:

- The income account(s) attached to the item(s) on the invoice are credited.

- The liability account attached to the discount item is debited.
- The A/R account is debited for the net balance due.

If you're maintaining subaccounts of your bank account to separate upfront deposits from operating funds, transfer the amount of the discount you applied to the operating funds. (See the instructions earlier in this chapter for transferring funds between bank subaccounts.)

Upfront Deposits that are Just Payments in Advance

Sometimes, a customer deposit is nothing more than an advance payment. This usually means that the job or product is delivered to the customer in a short time. (You shouldn't hold deposits for long jobs unless you treat the deposits as liabilities.)

In this circumstance, you can create an invoice, apply the advance payment, and then hold the invoice until you deliver the services or products. You don't have to treat the advance payment as a liability.

Creating an Advance Payment Item

To use an advance payment, you must create an item for it, as follows:

1. Choose Lists → Item List.
2. Press Ctrl-N to open the New Item dialog.
3. Select Payment as the Item type.
4. Name the item Advance Payment or Payment in Advance.
5. If you take credit cards, or receive cash, in addition to receiving checks, don't enter anything in the Payment Method field.
6. If you don't use the Undeposited Funds account, select the option Deposit To and enter the bank account (or subaccount) to receive this payment.
7. Click OK.

The description field is optional, but you should enter the text you want to appear in the invoice, to make it clear to the customer that the advance has been applied to the invoice.

Applying an Advance Payment to an Invoice

In QuickBooks, you receive an advance payment and create an invoice at the same time. The advance is not treated as a separate transaction, or as a payment against an existing invoice.

Enter the item(s) you're selling the customer, and then enter the Advance Payment item. Do *not* enter a minus sign; Payment type items are always automatically deducted, so QuickBooks automatically enters the minus sign. The invoice total is the net of the sale less the advance payment.

Depositing Advance Payments

When you apply an advance payment to an invoice, QuickBooks automatically deposits the money. If you linked the advance payment item to the Undeposited Funds account, the next time you use the Payments to Deposit window, the advance payment is there. The payment is differentiated by the code INV in the Type column.

Managing Escrow

Managing escrow funds differs from managing retainers and customer deposits in two respects:

- The funds belong to your client, but are not collected from that client. Instead, they're collected from a third party on behalf of your client.
- The rules for managing escrow funds are mandated by state law and the rules of your professional association.

All states require attorneys to maintain a separate bank account for escrow funds, and to impose bookkeeping procedures for tracking escrow funds as liabilities.

Professional associations and general conventions impose similar rules on other professions, such a realtors, agents, and others who collect funds on behalf of clients.

To manage escrow you must open a separate bank account for escrow funds. In QuickBooks, you must create the following accounts in your chart of accounts:

- A bank account for the escrow account.
- A current liability account to track escrowed funds (usually named Funds Held In Trust).

If you need more than one "real" escrow bank account, you must create a bank account in your chart of accounts for each escrow account.

If you have multiple escrow bank accounts, you can still use one liability account for escrowed funds. Because all transactions are linked to a customer, your customer reports make it easy to ascertain which funds in the liability account belong to which customer. On the other hand, you may be more comfortable using subaccounts to separate the liability account by category.

Customized Templates

The Premier Professional Services Edition offers several customized templates you can use to create transactions. You can use these templates as-is, or as the basis of further customizations.

Customized Invoice Templates

The customized invoice templates are designed to tweak standard Intuit invoice templates so they use the right jargon (which is a slick professional touch). For example, the Time & Expense invoice template has a column named Hours/Qty instead of the standard Qty heading that's more appropriate for product sales. The Fixed Fee invoice template has a simplified design that omits any columns for quantity, and adds a Date column.

Customized Proposal Template

If you create proposals, QuickBooks has a Proposal template available when you choose the Create Estimates command from the Customers menu or the Create Proposals & Estimates command from the Professional menu.

To use proposals you must enable the feature by choosing Edit → Preferences and selecting the Jobs & Estimates category in the left pane. In the Company Preferences tab, select the Yes option in the section labeled Do You Create Estimates?

The Proposal template has a column titled Est. Hours/Qty. If you wish, you can customize this template to eliminate the text Qty from the column heading.

TIP: *Use the Invoice button on the Proposal template to turn the proposal into an invoice automatically when it's time to invoice your customer.*

Customized Reports

The Premier Professional Services Edition includes a well thought out list of reports that have been customized for service providers. Choose Reports → Professional Services Reports to display the list. The reports are useful and relevant (and the titles are self-explanatory).

Chapter 15

Retail Edition

- Company file elements
- Recording sales
- Upfront deposits
- Layaways
- Gift certificates
- Selling on consignment
- Point of Sale add-ons
- Customized reports

The Premier Retail Edition is designed to help you track retail sales efficiently. While I wouldn't try to use QuickBooks to run a supermarket that has to track thousands of inventory items, the Premier Retail Edition works well for small retailers.

In this chapter, I discuss ways to understand and use some of the features and functions available in your copy of QuickBooks Premier Retail Edition software.

Company File Elements

Your company file needs to be set up with elements required to run your retail business. If you're just starting in QuickBooks, when you create your company file, either with the EasyStep Interview, or manually (by clicking Skip Interview when the EasyStep Interview starts), choose Retail as the industry type. This action automatically creates the basic elements you need to start running your business in QuickBooks.

In this section I'll provide a brief overview of a few of the important elements in your company file.

Chart of Accounts

You need to make sure your chart of accounts contains the accounts you need to run your business. When you create your company file in QuickBooks, many accounts are automatically loaded in the chart of accounts, but you have to create your bank accounts yourself.

You need to create an account of the type Bank for each bank account (operating account, payroll account, money market, business savings, etc.). In addition you need a bank account for the cash you keep in the register. You can name the account Cash in Register, Cash in Till, Petty Cash, or something similar.

For Assets, you need an account for inventory, and for fixed assets.

For Liabilities, you need Sales Tax Payable (which QuickBooks installs in your chart of accounts as soon as you set up sales tax items).

For income, you need an account of the type Income (name it Income). Usually, retailers have no need to track a variety of income types with additional income accounts. However, it's a good idea to have an account of the type Income named Sales Discounts. If you offer a discount for quantity, or for any other reason, you should track that amount so you can analyze the effect of discounts on your gross and net income.

You need an account for Cost of Goods Sold, which tracks purchases of goods for resale.

You need an account for tracking merchant card fees, and you should ask your accountant whether those fees should be posted to an account of the type Cost of Goods Sold, or Expense.

You need accounts of the type Expense for all your business expenses.

In addition, you may have to add accounts to track special circumstances, such as layaways, gift certificates, and so on. Those topics, and the accounts you need to create for them, are discussed later in this chapter.

Inventory

Inventory is a topic you must discuss with your accountant. For most small retailers, tracking inventory is more trouble than it's worth. You can probably work out a data entry system, with the help of your accountant, that lets you post purchases to Cost of Goods Sold (COGS) and periodically (yearly, at tax time) adjust your inventory and COGS accounts as follows: Debit Inventory and credit COGS for the amount (cost amount) of unsold Inventory.

Your accountant may want to handle this slightly differently, or start your inventory system with opening balances.

If you have a super-duper fancy cash register, and bar code readers, you can let that equipment track and report data. Then, turn that data over to your accountant, along with product purchasing totals, and have your accountant tell you how to enter the adjusting journal entry in QuickBooks.

If you want to track inventory, basic information about setting up inventory items is available in QuickBooks 2008: The Official Guide, which is available at your favorite bookstore. In this book, I don't cover the elementary, basic, setup tasks for QuickBooks (because the book is dedicated to the Premier editions features), but Chapter 7 of this book explains how to use sales transactions when inventory is enabled.

Items

You can't sell anything in QuickBooks without creating items, because all sales transactions require an item. You should create the following basic items:

- Sales-Taxable
- Sales-Nontaxable
- Customer Deposits
- Discount
- Subtotal
- Sales Tax
- Over and Short

Over and Short items are discussed in the section " Managing the Over and Short Problem", later in this chapter.

In addition, you may have to add items to track special circumstances, such as layaways, gift certificates, and so on. Those topics, and the items you need to create for them, are discussed later in this chapter.

Customers

Most small retailers don't track customers; instead, they create one generic customer in QuickBooks, named Customer, or Sale, or RetailSale. If you collect sales tax, make the customer's tax code Taxable.

If some of the products you sell aren't taxable, a customer who is configured as taxable isn't charged sales tax for the purchase of those products. Sales tax kicks in when both the customer and the item are taxable.

If you have customers who are not required to pay sales tax (such as nonprofit associations), create another customer named CustomerNoTax (or something similar). Configure that customer as nontaxable.

If you want to track some customers, especially if you extend credit for certain customers, create those customers in addition to the generic customers.

Payment Methods

It's important to create all the payment methods you need, because your bank deposits vary by payment method. For instance, cash and checks are deposited separately from credit card payments. Your Visa and Mastercard payments may be handled differently from American Express payments. Some retailers take checks to the bank with a deposit slip, but deposit cash in a bag provided by the bank.

To create a payment method, choose Lists → Customer & Vendor Profile Lists → Payment Method List. To create a payment method, when the list window opens press Ctrl-N to open a blank payment method dialog. Name the new payment method and select the appropriate payment type.

If you chose Retail as the industry when you created your company file, the list is already populated with payment methods commonly required for retailers (see Figure 15-1).

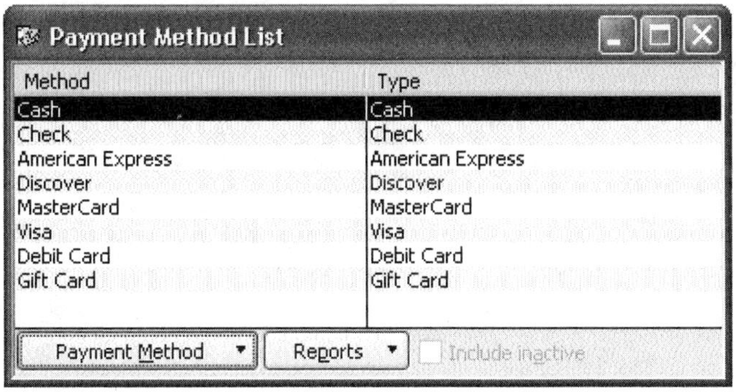

Figure 15-1: The payment methods displayed here cover the needs of most retailers.

Handling Over and Short

Most retailers find that when they count the money in the till at the end of the day, the recorded income doesn't match the cash in the till. This is a common problem with cash.

You have to know how to handle this in your bookkeeping system. QuickBooks is a double-entry bookkeeping system, which means the left side of the ledger has to be equal to the right side of the ledger. If you post $100.00 in cash sales but only have $99.50 to take to the bank, how do you handle the missing 50 cents? You can't just post $100.00 to your bank account (well, you could, but your bank reconciliation won't work and, just as important, you're not practicing good bookkeeping).

The solution to the Over/Short dilemma is to acknowledge it in your bookkeeping procedures. Track it. You'll be amazed by the way it balances — short one day, over another. (Of course, if you're short every day, and the shortages are growing, you have an entirely different problem, and the first place to look is at the person who stands in front of the cash register.)

Create Over and Short Accounts

To track Over/Short, you need to have some place to post the discrepancies, which means you have to create some accounts in your chart of accounts, as follows:

- Create an account named Over, using the account type Income.
- Create an account named Short, using the account type Income.

If you're using numbered accounts, use sequential numbers on the next level from your regular Income accounts. For example, use 41000 if your regular Income accounts are 40000, 40100, 40200, and so on.

If you want to see a net number for Over/Short (a good idea), create three accounts. Create the parent account first and name it Over-

Short (or Over&Short), and then make the Over and Short accounts subaccounts of the parent account. If you use account numbers, make the three numbers sequential; for instance:

- 41000 Over/Short (parent account)
- 41010 Over (subaccount)
- 41020 Short (subaccount)

Create Over and Short Items

When you track cash sales in a Sales Receipt transaction, you need items for your overages and shortages (in QuickBooks, you need items for everything that's connected with entering sales data in a transaction window). Create items for overages and shortages using the following guidelines:

- Create two Other Charge items, one named Overage, the other named Shortage.
- Don't assign a price.
- Make the item nontaxable.
- Link each item to the appropriate account (or subaccount) that you just created for Over/Short.

Now that you have the necessary accounts and items, use the Over and Short items right in the Sales Receipts window to adjust the difference between the amount of money you've accumulated in the cash-sale transactions and the amount of money you're actually depositing to the bank. Remember to use a minus sign before the figure when you use the Short item.

Recording Sales

The big difference between retailers and other types of businesses is the overwhelming presence of cash sales. A cash sale is a sale for which you don't have to create an invoice, because the exchange of product and payment occurs simultaneously. This also means that there's no period of time during which you have money "on the street". You can have a cash sale for either a service or a product, although it's far more common for retailers to deal exclusively in products.

There are two ways to handle cash sales in QuickBooks:

- Record each sale in its own transaction record.
- Record sales in batches (usually one batch for each business day). This method tracks income and inventory when you have no need to maintain historical information about each customer.

Recording Individual Sales

If you don't have a cash register capable of producing detailed information (that you can enter as a batch transaction), you can enter each sale in its own transaction form.

Create a generic customer and enter that customer on the sales form. Choose Customers → Enter Sales Receipts from the menu bar, which opens the Enter Sales Receipts transaction window (see Figure 15-2).

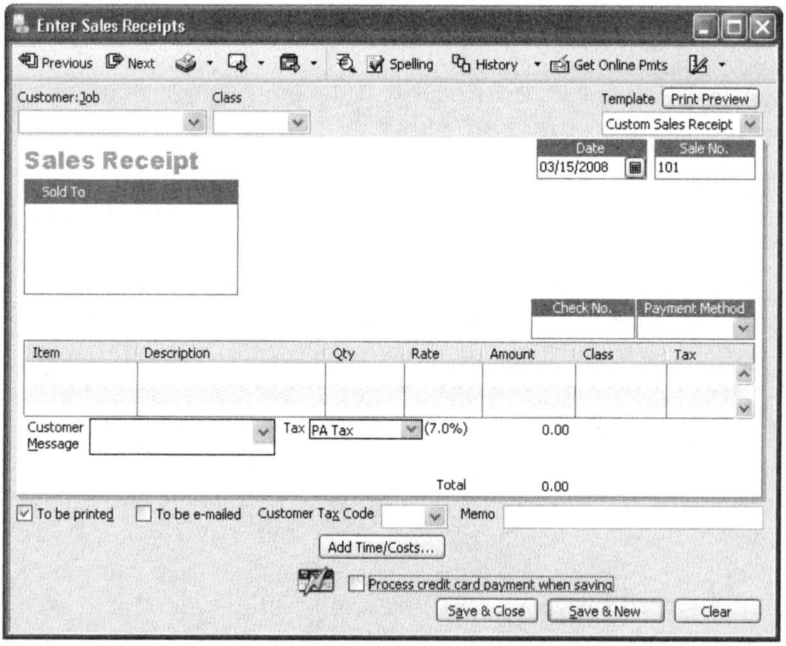

Figure 15-2: Use the Custom Sales Receipt template to track a single sales transaction.

Recording Sales in Batches

If your cash register gives you a breakdown of sales in terms of taxable and nontaxable, and also provides payment information (cash, check, and each credit card you accept), you have everything you need to enter your totals in QuickBooks.

The best way to make use of a cash register report is to include sales and payment information (bank deposit information) in one QuickBooks transaction form. The bottom line is zero (sales in, deposits out). To do this you have to set up a couple of accounts and items so that everything posts properly.

If your cash register can track the items you sell, you don't need to track those items in your QuickBooks sales transaction (you can periodically adjust item quantities separately, using journal entries or inventory adjustment transactions). Use the daily summary transaction to get the numbers into your general ledger.

Create Items to Match the Sales and Payments You Enter

You need to create items to use on your batch sales receipt transaction. I'll go over the simple method for this, and once you understand how it works you can add any additional items you want to track.

Sales Items

For sales, you need the following:

- An item for taxable sales
- An item for nontaxable sales

I use a Service item for both of these, because it's an easy item type to work with.

Sales Tax Items

For sales taxes, you need the following:

- A sales tax item or group (to apply, as a line item, to the total taxable sales). You probably already have this item configured in your company file.
- A "placeholder" sales tax item, with a zero rate, to apply to the transaction (because the real tax item is applied as a line item). You can name the sales tax "Placeholder", configure it for 0.0%, and create a vendor named Placeholder as the tax agency.

Payment Items

Payment items track payments, and to do so, they deduct amounts from sales transactions. This means you don't use a minus sign when you enter a Payment type item; QuickBooks automatically adds the minus sign. To track payments you need the following items of the type Payment:

- Cash
- Check
- Visa
- Mastercharge
- Other credit cards you accept
- Debit cards

To set up Payment items, take the following steps:

1. Open the Items List
2. Press Ctrl-N to open the New Item dialog.
3. Select Payment as the Item Type.
4. Enter the Item Name, such as Visa.
5. Select the appropriate payment method from the drop-down list.
6. Select the option labeled Group with other undeposited funds.

Repeat this for every payment type you accept.

To set up these Payment items, you must have created the appropriate payment methods (so they appear in the drop-down list of the Payment Item dialog). To accomplish this, choose Lists → Customer & Vendor Profile Lists → Payment Method List. Press Ctrl-N to create a new payment method if the payment method you need isn't available.

Creating the Summary Sales Transaction

Armed with the report from the cash register, choose Customers → Enter Sales Receipts. If you're using the Premier Retail Edition, select the Daily Sales Summary form from the drop-down list in the Template field. (Actually, the built-in Custom Sales Receipt form works just as well, although it's a bit crowded with columns and fields you don't really need.)

Select the generic customer named Retail or Sales (or whatever you named the generic customer). Technically, you don't have to enter a customer at all, but using a generic customer for your daily sales summary makes it easier to build reports.

If the customer isn't configured for the Placeholder tax item, change the tax item that appears at the bottom of the form to the Placeholder (zero rate) tax item. (When you save the transaction, QuickBooks will ask if you want to change the customer's tax item; click Yes so the Placeholder always appears when you select the transaction.

Then fill out the form as follows:

1. Enter the total of nontaxable sales.
2. Enter the total of taxable sales.
3. Enter the tax collected for taxable sales (when you enter sales tax as a line item, it automatically calculates the tax for the line above).
4. Enter the total payments for one of the payment types (in this example, I'll enter cash).
5. Enter the total payments for all the other payment types.

When you're finished entering sales and payments, the total for the transaction should be zero (see Figure 15-3).

If the total isn't zero, use the Over or Short item discussed earlier in this chapter to balance the transaction. Then save the transaction.

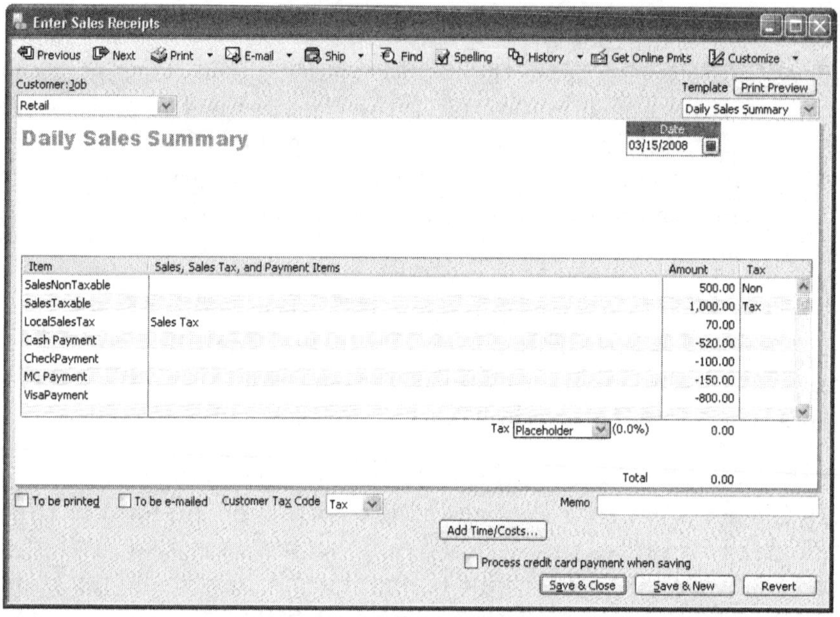

Figure 15-3: It's easy to summarize the day's activities when the sales and payments are equal.

Depositing the Day's Funds

When you choose Banking → Make Deposits, the Payments to Deposit window displays each payment method (see Figure 15-4), so you can select each method separately, to match the way deposits are listed on your bank statement.

If you deposit cash and checks together, select both items and click OK to add them to the Make Deposits window. Then click Save & New to return to the Payments to Deposit window

For a merchant card company that deducts the fee before depositing the proceeds, deduct the fee in the Make Deposits window before transferring the funds to the bank account:

1. In the line below the deposit, select your merchant card fee expense in the Account column.
2. In the Amount column, enter the fee with a minus sign.

3. The deposit totals the net payments, which matches what will show up in your bank account.

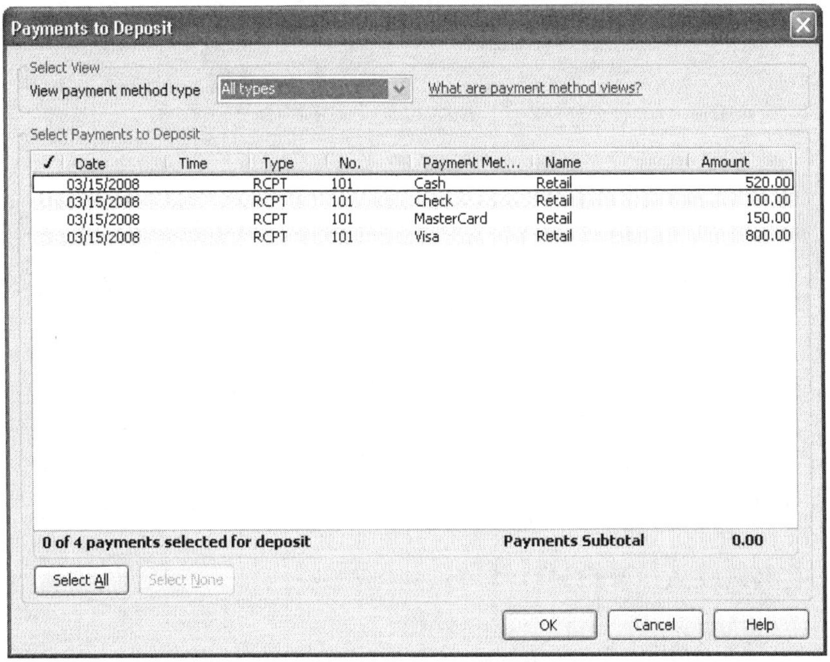

Figure 15-4: Select each payment method separately, so it's easy to reconcile your bank statement.

You don't need a calculator to determine the fee; you can let QuickBooks do the calculation for you:

1. In the Account column, select the merchant card fee expense account.
1. In the Amount column, enter the amount being deposited for this credit card (the amount directly above).
2. Press the asterisk key; QuickBooks immediately opens a calculator window.
3. Enter a minus sign, followed by the percentage rate for the fee for this credit card (see Figure 15-5).
4. Press the Tab key to enter the fee in the column, and save the deposit.

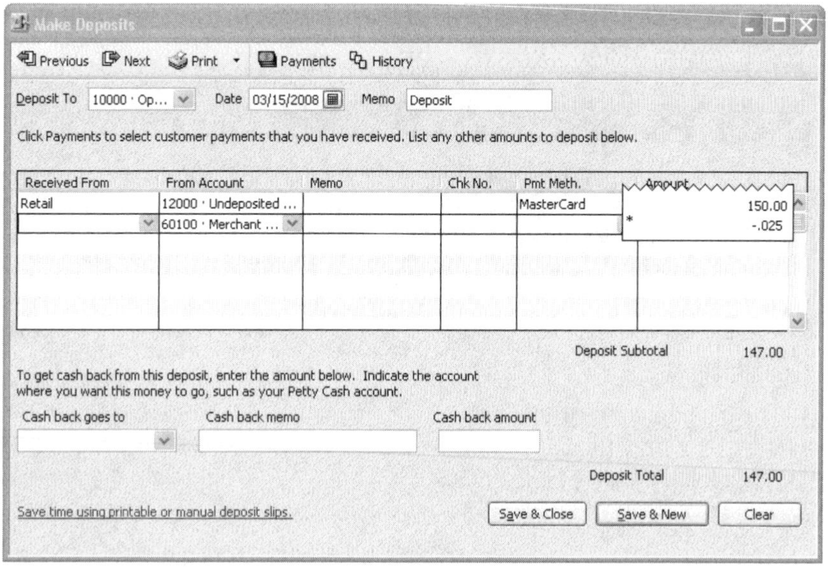

Figure 15-5: Let QuickBooks calculate your merchant card fees.

Handling Upfront Deposits

Deposits are funds a customer gives you before taking delivery of a product. It's common to ask for a deposit when you're selling a customized product that you have to special-order.

Theoretically, upfront money is money you've collected that continues to belong to the customer. Because the money isn't yours, it's a liability, and you must create a liability account to track those funds.

However, you can make your life easier if you treat upfront deposits as advance payments against invoices. This means entering the upfront deposit when you create the invoice. This assumes the entire transaction is completed in a timely fashion—unlike a layaway (covered later in this chapter.)

The easiest way to manage a sale that has an upfront deposit is to create a standard invoice, and then immediately accept the customer's deposit against it. Asking for a deposit is an acceptable and common way of doing business when a customer wants a special item.

Creating Items for Upfront Deposits

You need a way to enter the deposit you received from the customer in QuickBooks, and also let the customer know you've acknowledged the deposit.

A deposit is an item of the type Payment, and you need a payment/deposit item for each type of payment you accept (e.g. cash, check, credit card, etc.) To set up Payment items, take the following steps:

1. Open the Items List
2. Press Ctrl-N to open the New Item dialog.
3. Select Payment as the Item Type.
4. Enter the Item Name, such as Visa.
5. Select the appropriate payment method from the drop-down list.
6. Select the option labeled Group with other undeposited funds.

Repeat this for every payment type you accept.

To set up these Payment items, you must have created the appropriate payment methods (so they appear in the drop-down list of the Payment Item dialog). To accomplish this, choose Lists → Customer & Vendor Profile Lists → Payment Method List. Press Ctrl-N to create a new payment method if the payment method you need isn't available.

Because this is a payment, the money you receive for this Payment Type item goes into the bank, it's real money (cash, check, or credit card). If you use the Undeposited Funds account (always a good idea), select Group With Other Undeposited Funds. If not, select Deposit To and choose the bank account you use to enter funds for merchandise sales.

Applying an Upfront Deposit to an Invoice

In QuickBooks, when you receive an upfront deposit, you create an invoice at the same time. The upfront deposit is not treated separately as a sales receipt or a payment against an existing invoice.

Enter the item(s) you're selling the customer, and then enter the Upfront Deposit item you created. Do *not* enter a minus sign; Payment type items are automatically deductions, so QuickBooks automatically enters the minus sign. The invoice total is the net of the sale less the advance payment.

When you apply an advance payment to an invoice, QuickBooks automatically deposits the money. If you linked the advance payment item to the Undeposited Funds account, the next time you use the Payments to Deposit window, the advance payment is listed.

Managing Layaways

Layaways require you to take an item out of stock for the period of time that the customer makes payments. You should have a policy on layaways that clearly spells out the payment schedule, and what happens if the customer stops making payments. That policy should be printed and given to the customer along with the invoice or sales order.

Using Invoices for Layaways

The easiest way to manage layaways is with an invoice. Create an invoice for the sale (use the Memo field to indicate the sale is a layaway). As each payment arrives, use the Receive Payments transaction window to apply it.

If the item is an inventory part, the invoice decrements the inventory and increments cost of goods. Because the item isn't on the shelves, that's a logical approach. If the item is something you're likely to run out of before the customer has paid up and wants the product, you should move the item from the stock shelves into a special area for layaways.

However, your accountant may suggest that the item isn't really sold, and would prefer you didn't treat the layaway as a real sale. A real sale decrements the inventory quantity, applies the amount of the invoice to income, and applies the cost of goods. For a big-ticket item, such as furniture or major appliances, this is a significant amount of money. None of those things really occur for a layaway transaction. In that case, read the next section on using Sales Orders for layaways.

Using Sales Orders for Layaways

Technically, since a layaway isn't a completed sale until all the payments are made, you can consider a layaway a sales order. A sales order is a pending order, and doesn't post any amounts to accounts. The item isn't removed from inventory, but inventory reports display the item as linked to a sales order.

What's complicated about using sales orders for layaways is that you cannot accept payments against a sales order—the sales order, as I explained earlier in this chapter, is not a financial transaction.

If you want to use sales orders for layaways, the payments you receive are managed as credits, and when the final payment is made you can create the invoice, apply all the credits (creating a zero balance invoice) and give the customer the product.

After you create the sales order, you have two methods for tracking layaway payments:

- Use the Receive Payments transaction (receiving payments against a non-existent transaction, which creates a customer credit) and let the payments pile up until you create the invoice, at which point you can apply the payments to the invoice.
- Create a credit memo for each payment, and then apply all the credits against the invoice you create when the product is paid for.

Applying Payments Against a Sales Order for Layaways

You can enter each layaway payment as a payment receipt, even though you cannot accept payments against a sales order, and there's no invoice. Use the following steps to accomplish this:

1. Choose Customers → Receive Payments.
2. Select the customer from the drop-down list in the Received From field.
3. Enter the amount of the payment.
4. Enter Layaway Payment—# XXX in the Memo field (substitute the layaway sales order number for XXX).

5. If unpaid invoices that are not layaways are displayed for this customer, QuickBooks automatically selects them. Deselect the invoice(s)—this is not a payment against any existing invoice.

Since no invoice is selected, you've entered a customer payment that is larger than any transaction with a balance (by deselecting any existing invoices, there's a zero balance due from this customer). QuickBooks displays a message at the bottom of the transaction window asking if you want to use the overpayment as a credit, or refund the amount to the customer. Obviously, select the option labeled Leave The Credit To Be Used Later.

When you save the transaction, QuickBooks displays a message asking how you want to proceed (see Figure 15-6).

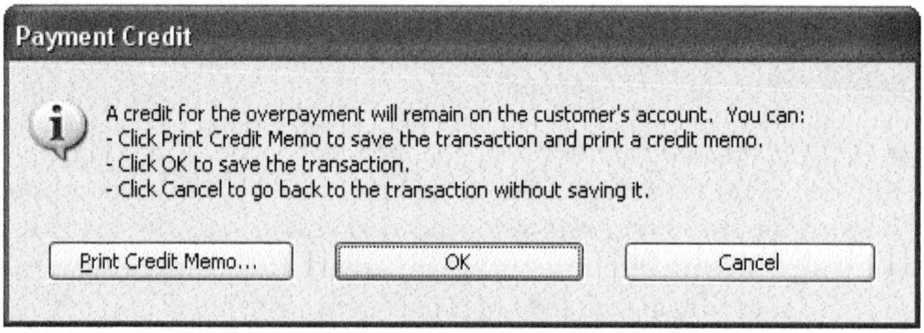

Figure 15-6: A customer payment that's not applied to an invoice is the same as a credit memo.

If the customer paid in person, definitely print a credit memo. You might also want to print and mail a credit memo if the customer's check arrived by mail.

Each time the customer sends a payment repeat this process. QuickBooks displays the total of the existing (past) credits in addition to presenting the current credit amount in the Overpayment message.

When the customer has finished paying off the layaway, turn the layaway order into an invoice and apply the credits, using the following steps:

1. Open the original layaway sales order.
2. Click the Create Invoice button on the transaction window to open the Create Invoice Based On Sales Order dialog.
3. Select Create Invoice For All Of The Sales Order(s), and click OK.
4. In the Create Invoices window, click Apply Credits.
5. QuickBooks displays a dialog telling you the transaction has changed and must be saved. Click Yes to save the transaction.
6. In the Apply Credits dialog select the credits to apply to this invoice (usually all of the credits, unless the customer has multiple layaway sales orders), and click Done.

The bottom of the invoice displays the total of payments applied to the invoice, as well as any balance due. (Often, layaway customers come in with the last payment when they're ready to pick up their merchandise.)

Save the invoice. If a balance exists, take the money, and use the Receive Payments transaction window to apply it against this invoice. Then give the customer the merchandise.

Tracking Customer Layaway Payments

If you posted customer layaway payments as payments against a layaway/sales order, you can keep an eye on the total payments in the Customer Center.

Open the Customer Center, and select the customer of interest in the Customer & Jobs tab. Then, in the right pane of the Customer Center, select the following options from the drop-down lists:

- In the Show field, select Received Payments.
- In the Date field, select whatever date range is appropriate.

The resulting display (see Figure 15-7) provides a quick look at the payments that have arrived against a layaway.

You can customize the columns in the right pane by right-clicking anywhere in the right pane and choosing Customize Columns. Add the Memo field to the columns so the specific sales order number you entered in that field is displayed.

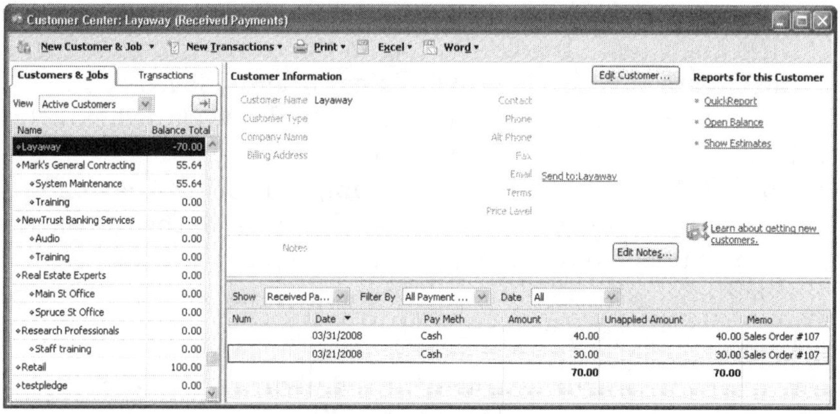

Figure 15-7: If a customer asks about layaway payments, the details are easy to find.

Service Charges for Undelivered Layaways

It's common, and perfectly acceptable, to assess a service charge if the customer doesn't finish paying for the layaway. When the customer shows up to tell you "I've changed my mind", you return the customer's money, less the service charge. (Some businesses call this a restocking charge, or a handling charge.)

If you want to assess a service charge, you must create an item for it. Make the item a Service or Other Charge item, and link it to an income account for service charges. Don't specify a price for the item; instead, when you invoice the customer for the charge, you can enter an amount that matches your layaway policy.

Managing Gift Certificates

To sell and redeem gift certificates, you need to set up accounts and items to manage those sales. A gift certificate isn't a real product, so when you sell a gift certificate, you haven't received money that qualifies as income. Instead, you've put cash on the street that can be redeemed for a product in the future.

You need to set up a liability account to track your gift certificates, and you also need items for selling and redeeming the gift certificates.

Creating an Account for Gift Certificates

The funds you receive for the sale of the gift certificate aren't yours; they belong to the certificate holder. Because you're holding funds that belong to someone else, you've incurred a liability.

You must create a liability account to track the sale and redemption of gift certificates. The account type is Other Current Liability, which you should name Gift Certificates or something similar. If you created your company in Premier Retail Edition, and selected Retail as the industry type, your chart of accounts already has the account, and it's named Gift Certificates Outstanding.

Creating Items for Gift Certificates

To sell a gift certificate, you need two items: One item for the certificate itself, and another item for the income you receive when you sell a certificate (so you can deposit the money you receive into your bank account).

Create the item for gift certificates with the following configuration options:

- The item type is Other Charge
- The item name is GiftCert, Gift Certificate, or something similar.
- Do not enter text in the Description field or the Amount field (you use those fields when you sell the gift certificate).
- The item is not taxable.
- In the Account field, select the liability account you created for gift certificates.

Because the item isn't linked to an income account, you don't record income for the gift certificate. Now you need a way to post the money you received to your bank account without creating a sale. QuickBooks offers an item type of Payment for this purpose.

Create another item, of the type Payment. Name it Paymt-GiftCert (or something similar). Configure the item for deposit to a bank account, or to the Undeposited Funds account, depending on the way you usually handle bank deposits.

Selling Gift Certificates

Usually you sell gift certificates over the counter, so a Sales Receipt is the appropriate transaction type. Most of the time, it's not necessary to track customer activity for this type of sale, so you can create a generic customer named GiftCertificate. Use the following steps to sell a gift certificate:

1. Choose Customers → Enter Sales Receipts.
2. Enter the customer name.
3. Enter the gift certificate item in the Item column.
4. Enter the gift certificate number in the Description column.
5. Enter the amount of the gift certificate in the Amount column.
6. On the next line, enter the payment item you created for gift certificates.
7. In the Amount column, enter the amount of the payment (which must equal the amount of the gift certificate). Don't enter a minus sign, because QuickBooks automatically assigns a minus sign to payment items.
8. Save the transaction.

As you can see in Figure 15-8, the transaction has a zero balance. When you save the transaction, QuickBooks makes the following postings:

- The gift certificate liability account is credited.
- The bank (or the Undeposited Funds account) is debited.

Redeeming Gift Certificates

When a customer redeems a gift certificate, use a sales receipt as the transaction type. Take the following steps to redeem the gift certificate:

1. Fill out the transaction window with the item(s) the customer purchased and the prices.
2. In the last line of the transaction, enter the gift certificate item.
3. Enter a negative amount for the gift certificate. Do not exceed the amount of the sale if the gift certificate is larger than the total sale.

- If the total sale is more than the amount of the gift certificate, the customer must pay the balance.
- If the total sale is less than the amount of the gift certificate, you should issue a new physical certificate for the balance (do not enter that certificate in QuickBooks).

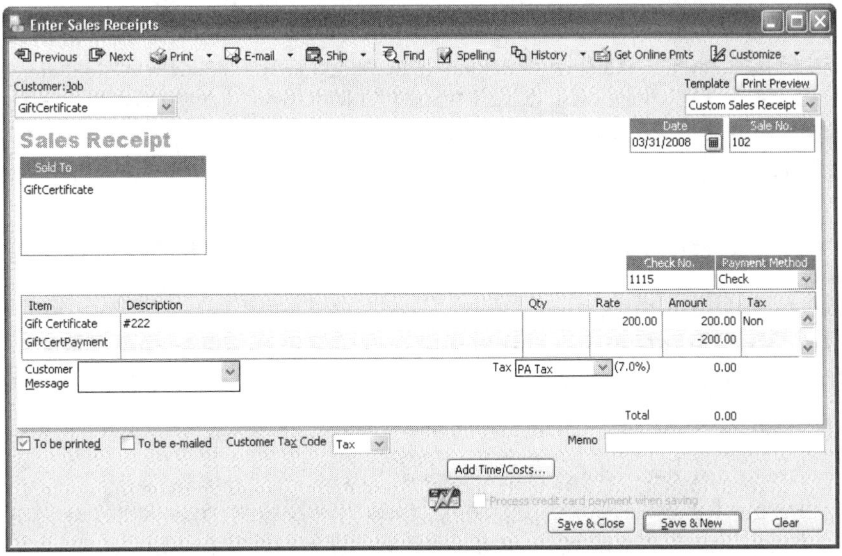

Figure 15-8: Create a sales transaction for a gift certificate.

When you save the transaction, QuickBooks makes the following postings:

- The gift certificate liability account is debited.
- The income accounts connected to the items you sold are credited.

If the gift certificate was larger than the sales total, and you entered an amount equal to the sales total, but smaller than the certificate, you didn't "wash" the entire amount of the certificate in the liability account.

Issue a new physical certificate for the balance due on the original certificate. When that certificate is redeemed (assuming it's not larger than the next sale), entering its amount will wash the rest of the original posting to the liability account.

Consignment Sales

A consignment sale is a sale you make on behalf of another seller. Instead of purchasing goods from the seller, you offer the products to your customers, acting as an agent for the seller. When (or if) the goods are sold, the seller is paid, and you get your commission.

You have several choices about the way you want to track consignment sales in QuickBooks. You should ask your accountant to help you decide which paradigm to follow. In the following sections, I'll go over some of the options available to you.

Configuring QuickBooks for Consignment Sales

To track consignment sales accurately, you need to create components in your company file that let you separate consignment transactions from the transactions involving your purchased products. You need the following components:

- A vendor record for each consignor.
- Items for consigned products (see the following sections regarding inventory and non-inventory consignment items).
- A custom field for items, to track the consignor.
- An income account to track consigned item sales.

***TIP**: In addition to setting up QuickBooks for consignment sales, you need to establish an identification system for consigned products. Each product must have a sticker or tag that identifies it as a consigned item, and identifies the consignor by name or by a code you've created.*

Custom Fields for Consigned Items

To facilitate transactions and reports, you should add a custom field to your Items list, and use it to track the consignor for consigned items. When you create a custom field in any item, it's available for all items and all item types. Use the following steps to accomplish this:

1. Double-click any item in the Item list to open its record.
2. Click Custom Fields. If this is the first custom field you're creating, QuickBooks displays a message telling you there are currently no custom fields. Click OK.
3. In the Custom Fields dialog, click Define Fields.
4. In the Define Custom Fields For Items dialog (see Figure 15-9), enter the text for the field's label (Consignor), and select the Use check box.
5. Continue to click OK until you close all dialogs and return to the Item list.

Figure 15-9: Create a custom field for items so you can track the consignor.

As you create consignment items, you can use the custom field to enter the name of the consignor. You should also add the custom field to the transaction templates you use to sell those items. See the section "Customizing Templates for Consignment Sales".

Consigned Products as Inventory Parts

If you want to track consigned products as inventory parts, you must separate the consigned inventory from your regular inventory (the inventory you purchased and own).

It's not a good idea to track consigned products as inventory if you have a large variety or volume of consignment sales. You'll find the amount of work involved is onerous if you sell more than a few consigned items a month.

Before you can set up consigned items as inventory parts, you have to create the following accounts:

- A separate inventory asset account named Consigned Inventory. (Inventory accounts are Other Current Assets.)
- A separate Cost of Goods account.

You assign those accounts to the inventory parts you create for consigned items.

Creating Inventory Items for Consigned Products

If you want to track inventory for consigned products, each product must have its own discrete item listing. Use the following guidelines when you create the inventory part:

- Use a special convention for the Item Name/Number to make it easy to identify consignment items in the drop-down list in transaction forms. For example, start each item name with **X-**.
- In the Cost field, enter the amount you have to pay the consignor.
- In the COGS Account field, enter the COGS account to use for this item.
- In the Preferred Vendor field, enter the name of the consignor.
- In the Sales Price field, enter the price of the item.
- In the Tax Code field, enter the appropriate tax code.
- In the Income Account field, enter the income account for consignment sales.
- In the Asset Account field, enter the inventory account for consignments.
- Click Custom Fields, and in the Custom Field labeled Consignor, enter the consignor's name, and click OK. (The data appears on your customized transaction templates.)

Click Next to create another consigned inventory part, or click OK if you're finished.

Receiving Consigned Products into Inventory

If you're tracking consigned products as inventory, you must receive the products into inventory. This action increments the value of your consignment inventory asset, and updates the quantity available for the items. Use the following steps to receive the items:

1. Choose Vendors → Receive Items to open the Create Item Receipts transaction window.
2. Select the vendor (consignor).
3. Move to the Items tab and select the item from the drop-down list in the Item column.
4. Enter the number of items in the Qty column. The cost should appear automatically from the item's record. If you didn't enter a cost when you created the item, enter the cost per item in the Cost column. (QuickBooks automatically calculates the quantity and cost to enter data in the Total field at the top of the transaction window.)
5. If necessary, continue to receive items for this shipment.
6. Click Save & New to receive another shipment. Click Save & Close if you're finished.

When you sell the items, QuickBooks automatically posts the cost of goods, and decrements the inventory asset.

Consigned Products as Non-inventory Parts

To manage your consigned items outside of inventory, use a Non-inventory Part type for the items.

You can create a special naming convention, such as a prefix of **X**, to separate your consignment items from your purchased items. Or, you can create a parent item, named Consigned, and make all your consigned items subitems. I think the subitem paradigm is easier to manage, and it also makes it easier to see totals in reports.

If you're using subitems, when you create the parent item don't enter any information except the expense and income account. Then, for the subitems, enter information about cost, price, description, and vendor, as follows:

1. Create a New Item of the type Non-inventory Part.
2. Name the item.
3. Select Subitem Of, and enter the parent consignment item.
4. Select the option This Item Is Purchased For And Sold To A Specific Customer:Job. Even though the option doesn't fit the way you sell consigned items, selecting the option changes the dialog by adding the cost fields you need.
5. Enter the Cost (your agreed upon share) and the account to which the cost is posted (usually Cost of Goods).
6. Enter the Preferred Vendor (the Consignor)
7. Enter the Sales Price, and the account to which you post the income.
8. Specify whether the item is taxable in your state.
9. Click Custom Fields and enter the consigner name.

Customizing Templates for Consignment Sales

You need a customized template for sales transactions, so you can track consignor information. Most retailers use a sales receipt template, so I'll go over the customizations for that form. However, if you use invoices, you can make the same changes to an invoice template.

To create a customized template, use the following steps:

1. Choose Lists → Templates to open the list of Templates.
2. Right-click the template named Custom Sales Receipt and choose Duplicate.
3. In the Select Template Type dialog, select Sales Receipt and click OK.
4. Double-click the new listing, named Copy Of: Custom Sales Receipt to open the Basic Customization dialog.
5. Click Manage Templates.
6. In the right pane, enter Consignment Sale in the Template Name field, and click OK to return to the Basic Customization dialog.
7. Click Additional Customization (at the bottom of the dialog), and then make the following changes:

- In the Header tab, change the text in the Default Title field to Consignment Sale.
- In the Header tab, deselect the check mark for the Project/Job field (the check mark is for the printed version of the sales receipt).
- In the Columns tab, go to the Consignor entry (the custom field you created for items), and click the Screen option. This puts the column on the on-screen version of the template so you can enter the consignor's name in order to track sales for this consignor.

Selling Consigned Items

When a customer purchases a consigned item, choose Customers → Enter Sales Receipt and select the template you created for consignment sales. Enter the item, and the rest of the row should be filled in automatically, using the information in the item's record.

Tracking Consigned Item Sales

You need a consignment sales report in order to pay your consignors. Several reports can be modified to produce information about your consignment sales. Here are the instructions for creating the customized report I install at client sites:

1. Choose Reports → Custom Transaction Detail Report (this report automatically opens in Modify Report mode).
2. In the Display tab, go to the Columns list and select Consignor. Then deselect all the selected columns except for the following:
    - Date
    - Item
    - Amount
4. In the Filters tab, make the following changes:
    - Select Account in the Filter box. Then select the income account to which you post your consignment sales.

- Select Item in the Filter box. If your consignment items are subitems, select the parent item. If you use items with special letters for the first character choose Multiple Items and select all the items.

5. Click OK to return to the report window.
6. In the Total By field, select Totals Only.
7. In the Sort By Field, select Consignor.

Unfortunately, there isn't any way to list costs (the amount you owe the consignor). However, when you pay the consignor, the cost information is available (see the next section on paying consignors).

Paying Consignors

The way you pay consigners depends on whether you set up your consigned items as inventory parts, or non-inventory parts. Regardless of your method, use the customized report on consignment sales you created as your basis of information.

Paying for Inventory Parts

If you use inventory parts, you received the items with the inventory item receipt transaction. To remit payment, choose Vendors → Enter Bill For Received Items. In the Select Item Receipt dialog, choose the Vendor, and the list of item receipt transactions appears in the dialog.

Choose the appropriate receipt and click OK to open the Enter Bills window. All of the data is filled in automatically.

The Qty column displays the Qty received. If you received more items than you sold, change the number to reflect only the number of sold items, and click Recalculate. Then follow the usual procedures to create or print the check.

Paying for Non-inventory Parts

To remit payment to consignors for non-inventory parts, it's easiest to write a check. Choose Banking → Write Checks. Enter the vendor, and move to the Items tab. Enter the items and quantities of the products you sold.

Point of Sale Add-ons

For many retailers, it's difficult to track everything you want to track without a robust POS add-on. In fact, I don't think it's possible to run anything beyond a small boutique retail business without help from a POS. There are two common POS approaches:

- A powerful cash register that provides detailed reports about sales. You manually enter the totals into your QuickBooks company file.
- A software add-on that runs the "front end" of your sales. The software should be able to integrate with QuickBooks, so you can transfer data into the general ledger of your company file.

A POS software program is more convenient, of course, and many applications are available for QuickBooks.

QuickBooks POS

Start by investigating QuickBooks POS, which is built from the ground up to integrate with your company file. QuickBooks POS runs the "front" –sales, inventory, and payments, while QuickBooks Premier Retail Edition tracks your postings and other accounting data.

QuickBooks POS transfers sales totals to your general ledger. In addition, as you add vendors, customers, and items into the POS software, that data is transferred to your company file.

You can learn more about this software by visiting www.QuickBooks.com, and following the links to the products.

Third Party POS Applications

A number of third-party developers have created POS applications that integrate with QuickBooks. You can investigate their offerings by traveling to www.marketplace.intuit.com.

Customized Reports

The Premier Retail Edition is chock-full of reports that have been customized for you. To see the list of available reports, choose Reports → Retail Reports. The report names listed on the submenu are self-explanatory. You can, of course, modify any of these reports to create memorized reports that provide exactly the information you need.

Appendix A

Importing Excel and CSV Files

Importing the contents of your lists is an efficient way to get the data you need into your QuickBooks company file, without going through all the work of entering each entry by filling out a dialog one entry at a time.

You can import data into QuickBooks directly from Excel or a CSV file. QuickBooks 2008 supports both .XLS and .XLSX (Excel 2007) files. In this appendix, I'll go over the steps for importing Excel/CSV files.

***NOTE**: Starting with QuickBooks 2008, there's an import feature that lets you open a spreadsheet in which you've been storing lists and copy them into a pre-formatted Excel worksheet. I'm not covering that feature in this appendix.*

Importing Excel or CSV Files

While the ability to import data directly into QuickBooks from Excel is attractive, it's a limited feature. You can only perform a direct import for the following lists:

- Chart of accounts
- Customer list
- Vendor list
- Items list

Additional limitations include the inability to import complex listings, such as nonposting accounts, or detailed information about entries (for example, custom fields). After you import your list, you have to open each list entry and fill in those details. However, if you hadn't been tracking that information anyway, this is an easy way to populate your QuickBooks company file with the important basic lists.

Configuring an Excel or CSV File as an Import File

The data format of your Excel/CSV file must follow a set of conventions and rules in order to be recognized as an import file by QuickBooks (covered next, in the section "Header Row").

In addition, some of the data in the import file must contain text that matches QuickBooks keywords (covered in the Section "Data Keywords").

NOTE*: Each worksheet (or spreadsheet, if only one worksheet exists) must contain data for a single list. Other lists you want to import must be in their own discrete worksheets or spreadsheets.*

Header Row

The top row must contain headers that categorize the data in each column. You can enter the header text that QuickBooks requires (header keywords), or leave the header text from the export file you created, and map that text to the QuickBooks keywords when you perform the import.

If your worksheet doesn't have a header row, insert a blank row at the top of the worksheet, and enter the QuickBooks column heading keywords. For Excel and CSV files, QuickBooks uses plain English phrases for keywords. All of the keywords are documented in this appendix.

NOTE*: For IIF files, QuickBooks requires specific (less user-friendly) keywords for each category. IIF files are covered in Appendix B.*

It's possible to import an Excel/CSV file without having a header row, because QuickBooks will use the Column Names that Excel displays (Column A, Column B, and so on) when it maps the categories. However, this means you either have to memorize the type of data in each column, or print at least one row of the spreadsheet to use as a reference.

Understanding Mapping

Mapping is the process of matching the text in your file that describes categories to the specific text QuickBooks requires. Specifically, it means matching the titles of the columns (column headings) in your spreadsheet document to the field names in the QuickBooks list.

For example, QuickBooks uses the text "Name" for an entry's name in the list. Your exported file may use different text for that category, such as CustName for a customer list. QuickBooks needs to know which column holds the data for the category Name, but your exported file has the column heading CustName. When you import the file, you map "CustName" to "Name". QuickBooks uses the data in the column named CustName as if the column were named Name.

Data Keywords

Mapping, the ability to match your text to the text QuickBooks needs, is only available for column headings (categories). Certain data in your file must match the text QuickBooks is expecting, called *keywords.*

The data categories that require keywords vary, depending on the list you're importing. For example, QuickBooks requires specific text for account types in the chart of accounts, and requires a Y or N (for Yes and No) in some fields of other lists (such as whether a vendor is configured for Form 1099). See the section "Keywords for Excel/CSV Import Files", later in this appendix, for details.

When your file is ready (with the data arranged in columns by category, and the data that requires keywords appropriately entered), save the file with an .xls extension or a .csv extension, depending on the spreadsheet program you use.

To import the data, open QuickBooks, and open the company file for the company into which you want to import the list. Before you begin the import, back up the company file (just in case something goes wrong during the import process).

Selecting the Import File

Select the file you want to import by choosing File → Import → Excel Files. The Add Your Excel Data to QuickBooks dialog opens. This dialog is aimed at people who want to copy and paste listings from an existing spreadsheet, which I'm not discussing in this appendix.

The dialog has a button labeled Advanced Import. Click that button to open the Import a File dialog seen in Figure A-1. (Even though the feature seems to be exclusively for importing Excel files, it also works for CSV files.)

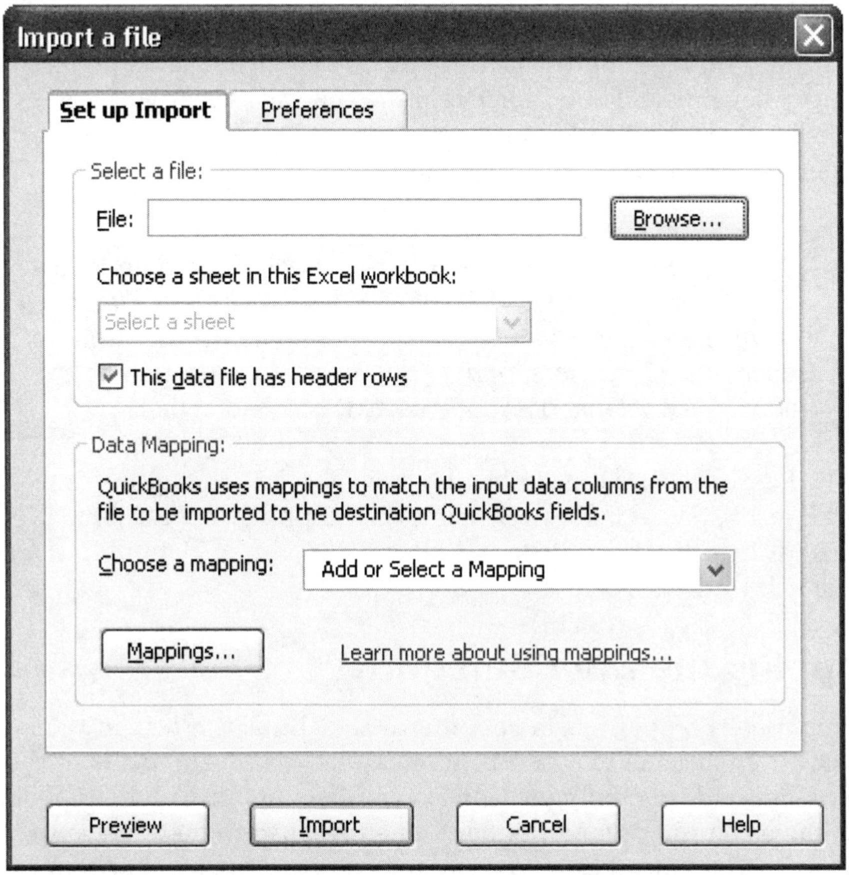

Figure A-1: The Import a File dialog can handle XLS and CSV files.

Click the Browse button and locate the file you want to use to import your list(s). When you select the file, QuickBooks enters the filename in the File field of the dialog.

If the file is an .XLS or .XLSX file, click the arrow to the right of the field labeled Choose a Sheet in This Excel Workbook. Then choose a worksheet from the drop-down list. (If the file is a CSV file, it only has one worksheet, so you can skip this step.)

Many Excel workbooks have multiple worksheets, so even if you only used one worksheet the other worksheets still exist (unless you deleted them). The drop-down list displays the names of all the worksheets in the selected file.

If you renamed the worksheet you used for your list, you'll see it on the drop-down list. If you didn't rename the worksheet you used, you see Worksheet1, Worksheet2, and so on. Select the Worksheet that contains the data for the list you're importing.

***TIP**: If you have multiple worksheets that contain data, open your spreadsheet in Excel before importing the list. Either rename each worksheet to specify the contents (e.g. Chart of Accounts, Customers, and so on), or make yourself a note about the contents of Worksheet1, Worksheet 2, etc.*

If the file doesn't have a header row, deselect the option labeled This Data File Has Header Rows. During the mapping process, QuickBooks will map the column labels (e.g. Column A, Column B, etc.) to the appropriate keyword text.

Mapping the Data Categories

A QuickBooks mapping is a set of data that links the text in the heading row of an import file to category names that match the fields of the list being imported. For example, if you're importing an Excel or CSV file that has a column named VendorName (because that's what your previous application used for vendor names), you must map that text to the QuickBooks text "Name" (which is the field name QuickBooks uses for the vendor name).

QuickBooks mappings are created for specific lists, so you must create a mapping for each type of list you're importing. You can save your mappings and use them again for re-importing the same type of list.

To create mappings for the list you're currently importing, click the arrow to the right of the Choose a Mapping field, and select <Add New> to open the Mappings dialog seen in Figure A-2.

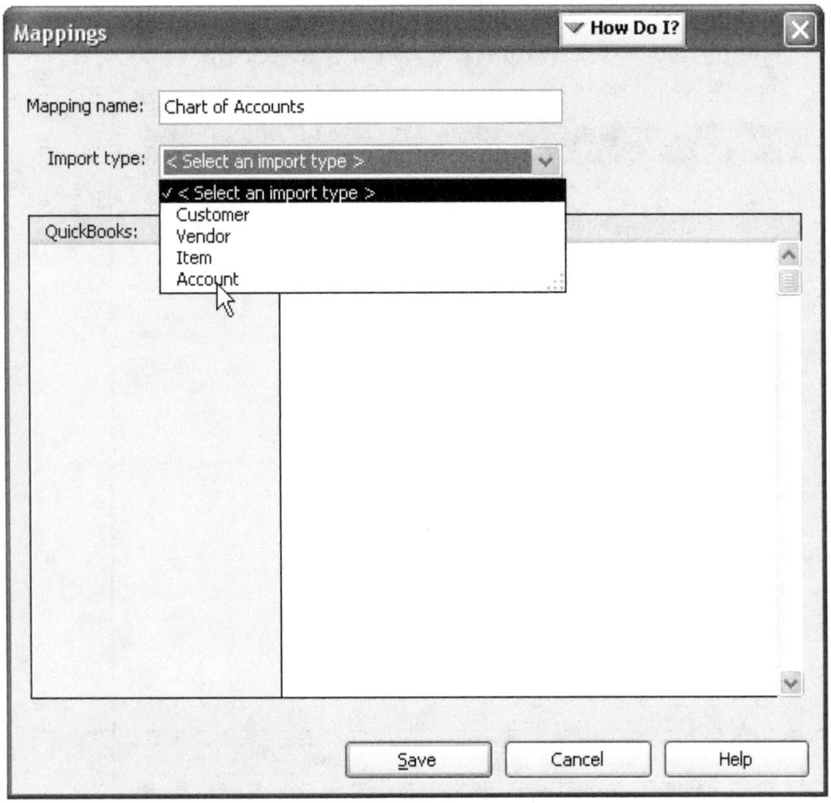

Figure A-2 Name the mapping scheme you're creating, and select the type of list you're importing.

Give the mapping scheme a name (make sure the name is a hint about the list it's intended for), and select the list you're importing from the drop-down list in the Import Type field.

***TIP**: Once you create a mapping scheme and name it, you can select it in the future for importing the same QuickBooks list. If a list you want to import in the future has different column headings in your file, you can edit this mapping scheme to change the text that maps to the appropriate QuickBooks fields. This is easier than building the mapping scheme from scratch.*

In the left pane, QuickBooks displays the text it uses for field names for the type of list you're importing (see Figure A-3).

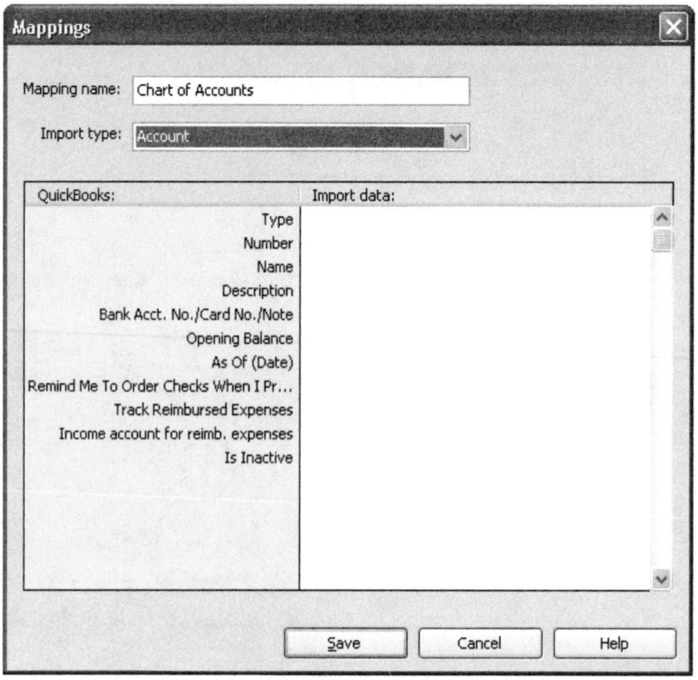

Figure A-3: The field names QuickBooks uses are displayed, and you need to link each field name to the text in your worksheet.

Click inside the Import Data column, to the right of the first QuickBooks field name for this type of import file. QuickBooks reads the column headings of your worksheet (or the column labels if you don't have a heading row) and displays them. Select the column heading that matches the QuickBooks field (see Figure A-4).

Continue to map your worksheet column headings to the QuickBooks text for the fields in this list.

Usually, QuickBooks offers more fields than your worksheet contains, because you weren't tracking all the information available in

QuickBooks. If you decide to enter data for the fields you haven't been using, you can edit each record after you import the file.

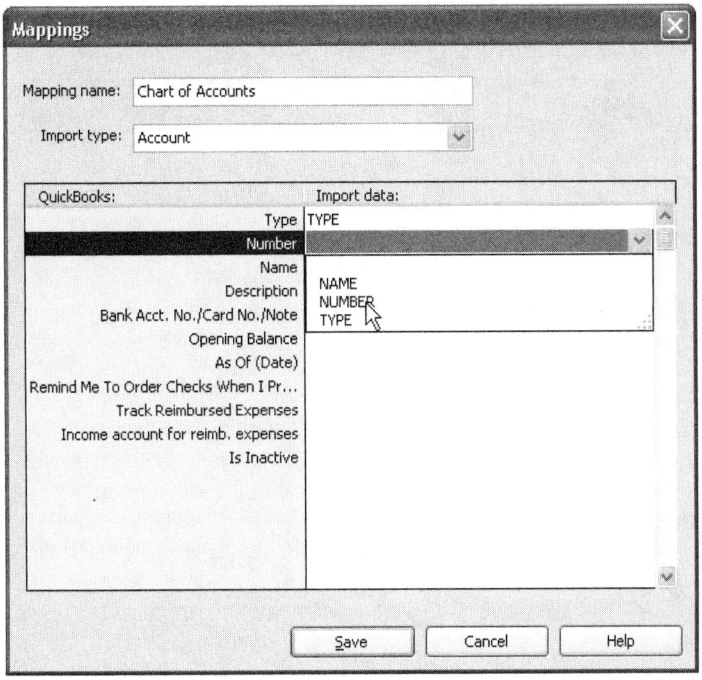

Figure A-4: Map the text in your column headings to the text QuickBooks requires for the list you're importing.

Click Save when you've finished mapping your column headings to the QuickBooks field names. Your mappings are saved, using the name you provided, and you're returned to the Import A File dialog.

Setting Preferences for Importing Data

Move to the Preferences tab of the Import a File dialog to specify the way you want QuickBooks to manage duplicate records and errors (see Figure A-5).

Duplicate records occur if your list already has entries that are also in your import file (QuickBooks creates a basic chart of accounts when you set up a company file). Errors occur if any data is incorrectly configured. For example, you may have the wrong text for a field that requires a QuickBooks keyword, or your data may use more characters than QuickBooks permits in a given field.

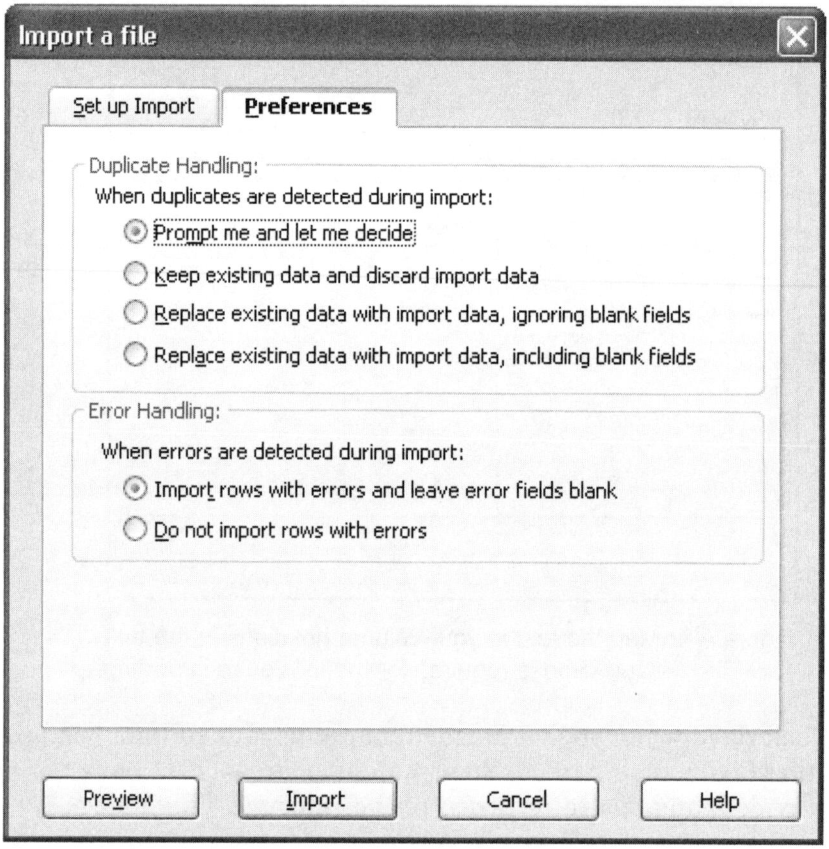

Figure A-5: Specify the way to manage problems.

Managing Duplicate Records

Here are the guidelines for selecting your options for duplicate records:

- **Prompt me and let me decide**. Don't select this option because the message you see (the prompting message upon which you're expected to make a decision) doesn't name the record in question. Blind guesses don't work well as a problem solving technique.

- **Keep existing data and discard import data**. This tells QuickBooks to skip the imported data and keep the existing record.
- **Replace existing data with import data, ignoring blank fields**. Existing data is replaced, and a blank field in the import file won't overwrite any existing data in that field.
- **Replace existing data with import data, including blank fields**. Existing data is totally replaced with imported data. If an existing field has data, but the import file field is blank, the blank field overwrites the existing data.

Managing Duplicate Records When You're Importing a List

If you're importing a list to get all your records into QuickBooks, the option Keep Existing Data And Discard Import Data is the best choice. It means that the import won't disturb any records you've already created.

If you don't have any records, and you're using the Import function to create a list from scratch, it doesn't matter which option you choose for managing duplicate records.

Managing Duplicate Records When You're Modifying a List

If you're importing a list for the purpose of modifying the data in an existing list, select either of the options that start with Replace existing data. You can decide which of those options to select depending on the current state of your QuickBooks list, and the data in your import file.

For example, you may be changing the numbering scheme for a chart of accounts, or you may be adding or changing the Type field in a customer or vendor list.

If you're changing the data in a list, it's often easier to export your original list, make changes in Excel, and then import the list back into QuickBooks. Excel has handy features for sweeping changes such as "Search and Replace". Importing the modified data back into QuickBooks is quicker and easier than opening every record in the list and making changes.

Managing Error Handling

Use the following guidelines for managing errors:

- **Import rows with errors and leave error fields blank**. This option works best. It means that, except for any fields that have data errors, your records are imported. You can edit the imported records later to enter the data that wasn't imported.
- **Do not import rows with errors**. If you select this option, the entire record is skipped if any field has an error. You'll have to enter the entire record manually.

Previewing the Import

It's always better to preview the import to see if your data has any problems. Click Preview to have QuickBooks test the data and display the results in the Preview dialog, which also tells you how many rows (records) were processed, and how many errors were found.

> ***TIP***: *Unfortunately, the Preview feature doesn't catch all errors, just some data entry errors. You could still have errors when you import the file.*

Managing Preview Errors

QuickBooks displays the results of the test import in the Preview dialog, along with the row number, and an explanation of the problem. By default, the Preview dialog shows all the import data, not just the errors, and you have to scroll through the list to find the errors.

To make it easier to locate errors, select Only Errors from the drop-down list in the field labeled In Data Preview Show, at the top of the dialog. Figure A-6 shows the result of a preview of an import of the chart of accounts. QuickBooks found a record with data errors.

In this case, I have to change the text "A/R" to "Accounts Receivable" (the QuickBooks keyword), and change the text "A/P" to "Accounts Payable (the QuickBooks keyword).

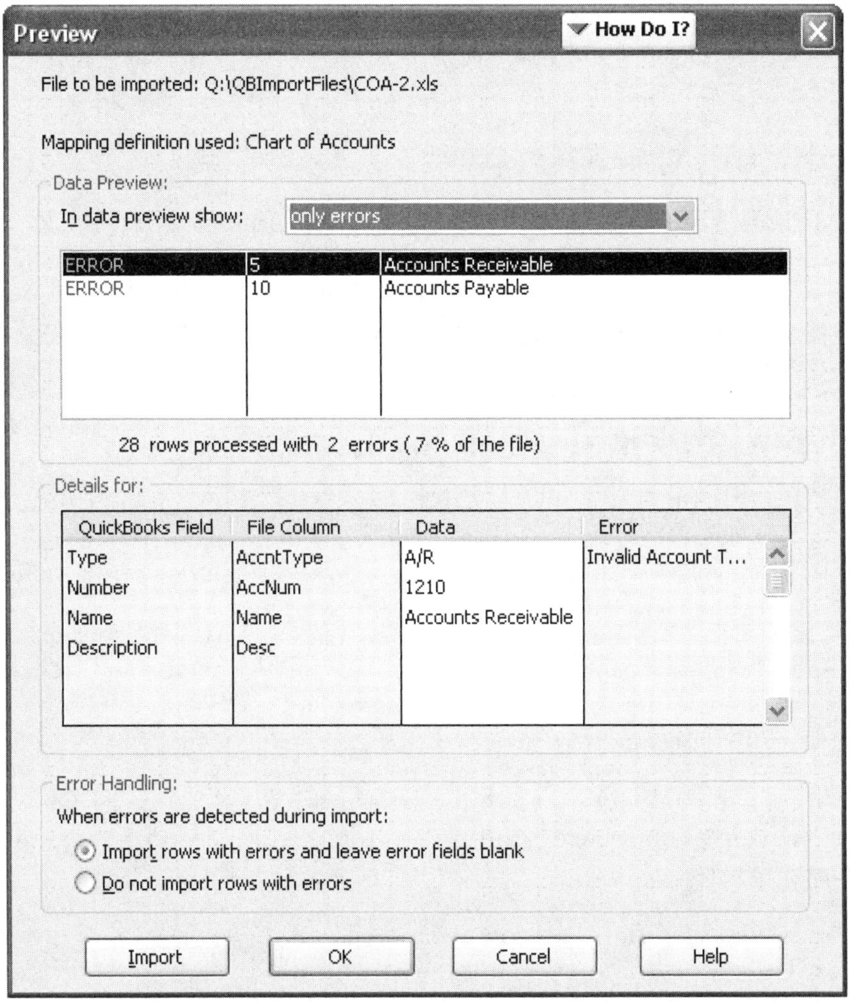

Figure A-6: In two records, the data in the Account Type field didn't match the text required by QuickBooks.

You can correct the problem right in the Preview dialog, instead of canceling the import, opening your worksheet, changing the data, and starting the import again.

To correct an error, select the record in the top part of the dialog, and then change the text in the Data column in the bottom part of the dialog. When you've made all the corrections, click Preview to see if any errors still appear (and fix them). If the errors are gone, click Import.

Importing the File

When there are no errors in your file, click Import. QuickBooks displays a message asking if you want to continue with the import, rather than cancel it in order to back up your company file. If you've just backed up the file, as I suggested earlier, click Yes to continue. Your list is imported into your QuickBooks company file.

Viewing the Import Error Log

After QuickBooks imports your data, it saves an error log that contains details about errors, or warnings about problems (if any were encountered). A message appears to ask if you want to save the error log.

Click Save, because you should always save and inspect the log. In the Save Import Error Log As dialog, select a location for the error file, and give the file a name. The file is saved as a CSV file, which you can open in your spreadsheet program.

Open the error log to examine the problems. In many cases, an error prevents the record from being imported. Here are some of the common errors:

- A required field had no data
- The record name (or number, if the file is a chart of accounts with account numbers) is already in use
- The format of the data did not match QuickBooks requirements, which is frequently a problem with the way you enter dates
- The number of characters your data uses exceeds the number of characters allowed in the field
- A job or subaccount was not imported because the parent account did not exist. This means the parent account may have had a data problem and was not imported, or it was listed below the subaccount in your worksheet—it must be listed first.

You can correct the problems in your worksheet, and re-import, but if you only have a few errors it's easier to open the list in QuickBooks and manually edit or enter data.

Re-using Mappings

Once you save a mapping, you can use it again for another import of the same list. As long as the worksheet you're importing uses the same columns, and has the same heading text as the existing map, QuickBooks will import the data to any company file.

If you plan to import lists to multiple companies (a common task for accountants), use a generic name when you save the mapping. For example, you can name the mapping for a chart of accounts "COA". Essentially, you're creating a mapping template.

Editing a Mapping

If a new worksheet is slightly different from the saved mapping, you don't have to create a whole new mapping. Instead, you can edit an existing mapping. For example, if you receive the data for a list from your client you may face one or more of the following scenarios:

- The worksheet uses different text for one or more of the column headings.
- The worksheet omits a column that exists in your mapping.
- The worksheet contains a column that doesn't exist in your mapping.

To edit a mapping so it matches the worksheet you want to import, follow the steps enumerated earlier in this appendix to import an Excel/CSV file. When all the fields on the Import a File dialog are populated with data, follow these steps:

1. Choose Edit from the drop-down list in the field labeled Choose a Mapping to open the Mappings dialog.
2. Select the mapping you want to edit.
3. Change whatever needs to be changed.
4. Click Save to return to the Import a File dialog.
5. Preview, and then import, the list.

Deleting a Mapping

To delete a mapping, click the Mappings button on the Import a File dialog to open the Mappings dialog. Select the appropriate mapping name and click Delete. QuickBooks asks you to confirm the fact that you want to delete the mapping. Close the Mappings dialog to return to the Import a File dialog, where you can create a new mapping, editing an existing mapping, or close the dialog if you're not ready to import a file.

Keywords for Excel/CSV Import Files

Two types of keywords are required for a direct import of an Excel or CSV file:

- Heading keywords, which are category names, and they match the names of the fields in the list. In your worksheet, these appear as column headings. You don't have to use the keywords in your spreadsheet document, because you can map your text to the keyword text QuickBooks needs.
- Data keywords (only for certain fields), which are the text entries that must match text that QuickBooks expects (keywords).

The heading keywords are the name of the field for each component of the data record. When you import a list using an Excel/CSV file, QuickBooks uses plain English that matches the text you see if you're creating list entries directly in QuickBooks. If the heading row of your import file doesn't match the text QuickBooks requires, you can map your text to the QuickBooks text (as described earlier in this appendix).

For the data keywords (which are actually the choices you see in drop-down lists in the dialog when you're creating an entry directly in QuickBooks), you must be sure to use the keyword text in your worksheet data. In the following sections, I'll provide the data keywords you need for each list you can import via an Excel or CSV file.

Chart of Accounts Excel/CSV Headings

When importing the chart of accounts, you must enter data in all required fields, and can optionally enter data in the other fields. Table A-1 describes the headings and data requirements for the chart of accounts.

Heading	Data
Account Type (Required)	The type of account. You must use the text QuickBooks expects for the account type (covered in the next section).
Account Number	The number you want to assign to the account.
Account Name (Required)	The account name.
Description	A description of the account.
Bank Acct. No/Card No./Note	The number for a bank account, credit card, or loan.
Opening Balance	Don't use this field; see the discussions in this book about the reasons to avoid opening balances.
As Of (Date)	The date for the opening balance you're not going to enter.
Remind Me To Order Checks	The check number you'll be entering at the point you want to be reminded to order checks.
Track Reimbursed Expenses	Enter Yes or No to specify whether you want to track reimbursed expenses for this account. See the section "Understanding Reimbursed Expenses Accounts".
Income Account For Reimb. Expenses	The name of the income account to use to track reimbursed expenses.
Account Is Inactive	Enter Yes or Not-Active to hide the account; Enter No or Active to make the account active.

Table A-1: Headings and data requirements for importing the chart of accounts.

Account Type Keywords for Excel/CSV Files

The data in the Account Type column must match the text QuickBooks uses in the drop-down list. Use the following text for account types:

- Accounts payable
- Accounts receivable
- Bank
- Credit card account
- Cost of goods sold
- Equity
- Other expense
- Other income
- Expense
- Fixed asset
- Income
- Long term liability
- Other asset
- Other current asset
- Other current liability

QuickBooks also supports an account type of non-posting, but it's not in the drop-down list of the New Account dialog when you create an account manually, so you cannot import non-posting accounts with an Excel/CSV import file (you *can* import non-posting accounts with an IIF file).

Understanding Reimbursed Expenses Accounts

When you're posting expenses, either by entering vendor bills or direct disbursements, you can assign the expense to a customer:job, and invoice the customer for the expense. In addition, QuickBooks provides a feature that lets you post the income from those reimbursements to an income account, instead of "washing" the expense account. In order to implement the feature, you have to take the following steps:

- Enable the ability to track reimbursed expenses as income. This option is in the Company Preferences tab of the Sales & Customers section of the Preferences dialog.
- After the option is enabled, when you create or edit an expense account you see additional fields: a check box to track reimbursements to this expense account as income, and a text box in which

you enter the name of the income account that receives the postings for reimbursed expenses.

You must create an income account for each expense account you've marked as tracking reimbursements as income. That means a separate income account for each expense account so marked; you cannot post all reimbursed expenses to a single income account. (QuickBooks 2008: The Official Guide from McGraw-Hill Publishing has detailed instructions on configuring this feature and implementing it during customer invoicing.)

Tips for Importing the Chart of Accounts from Excel/CSV Files

Data in your chart of accounts import files should follow certain protocols in order to ensure a successful import, and/or to make sure the data in the list is consistent and easy to work with.

Using Account Numbers

If you're planning to use account numbers, and have entered account number data in the appropriate column, QuickBooks imports the account numbers and saves them, even if account numbers aren't enabled in your company file.

By default, QuickBooks does not enable account numbers, and if you haven't changed the setting in the Accounting section of the Preferences dialog, you won't see your account numbers when you open the chart of accounts after you import the file. Don't panic, QuickBooks stored the account numbers you imported, and as soon as you enable account numbers, they'll show up.

Import the Chart of Accounts First

If you're planning to import the Items list, you must import the chart of accounts before you import the Items. Some of the data connected to an item includes account numbers (income account, cost of goods sold for inventory items, and so on).

Importing Subaccounts

If you want to import subaccounts, you must list the parent account first, and then list the subaccount(s) in the following format (make sure there are no spaces before or after the colon):

ParentAccountName:SubaccountName.

If any subaccounts are listed above the parent account, when you preview the import you won't see any errors. However, when you perform the import, any subaccounts listed above the parent account aren't imported. The error log indicates that the parent account didn't exist, so the subaccount wasn't imported.

Remember that the colon means "subaccount" to QuickBooks, so don't use colons in account names. It's a common writing technique to make text clear by using a colon, and you may find it logical to name an account Insurance:Automobile. However, because QuickBooks only uses a colon to indicate a subaccount, the account won't be imported if you didn't list a parent account named Insurance in a row above the listing for Insurance:Automobile. If you want to use text to clarify names, use a hyphen (Insurance-Automobile).

Retaining Leading Zeroes

Many users like to enter the account number in the Bank Acct.No/Card No./Note field of bank accounts, current liabilities (loans), and credit card accounts. If the account number begins with one or more zeroes, after you enter the number and move to the next cell, the leading zeroes are removed, because the default format for cells is General (which doesn't support leading zeroes).

Before you begin entering data, select the entire column for this heading and change the format of the cells to Text. The data in Text cells is retained exactly as it's typed.

Customer:Job Headings for Excel/CSV Files

The QuickBooks headings that map to your column headings are represented in Table A-2, along with the data requirements.

Heading	Data
Job or Customer Name (Required)	The customer name, or the job name.
Opening Balance	Don't use this field; see the discussions in this book about the reasons to avoid entering opening balances in lists.
Opening Balance As Of	The As Of date for the opening balance you aren't going to enter.
Company Name	The company name.
Salutation	Mr., Mrs., etc.
First Name	Customer's first name.
Middle Initial	Customer's middle initial.
Last Name	Customer's last name.
Contact	Your contact name for the customer.
Phone	Phone number.
Fax	FAX number.
Alternate Phone	Alternate phone number.
Alternate Contact	Alternate contact name.
Email	Contact's e-mail address (used to e-mail transactions if you choose that Send Method).
Billing Address 1 Through Billing Address 5	Each line of the customer's billing address.
Shipping Address 1 Through Shipping Address 5	Each line of the customer's shipping address.
Customer Type	Customer type.
Terms	Terms for this customer.
Sales Rep	Sales rep assigned to this customer.
Preferred Send Method	Preferred send method for invoices, estimates, statements, etc.
Tax Code	Customer's Tax Code.
Tax Item	Tax item for this customer.
Resale Number	Resale number if the customer is not taxable.
Price Level	Price level for this customer.
Account Number	Your account number for this customer, if you use account numbers (can contain both letters and numbers).
Credit Limit	Credit limit for this customer.
Preferred Payment Method	Preferred payment method.
Credit Card Number	Customer's credit card number, appended with a single quotation mark (').

Credit Card Expiration Month	Expiration month with two digits (e.g. January is 01).
Credit Card Expiration Year	Expiration year with four digits.
Name On Card	Name on the credit card.
Credit Card Address	Address for the credit card.
Credit Card Zip Code	Zip code for the credit card.
Job Status	Job status (for jobs).
Job Start Date	Start date for the job.
Job Projected End	Expected completion date for the job.
Job End Date	Actual end date for the job (if completed).
Job Description	Description of the job.
Job Type	Job type.
Is Inactive	Enter Yes or Not-Active to hide the customer's listing; enter No or Active to display the listing.
Note	Notes connected to the customer.

Table A-2: Columns (categories) for importing customers and jobs.

Customer:Job Data Mappings for Excel/CSV Files

Customer and job records have quite a few keywords that are useful for defining customers, or for tracking information about customers so you can create transactions quickly. Unfortunately, the keywords aren't preconfigured in QuickBooks; instead, they are the data entries in other lists. The other lists cannot be imported with an Excel/CSV file; instead, you must enter everything manually (or import the list with an IIF file).

Your text must match the text of the entries in the lists described in Table A-3. The list entries must have been created before you import the customer list. Except for the Sales Tax items, all of the lists are in the Customer & Vendor Profile Lists submenu. The Sales Tax Code list is on the Lists menu, and Sales Tax Items must be predefined in the Items list (or included in an import file for Items).

QuickBooks prepopulates some of the lists (e.g. Terms and Payment Methods). If you use a predefined company file (available in some Premier editions), other lists, such as Customer Type, may also have some prepopulated data. However, you may have added entries to any of these lists, or renamed or removed pre-loaded entries. To have the correct text available when you create your import file, print each list's contents by opening the list window and pressing Ctrl-P.

Heading	List Name
Customer Type	Customer Type List
Preferred Payment Method	Payment Method List
Price Level	Price Level List
Sales Rep	Sales Rep List
Tax Code	Sales Tax Code List
Tax Item	Items List
Terms	Terms List

Table A-3 These lists must be populated before you import customer data that includes entries from the lists.

Job Keywords for Excel/CSV Files

Jobs have two data fields you can use to categorize the job record, and your data must match the text in the associated lists:

- Job Type, which is a list in the Customer & Vendor Profile Lists submenu.
- Job Status, which is a descriptive phrase that appears in the Jobs & Estimates Preferences dialog which you access by choosing Edit → Preferences.

Tips for Importing the Customer:Job List from Excel/CSV Files

Your QuickBooks tasks will be easier if your customers and jobs are set up for efficiency, so you need to pay attention to some protocols as you create your import file.

Jobs are Like Subaccounts

Jobs don't stand alone; they're subordinate to customers. To import jobs, the data must be in the format CustomerName:JobName (no spaces around the colon). This is similar to the way subaccounts are managed in an import file for the chart of accounts. The customer must exist in order to import a job, so you must be sure to list the customer name before the job name in your import file.

Customer Financial Information

As described earlier, your import file contains columns for financial information about the customer. Here are some guidelines for entering this data:

- **Credit Limit**. Enter the amount without a dollar sign.
- **Credit Card Number**. Don't use this field, it's dangerous. In fact, it's probable that either your merchant account agreement, or state law (or both), makes it illegal to have this information stored in plain text. The laws and rules that govern computer storage of credit card numbers usually limit you to storing the last four digits only (either omitting the other digits or using XXXX to replace them).

QuickBooks 2008 has a feature called Customer Credit Card Protection, which configures your company file and user logins/permissions to protect customer credit card information. To access the feature, choose Company → Customer Credit Card Protection.

Vendor Headings for Excel/CSV Files

QuickBooks will map your column headings to the QuickBooks field names, if your column headings don't match those in Table A-4. Mappings represent the columns that QuickBooks will import, which in turn represent the fields available in the Vendor dialog you work in if you're entering vendors one-at-a-time in QuickBooks.

Mapping	Data
Name (Required)	Vendor name (your vendor code).
Opening Balance	Don't use this field; see the discussions in this book about the reasons to avoid entering opening balances in lists.
Opening Balance (As Of)	The As Of date for the opening balance you aren't going to enter.

Company Name	Company name.
Salutation	Mr., Ms., etc.
First Name	Vendor's first name.
Middle Initial	Vendor's middle initial.
Last Name	Vendor's last name.
Address 1 Through Address 5	Each line of the vendor's address.
Contact	Your contact name for the vendor.
Phone	Phone number.
Fax	FAX number.
Alternate Phone	Alternate phone number.
Alternate Contact	Alternate contact name.
Email	E-mail address.
Print On Check As	Vendor's name as printed on a check.
Account Number	Your account number with this vendor.
Vendor Type	Vendor types.
Terms	Terms
Credit Limit	Your credit limit with the vendor.
Tax ID	Tax ID number.
Vendor Eligible For 1099	Yes or No.
Is Inactive	Yes to hide the vendor's listing; No to display the listing.
Note	Your notes about the vendor.

Table A-4: Columns (categories) for importing vendors.

Vendor Data Keywords for Excel/CSV Files

Some of the data referenced in Table A-4 (vendor categories) requires you to enter text that matches existing data in other existing lists, to wit:

- Vendor Type
- Terms

Be sure to populate those lists before importing your vendor list.

Tips for Importing the Vendor List from Excel/CSV Files

To make sure it's easy to enter transactions and get the reports you need, you must be careful to import your vendor list accurately, using all the data you'll need. While you can always correct or add data by editing each vendor's record, that's a time consuming, annoying task.

Enabling 1099 Tracking

If your vendor data includes references to Form 1099, you must enable 1099 tracking. This option is in the Company Preferences tab of the Tax 1099 category of the Preferences dialog. You must also configure the expense accounts that are associated with Form 1099 tracking. Detailed instructions for setting up, configuring, and printing Form 1099 are available in various chapters of QuickBooks 2008: The Official Guide.

> ***TIP**: If a vendor is not eligible for Form 1099, you don't have to fill in data for the Tax ID category.*

Account Number Means Your Account Number

The Vendor Account Number is your account number (your customer number with the vendor). The text you enter in this field is automatically printed on the Memo line of checks (if you print checks), and this is the commonly accepted method of providing your account number to the vendor when you pay bills.

If you use online bill paying, the Account Number field must contain your customer account number with the vendor. The data is included in the online bill paying information, and it's the only way the vendor can identify your payment.

E-Mail Address is for Sending Purchase Orders

QuickBooks offers a method of sending purchase orders to vendors via e-mail. The e-mail has message text, and the purchase order is attached as a PDF file. If you plan to use this feature, enter the e-mail address of the person who receives purchase orders from you in the Email field of your vendor import file. Complete instructions for setting up and using e-mail for invoices, estimates, purchase orders, and other transaction forms are of QuickBooks 2008: The Official Guide.

Vendor Name as Printed on a Check

The vendor name you assign a vendor should be a code, and your protocols for entering vendor codes should be consistent. However, the name/code probably won't work for addressing mail, nor for printing the payee name on checks. The field Vendor Name As Printed On Checks is a nifty solution.

When you're entering vendors directly in QuickBooks (using the New Vendor dialog), after you enter the text for the Company Name field, QuickBooks automatically copies that text to the Vendor Name As Printed On Checks field. That's almost always appropriate. Therefore, to save a little time when you're creating your import file, use the Copy feature in Excel to copy the Company Name text to the Vendor Name As Printed On Checks field.

Item Headings for Excel/CSV Files

For importing items, the QuickBooks headings that map to your column headings are represented in Table A-5, along with the data requirements.

Mapping	Data	Data Requirements
Type (Required)	Item type.	Must match keywords (see the section "Item Type Keywords")
Name (Required)	Item name	
Is Reimbursable Charge	Yes or No	For services performed by others, item type should be Service. For reimbursable expense, item type should be Other Charge
Description/Description on sales transactions	Item description	
Tax Code	Three character tax code from the Sales Tax Code lists	Data must match existing Tax Code text in the Tax Code list
Account/Income account (required)	Name of account linked to this item	Account name must match existing account
Expense/COGS Account	Name of expense account linked to this item	Account name must match existing account
Asset account	Name of asset account linked to this item	Account name must match existing account
Deposit To (Account)	Name of bank account for deposits	Account name must match existing account
Description On Purchase Transactions	Description.	For Inventory Part only
On Hand	Number on hand.	For Inventory Part only
Cost	Cost amount	For Inventory Part only

Preferred Vendor	Vendor's name.	Vendor name must match existing vendor
Tax Agency	Tax agency (vendor)	Name must match existing vendor
Price/Amount Or %/Rate	Price or percentage rate .	To enter a percentage, the Cost category must have data. For inventory items or reimbursable expenses, data must be a dollar amount.
Is Inactive	Yes or No	
Reorder Point	On hand number that kicks in the reorder reminder	
Total Value	The number representing the value of this item	Inventory parts only —You can manually enter a number, but it's better to let QuickBooks calculate this amount by multiplying the number on hand by the cost of each item
As Of (Date)	Effective date of Total Value	
Payment Method	Default payment method	Text must match existing entry in Payment Method List

Table A-5: Columns (categories) for importing items.

Item Type Keywords for Excel/CSV Files

For item type, the text in your file must match the keywords for item types. Following are the keywords for item types:

- Service
- Inventory Part
- Inventory Assembly
- Non-inventory Part
- Other Charge
- Subtotal
- Discount
- Payment
- Sales Tax Item

Tips for Importing the Item List from Excel/CSV Files

The Item list is rather complicated, especially if you want to import information over and above the required fields. If you have a product-based company, it might be less complicated to import only inventory parts, and enter other types of items manually.

Import or Create Other Lists First

Be sure you install (or import) the chart of accounts before you import the Item list. The accounts linked to items are required entries, and the account names in your Item list file must already exist in your company file. Otherwise, the import fails.

***WARNING**: The data for the account names in your Items list import file must be exactly the same text as the account name in your already-installed chart of accounts.*

Table A-5 notes the other lists that impact the Item list, and you must either import those lists with an IIF file, or enter the data manually.

Importing Subitems

If you want to import subitems, you must list the parent item first, and then list the subitems(s) in the format ParentItemName:SubitemName. Be sure there are no spaces before or after the colon. QuickBooks recognizes the colon as the format for a subitem.

If any subitems are listed above the parent account, when you preview the import you won't see any errors. However, when you perform the import, any subitems listed above the parent account aren't imported. The error log indicates that the parent account didn't exist, so the subaccount wasn't imported.

Group Items Cannot be Imported

If you check the drop-down list for item types in the New Item dialog, you'll notice that when I listed the keywords for item types earlier in this section, I omitted two item types: Group, and Sales Tax Group. You cannot import a group item type with an Excel/CSV file. Import the items, and then manually create the group items you need.

Appendix B

Importing IIF Files

You can import data into QuickBooks directly from a tab-delimited text file that has the filename extension .IIF. The file must be configured properly for importing to QuickBooks.

In this appendix, I'll go over the steps for creating and importing IIF files into a QuickBooks company file. I'll also provide the keywords and format information for the commonly imported lists.

About IIF Import Files

IIF import files are a bit complicated to create, but they are more powerful as an import tool than the Excel or CSV files discussed in Appendix A.

Unlike importing an Excel or CSV file, QuickBooks does not preview or error-check the contents of a tab-delimited text file. If the import fails at some point, it just fails. Therefore, you must be careful about the way you create the file.

On the other hand, using a tab-delimited file means you can import all the data you need to set up a company, instead of being restricted to the few lists provided in the Excel/CSV import feature, each of which is limited in the number of fields it accepts. An IIF file can contain data to populate every list in QuickBooks, including detailed information about each record in the list.

Sadly, starting with QuickBooks 2006, Intuit stopped updating IIF file data standards (keywords and required entries) for new fields introduced in the software. Any attempts to gain information about the missing data results in advice to use the Software Developer Kit (SDK) and develop programs to import files.

Few accountants or business owners have the time or desire to become programmers, and many have contacted me to express their displeasure over this attitude, as well as ask for advice and information. Unfortunately, I can't "invent" IIF data standards-that's up to Intuit-so I haven't been able to provide any assistance.

Luckily, the limitations imposed by this decision aren't enormous-only a few data fields are affected (so far) and I've found that they're fields that aren't commonly used, or aren't commonly imported. From the e-mail I receive, and the discussions I have at seminars and CPE courses, thousands of accountants apparently share my hope that Intuit reverses their attitude about IIF files for lists-I think it's appropriate to encourage users to turn to the SDK for importing transactions, but not for lists.

Accountants and IIF Files

An IIF file is a great way for accountants to provide all the data required for a client's company file. It's like creating a perfect company file from scratch in QuickBooks, and delivering the file to the client.

Entering data in a spreadsheet is faster and easier than going through all the work involved in creating a company file in QuickBooks. Entering data in rows and columns in an Excel worksheet is faster than opening one QuickBooks list window after another, and then opening one dialog after another within each list.

Most accountants are extremely comfortable working in a spreadsheet application, and after they've created a series of boilerplate import files for different types of companies, they can zip through the process of customizing a boilerplate for any particular client. Do your work in a regular spreadsheet file, saving it as an Excel file, so you can avoid all those reminders from Excel about text files not having all the features of a regular spreadsheet file. Then, save the file as a tab-delimited text file (with the extension .IIF) when you're ready to create an import file for QuickBooks.

Format of an IIF File

To work correctly as an import file, an IIF file has to follow a certain format. Figure B-1 is an Excel worksheet for the chart of accounts that displays the proper format.

Notice the following characteristics of this sample IIF file:

- The list being imported is identified by that list's keyword in Cell A-1 (identified by the exclamation point)

- Each record (row) indicates the list into which the data is being imported (keyword in Column A).
- Each category (column header) has the keyword for the field into which the data in that column is imported.

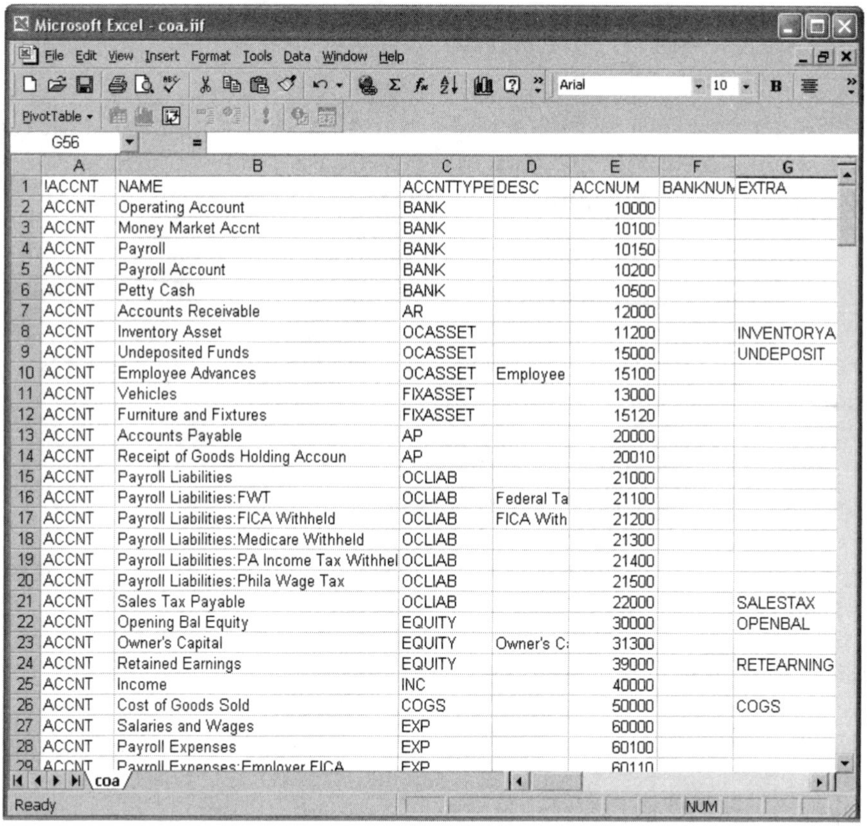

	A	B	C	D	E	F	G
1	!ACCNT	NAME	ACCNTTYPE	DESC	ACCNUM	BANKNUM	EXTRA
2	ACCNT	Operating Account	BANK		10000		
3	ACCNT	Money Market Accnt	BANK		10100		
4	ACCNT	Payroll	BANK		10150		
5	ACCNT	Payroll Account	BANK		10200		
6	ACCNT	Petty Cash	BANK		10500		
7	ACCNT	Accounts Receivable	AR		12000		
8	ACCNT	Inventory Asset	OCASSET		11200		INVENTORYA
9	ACCNT	Undeposited Funds	OCASSET		15000		UNDEPOSIT
10	ACCNT	Employee Advances	OCASSET	Employee	15100		
11	ACCNT	Vehicles	FIXASSET		13000		
12	ACCNT	Furniture and Fixtures	FIXASSET		15120		
13	ACCNT	Accounts Payable	AP		20000		
14	ACCNT	Receipt of Goods Holding Accoun	AP		20010		
15	ACCNT	Payroll Liabilities	OCLIAB		21000		
16	ACCNT	Payroll Liabilities:FWT	OCLIAB	Federal Ta	21100		
17	ACCNT	Payroll Liabilities:FICA Withheld	OCLIAB	FICA With	21200		
18	ACCNT	Payroll Liabilities:Medicare Withheld	OCLIAB		21300		
19	ACCNT	Payroll Liabilities:PA Income Tax Withhel	OCLIAB		21400		
20	ACCNT	Payroll Liabilities:Phila Wage Tax	OCLIAB		21500		
21	ACCNT	Sales Tax Payable	OCLIAB		22000		SALESTAX
22	ACCNT	Opening Bal Equity	EQUITY		30000		OPENBAL
23	ACCNT	Owner's Capital	EQUITY	Owner's C:	31300		
24	ACCNT	Retained Earnings	EQUITY		39000		RETEARNING
25	ACCNT	Income	INC		40000		
26	ACCNT	Cost of Goods Sold	COGS		50000		COGS
27	ACCNT	Salaries and Wages	EXP		60000		
28	ACCNT	Payroll Expenses	EXP		60100		
29	ACCNT	Payroll Expenses:Employer FICA	EXP		60110		

Figure B-1: This file is formatted properly for importing the chart of accounts.

***NOTE**: As I discuss each list I'll present the Header Keywords and the other keywords for each. As a reference, a summary of Header Keywords for the lists I discuss is at the end of this appendix.*

To create an IIF file from scratch, make sure you've set up your columns properly, with the appropriate headings (using keywords). When you enter data, remember that some data requires special handling (keywords again). The documentation for those keywords is in this appendix.

Unlike the Excel/CVS column heading text covered in Appendix A, an IIF file doesn't use the field names you see when you're entering entries into a list in QuickBooks. Instead, the column headings (field names) are indicated by specific keywords. The keywords for each list are documented in this appendix.

Exporting Data into an IIF File

You can export data from another application and specify a tab-delimited file for the exported file format. The application could be another accounting software application, or a spreadsheet in which you've been keeping customer information, inventory information, etc.

To open a tab-delimited file in your spreadsheet application, right-click the file's listing in My Computer or Windows Explorer and choose Open With. Then choose Microsoft Excel (or another spreadsheet application if you don't use Excel).

Creating Multiple Lists in One IIF File

You can actually create an entire company in one IIF file, by having all the entries for all the lists you want to import in one worksheet. If you're an accountant, this is a good way to deliver a "company in a worksheet" to your clients.

Each list must be in its own contiguous section of rows, with the appropriate keyword headings as the first row of each section. To make it easier to work with the file, insert a blank row between each section (list).

Many accountants who work in Excel save the file as a standard Excel (.xls) file while they're building import files. It's common to create a separate worksheet for each list being created. This method is more efficient, and lets you build boilerplate worksheets for each QuickBooks list.

However, you can't save multiple worksheets when you save a document as a tab-delimited file. When you're ready to turn your Excel document into QuickBooks import files, you can either save each worksheet as a separate IIF file, or you can copy the contents of every worksheet into a single worksheet in a new Excel document. Then, save the new combined document as an IIF file.

Importing an IIF File

Importing an IIF file is an uncomplicated process, and takes only a few easy steps. It's even easier if you copy the file to the folder in which the QuickBooks company file is installed, so you don't have to navigate through the computer to find the file. Use the following steps to import an IIF file:

1. In QuickBooks, open the company that needs the imported file.
2. Choose File → Utilities → Import → IIF Files.
3. Double-click the listing for the IIF file you want to import.

QuickBooks automatically imports the file and then displays a message indicating the data has been imported. Click OK.

IIF File Keywords for Lists

In the following sections, I'll provide the keywords and instructions for building IIF files for QuickBooks lists. For many lists, I'll provide only the keywords for fields that are commonly imported, instead of covering the full range of possible keywords.

For example, all lists accept data in a field (column) named HIDDEN, and you enter Y (meaning "yes it's hidden") or N (meaning "no, it's not hidden") for each entry (row) to indicate whether the entry is active (not hidden) or inactive (hidden). It's normal to omit that column in an import file. In the absence of information about the active status, QuickBooks assumes the entry is N (not hidden.)

For lists that permit custom fields in the names lists and the items list, QuickBooks has keywords you can use to import that data. However, it would be unusual to take the trouble to create these in a worksheet. It would also be unusual for a file imported from another application to contain this information. Custom fields are usually specific to a particular company and its company file.

Profile Lists Import Files

Profile lists are the lists that contain entries to help you categorize and sort major lists. The entries in profile lists are fields in major lists, such as Terms or Vendor Type. You can see the profile lists by choosing Lists → Customer & Vendor Profile Lists.

I'm starting the discussion of importing lists with the profile lists, because if you import the profile lists, you can use their contents in other lists. For example, if you import your Customer Type List, you can enter data in the customer type category of your customer import list. However, I'm not covering all the profile lists; instead, I'll discuss those that are commonly imported.

Customer Type List Import File

The Customer Type List has one keyword: Name. Your worksheet needs only two columns:

- Column A contains the list keyword !CTYPE in the top row, and the entry keyword CTYPE on each entry row.
- Column B contains the data keyword NAME on the top row, and the data (the name you've created for a customer type) is in each following row.

Vendor Type List Import File

The Vendor Type List is almost exactly the same as the Customer Type List:

- The list keyword for the first row of Column A is !VTYPE and the entry keyword in Column A for each row of data is VTYPE.
- Column B contains the data keyword (NAME) on the top row, and the data in each following row is the name of the type.

Job Type List Import File

The Job Type List is also similar to the Customer Type list:

- The list keyword for the first row of Column A is !JOBTYPE and the entry keyword in Column A for each row of data is JOBTYPE.
- Column B contains the data keyword NAME on the top row, and the data in each following row is the name of the type.

Sales Rep List Import File

The Sales Rep List has the following format:

The list keyword for the first row of Column A is !SALESREP and the entry keyword in Column for each row of data is SALESREP.

- Column B contains the data keyword INITIALS on the top row, and the data (1-5 initials) is in each following row.
- Column C contains the data keyword ASSOCIATEDNAME on the top row, and the data (the name of the sales rep) is in each following row.
- Column D contains the data keyword NAMETYPE on the top row, and the data (a code representing the list the name listed under ASSOCIATEDNAME is a member of) is in each following row.

The NAMETYPE codes are:

- 2 if the rep is in the Vendor List
- 3 if the rep is in the Employee List
- 4 if the rep is in the Other Names List

Because the list references other lists, import the Vendor, Employee, and Other Names lists before importing the Sales Rep list.

Ship Method List Import File

The Ship Method List (which supplies data for the Ship Via field in transactions) is also similar to the Customer Type list:

- The list keyword for the first row of Column A is !SHIPMETH and the entry keyword in Column A for each row of data is SHIPMETH.
- Column B contains the data keyword NAME on the top row, and the data (UPS, FedEx, Truck, etc), is in each following row.

Terms List Import File

The Terms List import file must contain all the information for each named set of terms. The terms you include must cover the terms you need for both customers and vendors (QuickBooks doesn't provide separate Terms files for customers and vendors).

- The list keyword for the first row of Column A is !TERMS and the entry keyword in Column A for each row of data is TERMS.
- The remaining columns contain the data keywords on the top row, and the data is in each following row. The data keywords for columns are explained in Table B-1.

Keyword (Column Title)	**Data**
NAME	(Required) The name for the terms.
TERMSTYPE	The type of terms. **0** = standard terms (payment within a specific number of days). **1** = date driven terms (payment by a certain date of the month).
DUEDAYS	When TERMSTYPE = 0, the number of days in which payment is due. When TERMSTYPE = 1, the day of the month by which payment is due.
DISCPER	The discount percentage earned for early payment. The data is a number and the percent sign (e.g. 2.00%).
DISCDAYS	The number of days by which the discount specified by DISCPER is earned.

Table B-1: Terms list import file keywords.

Standard Lists Import Files

The information in the following sections covers the commonly imported lists that are displayed on the Lists menu. After your profile lists are imported, the data in some of the "regular" lists can be linked to the data in the profile lists.

Chart of Accounts Import File

The chart of accounts import file is not terribly complicated:

- The list keyword for the first row of Column A is !ACCNT and the entry keyword in Column A for each row of data is ACCNT.
- The rest of the columns on the first row contain the data keywords. The data is in each following row.

Table B-2 shows the important column headings for importing a chart of accounts.

Keyword (Column Title)	Text
NAME	(Required) The name of the account.
ACCNTTYPE	(Required) The type of account. The text must match keywords (See Table B-3).
DESC	Description of the account.
ACCNUM	The account number.

Table B-2: Keywords for the chart of accounts.

The ACCNTTYPE entry is required and your text in that column must match the keywords in Table B-3.

Account Numbers in COA Import Files

If the company file into which the chart of accounts is imported has enabled account numbers, the numbers in the IIF file are displayed in the chart of accounts window and the drop-down lists in transaction windows.

Section	Account Type	Keyword
Assets		
	Bank	BANK
	Accounts Receivable	AR
	Other Current Asset	OCASSET
	Fixed Asset	FIXASSET
	Other Asset	OASSET
Liabilities		
	Accounts Payable	AP
	Credit Card	CCARD
	Other Current Liability	OCLIAB
	Long-Term Liability	LTLIAB
Equity		EQUITY
Income		INC
Cost Of Goods Sold		COGS
Expense		EXP
Other Income		EXINC
Other Expense		EXEXP
Non-Posting Accounts		NONPOSTING

Table B-3: Keywords for account types.

If account numbers are not enabled in the company file, QuickBooks stores the account number data that was imported. When (or if) the user enables account numbers, the imported account numbers are available.

EXTRA Account Keywords

You can include a column named EXTRA to import accounts that QuickBooks automatically creates when such accounts are needed (when specific features are enabled).

For example, when a QuickBooks user enables the inventory feature, QuickBooks creates an account named Inventory Asset Account in the Assets section of the chart of accounts.

To use these accounts in an import file, the text you enter in the EXTRA column must match the required keywords. If the text doesn't match the required keyword, QuickBooks will create another account when the user enables the appropriate feature. Table B-4 contains the keywords required in the EXTRA column when you create these special accounts.

Account	EXTRA Column Keyword
Inventory Asset	INVENTORYASSET
Opening Balance Equity	OPENBAL
Retained Earnings	RETEARNINGS
Sales Tax Payable	SALESTAX
Undeposited Funds	UNDEPOSIT
Cost of Goods Sold	COGS
Purchase Orders	PURCHORDER
Estimates	ESTIMATE

Table B-4: Keywords for configuring the EXTRA column for special accounts.

Although QuickBooks adds these accounts automatically when needed, including them in the import file lets you control their account numbers. If you're an accountant, you can create boilerplate import files by client type, and include the appropriate EXTRA accounts. For example, product-based businesses need inventory and purchase order accounts, and some service-based businesses may need estimates.

Customer:Job List Import File

If you've been keeping a customer list in another software application, you can avoid one-customer-at-a-time data entry by importing the list into QuickBooks. This is only possible if your current application is capable of exporting data to a tab-delimited text file.

Load the tab-delimited text file into a spreadsheet program (I'm assuming you use Microsoft Excel), and use the instructions in this section to create an .IIF file.

A QuickBooks customer import file can contain all the information you need to fill out all the fields in the customer dialog, such as customer type, sales tax status, and so on.

However, it's unlikely you've kept records in a manner that matches these fields. Therefore, I'll provide the keywords and instructions for basic customer information. I'll include some of the additional fields so you can fill them in manually if you wish (or skip the keyword column for any data you don't want to import).

Customer Import File Format

If you're dealing with data from another source, after you import the data to Excel, you need to format the worksheet as follows:

- To make room for the QuickBooks keywords you need, insert a column to the left of the first column, and insert a row above the first row.
- In cell A1, insert the text !CUST (the exclamation point is required). This is the code that tells QuickBooks the import file is a Customer:Job list.
- In the remaining cells in the first column, for every row that has data, insert the text CUST. This identifies the data in that row as data for a Customer:Job list.
- In the first row, starting with the second column (the first column contains !CUST), enter the QuickBooks keywords for customers.

Table B-5 describes the keywords and the text that belongs in the column under each keyword.

***TIP**: The only required entry is the customer name, which is linked to the keyword NAME. If that's the only information you have, use it to import your customers-you can fill in the rest of the fields as you use each customer in a transaction.*

QuickBooks supports multiple shipping addresses for customers, and when you're creating customer records you can name each shipping address. The import file can only manage one shipping address. When you import the file, the shipping address data becomes the default shipping address. However, there is no keyword for the shipping address name.

Keyword (Column)	Text
NAME	The customer name (the code you use for the customer).
COMPANYNAME	Name of the customer's company.
FIRSTNAME	Customer's first name.
MIDINIT	Customer's middle initial.
LASTNAME	Customer's last name.
BADDR1	First line of the customer's billing address, which is usually a name (customer's name or company name).
BADDR2	Second line of the customer's billing address, which is the street address.
BADDR3	Third line of the customer's billing address, which is either additional street address information, or the city, state, and zip.
BADDR4	Fourth line of the billing address, which is either additional street address information, or the city, state, and zip.
BADDR5	Fifth line of the billing address, which is either additional street address information, or the city, state, and zip.
SADDR1	First line of the default shipping address.
SADDR2	Second line of the default shipping address.
SADDR3	Third line of the default shipping address.
SADDR4	Fourth line of the default shipping address.
SADDR5	Fifth line of the default shipping address.
PHONE1	Phone number.
PHONE2	Second phone number.
FAXNUM	FAX number.
EMAIL	E-mail address of a contact.
CONT1	Name of the primary contact.
CONT2	Name of another contact.
CTYPE	Customer Type (must match text in the Customer Type import file).
TERMS	Terms (must match text in the Terms import file).
TAXABLE	Y or N
SALESTAXCODE	Tax code (must match text in the Tax Code import file)
LIMIT	Credit limit (e.g. 5000.00)
RESALENUM	Resale number for tax exempt customers

Table B-5: Keywords for a Customer:Job import file.

Importing Jobs

A job is like a subaccount, it's linked to a parent, and the text must be in the format **customer:job**. Notice that no spaces exist before or after the colon.

To import jobs, you must make sure the customer is imported first; the text for the customer must appear in the Name column before the text for the job. For example, if you have a customer named LRAssocs with jobs named Consulting and Auditing, enter the following in the Name column:

LRAssocs

LRAssocs:Consulting

LRAssocs:Auditing

Most jobs have the same basic information (address, taxable status, and so on) as the customer, so you don't have to enter text in the other columns. However, if any specific information is different, such as the name of the primary contact, or the job type, enter the text in the appropriate column.

Vendor List Import File

If you're exporting your vendor list from another software application, follow the formatting rules described earlier for the customer file.

- The list keyword for the first row of Column A is !VEND and the entry keyword in Column A for each row of data is VEND.
- The remaining columns contain the data keywords on the top row, and the data is in each following row.

The data keywords are explained in Table B-6.

Keyword	Data
NAME	The Vendor Name (the vendor code).
PRINTAS	The Payee name that prints on checks.
ADDR1	First line of the vendor's address.
ADDR2	Second line of the vendor's address.
ADDR3	Third line of the vendor's address.
ADDR4	Fourth line of the vendor's address.
ADDR5	Fifth line of the vendor's address.
VTYPE	Vendor Type (must match text in the Vendor Type import file).
CONT1	Your primary contact.
PHONE1	Phone number.
PHONE2	Second phone number.
FAXNUM	FAX number.
EMAIL	E-mail address of a contact.
NOTE	The text you want to print in the Memo field of checks (usually your account number with the vendor).
TERMS	Terms (must match a name in the Terms import file).
TAXID	Tax identification number for a 1099 recipient.
SALUTATION	Salutation or title.
COMPANYNAME	Vendor's company name.
FIRSTNAME	First name.
MIDINIT	Middle initial.
LASTNAME	Last name.
1099	Specifies whether this vendor receives a 1099-MISC form. Enter Y or N as the data.

Table B-6: Keywords for importing vendors into QuickBooks.

Items List Import File

If you've been keeping your items in a software application (usually this means inventory items only), you can import those items, saving yourself some manual work. Use the instructions earlier in this chapter to format the file.

The required keywords for items import files are the following:

- NAME-the item name
- INVITEMTYPE-the item type

- ACCNT-the account to which you post transactions for the item

Some QuickBooks item types don't have an account (such as prepayments or tax items).

The keyword for the item list is !INVITEM on the heading row, and each record (row) must have INVITEM in the first column. Table B-7 describes the keywords for the rest of the columns on the first row of the import file. Table B-8 (referenced in Table B-7) has the keywords for the Item Type required in the import file.

Keyword	Data
NAME	Item Name or Number
INVITEMTYPE	Item type. The data must match the keywords in Table B-8.
DESC	The description that appears on sales forms
PURCHASEDESC	(Inventory part items only) The description that appears on purchase orders
ACCNT	The income account you use to track sales of the item
ASSETACCNT	(Inventory part items only) The inventory asset account
COGSACCNT	(Inventory part items only) The cost of goods account
PRICE	The percentage rate or price of the item (not for Group, Payment, or Subtotal type).
COST	(Inventory part items only) The unit cost of the item.
TAXABLE	Specifies whether the item is taxable—enter Y or N.
PREFVEND	(Inventory part items only) The vendor from whom you normally purchase the item.

Table B-7: Keywords and data information for an Item List import file.

Several item types have additional options when you create them in the standard dialog while working in QuickBooks. When you select any of these options, the dialog changes to include fields for Cost, Expense Account, Purchase Description, and Preferred Vendor.

- A Non-Inventory Part item type has an option labeled This Item Is Purchased For And Sold To A Specific Customer:Job.
- A Service item type has an option labeled This Service Is Performed By A Subcontractor, Owner Or Partner.

- An Other Charge item type has an option labeled This Is A Reimbursable Charge.

Keyword	Item Type
ASSEMBLY	Inventory Assembly item
COMPTAX	Sales tax item
DISC	Discount item
GRP	Group item
INVENTORY	Inventory part item
OTHC	Other charge item
PART	Non-inventory part item
PMT	Payment item
SERV	Service item
STAX	Sales tax group item
SUBT	Subtotal item

Table B-8: Item Type keywords.

You can set these options in your import file by creating a column with the keyword ISPASSEDTHROUGH. The data for this column is either Y or N (for Yes or No). For any item that has a Y in this column, you can enter data that is marked Inventory part items only in Table B-7.

Employee List Import File

When you import the Employee List, you can only import basic data about the employee. Wage, tax, deductions, and other financial information have to be set up in the Employee record in QuickBooks. However, importing the basic information saves you quite a bit of work.

The keyword for the employee list is !EMP on the heading row (Cell A1), and each record (row) must have EMP in the first column. Table B-9 describes the keywords for the rest of the columns on the first row of the import file.

The Mystery of Employee Initials

QuickBooks' documentation for IIF files says that the INIT data (employee initials) is a required entry for an employee list import file. It's not;

I've imported many Employee Lists without it. In fact, the field doesn't appear in the employee record dialog when you create an employee in QuickBooks, or view an existing employee's record. If you've consulted the QuickBooks documentation to build IIF files, you can ignore this requirement, and omit the column from your import file.

Keyword	Data
NAME	(Required) Employee's name.
ADDR1	First line of the address.
ADDR2	Second line of the address.
ADDR3	Third line of the address.
ADDR4	Fourth line of the address.
ADDR5	Fifth line of the address.
SSNO	Social Security number (XXX-YY-ZZZZ).
PHONE1	Phone number.
PHONE2	Alternate phone number.
FIRSTNAME	First name.
MIDINIT	Middle initial.
LASTNAME	Last name.
SALUTATION	Salutation (Mr., Ms., Mrs., etc.).

Table B-9: Keywords for Employee List import file.

I think it's probable that the INIT data requirement dates back to earlier versions of QuickBooks when sales reps had to be employees, and sales reps are listed by initials in drop-down lists.

Other Names List Import File

Some companies never use the Other Names list, but this list is necessary for some company types, and handy for others. For proprietorships and partnerships, or any business in which a draw occurs, the owners should be in the Other Names list instead of the Vendors list.

Companies that occasionally issue non-payroll checks (such as loans or reimbursement of expenses) to employees must add the employees to the Other Names list. That entry is the payee for non-payroll disbursements.

The keyword for the Other Names list is !OTHERNAME on the heading row (Cell A1), and each record (row) must have OTHERNAME in the first column. Table B-10 describes the keywords for the rest of the columns on the first row of the import file.

Keyword	Data
NAME	(Required) The name.
BADDR1	First line of the address.
BADDR2	Second line of the address.
BADDR3	Third line of the address.
BADDR4	Fourth line of the address.
BADDR5	Fifth line of the address.
PHONE1	Phone number.
PHONE2	Alternate phone number.
FAXNUM	FAX number.
EMAIL	E-mail address.
CONT1	Primary contact (if a company).
SALUTATION	Salutation, or title (Mr., Ms., Mrs., etc.).
COMPANYNAME	Company Name (if a company).
FIRSTNAME	First name.
MIDINIT	Middle initial.
LASTNAME	Last name.

Table B-10: Keywords for the Other Names List import file.

Price Level List Import File

Price levels are assigned to customers and sales transactions, and the IIF file has the following format:

- The list keyword for the first row of Column A is !PRICELEVEL and the entry keyword in Column A for each row of data is PRICELEVEL.
- Columns B and C contain the data keywords NAME and VALUE.

The data is percentages, such as 10.00%, 5.50%, etc. A discounted price level has a minus sign.

Sales Tax Code List Import File

Sales tax codes are assigned to customers and items, and indicate whether sales tax should be imposed. These are not the sales tax items, which determine the rate (those are in the Item List).

Sales tax codes only need to be imported if you need more tax codes than QuickBooks provides automatically. QuickBooks preloads the entries Tax and Non, which suffice for many businesses. However, for businesses in states that require explanations for nontaxable sales, you need additional codes. Here are some examples of sales tax codes you can assign to customers:

- NPO for nontaxable nonprofit organizations.
- GOV for nontaxable government agencies.
- RES for customers who are nontaxable because they resell products (your customer record should include the resale tax number).

The list keyword for the first row of Column A is !SALESTAXCODE and the entry keyword in Column A for each row of data is SALESTAXCODE.

The following keywords are used in this import file:

- CODE is the name of the code (and is required data). Data entries cannot exceed three characters.
- DESC is an optional description of the code.
- TAXABLE specifies the taxable or nontaxable status (and is required data). The data is Y or N.

Class List Import File

Classes are assigned to transactions in order to track income and expenses by class. The list keyword for the first row of Column A is !CLASS and the entry keyword in Column A for each row of data is CLASS.

The column heading for Column B is NAME and the data in the rest of Column B is the class name.

Summary of List Headings

Table B-11 contains the HDR keywords for importing lists via IIF files. The data in the column labeled HDR must be in cell A1 of your IIF import file.

HDR	List
!ACCNT	Chart of accounts.
!CUST	Customers & Jobs List
!VEND	Vendors List
!EMP	Employees List
!OTHERNAME	Other Name list.
!CLASS	Class List
!CTYPE	Customer Type List
!INVITEM	Items List
!INVMEMO	Customer Messages
!PAYMETH	Payment Method List
!SHIPMETH	Shipping Method List
!TERMS	Payment Terms List
!VTYPE	Vendor Type List

Table B-11: Header keywords that identify the list you're importing.

Appendix C

Tips & Tricks for Accountants

Helping clients with complicated features

Troubleshooting

Accountants who support QuickBooks users (or users of any accounting software application) spend a lot of time troubleshooting problems. Most of the problems are user-induced rather than software bugs. Some of the predicaments users find themselves in are the result of plunging ahead on a task without calling an accountant first.

In this appendix, I present tips, tricks, workarounds, and troubleshooting techniques that I've used, or learned about from accountants who attend my seminars and CPE classes. It's impossible to cover every possible dilemma, and it's even impossible to cover every possible facet of a particular predicament (users are *so* inventive), so you'll have to view this appendix as a much-shortened course in QuickBooks problem solving techniques.

The topics that are presented are those about which I receive the largest number of queries or comments. They're presented in random order, because it's difficult to create logical groups out of the subject matter offered here.

Updating Lists with Import Files

Do any of these scenarios seem familiar?

- A client needs to track certain information about customers, and you've suggested a custom field. You created the custom field for the Customers & Jobs list, and added it to sales transaction windows by customizing the templates. The client has 500 customers to update with data for the new field.
- A client has created price levels and wants to assign a price level to many of the 200 customers in the system. Or, instead of price levels, it's sales reps (or both).
- A client tracks jobs and doesn't have the same rep on every job for the same customer. QuickBooks doesn't provide a Rep field for jobs; instead, the Rep for the customer is automatically the Rep for the job.

Tweaking and updating information in lists is a common practice as users become more familiar with QuickBooks, and the additional data can be the solution for producing more sophisticated detailed reports.

Performing these tasks on a customer-by-customer, vendor-by-vendor, or item-by-item basis means opening each record, moving to the appropriate tab, entering the data, closing the record, opening the next record, and... you get the picture.

Not only is this time consuming, but the user is likely to be inconsistent about data entry in the custom field, making it hard to track the needed information. The fastest, most accurate method for upgrading data in lists is to import the information.

Any field in any list can be updated with an .IIF file. For example, you may create a Customer Type that you want to use to sort customers in reports, or to prepare mailings. Or, you might create a custom field and have to enter data in that field for most (or all) of the entries in a list. Working in QuickBooks means opening the record for each entry in the list, moving to the right tab in the record's window, typing in the data, closing the record, selecting the next record, etc. etc. This could take days if the list is large.

For some lists, you can use an IIF file, an Excel XLS/XLSX file, or a CSV file. Only the following lists can accept XLS imports:

- Customer
- Vendor
- Items
- Chart of accounts

However, not all fields are available for import when you use an Excel import file. For example, you cannot import data for custom fields, which is a severe limitation. As a result, I use IIF files for all of these tasks.

Creating Import Files to Update Existing Lists

Start by exporting the appropriate list from the company file. Choose File → Utilities → Export → Lists to IIF Files. Do not export multiple lists, even if you want to update more than one list; instead, update the lists one at a time.

Open the resulting .IIF file in Excel and look for the first row of "real" data, which has the list name preceded by an exclamation point.

Select all the rows above that row and choose Edit → Delete to remove those rows from the worksheet. This data isn't necessary in an import file, and removing it makes it easier to work with columns (because the column names for the rows you're deleting are not the same column names you'll work with as you add data). Figure C-1 displays a customer list where all the rows above !CUST (the list header) have been selected for deletion.

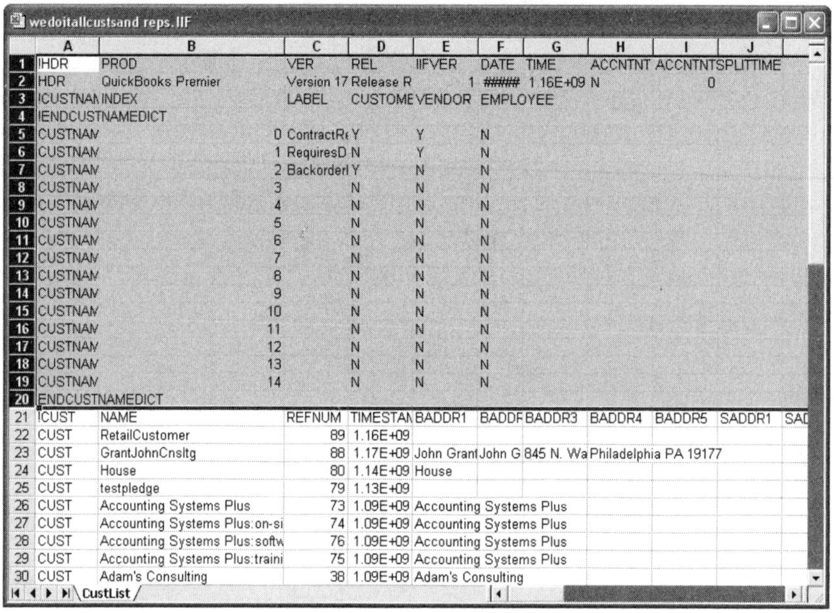

Figure C-1: Find the first row of real data, and eliminate every row above it.

To add data, you must be able to see the NAME column. Freeze the column that holds the names so that as you scroll through the columns the NAME field stays visible. Use the following steps to freeze the column:

1. Click the column heading of the column to the right of the NAME column to select it.
2. Choose Window → Freeze Panes.

Adding and Modifying Data

Except for data going into custom fields (covered in the next section), the data you enter in any column must match the data already in the QuickBooks file.

For example, if you're adding Customer Type data to your customer list, the data must match the Customer Type entries you created in the Customer Type list. If you created a Customer Type named Stmnt (to indicate customers who should receive statements), the text you enter must be Stmnt; you cannot enter Statement, Stamnt, or any other text. The same is true for Terms, Price Level, and other data contained in QuickBooks lists.

To make sure you enter data correctly, open the list and press Ctrl-P to print the list. Then, with the entries in the Customer Type, Price Level, etc. list in front of you, you'll be able to enter the text correctly.

Chapter 9 of *Excel for Accountants*, published by CPA911 Publishing, has instructions for creating a drop-down list in the cells of the column you're working on. Create the drop-down list to match the text that exists in the list you're using. For example, if you're adding Vendor Type entries to a Vendor List, you can display all the vendor types that exist in the Vendor Type List. Using the drop-down list in each cell means you can be sure the data you're entering matches the text you need. You can buy *Excel for Accountants* at your favorite bookstore, or from our website www.cpa911publishing.com.

***WARNING**: If the data you're entering or changing is a QuickBooks Keyword you must use the keyword. Appendix B documents all the keywords for all the list files.*

When you're working in Excel, you can take advantage of the Windows clipboard and the Excel data entry tools to enter data.

1. After you enter data in the first row (record) for which you're entering or modifying text, select the cell and press Ctrl-C (or

right-click in the cell and choose Copy) to copy the text to the clipboard.

2. Find the next row that needs the same data, and press Ctrl-V to paste the text (or right-click in the cell and choose Paste).
3. Move to the next row that needs the same data and press Ctrl-V to paste the text there. Continue to paste until you've pasted this text into all the records that should have it. (Once you have text in the Windows clipboard, you can continue to paste it endlessly, as long as you don't stop pasting to perform another task.)
4. Enter the next data text into the appropriate row, and follow the same pattern to paste that text into every row that's appropriate.

If you have a section of contiguous rows that require the same data (e.g. all the jobs listed below a customer), enter the data in the first row, and then select that cell. Position your mouse in the lower right corner of the cell, and when your pointer turns into vertical and horizontal intersecting lines drag down to fill all the cells with the same data.

Working With Custom Fields

The Custom Field columns do not have the name of the custom fields you created. The columns are labeled CUSTFLD1, CUSTFLD2, and so on. Open the custom field list in QuickBooks to see the names of the custom fields you created. The top custom field is CUSTFLD1, the next is CUSTFLD2, etc. Write down the names of the custom fields so you know the type of data you have to enter as you update the list.

- In the Items list, open any item, and click the Custom Fields button to see the custom fields.
- In a Names list, open any entry in the list and move to the Additional Info tab to see the custom fields.

When you enter data into custom fields, you must be consistent, or else it will be difficult to create reports on the contents of the fields. For example, if you have a custom field in your Customer & Jobs list named Backorder (to indicate which customers will accept backorders), devise a protocol for the data. For customers that do not accept backorders, if you use the text NoBO, don't also enter text No BO (note the space), or just No (see Figure C-2).

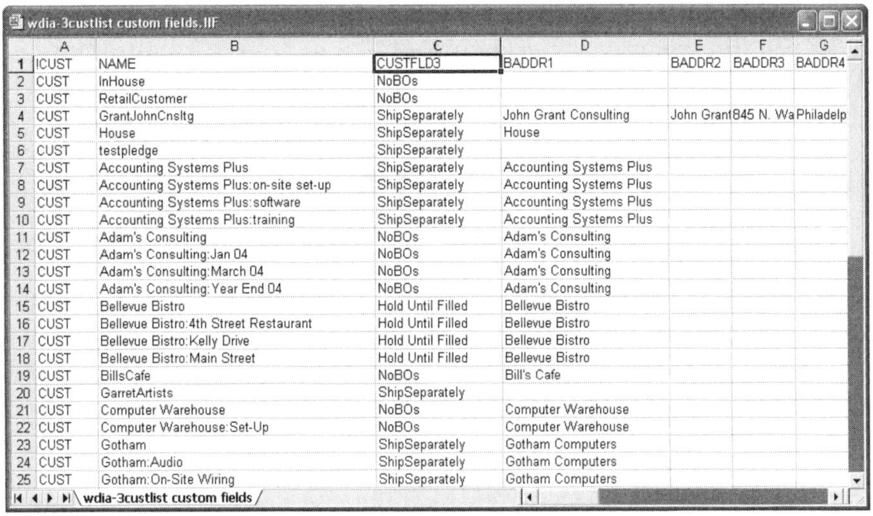

wdia-3custlist custom fields.IIF

	A	B	C	D	E	F	G
1	!CUST	NAME	CUSTFLD3	BADDR1	BADDR2	BADDR3	BADDR4
2	CUST	InHouse	NoBOs				
3	CUST	RetailCustomer	NoBOs				
4	CUST	GrantJohnCnsltg	ShipSeparately	John Grant Consulting	John Grant	845 N. Wa	Philadelp
5	CUST	House	ShipSeparately	House			
6	CUST	testpledge	ShipSeparately				
7	CUST	Accounting Systems Plus	ShipSeparately	Accounting Systems Plus			
8	CUST	Accounting Systems Plus:on-site set-up	ShipSeparately	Accounting Systems Plus			
9	CUST	Accounting Systems Plus:software	ShipSeparately	Accounting Systems Plus			
10	CUST	Accounting Systems Plus:training	ShipSeparately	Accounting Systems Plus			
11	CUST	Adam's Consulting	NoBOs	Adam's Consulting			
12	CUST	Adam's Consulting:Jan 04	NoBOs	Adam's Consulting			
13	CUST	Adam's Consulting:March 04	NoBOs	Adam's Consulting			
14	CUST	Adam's Consulting:Year End 04	NoBOs	Adam's Consulting			
15	CUST	Bellevue Bistro	Hold Until Filled	Bellevue Bistro			
16	CUST	Bellevue Bistro:4th Street Restaurant	Hold Until Filled	Bellevue Bistro			
17	CUST	Bellevue Bistro:Kelly Drive	Hold Until Filled	Bellevue Bistro			
18	CUST	Bellevue Bistro:Main Street	Hold Until Filled	Bellevue Bistro			
19	CUST	BillsCafe	NoBOs	Bill's Cafe			
20	CUST	GarretArtists	ShipSeparately				
21	CUST	Computer Warehouse	NoBOs	Computer Warehouse			
22	CUST	Computer Warehouse:Set-Up	NoBOs	Computer Warehouse			
23	CUST	Gotham	ShipSeparately	Gotham Computers			
24	CUST	Gotham:Audio	ShipSeparately	Gotham Computers			
25	CUST	Gotham:On-Site Wiring	ShipSeparately	Gotham Computers			

wdia-3custlist custom fields

Figure C-2: Entering data for the custom field for backorders keeps customer preferences straight (the field appears on transaction templates to make it easy to track the information).

Saving the Import File

I always use the Save As command in Excel to save the file in order to retain the original exported data (in case I have to repair a mistake I made). I usually add a dash and a number to the original filename (such as custlist-1, if the original exported file was named custlist).

Save the file as a Text (Tab Delimited) file with the extension .IIF. Excel issues warnings about text files not holding on to formatting, etc. Just ignore the warnings. Then close Excel.

Importing Updated Data into QuickBooks

Before you import data in batches with an import file, back up the company file. If anything goes amiss, you can restore the backup and continue to work in the file. Then examine your import file to find any errors, and try again (backing up the file again first, if you've worked in the file).

To import the file, choose File → Utilities → Import → IIF files. Select the file you created and click Open. QuickBooks automatically imports the data. Open the list you tweaked and make sure everything is as you expected.

Disbursements Report Mysteries

In Chapter 6, I wrote about the problems you can run into when you're trying to create reports on job costing, after you use JEs for job costing. I won't repeat the entire section here, but I'll provide a summary of the solution to jog your memory if you already read Chapter 6. If you didn't read the section, here's the summary of the solution presented in Chapter 6.

All transactions in QuickBooks have a source and a target, and if you don't get them right, you end up with unexpected results.

The source is the account where the transaction originates, and the target is the account where it is completed. When you write a check to a vendor, the bank account is the source (it's where the money starts) and the expense account is the target (it's where the money ends up).

If you attach additional information to the check, it travels with its source or target counterpart. For example, assigning a customer to the line that contains an expense account (for job costing) links the customer information and the amount to the target (because a line item, in which this data exists, is part of the target).

For JEs that perform job costing allocations there are two important facts to remember:

- QuickBooks assigns job costing or other information when it's part of the target, and ignores it when it is part of the source.
- The first line of a JE is the source and all other lines are targets.

This means that if you're moving job costing information from one customer to another or from one job to another for the same customer, you will almost certainly end up with one or more incorrect postings.

The solution is to make sure you don't enter real data in the first line of a JE; instead, insert data in the Memo column only.

Here's another mystery that's solved if you understand the QuickBooks source/target paradigm. Unfortunately, solving the mystery doesn't always remove the problem. Here's a puzzle I was presented with. To guess how I solved it, you have to remember that the target, not the source, has dibs on reports about postings.

An accountant called me from a client site. He was grumpy. Here's the transcript of our conversation.

Him: I'm looking at a trial balance and my client has several expense accounts that have postings for consultants that get 1099s so I'm checking his 1099 payments. When I double-click one of those accounts, I get a QuickReport.

Me: Right, that's what's supposed to happen.

Him: The payees are wrong. I asked my client who Sam Smith is and why he's not listed as a 1099 vendor, and he tells me Sam Smith is a customer. I asked him why he was writing checks to Sam Smith, and he says he's not.

Me: Double-click the listing for the check to Sam Smith - you'll see the original check.

Him: OK, the check is made out to somebody else, why does the report say Sam Smith?

Me: Check the columns in the line item section. I'll bet he linked the expense to a customer named Sam Smith.

Him: That's right. So I have to keep double-clicking every single entry, all hundreds of them, to find out who the payee really is because this report is wrong?

Me: Nope, click Modify Report and deselect the Name listing and select the Source Name listing.

Reports on disbursements should provide information on the source name by default, saving the use of the target name for job costing reports. I've passed my thoughts on this to Intuit, but I haven't received any response.

You need to be aware of the fact that when you create a report to get information about disbursements and expenses, you may end up with some very confusing data in the report. If an expense is linked to a customer (target data), that's the name that appears on the report. If no expenses are linked to customers or jobs, the payee (source data) appears. Most of the time, modifying the report to display Source Name instead of Name (which really means target name if a target name exists) cures the problem.

If you have some reason to know both the source and target names, select both from the Display list. For those transactions without a posting to a target name, both columns have the same data (the source name)—but it would be clearer if the target name column were blank.

Inventory Issues

Whether you're helping a client set up inventory, or troubleshooting inventory reports that don't make sense, you need to understand where clients can go wrong with inventory transactions.

Work in Process Inventory

It's possible to set up a QuickBooks system to track WIP and then transfer finished goods to inventory, but QuickBooks doesn't make it easy. The software has no built in "WIP to Inventory" process. That's understandable, because QuickBooks isn't intended for use in complicated manufacturing businesses.

Don't try to do this if the business has more than a few inventory products that are tracked via WIP. In that case, buy a separate software application to track these manufacturing steps. Check the QuickBooks Marketplace Solutions web pages to find a QuickBooks add-on that will work for you.

To track WIP, create a WIP account in addition to the Inventory account QuickBooks creates when you enable inventory tracking. Both accounts are Other Current Assets.

Tracking WIP Transactions

Products or services purchased to create inventory items should be posted to the WIP account, not to COGS or an Expense account.

Purchase products and services for WIP without using POs to avoid having to create an item. (Items need COGS and income accounts, which makes tracking WIP much more complicated.) Use the Memo field on each transaction to note the product for which you're making the purchase.

If you purchase the same products and services for multiple inventory items, split the purchase amount in order to be able to note each product in the Memo field. This makes it easier to transfer inventory from WIP to the inventory account.

Moving Finished Products into Inventory

When the parts and services have been purchased and you're ready to move a product into inventory, create a report to determine the cost of inventory, and then perform an inventory adjustment to add the product to your inventory at the right cost.

Creating WIP Reports

To gather the information you need about the total cost of parts and services for an inventory product, customize a report to eliminate transactions not included in your WIP system.

Choose Reports → Vendors & Payables → Vendor Balance Detail, and click Modify Report. Make the following changes:

- In the Display tab, select Memo in the Columns drop-down list.
- In the Filters tab, select Account in the Choose Filter list, and then select the WIP account.
- In the Filters tab, select Transaction Type in the Choose Filter list, select Selected Transaction Types, and then select Bill and

Check. (The transaction types Bill and Check cover vendor bills you entered and checks written as direct disbursements.)

The resulting report displays the total cost of an inventory product. If the report covers more than one inventory product (the memo field indicates the product), you can grab a calculator and work out the totals manually, or export the report to Excel, where you can re-sort the data and create formulas for totals.

Adjusting Inventory

With the total cost known, move the product(s) into inventory by choosing Vendors → Inventory Activities → Adjust Quantity/Value on Hand. In the Adjust Quantity/Value on Hand dialog (see Figure C-3), take the following actions:

1. Select the option Value Adjustment (on the bottom left of the window).
2. Select the item you're bringing into inventory.
3. In the New Qty column enter the number of units you're transferring to inventory.
4. In the New Value column enter the total cost of the item (the total of all postings for this item in the WIP account).
5. In the Adjustment Account field, enter the WIP account.

When you sell the product, QuickBooks divides the total value by the number of units, and posts that amount to COG. In the future, as you move additional units from WIP into inventory, the New Value amount you enter is the total value. That means you must add the results of your new WIP cost report to the existing value.

Inventory Adjustment Account

When you select the WIP Inventory account, QuickBooks displays a message telling you it expected an expense or income account (see Figure C-4). The same message appears if you select a COGS account when you're doing an inventory adjustment after a physical count.

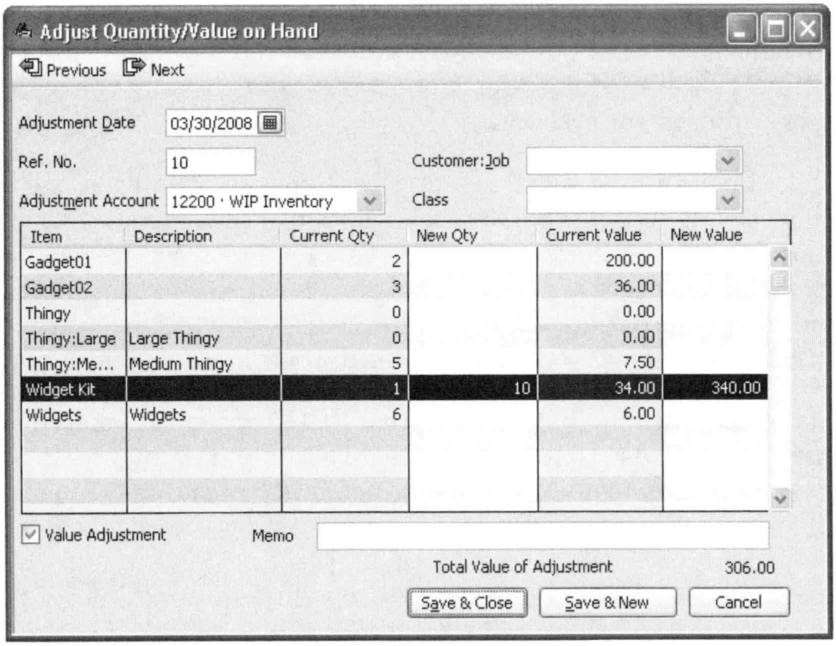

Figure C-3: Enter the new quantity and value of an inventory item you're moving from WIP into inventory.

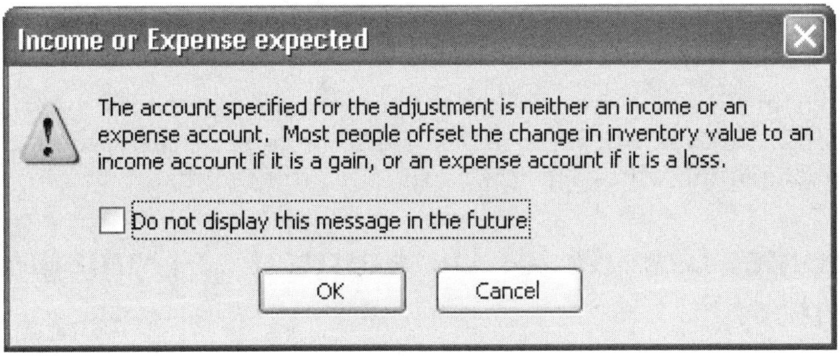
Income or Expense expected
The account specified for the adjustment is neither an income or an expense account. Most people offset the change in inventory value to an income account if it is a gain, or an expense account if it is a loss.
Do not display this message in the future
OK
Cancel

Figure C-4: QuickBooks objects to using any account type except Income or Expense for inventory adjustments.

You can select the option Do Not Display This Message In The Future before you click OK so you're not bothered with this message in the future. However, this raises a question about the way you set up the inventory adjustment account.

QuickBooks automatically creates an Expense account as the inventory adjustment account. Some accountants use that account, whether the adjustment is an increase or a decrease, so the account tracks the net changes. I haven't met many accountants who agree that an Income account is an appropriate adjustment account; they tell me that increasing stock doesn't result in income (potential income isn't real income).

Many accountants prefer to create a COGS account named Inventory Adjustments, and use that account for inventory adjustments. In addition, there are circumstances under which other accounts can be used as the inventory adjustment account.

If you send a sample to a potential customer, that's a marketing device. You have two choices about the way you post the transaction:

- Create a zero amount invoice for the inventory item. No income results and the COGS account tracks the cost of the item. Enter a notation in the Memo field to indicate this is a sample product.
- Adjust the inventory by reducing the stock by one, and use the Marketing Expense account as the inventory adjustment account.

The same options are available if you provide inventory to a charitable organization for a door prize or a raffle (if you use the second method, use the Charitable Gifts account as the inventory adjustment account).

Customer Credits for Unreturned or Damaged Inventory

Usually, when a customer returns an inventory product for credit, the process of creating and applying the credit is straightforward. When you enter the inventory item in the credit transaction, QuickBooks returns the item by incrementing the inventory account and decrementing the COG account (in addition to the postings to sales and A/R).

If the customer reports a damaged item, most companies tell the customer not to bother returning it to avoid paying the shipping cost for something that can't be resold. Even if the customer returns the damaged item, you can't put it back into inventory.

To create a customer credit without involving the original inventory item, you need to create an account and an item.

- Create an income account named Returns (some accountants prefer the name Returns and Adjustments). You can make this account a subaccount of the income account that tracks product sales so your P & L reports display the net amount.
- Create an Other Charge item named Adjustments (or Sales Adjustments). In the income account field for this new item, enter the new sales returns account you created. Do not enter an amount, and make the item taxable if your products are taxable.

To create the credit memo, use the new item in the transaction, filling in the amount based on the amount of the unreturned or damaged item. If the customer originally paid for shipping, enter the shipping costs to refund that amount too.

When you save the credit memo, you can apply the amount to another invoice, leave the credit as a floating credit, or issue a refund check.

Purchasing and Selling in Different Lot Sizes

In many accounting software applications designed for wholesale and distribution businesses, an automated conversion chart is available so you can track inventory for a product that you buy in bulk, and sell in individual units. The software automatically converts the bulk purchase cost and price when you sell the individual items.

QuickBooks supports a similar function with the Unit of Measure feature. However, your clients using QuickBooks Pro don't have access to the Unit of Measure feature

Some Pro users have created two items: one for the bulk purchase (a gross of items), and one for the sales (an individual item). However, that solution doesn't work, because the resulting inventory postings and reports are for two separate items, which is incorrect.

The solution is to make sure that both the purchase of items and the sale of items are decrementing the same inventory item, and applying cost of goods correctly.

In QuickBooks Pro, the only way to accomplish this is to create an item for sales, and then create a group for that item for purchases.

Create the individual item (for sales). Then, create a group item (for purchases) that includes only the individual item, but uses the appropriate quantity. For example, if you sell a widget that you purchase by the gross, the group item is the widget with a quantity of 144.

Inventory Item Quantities Display Half an Item

I've seen quite a few inventory reports in which the amount of available stock for an item is 12.5, or 9.3. How can you have a half or third of a physical item? You didn't sell half an item, or two-thirds of an item.

Inventory quantities end up with this problem as the result of progress invoicing on estimates. When you create a progress invoice, QuickBooks asks you to specify the percentage of the job that's completed so you can send an invoice reflecting that percentage. If products are included in the invoice, the percentage is applied to them, too.

Click the Progress icon on the toolbar of the Create Invoices window. This opens a dialog that allows you to reconfigure the line items. You can change the quantity, rate, or percentage of completion for any individual line item. Use this function to change line items that contain products, to make sure you're invoicing for "whole" products.

Assembly Costs Not Updated

If you have clients using assemblies, when they create the assemblies QuickBooks automatically uses the current costs of the components. When they build the assemblies, QuickBooks uses the same costs.

If your clients have received additional shipments of the components at a higher cost, this changes the average cost of each component (QuickBooks manages inventory costs with Average Costing).

However, the assembly Bill of Materials data doesn't change, so as assemblies are built, the costs are incorrect. This is even more troublesome when the price of an assembly is configured as an automatic markup. Open the item and manually change the costs in the Bill of Materials section.

Vendor Transaction Troubleshooting

According to the e-mail I receive, and the questions I'm asked in seminars, it's common to encounter some difficult situations in vendor transactions and vendor balances.

Voided Vendor Checks—Don't Use a JE

An accountant asked me to solve a problem that involved a check sent to a vendor that wasn't cashed, and never would be cashed. The check was written to pay a bill that had been previously entered in QuickBooks.

The accountant voided the check in the bank account, which, of course, put the vendor bill back into the "Bills to Pay" window, and also put the bill into A/P aging reports. When the A/P manager brought this to the accountant's attention, he did what accountants often do — he created a journal entry. (Accountants seem to gravitate to JEs automatically, even though they're frequently not the right tool.).

The journal entry debited A/P and credited the original expense account, and the accountant entered the Vendor name in the JE. Now the A/P aging reports showed correct totals, but the A/P manager reported that the bill continued to appear in the Pay Bills transaction window, and on QuickReports for this vendor. The accountant told her to ignore the bill's listing because the company's books were in balance (the A/P totals were correct).

However, the A/P manager insisted that the bill be removed from the Pay Bills window, and the accountant didn't know how to proceed.

To remove a bill from the Pay Bills window, you have to pay the bill, either with a check or a credit. When the accountant created the JE with the vendor name, a credit was created for the amount posted to A/P.

The credit is floating, so all the bills from this vendor in the Pay Bills window are eligible for the credit. Obviously, the credit should be applied to the bill that was paid with the voided check, and that bill is the same amount as the floating credit (making it easy to select it in the Pay Bills window).

Select the bill, click Set Credits, apply the credit, and click Pay & Close. When the Pay Bill window closes, QuickBooks issues a message telling you that one or more bills were paid by credits and no check was issued. That's what you wanted to happen, so click OK.

The best approach to this is not a JE, which only creates the extra step of the JE. All the postings are correct if you create discrete transactions that are linked to the vendor.

Void the check, which puts the original bill back into its unpaid state. If you're not going to reissue a check to pay this bill, create a vendor credit. Then open the Pay Bills window and use that credit to pay off the bill that reappeared when you voided the check.

Reimbursed Cost of Goods

It's unusual to encounter a situation in which a customer is invoiced for reimbursement of cost of goods, but after receiving several inquiries from business owners and accountants on this subject I figured out a way to do this.

In each case, the object was to charge the COGS account, not to worry about moving an inventory item in or out of inventory. I'm assuming that these inquiries involve businesses that aren't tracking inventory items, and are posting COG amounts directly when they have an expense directly connected to sales items or services.

Each inquiry I received included the information that when the COGS account was selected in the Enter Bills or Write Checks transaction window, QuickBooks did not permit the transaction line to be marked as "billable" after the user entered a customer name. Therefore, the amount never showed up in the Time/Costs list when the customer's invoice was created.

QuickBooks doesn't recognize a COGS account as a customer-reimbursable expense if you enter the account in the Expenses tab in the Enter Bills or Write Checks transaction window. The workaround is to use the Items tab in the transaction window.

Fixing Vendor Bills Paid with Direct Disbursements

Sometimes users write direct checks to pay vendors for whom they've entered bills, instead of using the Pay Bills feature. Most of them use the bank account register to record checks they wrote manually.

When you enter a vendor name in the Write Checks window, QuickBooks warns you to use the Pay Bills feature if there are outstanding bills for this vendor, which many users ignore <sigh!>, but you see no warnings if you record checks directly in the register.

After a while, these users notice they have a very large Accounts Payable balance, and running an A/P report displays names of vendors who have actually been paid.

In addition, expenses are higher than they should be, because the expense was posted when the bill was entered, and then posted again with the direct disbursement.

***TIP**: Most people who do this use the vendor's physical bill to create the check. Insist that clients mark the physical bill to indicate the fact that the bill was entered into QuickBooks in the Pay Bills transaction window, so they can avoid this problem. Put a 'Q' or a 'QB" on the part of the bill that's retained (not the portion returned to the vendor).*

The easiest way to fix the problem is to replace the direct disbursement check with a "pay bills" check. In order to do this, you need to create a list of checks so you know where the problems are.

Choose Reports → Banking → Check Detail report (on the Banking submenu of the Reports menu), and modify it as follows to make it easier to find the direct disbursements.

1. Change the date range to go back to the date of the first incorrect direct disbursement.
2. Click Modify, and then click the Filters tab.
3. In the Filter List, select Transaction Type, and select Check from the Transaction Type drop-down list. (This eliminates the checks that were correctly written as the type Bill Payment).
4. If there are only a few vendors that are affected, select Name from the Filter List, and then select Multiple Names in the Name drop-down list. When the Names list appears, select the affected vendors. If many vendors are involved, skip the vendor selection.
5. Click OK to return to the report window, and print the report.

Now that you have a list of the checks, and their check numbers you can open the Pay Bills window and begin paying the bills that were already paid by a direct disbursement.

1. Select each vendor's bill (or multiple bills if the check covered more than one bill). If credits were applied when the check was written, click the Set Credits button to apply those credits.
2. Change the date to match the date of the check that was written and sent.
3. When the bills are selected, and the amount of the check matches the direct disbursement check, select the option Assign Check No. at the bottom of the Pay Bills window.
4. Click Pay & Close (or Pay & New if you have to do this again for another check).
5. In the Assign Check Numbers dialog, enter the check number that was used for the direct disbursement (the Check Detail report has the check number).
6. When QuickBooks warns you that the check number has already been used, select Keep Number.

When you're finished paying the bills that were already paid, using the check numbers you've already used, open the check register. Here's what you'll find:

- The bank balance is much smaller than it should be.
- Each check number you just used appears twice, once for the direct disbursement (check type CHK), and once for the bill payment you just made (check type BILLPMT).

Void or delete every duplicate check that is of the type CHK. The bank balance returns to its proper amount, and the expense account is adjusted to reflect only the expenses posted when the vendor bills were originally recorded.

Vendor Pays Off a Credit with Checks

This solution arose from a problem presented by a reader's e-mail, which is always the type of challenge we enjoy.

The reader has an open credit with a vendor for a large amount. She no longer uses this vendor, so the vendor has agreed to refund the credit amount in installments. She asked how to enter each check, deposit it into the bank, and reduce the credit at the same time. She wants to be able to track the history of this credit and the installment payments against it (which is a good idea, because it means that any disputes with the vendor can be easily resolved).

This is actually quite easy to accomplish, and if you run into the same situation, here's the "fix".

I'm assuming that when you created the credit, you used the Enter Bills transaction window, selected the Credit option, and posted the credit amount to the expense account that was originally used for the purchase.

Now, checks from the vendor begin to arrive. To pay down the credit, when each check arrives, open a General Journal Entry window (Banking, Make General Journal Entries), and proceed as follows:

1. In the Account column, choose the bank in which you're depositing the funds, and debit it for the amount of the check. This deposits the money into your bank account.
   You can also debit the Undeposited Funds account, instead of the bank account, and when you open the Make Deposits window, this amount is on the list of payments to deposit.
2. In the Name column of the GJE window, enter the name of the vendor.
3. On the next line, choose Accounts Payable. QuickBooks will automatically insert a credit equal to the debit you entered. Enter the vendor in the Name column.
4. Save the JE.

Do this each time you receive a check. When you check the A/P balance of this vendor, you'll notice the credit balance has declined by the amount of the check.

Open the Pay Bills window, where the entry you made shows up as a payable (an open bill). When you select that bill, QuickBooks displays a message saying there's a credit available. Select the Set Credits window, and apply the appropriate amount (the amount of the bill you selected). Eventually, the last check will pay off the vendor credit balance. If the checks don't continue to arrive, you'll have an accurate record of the balance the vendor still owes, and an audit of the transactions to date.

Applying Additional Credits to a Paid Bill

After entering a credit and applying it to a vendor's bill, you create the check in the Pay Bills transaction window. Then you realize you need to add more credits to the bill. After voiding the check, the credit already applied to the bill disappears, and it seems as if you can't apply it. What's going on?

When you create a credit for a vendor, and then use the Pay Bills window to apply the credit, the resulting check is for the net amount. For example, if the original bill is $1000.00, and you apply a credit of $100.00, the check amount is $900.00 after you use the Set Credits feature to apply the credit you created.

To add more credits after you void the check, open the Enter Bills window, select the Credit option at the top of the window, and enter another credit for this vendor (for this example, $100.00). You've now applied a total of $200.00 credits to this vendor, and the vendor had originally submitted a bill of $1000.00, so you should only have to pay the vendor $800.00.

When you open the Pay Bills window, the bill listing that appears for this vendor is for $900.00, not the original $1000.00. That first $100.00 credit has been "absorbed" into the current balance due. If you select the bill's listing and click Set Credits, you'll see the second $100.00 credit you created. The window also displays the bill's "history" - the original amount, the first credit, and the current balance due. The current balance due should equal the original amount less the original credit that was applied. Just apply the second credit to change the new balance due.

The net amount of the check will be mathematically correct – you just don't see the individual listing for the credit you originally applied, because it's been taken into account for this bill.

If you really want to start over and enter all the available credits just before paying the original bill, you could void the original credit transaction after voiding the check. But that's extra work, and unnecessary, because QuickBooks is tracking the net amounts.

If you select the Vendor's listing in the Vendor List and press Ctrl-Q, you see a list of all the transactions, including the bill, the original credit, and the additional credit(s).

Property Management

This is another topic that produces many questions from readers, so I'm assuming that QuickBooks is a popular choice of software for people who manage properties. The questions are almost always about setup, not about transaction entries. If you have clients who are using QuickBooks to manage property, the way you set up the company file depends on how the management business is run.

Property Owners

If the client owns the properties, you want to be able to report on the profit for each property. Use the following guidelines for company file setup:

- Enable Class Tracking in the Accounting category of the Preferences dialog.
- Be sure the option Prompt To Assign classes is checked. This is a reminder to assign a class to every income and expense transaction.
- Create a class for each property.
- Create a class for administration (so that transactions not directly related to a property receive a class assignment).

Every expense directly linked to a property is assigned to that property's class (mortgage, interest, repairs, utilities, and so on). All other expenses are assigned to the administration class.

Each month, or quarter, or year, create a JE to allocate appropriate expenses from the administration class to each property. You do not have to clear the entire amount in the expense account, the amount of expense you allocate is a financial judgment based on knowledge of the way the client's overhead applies to each property.

You can then create a P & L statement for the properties by choosing Reports → Company & Financial → Profit & Loss By Class.

***TIP**: To create and print a separate report for each property, modify the report by going to the Filters tab and select Class from the Filter list. Select one class (property) and memorize the report. Repeat for each class. Name the memorized reports with the property address.*

Property Management Companies

If the client is a property management company and manages properties for multiple owners (customers), you need to be able to report on the profit for each customer, as well as for each property owned by that customer.

Use the guidelines described here, but in addition to creating the owners as customers, create a class for each owner, and create a subclass for each property.

Create a customer for each tenant, but as tenants move and are replaced, make the old tenants inactive customers. On the other hand, you can create a generic customer named Tenant and keep information on the tenant (telephone, employer information, etc.) outside of QuickBooks.

Paying Sales Reps

I think the reason I'm asked so often about managing commissions for outside sales reps is the lack of an automatic commission calculator in QuickBooks. Some accounting applications let you enter the commission rate in the rep's record, and then automatically calculate the commission (and some software automatically creates the checks). QuickBooks doesn't, which makes the issue of sales reps and commissions seem more complicated than it is.

Configuring QuickBooks to Track Reps

In order to track sales for which outside reps receive commission, you must create sales reps, and enter the rep on every affected sales transaction. (Chapter 3 covers setting up sales reps).

To enter the reps when you're creating transactions, you have to add the Sales Rep field to all the sales transaction templates you use (Sales Orders, Invoices, Sales Receipts, etc.). Some of the industry specific Premier editions provide a sales order template with the rep field included, but if such a template isn't available, create customized templates that contain a Rep field.

When a sales rep is linked to a customer, the rep's initials are automatically placed in the Rep field when that customer is selected in a sales transaction template. However, even if the rep is linked to that customer, if you use a transaction template without a Rep field, the transaction is not linked back to the rep.

***WARNING**: You cannot split a sales transaction among multiple reps. If you need to pay commissions to more than one rep, create a rep that is an alias for two reps, and then split the commission appropriately for that "fake" rep.*

Sales Transactions and Sales Rep Commissions

Most of the time, all the items (services and products) in a sales transaction can be posted to the sales rep's record, so the rep gets a commission on the total sale. QuickBooks does not include sales tax amounts in the sales total posted for commission tracking.

Sales Reports for Reps

To create a report on sales by rep, choose Reports → Sales and then select one of the following reports:

- Sales By Rep Summary, which displays the total amount of sales credited to each rep for the period selected in the report.
- Sales By Rep Detail, which displays every sales transaction for each rep, totaled for each rep.

You can use a calculator to add the amounts and multiply by the commission rate. If you have a lot of sales reps and a lot of sales, export the report to Excel and perform your calculations there.

Write the commission check, posting the amount to the account you set up for that purpose (usually an expense account, but sometimes a COG account). For sales reps that receive 1099 forms, use an expense account that you've configured as a 1099 account.

Remittance Documents for Reps

You can attach a detailed report with the rep commission payment by modifying the Sales By Rep Detail report for each rep as follows:

1. Choose Reports → Sales → Sales By Rep Detail.
2. Click Modify and move to the Filters tab.
3. In the Filter column, select Rep.
4. In the Rep field, select a rep.
5. Click OK to return to the report window, where only this rep's sales are displayed.
6. Click Memorize and memorize the report, using the rep's name.
7. Repeat for every rep.

Each time you issue rep commissions, select the appropriate report from the Memorized Reports list, print it, and attach it to the check.

TIP: *Create a Memorized Reports Group for rep commission reports, and put all these memorized reports in that group. This makes it easier to find the report you need when you pay the commissions.*

Paying Reps Who Collect Payments

Some reps bring invoices to customers when they deliver goods, and collect cash payments from some customers. The reps want to deduct their commissions from the total collection, and remit the balance to the business owner.

That's a common situation, and it's not difficult to manage it in QuickBooks, as long as you understand the basic rules:

- The customer's invoice must be totally paid off in QuickBooks.
- The reps must have their commissions tracked (especially if they're 1099 recipients).
- You must deposit the money to Undeposited Funds, not directly to a bank; otherwise you cannot deduct the commission the rep already took.

When you receive the money from the rep, open the Receive Payments window, enter the customer's name, select the appropriate invoice, and indicate the full amount of the invoice as the amount received.

Choose Banking → Make Deposits to open the Payments to Deposit window. Select this payment for deposit, and click OK.

In the next Make Deposits window, make the following entries in the row below the deposit listing:

- Select the Rep's name in the Received From column.
- Select the account you use for posting commissions in the From Account column (this account is linked to 1099 payments if the Rep gets a 1099).
- Optionally, enter a comment in the Memo column (e.g. Commission on Inv1234).
- Skip the Check Number column.
- Optionally, choose Cash in the Payment Method column (it's not essential, but you may want to track this as cash).
- Assign a class in the Class Column (if you're tracking classes).
- In the Amount column, enter the amount the Rep kept, *using a minus sign.*

The net amount is transferred to the bank account as a deposit. Your customer's record are accurate, your rep's records are accurate, and your 1099's will be accurate.

Bartering

It's amazing how much e-mail we receive asking how to manage relationships with customers who are also vendors. Bartering isn't complicated if you configure QuickBooks properly to manage it.

Bartering kicks in when you send an invoice to a customer, and your customer contacts you to buy something from his company. You buy the product or service and then either you or your customer suggests that a credit against the invoice is the easiest way to pay (either partially or in full, depending on the amounts) for the purchases. It works the other way around, too — you may have a vendor who wants to buy your products or services and use a credit for payment or partial payment.

Configuring Elements for Bartering

To manage bartering, you need the following elements in your QuickBooks company file:

- A duplicate customer account for each vendor with whom you barter (and the other way around, a duplicate vendor account for each barter customer). Use the same text in the Name field for both, adding "V" and "C" to the names to make the names unique.
- An account to track barter transactions, of the type Other Current Asset. Name the account Barter or Exchanges.
- An item to use in transactions, of the type Other Charge. Name the item To/From Exchange (or Barter, or whatever text works for you). Link the item to the Other Current Asset account you created.

Entering Barter Transactions

Once you've agreed to barter transactions with your Customer/Vendor, entering transactions is the same as it was before. When there's a barter balance, you credit the appropriate transaction using the barter item. You have to follow two rules to make this work:

- Always use an invoice when the customer purchases goods or services—never use a sales receipt. You can only apply credits against invoices.
- Always use a bill when you purchase from the vendor—never use a direct disbursement. You can only apply credits against bills.

I'll go through the processes so this is all becomes clear.

1. You sell a customer (who is also a vendor) products or services, and the total invoice is $540.00.
2. You order a product or service from the vendor (same as the customer in Step 1) for $400.00, and agree to a barter arrangement.
3. The Vendor sends a bill for $400.00, which you enter in the Enter Bills transaction window.

QuickBooks now shows that you have an A/R entry in the amount of $540.00 and an A/P entry for $400.00, which in "barter-speak" means you have an A/R for $140.00. (This works identically the other way around—when the A/P is a larger amount than the A/R.)

Now you have to take $400.00 off the original invoice, and clear the vendor bill because you're not going to write a check to pay the bill.

1. Choose Customers → Create Credit Memos/Refunds.
2. Select the barter customer.
3. Select the barter item you created and enter the amount (in this case $400.00).
4. Save the transaction.
5. QuickBooks displays a message asking how you want to apply the credit. Choose Apply To An Invoice and click OK.
6. In the Apply Credit to Invoice dialog, select the original invoice (in this case, for $540.00) and click Done.

QuickBooks debits $400.00 to the Barter account. Now you have to enter a vendor credit and apply it to the vendor's bill. QuickBooks will credit the Barter account, which ends up with a zero balance.

1. Choose Vendors → Enter Bills to open the Enter Bills transaction window.
2. Select the Credit option at the top of the transaction window.
3. Select the vendor.
4. Move to the Items tab and enter the Barter item.
5. Enter the amount of the credit (in this case, $400.00).
6. Save the transaction.
7. Choose Vendors → Pay Bills
8. Select the vendor bill that is part of the barter agreement.
9. Because the existing credit is the same amount as the bill, QuickBooks immediately applies the credit and displays a message telling you that no check will be created.
10. Click OK.
11. Click Pay Selected Bills. QuickBooks displays a summary of the Pay Bills activities, including this bill (which has no real payment).

Once you're rolling along with barters, it's not this "neat and clean", of course, because you won't always have near-simultaneous barter transactions. The invoices and bills you create, and the credits you enter against them for barter activities, produce balances on one side or another of the Barter account. Sometimes you'll enter a customer credit with no existing invoice, saving the credit for future use. At other times, you'll enter a vendor credit with no existing bill. This is normal for ongoing bartering.

When needed, you can enter the Barter item as part of a normal invoice to your customer, in addition to the services or products that appear on that invoice. You can also enter the barter item as an A/P credit and use it against any invoice from the vendor (if you've received multiple invoices). When the vendor credit is less than the amount owed, apply the credit and QuickBooks creates a check for the balance due.

Tracking Barter Balances

To see the current state of the barter balances, create a QuickReport on the Barter Item (select the item in the Items list and press Ctrl-Q). Choose All as the date range to see a report on the item's transactions.

***TIP**: Change the Sort By field to Name so you have all the customer side and vendor side transactions listed contiguously.*

The balance displayed in the QuickReport should always match the current balance of the Balance account.

Troubleshooting Online Banking

The most frequent complaint or query about online banking is dealing with unmatched transactions that will never be matched or added to the register, but remain in the download file.

The second most frequent complaint (in fact the only other complaint we ever hear about) is the inability to recover from a session that was abnormally terminated.

Removing Unmatched Transactions

By the time we hear from the user, the list of unmatched transactions is very long, and some of the listings are quite old.

Users can't add these unmatched transactions to the register because it would duplicate transactions already in the register. For example, the register shows three checks deposited on a certain date, and the download file shows one deposit that equals the total of the three checks. Realizing this, the user knows that adding the downloaded deposit to the register would falsely increase the bank balance. But there's no way to delete the listing.

The unmatched transactions remain in the download file and will still be there when you next download. If additional transactions in the next download can't be matched, the number of unmatched transactions grows and grows.

(Many users think that the old unmatched transactions are downloaded again, but that isn't what happens; instead the unmatched transactions are saved on your computer and continue to appear in the list of unmatched transactions in future downloads.)

TIP: *When the unmatched transactions are deposits, it's usually the result of the failure to use the Undeposited Funds feature. If you specify a bank account when you create income transactions (sales receipts and receipt of payments against invoices), each individual transaction is posted to the bank account. When you go to the bank and deposit all the checks, the bank and the download file show the total deposit.*

To resolve the problem, in the next download file match all the items that can be matched. Click Done, and when QuickBooks asks if you're sure you're done (because you haven't matched all the transactions), click Yes.

Then click the Delete button in the Items Received section of the Online Banking Center. QuickBooks asks you to confirm your action. When you click Yes, the file, which contains all the unmatched transactions, is deleted. The next time you download, only new transactions appear in the download file.

Recovering From an Interrupted Online Banking Session

Sometimes (not always) after an online banking session terminates abruptly, the user is unable to reconnect to the bank in the future. Every time an online banking session is initiated, QuickBooks displays an error message explaining that the system cannot recover from the incomplete session. The dialog requesting the PIN never appears, so you can't get online. This is a QuickBooks system problem, but you can fix it as follows:

1. Press and hold the Ctrl key as you open the Online Banking Center (Banking → Online Banking → Online Banking Center).
2. Continue to hold down the Ctrl key as you click Go Online.
3. Continue to hold down the Ctrl key until the dialog requesting your PIN appears.
4. Release the Ctrl key, enter your PIN and proceed.

Online Bill Payments: How They Work

I've had many queries from accountants and users about online bill payments, usually after an online payment doesn't reach the vendor. You can't resolve the problem unless you understand how online bill payments work, whether they're created within QuickBooks or at your bank's website.

When you send your own checks to vendors, the money isn't removed from your bank account until the check is presented to your bank for payment by the payee's bank. This means the payee has received, endorsed, and deposited the check.

When you create an online payment (either in QuickBooks or on your bank's website), the money is immediately removed from your checking account and placed into the bank's checking account.

The bank sends the check to the payee, and after the payee deposits it (in its own bank account), the check is sent to the bank's checking account for payment and clearance. No notification is sent to you when the check is presented for payment.

It's important to know that very few banks manage online payments directly; instead they outsource this process (as well as most other software-based processes including setting up online bank accounts for customers, statement preparations, etc.) to large, high-tech software companies that specialize in bank "back-end" processes. These companies are "bank processors" and are usually referred to as "processors" by bank personnel. This means when you contact your bank about a problem with an online payment, the bank has to contact the processor to get you the information you need (which may delay the response). In this section, when I use the term "bank" you should think "processor." For example, when I say that money is removed from your bank account and placed in the bank's bank account, it's almost certainly placed in a bank account that belongs to the processor, not into a bank account that belongs to your bank.

When you download bank transactions, you see the deduction for the online payment. However, unlike deductions you see for the checks you create and send, this doesn't mean that the vendor has received and deposited your payment; instead it means the bank has moved the money from your account to its account.

***NOTE**: If you create an online payment that is an e-payment, the same process applies; that is, the money is removed from your account before the e-payment is transmitted.*

When you get your statement from the bank, you don't see physical checks or pictures of checks (depending on the way your bank sends you checks with the statement) that were online payments. Those checks are sent to, and retained by, the bank (because it's the bank's checking account that processed the check).

If a Vendor Doesn't Receive Online Payment Checks

If you create and mail your own checks, when a vendor calls to say that the check wasn't received, you can check with your bank to see if the check cleared. If it didn't clear, you can stop payment and issue a new check. If it cleared, you can request a copy of the back of the check in order to see the endorsement. When you send the endorsement information to the vendor (a copy of the back of the check), the vendor can correct its records to apply your payment. If the vendor claims the endorsement is bogus, your bank has procedures for recovering the funds and you can send another check to the vendor.

It's not quite as straightforward when the check is an online payment, but your bank has procedures that cover this situation. However, when you talk to your bank's personnel about problems with online services, the banker you speak to almost certainly has to convey your query or complaint to the processor, which means you may not get an answer immediately (although the delay should never exceed a business day).

***NOTE**: You can determine the current status of an online payment you uploaded from QuickBooks by choosing Banking → Online Banking → Inquire About Online Banking Payment. The message you see tells you whether the payment is in process (which means the bank has it but has not yet created the check) or has been processed (the check has been created and mailed). This information does not tell you whether the check has been deposited by the payee, or whether it has cleared the bank's bank account.*

If an online payment check is not presented for payment to the bank's bank account within 90 days, a flag goes up in the bank's software (some processors may use a different number of elapsed days, but 90 days is the common interval). The money is automatically returned to your bank account, and a "stop payment" order is issued within the bank's bank account (not your bank account).

Ninety days is a long time, and well before this automatic stop payment is issued, you're being dunned by the payee. You have to remit payment immediately. Go to your bank and explain the problem. Your bank should offer you the following options:

- The bank will reissue the check and send it to the payee using the funds that were removed for the original payment. The money doesn't have to be withdrawn from your account again because the bank still has it, since the check wasn't presented for payment by the payee's bank.
- The bank will return the money to your account so you can issue your own check (or cash) to the vendor.

***NOTE**: Most banks call you or the vendor to check the vendor's address in case a bad address is the problem; if so, the check is reissued to the corrected address.*

If the bank discovers that the check it sent was presented for payment, the procedures are the same as if this happened with your own check. The bank will provide a picture of the endorsement that you can send to the vendor. The vendor will either discover its mistake in entering your payment, or will claim the endorsement is bogus (and the same remedies are available as for your own checks that have forged endorsements).

Index